FISHING SOUTHERN SALT WATERS

Also by Thomas Helm 〰〰〰〰〰〰〰〰

Thomas Helm ~~~~~~~~~~

~~~~~~~~

~~~~~~~~

FISHING
SOUTHERN SALT WATERS

Illustrated with photographs and drawings

~~~~~~~~ *Dodd, Mead & Company · New York*

Photographs are credited to the following sources as indicated: Joel Arrington: pages 44, 48, 64, 187; Bahamas News Bureau, William Roberts: page 108; Florida Development Commission: pages 135, 145; Florida News Bureau: pages 12, 23, 32, 51, 102, 103, 105, 139, 143, 157, 169, 181, 183, 262, 264, 267, 270, 272, 275; Dorothy L. Helm: page 197; Thomas Helm: pages 3, 4, 6, 27, 61, 124, 153, 163, 204, 209, 306, 308, 331, 368, 383, 388; Louisiana Tourist Development Commission: pages 289, 359; Marine Studios, Marineland, Florida: pages 213, 216, 312; National Park Service: pages 240, 242, 245; U. S. Navy: page 195.

Drawings of fish on the following pages are reproduced from *The Fishes of North America and Middle America* by David Starr Jordan and Barton Warren Evermann, reprinted 1963 for the Smithsonian Institute by T. F. H. Publications, Inc., Jersey City, New Jersey: 2, 11, 17, 21, 34, 42, 50, 58, 71, 78, 84, 91, 111, 118, 125, 128, 134, 146, 209, 293, 311, 320, 321, 323.

All other fish drawings are by Thomas Helm.

To my wife, Dorothy ~~~~~

ACKNOWLEDGMENTS
OF ILLUSTRATIONS

Photographs included in this book have come from many different sources including a considerable number from the author's personal files. In sorting through literally hundreds of pictures the fundamental objective was not to select ones that simply showed large numbers of fish. Instead, it was to choose those that seemed best to illustrate certain species of fish and the methods of angling which are most frequently employed by those who fish southern salt waters.

For their assistance in providing just the right photographs of particular subjects, the author would like to extend his gratitude to each and everyone personally involved. He would also like to say a special word of thanks to the following:

Al Hackett, sports editor of the Florida State News Bureau; Joel Arrington, outdoor editor of the North Carolina Department of Conservation; Gus Cranow of the Louisiana Tourist Development Commission; Bob Conwell of the Corpus Christi Area Tourist Bureau and Doug Whalen of Portsmouth, Virginia. Thanks for certain photographs also go to the Texas Highway Department, Bahamas News Bureau, the Georgia Department of Industry and Trade, Marine Studios, Florida, and the U.S. Navy.

In most instances the drawings identifying fish are after those which appear in *The Fishes of North and Middle America* by David Starr Jordan and Barton Warren Evermann, reprinted 1963 for the Smithsonian Institution.

PREFACE

If you put your boat in the water on the Atlantic side of Chincoteague Island on Virginia's Eastern Shore peninsula at about the 38th parallel and followed the coastline south along the Atlantic to Key West, and then doubled back up along the Florida Keys and on around the perimeter of the Gulf of Mexico to the Rio Grande River at the southern end of Texas, you would have covered 2,911 miles of coastline.

Nearly three thousand miles of coastline constitute a lot of open-water fishing, but it is not even a drop in the minnow bucket when you stop to consider that there are actually more than ten times that many miles of saltwater coastline contained in the same area. Actually, when the perimeters of islands and peninsulas in the nine southern coastal states are considered, you come up with a grand total of 32,382 miles of saltwater coastline.

Over the many years that I have pursued the sport of saltwater angling, I have become increasingly aware of the analogy that exists between fish and the weather. Both are predictable up to a point, but just when you are convinced a given set of conditions will produce certain effects, something is bound to knock your firmest conclusions into a cocked hat. Then, too, as with meteorology, angling is highly regional. The most dependable atmospheric signs and guideposts used by the weather forecaster in Seattle might be of scant value to his counterpart in Providence or Tampa. Similarly, an angler might become an expert in one region of the country only to discover his hard-earned knowledge was contrary or only statistically applicable to fishing in distant waters.

Much as many saltwater anglers in other sections of the country may not like the fact, it is true that there is a greater variety of game fish in southeastern salt waters than in any other region of the United States. Of even greater significance, the fish are annually caught in far greater numbers by the sportsman here than anywhere else. One of the primary reasons is that there are simply so many more "fishable" days on the calendar in the warmer climes.

It would indeed be grossly presumptuous for anyone writing a book about the subject to state unequivocally that such-and-such and so-and-so constitute the only acceptable methods of catching any one kind of fish. What such a book can do and should do, however, is to acquaint the reader with the basic habits of certain desirable fish. It can also enumerate many of the trials and errors and suggest some of the ways that have proved most successful on numerous fishing trips.

In his book *The Compleat Angler*, Izaak Walton made an observation that is as true today as it was well over three centuries ago: *"For* Angling *may be said to be so like the* Mathematicks, *that it can ne'r be fully learnt; at least not so fully, but that there wil stil be more new experiments left for the trial of other men that succeed us."*

That, in brief, is what the game of fishing is all about. It provides an opportunity to experiment with new methods that sometimes succeed and sometimes result in dismal failure. Each of these techniques has in all likelihood been tried before by other anglers, but as long as it is new to the person performing the experiment, then it is interesting and often worth the effort.

Should I count the number of hours I have spent in pursuit of fish I am sure I would be appalled to realize what a considerable portion of my life has been devoted to the sport. I am equally certain that not a moment of this time has been wasted.

I do not mean to imply that I always return home with a stringer burdened with many large fish. By going fishing, however, I have added years of pleasure to my life that might otherwise have been wasted in some less rewarding pastime.

A popular misconception held by those not thoroughly acquainted with the art of angling is that failure to catch fish in abundance on a particular day is tantamount to losing the game. They have missed the overall objective which, to my way of thinking, is the opportunity to commune with a phase of nature that has remained largely unchanged since man first appeared on earth. The simple act of capturing a fish or several fish while thus engaged is but a small bonus to be garnered from the sport.

I became absorbed in the art of angling while still very young, and the interest has never waned. Although I frequently return to the same stretch of coastline at the same season and in quest of a species of fish I have caught many times, I have never found two fishing trips to be the same. Each presents different challenges and never have I failed to learn something new and interesting. I am convinced that the longer one fishes, the more one's interest in the sport will grow.

It is toward that end this book is written.

CONTENTS

ILLUSTRATIONS

Photographs

Drawings

FISHING SOUTHERN SALT WATERS

Nomenclature

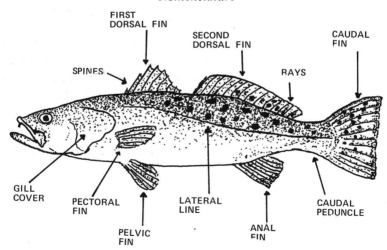

∿∿∿∿∿∿
∿∿∿∿∿∿

INSHORE

SPECKLED TROUT

There are few saltwater game fish about which one can make a wide, sweeping statement without expecting contradiction from some quarter. I will, however, say unequivocally that the spotted weakfish *(Cynoscion nebulosus)* is the most sought-after game fish that swims in southern salt waters.

Not only is he found throughout the entire range from Chesapeake Bay to the mouth of the Rio Grande, but he is plentiful, beautiful, and fine table fare. What is more, he is one of the gamest fish for his size that is to be found anywhere. This was the first game fish I ever saw caught and even though it was a number of years ago, I have total recall of the event.

It was late afternoon and there was a touch of fall in the air. I was about five years old—going on six—when my dad and I walked out to the end of a rickety old wharf near St. Andrew on Florida's panhandle. Dad had just bought a new bait-casting rod and reel and was anxious to try out the rig to see if it measured up to his expectations.

To keep him company, I trudged along behind with my trusty cane pole and a can of fiddler crabs. From past experience—you don't have much past experience when you are only five, but you do have some —I felt reasonably confident that I was going to catch a few shiners, and of course there was always the hope that I would bring in a sheepshead. What I did not know was that in a very few minutes I was going to be introduced to one of the sportiest game fish that swims in the Gulf of Mexico.

When we reached the end of the dock, I proceeded to pin a fiddler on my hook and flip it out a few feet from the nearest piling. Even at that age I had already caught a lifetime case of fishing fever, and while my catch was generally on the small size I was at least a champion in the eyes of the family cat.

While I kept watch on my cork bobber, I was aware that Dad was rigging up his new tackle. He clipped a red-and-white surface plug to the end of a 2-foot gut leader and made a few experimental casts to "get

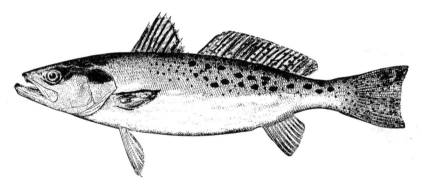

Spotted Weakfish

the feel" of his new rig. On about the seventh or eighth cast, the bottom of the bay seemed to explode at the precise spot where the plug landed.

Not only did the water explode, but it kept on exploding one time after another and in the middle of all the confusion I could see something big thrashing about with that red-and-white plug clamped in his jaws. On the dock beside me, Dad was holding the rod tip high and I

History has a way of repeating itself. Here, the author's father prepares to return a small speckled trout to the water. A goodly number of years and hundreds of fishing trips have intervened, but it was a "speck" caught on the same type of bait-casting tackle by the same man that introduced the author to salt water fishing.

thought I detected him muttering a few words and phrases that I was not accustomed to hearing him use around the house.

Probably it was only a matter of seconds, but it seemed like many long minutes later when Dad lofted a huge flopping fish up onto the wharf.

"Speckled trout!" Dad said, pinning the fish down and removing the plug. "He's a nice size one, too. Might even go four pounds."

During that autumn afternoon I pulled a few pinfish and small sheepshead up onto the wharf, but what I remember most vividly is that before the sun was down, Dad had brought in three more trout. As we walked home, I got the impression he was thoroughly pleased with the new rod and reel he had bought. For me, it was the beginning of a love affair with a fish that has endured through the years, and even today I get that same thrill whenever I make contact with old *Cynoscion nebulosus.*

The spotted weakfish is known by several different names, such as speckled trout, spotted trout, and sea trout. He also has several near relatives including the sand sea trout *(Cynoscion arenarius),* and silver sea trout *(Cynoscion nothus);* and along the Atlantic coast is another immediate member of the weakfish family regionally known as the

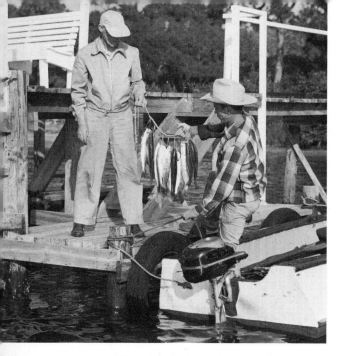

It could be October, February, or June. It could be Corpus Christi, St. Petersburg, or Savannah. The speckled trout is truly a game fish for all seasons and one ready to provide sport for the angler who fishes southern salt waters.

yellowfin trout, the squeteague, and the gray weakfish. Scientifically, he is *Cynoscion regalis* and bears a close resemblance to the spotted weakfish. The International Game Fish Association (IGFA) records show that *regalis* is the larger, with one weighing 19 pounds 8 ounces caught by Dennis B. Hall on April 13, 1962, while fishing out of Trinidad. The record for the spotted weakfish was set on January 13, 1949, at Fort Pierce, Florida, by C. W. Hubbard. It weighed 15 pounds 3 ounces.

Of the four fish mentioned above, the spotted or speckled trout is the one that provides the most sport for the largest number of anglers over the widest range and will therefore be the one concentrated on in this chapter.

The question most often asked by the beginning saltwater angler is: Why is such an active and worthy game fish called a weakfish? In this case, contrary to those of many other fish, there is a reasonably logical answer. The name certainly does not have any bearing on the stamina and agility of the fish, but applies simply to the structure of the mouth. The membrane connecting the jawbones is thin and easily torn and many fish go free before they reach the net by the hook being torn out of their mouths. Of course, if they are solidly hooked in a fleshy part of the mouth, no amount of thrashing by the fish or inept rod handling by the angler will result in their loss. This, however, is a condition that cannot be known until the trout is safely in the net. On numerous occasions I have seen the hook actually drop out of their mouths the moment the line is allowed to go limp.

With these thoughts in mind, the angler would do well to maintain a constant tension on the line from the instant of the strike until the fish is landed. Yet, at the same time, all effort should be made to avoid horsing the trout while the fight is on.

Having dispensed with the reason for the name weakfish, the second logical question is: Why the name trout? This is a misnomer, but one that is so popular and widespread that it is not likely to vanish from the vernacular of those who fish southern salt waters. Here again, there is reasonable validity for the name because of the resemblance to the well-known brown trout *(Salmo trutta)* found in freshwater streams and lakes throughout the world. While there is considerable difference in the body fins of the two fish, the general shape of the body is similar as are the square caudal fin and the pronounced black spots.

The spotted weakfish, or speckled trout, as he is widely known, is a handsome fish, bluish gray on the back and shading to silver white on the sides and belly. The numerous black spots on the upper part are generally round and vary in size and are also present on the soft rays of the second dorsal and caudal fins. The first dorsal usually has ten spines and the second dorsal has one spine, followed by about twenty-five soft rays. The bottom jaw protrudes and there are two prominent canine teeth in the front of the upper jaw.

One of the factors that contributes to the popularity of the trout is that he is a worthy opponent of a wide variety of tackle, ranging from the humble cane pole to the most sophisticated fly rods. Today, in sport fishing, the vast majority are taken with light spinning and bait-casting tackle.

Of equal importance is the fact that he is within range of almost all saltwater anglers. He is caught with pleasing frequency by those fishing from small boats, wading the shallows, casting from shore and jetties, or dangling a line from piers and bridges. He is basically a bay dweller, but is also caught in the surf and in tidal creeks.

His choice of bait covers a wide spectrum that includes chunks of fish flesh, live minnows, small crabs. Where natural bait is concerned, there is little question but that shrimp—especially live ones—consistently take the most trout. Close behind the shrimp is cut mullet. About the only requirement a trout insists upon is that what the angler offers him

The speckled trout bears a distinct resemblance to the well-known brown trout found in fresh water streams and lakes throughout the world. For the most enjoyment use only light tackle and bring home only the ones you want for the table.

must be fresh. This means that those not equipped to carry along a supply of live bait should keep whatever bait they use on ice if the weather is warm.

Numerous types of artificial lures attract the trout. These include top water plugs, popping bugs, streamer flies, deep-running minnows, spoons, and bucktails.

Just because the trout shows a willingness to cooperate in so many aspects of fishing, however, should not lure the angler into the belief that Old Specks is a bumbling oaf that can be caught anytime a hook and line is tossed in the water. He can be, and often is, just as temperamental as any fish that swims, and at times he has one set of rules and again he has another. If you want to play games and stand a chance of winning with him, you are going to be required to learn to anticipate him and catch him off guard. Further still, you should be aware that he is not beyond changing signals right in the middle of the game for reasons known only to him.

The trout's spawning period begins in early spring and continues well into the fall. The eggs are cast in shallow waters of bays and lagoons, almost always where there are ample bottom grass and other forms of aquatic vegetation. It is in this same area, often only a couple of hundred feet from shore, that the larval stage develops, and here that the young trout remains for a considerable length of time. During this period the grass provides him with shelter and numerous forms of crustaceans upon which he feeds.

It is because these shallow areas are literally the nursery for young trout and other important game fish that the conservation-minded angler and the land developers along coastal regions are often at loggerheads with one another. In Florida, where waterfront property is at a premium, the land developers have long indulged in the practice of dredging and filling.

Dredge and fill mean simply what the words say. The shallow bottom ground close to shore is dredged and used to fill out the shoreline. This practice has a twofold adverse effect on the fish nurseries. One is that it forever removes the shallows so important to fish culture, and the second is that during the period while dredging machinery is in operation, the surrounding waters are filled with vast clouds of silt. This silt drifts with the current and eventually settles back to the bottom. In a sense, it is much the same as a rain of volcanic ash that can lay waste an otherwise fertile countryside.

When this roiled silt settles in sufficient amounts, it destroys other grass flats considerable distances from the actual scene of operation. Thus, not only are the immediate areas actually removed, but countless others are at least temporarily rendered barren. Eggs covered by the silt fail to hatch and the protective vegetation is covered to the extent that the tiny fish are robbed of their shelter and source of food.

The land developer views a vast expanse of mud flats that lie exposed at low tide and knows that if a seawall were built around them and sufficient amounts of bottom ground pumped into the enclosed area, it would be transformed into valuable living space for people. In all honesty, he points out that many populated urban areas of today would be untenable coastal marshes had it not been for the practice of dredging and filling.

It is a debate that continues to grow more heated with the passage of time. Fortunately for the maintenance of a somewhat balanced ecology, however, the state and many municipalities are taking an increasingly firm stand on the subject. The result is that it is becoming more difficult for the land developer to ravish the bays to satiate his appetite for more and more expensive waterfront property. It should be pointed out, however, that the problem is not peculiar only to the state of Florida.

Many other southeastern states are wrestling with similar problems. In fairness to the land developer, it should be emphasized that man and his machines have, by dint of dredge and fill, opened many areas to the angler by building causeways linking islands to the mainland and often making those islands habitable. The conscientious saltwater angler is aware of this, but at the same time he refuses to sit idly by and watch the march of progress trample wantonly over nature.

With the onset of cold weather the juvenile trout forsakes the shallow nursery flats and moves into deeper water. Some trout leave for the Gulf or the Atlantic with the coming of winter, but the majority remain in the bays and sounds throughout the year, dropping to lower levels in holes, passes, and deep tidal creeks to escape the shallow water which is more quickly affected by falling temperature.

Both young and adults follow the same practice in the heat of summer. Therefore, the best fishing in both very cold and very hot weather is to be found in deep water. Basically, however, the grass flats are the primary feeding grounds of the trout and it is over these areas that the largest catches are made, especially in spring and fall. Even a temporary moderation in either extreme of the weather will send the fish back onto the grassflats.

One of the most productive forms of trout fishing in moderate weather is to let the boat drift along with the flow of the tide. With natural bait such as cut mullet or live shrimp there is seldom need for sinkers, since the weight of the bait will cause it to drop to sufficient depths. Experience will prove that often certain areas of a given bay will be far more productive than identical bottom conditions a half or even a quarter of a mile away. When such locations are found, the angler will do well to drift over the productive grounds until the action tapers off and then crank up the engine and return to the original starting point.

As previously mentioned, trout will strike a wide variety of artificial lures. One of the facts that makes angling for this fish so interesting is that you may successfully use a particular lure for several days in a row, only to return to the same spot on the same tide and under similar weather conditions and have absolutely no luck whatsoever. At such times it is necessary to accommodate to the trout's wishes, because he is certainly not going to conform to yours. Often it only requires the change of color or size of a bucktail or plug to meet his approval.

Far more frequently, however, when a trout changes his mind, the problem of discovering what will fool him is considerably more complicated. This is one of the occasions when a well-stocked tackle box pays off. If he has not moved to a different location it may necessitate experimenting with as many as a dozen lures before the right one is presented.

One trick that often produces results when all else fails is to select a small artificial minnow and attach a bucktail trailer onto it. The bucktail should be tied to about twelve inches of nylon leader and this is made fast to the hook ring at the rear of the plug. Frequently when the water is clear you will see the trout surge up toward the minnow and turn away without striking. If the plug has a bucktail or small spoon trailing behind, the fish will be provoked into striking this instead of the plug.

"Splashing" is still another method that many consistently successful trout fishermen swear by. In order to use the "splashing" method a cork or plastic bobber the size of a hen's egg, or even larger, is attached to the line about four feet above the bait or lure. The angler casts and lets the float lie motionless for a long moment. If nothing happens he gives the rod a sharp jerk, causing the float to make a splashing sound on the surface. This is repeated at intervals of about thirty seconds. Hopefully —and it often works—the trout will be attracted by the disturbance and come over to investigate. Thus attracted, he will catch sight of lure or bait and grab it.

The same general idea often works by using a floating plug. In this case, the artificial is splashed, allowed to float motionless for a few seconds, and then retrieved several yards and the procedure is repeated until it is time to make another cast.

Night fishing from piers and bridges is frequently good. The chances are enhanced in such cases if a gasoline lantern is lowered to about five feet over the water. The light will almost always attract small bait fish and the trout will come to feed on the minnows. They will often be seen rising swiftly from the depths to grab one of the light-dazed minnows. Again, they will patrol the outer perimeter of the light circle and dart in every so often on a hit-and-run attack. When fishing with a dangling lantern it is best to fish just outside in the shadows. Live minnows or shrimp are best under these conditions, but jigging an artificial also produces good results.

The angler who uses heavy tackle for trout is spoiling most of the fun. My favorite rig is a light spinning rod with 4- or 6-pound monofilament line. The trout has a large mouth and a 3/0 or 4/0 hook is a good size, especially when natural bait is used.

One of the important techniques in casting for this speckled battler is to make every cast count, and do not be in too much of a hurry. A short jerky retrieve, often letting the lure sink all the way to the bottom, is the method most likely to provoke a strike. The lure should be played right up to the moment of lift-out. Trout will often seem quite oblivious to the boat or a wading angler and will refrain from striking until they sense they are about to lose the lure they have been following.

Because the trout is frequently such a willing fish, there is often the temptation on the part of some anglers to bring home as many as they can catch. Sometimes this is well above any reasonable number. The true sportsman will find pleasure in releasing far more than he is able to catch. And the trout is an easy fish to release unharmed. He may be simply led into the net and the hook removed from his jaws even before he is lifted entirely out of the water.

SHEEPSHEAD

The sheepshead is one of the most difficult fish to catch on hook and line, and conversely, one of the fish most frequently caught by those who angle in southern salt waters. Such a seemingly paradoxical statement is admittedly confusing, but nonetheless true for two very good reasons.

The first concerns the range, plentifulness, and habitats of the sheepshead. He is abundant all along the Atlantic and Gulf coasts and often congregates in considerable numbers close to wharfs, piers, and bridges. This puts him in easy reach of the largest number of fishermen.

On the other hand, there is a decided art to hooking a sheepshead, and the angler who is not acquainted with the habits of this fine fish can *almost* catch several dozen in an afternoon and still fail to land a single one. It is only after a period of apprenticeship that the fisherman

Sheepshead

can sally forth on a sheepshead mission and accomplish it with any degree of satisfaction.

Oddly enough, for a popular fish with such an extensive range, the sheepshead, unlike many others, is not burdened with an abundance of local names. About the only sobriquet he is saddled with is *convict fish,* inspired by his distinct black-and-white vertical bars that comprise his coloration and are suggestive of the prison garb worn by the "chain gangs" of yore. The name sheepshead is obviously derived from the simularity between the fish's head and that of a sheep.

Specifically, there are two species of sheepshead found in the continental waters of the eastern part of the United States. The first is *Archosargus probatocephalus* and is found in the Atlantic, around Florida, and up into the northern Gulf of Mexico. The second, *Archosargus oviceps,* overlaps the former in the northeastern Gulf and extends westward to Mexico.

The average sheepshead ranges in weight from two to five pounds, but records of fifteen to twenty-five pounds have been set along both the Atlantic and Gulf coasts.

Aside from the six or seven vertical black bars on a silvery white background, the incisor teeth are one of this fish's easily recognizable features. They are pronounced and protrude slightly. He uses them to gather and crush food such as crabs and mollusks, and to cut barnacles off pilings and rocks.

Anyone who has taken the time to inspect a rock barnacle immediately realizes the strength of tooth and jaw any fish must necessarily possess to include them as a major part of his diet. The barnacles are shaped like a miniature volcano and are composed of a hard, limestone-like shell which attaches itself to pilings, hulls of boats and ships, rocks, and even turtles and whales.

The top of the barnacle cone consists of movable plates that are opened and closed at will. They dwell on objects in the tidal zone and can tolerate being exposed to air for long periods when the tide is at ebb. When they are covered with water the trapdoor plates at the top open to release modified feathery feet or legs which they wave about to collect the minute planktonic organisms on which they feed.

One of the most interesting and provocative features of the barnacle is the substance with which it adheres to solid objects. Some investigators believe that when this adhesive is fully understood and capable of being reproduced, it will have wide application in many phases of dentistry where fillings and caps are used on human teeth.

Inside the shell the animal is composed of both male and female organs, thus the fertile eggs are expelled from the same barnacle. In the

Well-known outdoor writer and sports fisherman in the truest sense of the word, Vic Dunaway holds a big sheepshead in his right hand and a small channel bass in his left. Because of the vertical black bands, the sheepshead is also known as the "convict fish."

larval stage it is free swimming and after a short period it attaches itself to some object and begins to produce its own protective shell. Barnacles are the curse of boat owners because the dense growth of shells forms a drag that reduces speed, and boats must be periodically hauled out of the water and scraped. Antifouling paints are helpful in retarding the barnacle growth, but their effectiveness soon wears off and the scraping and repainting has to be repeated.

Despite the extremely hard shell and the powerful adhesive, the sheepshead is able to crack the barnacle and extract the fleshy animal that lives inside. While the ubiquitous barnacle is the main attraction that causes sheepshead to congregate around piers, jetties, and bridges, the fish is ever on the lookout for dock spiders, small shrimp, and other creatures that inhabit such places.

The sheepshead is attracted to a variety of bait that includes chunks of clam flesh, oysters, which can be secured to a hook with a small rubber band, and sea worms. In areas where fiddler crabs (see chapter on natural bait) are plentiful, they are one of the best sheepshead bait to be found. It is best to push the hook through from the underside near either of the rear corners of the crab.

When fishing from piers and bridges, it is well to note the flow of the tide so that the bait will drift close to, but not beyond, the nearest piling. A float is frequently used advantageously to prevent the bait from sinking too deeply. The best depth is three or four feet beneath the surface.

It is the manner in which a sheepshead takes the bait that is frequently perplexing to the uninitiated angler. Croaker, channel bass, trout, and other fish will simply grab the bait and run. The fisherman strikes back and the battle is on. Not so with the sheepshead. His nature causes him to be somewhat suspicious to the extent that he will often simply nudge the bait and usually cause a slight tug on the line. The natural impulse of the angler is to pull back instantly.

To follow this standard procedure usually results in failure to set the hook. Those who have practiced the art to a point of near perfection ignore the first tentative nibble and wait several seconds until the second nudge is felt—only then do they strike. If the point of the hook is needle sharp and exposed, as it should be, it will likely be driven into the lip of the fish. The result will be a well-hooked sheepshead that will have little chance of escaping.

If the angler waits until the fish has the bait inside his armor-plated mouth, it is less likely to penetrate and the sheepshead often shakes free. It is because of this skill, or lack of it, as the case may be, that two anglers will occasionally be seen fishing with virtually the same type of tackle and identical bait, with one catching sheepshead frequently while the other spends most of his time putting on fresh bait and wondering if he is quite the fisherman he imagined himself to be.

One of the first fish I can recall catching was a sheepshead in St. Andrews Bay when I was living in Panama City, Florida. I was about five years old at the time, and my tackle consisted of a cane pole, hook, line, and sinker with a cork stopper for a float. In the years that followed I have caught many more. One of the most productive trips I remember was in the pass between Longboat and Anna Maria keys on the west coast of Florida just north of Sarasota. I had not intended to go fishing that day, but I became engaged in a conversation with a man and his young son when the three of us just happened to stop at the same roadside snack shop.

The talk quickly drifted to local fishing conditions and the man mentioned that he and his son were planning to go out in the pass and catch a mess of sheepshead. "Are you a fisherman?" he asked.

I entered a guilty plea and admitted to having a bait-casting rod and tackle box in my car.

"Me and the boy got a skiff up at the pass," he said. "If you're a mind to, you can come along. We got two buckets full of fiddlers and with the tide coming in like it is there oughta be plenty of fish."

The chance of catching a fish is something I seldom pass up whenever the opportunity presents itself and I quickly accepted the invitation. Several minutes later we were in the boat and underway.

"Used to be an old bridge 'cross this pass before a storm washed it out a few years back," the man said. "The road department come along and put a new one up but they left some of the old pilings still stuck in the bottom. We anchor close to where the old bridge was and then do a little chumming for a few minutes and all at once we got a lot of fishing to do."

Whenever I go fishing with someone I always observe what they do and try out their methods, because there is always something to learn if you are willing to listen. As soon as the anchor was set I watched with interest as the man went about the chumming process he had mentioned. Pulling a stained cotton glove on his right hand, he reached into one of the two buckets and grabbed a handul of the live fiddler crabs, crushed the mass slightly, and tossed it over the side. He continued to do this for a couple of minutes and then said:

"That ought to be enough to get 'em good and hungry so we better get some bait on our hooks and start fishing."

The man and boy were using boat rods with small star-drag reels and it made my freshwater rig look woefully inadequate by comparison. I paid particular attention to the type of terminal tackle they were using —2/0 hooks with clip swivels and about three feet of limp wire leader. Scrambling around in my own tackle box, I matched their rigs as closely as possible with a No. 1 hook, 12-pound test leader, and a 1-ounce barrel-type sinker attached to the line above the swivel at the top of the leader.

Thus rigged, I picked out one of the live fiddler crabs and pinned him on so that the hook went through the bottom shell and barely broke the surface on the carapace.

Letting the line slide off the reel, I waited until I felt the sinker touch the bottom and then wound in enough line to allow the bait to drift about a foot off the bottom. Had the fishing been from a bridge I would not have gone so deep, but in this case the target area was the stubs of old piling on the bottom.

As if someone had touched a button, all three of us had strikes almost at the same instant. I lost my fish within a couple of seconds after I felt the tug, because I made the mistake of striking too quickly. Hurriedly, I reeled in and rebaited the hook. Just at that moment the boy lost his sheepshead right at the side of the boat while he was trying to grab the leader.

I saw the man's rod dip and bend while he fought the reel handle and I was willing to guess he had tied onto a fish that would weigh at least seven pounds. When he finally lofted it over into the skiff, we put it on the scales, and I was surprised to see that it did not quite reach the 3-pound mark.

At the same instant, the boy was swinging into action again. If his father's rod had been doing a jig, the boy's rod was in the middle of a red-hot war dance.

"If you haven't had a bump since you let your line down you might as well reel in and put on another fiddler," the man said. "You shore ain't gonna catch nothing with a bare hook."

I had been so busy watching the action that I temporarily forgot about my own line. The man was right, of course. When I reeled in to check I discovered my hook had been cleaned.

"Funny thing 'bout sheepshead," the man said. "They fight like all git-out once they're hooked, but they can nip off a chunk of bait so light that you sometimes don't even know its been looked at."

By the time the boy had boated his second fish, the man was fast onto his next one and I had lost three more fiddler crabs.

"There's a real knack to hooking a sheepshead," the man chuckled. Every fisherman becomes an expert when he's catching fish and some-one nearby isn't, and the man could not resist the opportunity to do a little instructing. "When you feel the slightest little nibble," he continued, "you ease out on your line until you figure he's just 'bout ready and then you really sock it to him. If you jerk back too quick you lose, and if you give him enough time he'll feel the hook and spit it out."

Determined not to be outdone, I fastened on still another of the tiny crabs and let my line down. There it was—a bite, almost the instant the sinker touched bottom! I let the reel run slack for about two seconds and then heaved back on the rod with my thumb tightly clamped on the reel spool.

"See what I told you?" the man laughed. "This time you got him. Just keep on fighting him, though, 'cause if you give him half a chance he'll run around one of those old barnacle-crusted logs down there and saw your line in half 'fore you can say jackrabbit."

Before the fight was over I could fully understand why the man and his son were using the heavy tackle, but I had to admit secretly that I favored my lighter tackle.

"Beginner's luck," the boy grinned. "You got me and Pop beat on size so far."

I didn't care what kind of luck it was. My fish weighed an even eight pounds.

"Let me give you a little word of warning," the man cautioned. "Don't go sticking your finger in his mouth 'cause his teeth are sharp as knife blades and his jaws are strong enough to bite the end off your finger. I had a big one on once and he bit the hook clean in half just as I was hoisting him over the side."

Of course, I had known the sheepshead for a long while, but as I said earlier, there is always something to learn if you are willing to listen, and I did learn a few new angles on that trip.

So far as edibility is concerned, these fish are rated as excellent so long as they are in the 2- to 5-pound range. In fact, many piscatorial gourmets rate the flesh of small sheepshead right along with that of red snapper. As they grow larger, the meat becomes coarser. With all due respect to these convict fish, it must be stated that they are one of the hardest fish there is to scale. The easy way around this is simply to skin the fish and forget about the scaling knife.

Whatever the bait, and no matter whether you fish from a boat or dangle your line around the pilings of an old dock, the sheepshead is sure to provide you with some exciting fishing. He is a game fish all the way.

LADYFISH

My Dad and I had been trolling for mackerel without much luck in the vicinity of Hurricane Pass out from Dunedin on the west coast of Florida. I shut off the motor and we sat there wondering which way to go next when suddenly about an acre of smooth surface of the water on the Gulf side of the pass shattered, and a sound like someone shooting a stream of water in an empty bucket filled the air.

As quickly as it had begun, the noise and action subsided. A minute later the same disturbance occurred.

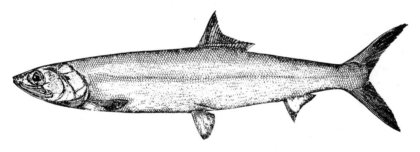

Ladyfish

"Are you thinking the same thing as I am?"

"Exactly," I said in reply. "You rig up the spinning rods and at least we will catch fish before this day is done."

Starting the engine, I nosed around a shallow bar and felt the sweep of the outgoing tide nudge the bow of the boat. Holding back on the throttle, I let the boat move along through the pass and twice more we saw the froth kicked up on the surface and heard the swishing sound of the attacking fish. When we were a couple of hundred yards away, I cut off the power and we rode the tide toward the target area.

Dad took aim and shot a small shiny plug toward the place we had last seen the fish break. It hit the water with a slight bounce and before it had time to settle the action was on. Out came the first ladyfish in a series of three fast jumps, shimmering like polished silver in the morning sunlight. These aerial acrobatics were followed by a long run to the north that stripped half the spool of 4-pound monofilament. More jumps, more line ripped off the reel, and then Dad began gaining on the fish. I could stand it no longer and offered the unseen school a yellow bucktail.

Two turns on the reel crank and out came the second ladyfish, but the bucktail did not hold. It shot out of the fish's mouth and was fielded by a second one the instant it hit the water. This time it held.

Both of us were now tied into a pair of the fightingest fish ever to honor southern salt waters with their presence. Both were running, turning, jumping, and in the middle of it, the entire school churned the surface again right ahead of the skiff.

"On this kind of tackle," Dad said, holding the rod butt almost over his head and fighting to regain some of his line, "I believe I would rather catch ladyfish than tarpon on heavier gear."

There was no time to indulge in the amenities of assisting one another in bringing the quarry aboard. When Dad had his fish close to the side of the boat, he held the rod with his left hand and fumbled around under the stern seat until he found the landing net.

"Good," he said, cautiously taking hold of the fish. "There is only one hook in his jaw." He slipped the plug free and eased the net back down into the water. For a moment the fish lolled motionless and then darted for the depths.

"Throw me the net before you catch another," I said. "This one is ready to come in."

For the next half hour we battled it out with well over a dozen of the fighting ladies and during the process we drifted into the middle of the school. I was glad because I wanted to see what kind of bait fish they were attacking.

"Glass minnows," Dad said, shading his eyes against the glare. "There must be thousands of them out here."

"More like millions," I countered.

We sat motionless in the small boat and watched the little transparent minnows sweeping around us in a vast surface-swimming swarm. Time after time we could see the ladyfish coming up en masse. Our boat did not seem to bother them in the least and during their brief raids the sound was almost deafening.

Here again is the fascinating question of where fish get their names. Swordfish, sailfish, and bluefish are easily understood. Others undoubtedly have their origin in foreign languages that reach far back into history. The drum and croaker and grunts make noises that give them a reasonable excuse for being called what they are. If you analyze it, most fish names are reasonable, but I have never been able to find even the flimsiest excuse for ladyfish *(Elops saurus)*.

Also, you feel a bit foolish holding one up and saying, "How about this ladyfish! Isn't he a beauty?" I have never investigated and I seriously doubt that anyone else has, but I am reasonably certain there are just about as many males in a school of ladyfish as there are females. What is more, in using a name that smacks of the distaff one is prone to think maybe it was applied because the fish was possessed of a gentle nature. Far be *that* from the truth.

Then, as if to cloud the issue even more, the ladyfish has another popular name that makes about as much sense as the first. For some reason, they are also called ten-pounders. Why? I don't have the faintest idea, because the overwhelming majority of ladyfish, or ten-pounders, if you will, are well below the ten-pound mark where weight is concerned. In fact one weighing three or four pounds is a big one. There is a record of one being caught that weighed twelve pounds, and off the southeastern coast of Africa they are known to exceed twenty-five pounds. And those weighing seven or eight pounds are not unheard of in the Bahamas.

The only nickname they have that makes any sense at all is *bonyfish.* This they certainly are. The name bonyfish, however, is often confused with bonefish *(Albula vulpes),* to which they are not at all related. Like the true bonefish, however, they are literally filled with bones and fall into the class of fish that you would eat only if you were stranded on a desert island and that was all you could catch.

In general appearance, ladyfish look like pint-sized tarpons. They are dark on the back and silver on the sides and belly. The fins, including the caudal, are similar to the tarpon with the exception of the elongated posterior ray peculiar to the tarpon's dorsal fin. The mouth with the upturned lower jaw is also similar to that of the tarpon.

They frequent shallow water and bays and are numerous in south Florida waters. Their range extends well up the Atlantic coast and in the Gulf. They are frequently caught by casting from the beach, especially near passes, in tides sweeping under bridges, and from piers.

To be fully enjoyed, they must be caught on light tackle—spinning, bait, or fly casting. Of course, because of their size, they could not match the tarpon for big-time rugged fighting that often pits brawn against speed and agility. But everything in fishing is relative and if the tackle is light, the ladyfish can be a worthy opponent.

They are occasionally caught on live bait, but this seems to be a waste of time with a fish that is so willing to strike artificials. The fly-rod angler is well equipped, even with his freshwater wand. My favorite is freshwater spinning tackle with a wide assortment of small lures that include spoons, jigs, plugs, and spinners. If there is a school nearby, get set for some fast and furious action. If your casting platform is a boat, it is important to approach the feeding school with caution. Along a jetty, beneath a bridge, or on the beach you may see a school coming, or they may just suddenly begin to strike from deep water.

The outgoing tide is favored, although they are often caught by trolling in bays. It has been my observation that they come into bays with the tide and fan out over wide areas while the flood is on. With the change, they seem to re-form into schools and head for open water.

It is important to use a short length of thin wire leader because of the sharp gill covers. Those same gills should be avoided when handling the fish. Here again is a fine game fish that should be released after you have won the battle, because they serve no practical use ashore except to fertilize the petunia bed. Now and then one will be so deeply hooked that it has to be killed to remove the lure. Even then, they might as well go back over the side because nothing in the way of fish flesh is wasted in the sea.

SNOOK

There are two ways to catch snook *(Centropomus undecimalis).* One is to make a long, exhaustive study of the fish, his habits, his peculiarities, where he is likely to be found, what his favorite foods are, which artificials are most likely to fool him, the best stage of the tide to fish for him, and in fact, become an expert on snook fishing.

The other is to know absolutely nothing about the fish and just catch one right after another. I am still not quite sure which is the best, because I have seen it happen both ways too many times to count.

Let's take an episode that occurred one spring day not long ago when I was trolling for mackerel off the southern tip of Anclote Key near the Florida sponge-fishing town of Tarpon Springs. I was not having much luck, so I rounded the tip of the island near the old lighthouse and shifted to light spinning tackle with the idea that I could at least catch a few speckled trout before calling it a day.

The tide was nearing the flood stage, and the wind was out of the northeast. I picked out a wide grassy plateau, shut off the motor, and was beginning to cast when I noticed a man standing up in the middle of a stern-drive boat that looked so new it conceivably could have been on the dealer's showroom floor the day before. He was waving his outspread arms up and down in what I interpreted to be some kind of distress signal.

Deciding he was either out of gas or had engine trouble, I put my spinning tackle down and moved over to see if I could be of help.

"I hate to interrupt your fishing," the man said, "but I wonder if you can tell me what kind of fish this is. I think its a barracuda, but I'm

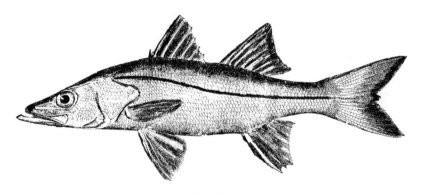

Snook

pretty new at this fishing business and I'm not quite sure." As he spoke he stooped over, lifted a large fish from inside his boat, and held it up for me to see.

"That's a snook," I said, "and a fine one at that. It must weigh ten pounds or better."

"Fourteen pounds exactly," the man said, nodding toward an open tackle box on one of the boat seats. "I have one of those fish scales and I just weighed him." Putting the fish back down, the man wiped his hands on a small bath towel and proceeded to light a cigar. "I thought all the time I was catching a barracuda."

"What did you catch him on?" I asked, suppressing the urge to say something about beginner's luck.

"Caught all of them on this big old artificial plug," he replied in a cloud of cigar smoke. "My granddaddy whittled this out of a block of wood years ago back in Ohio, and when we moved down here to Florida I stuck it in my tackle box."

The plug was a monstrosity if ever one existed. It was nearly five inches long with a head painted a bilious blue and white body speckled with red polka dots.

"When you say all of them," I said, "do you mean you caught more than that one snook?"

"Oh, heavens yes," the man said, reaching for a line tied to a cleat on the far side of his boat. "I have six on the stringer and this one in the boat makes seven. I guess this is what they mean when they talk about fabulous Florida fishing." He hefted a stringer of snook that must have totaled somewhere between thirty and forty pounds. "Do they always bite this well and what did you say they were?"

"To answer your questions one at a time," I said, staring at the great mass of fish the man was holding, "no, they don't always bite that well and the fish is called a snook." I paused, trying to think of the proper way to phrase what I knew I must say. "You are a lucky fisherman in more ways than one," I finally said.

"What do you mean?" the man asked, letting the stringer back down into the water.

"I mean that it is lucky for you that I'm not a fish and wildlife officer because if I were you would be headed for court and most likely be fined. Snook," I continued, "were designated as a game fish back in 1957 and there is a bag limit of four per fisherman in a day's time."

"Oh, good heavens!" The man tossed his freshly lighted cigar over the side. "I had no idea I was breaking the law." He pulled out his pocketknife and before I hardly knew what he was getting ready to do, he cut the bottom ring off his stringer and let the six half-dead snook spill back into the water. "Thanks for the warning." He picked up the seventh fish from the bottom of the boat and looked at it for a moment. "I think I'll take this one back to show my wife. When I bought this

If the angler with the light spinning tackle is lucky the rambunctious snook in the above photo will head for deep water. If the fish elects to make a dive for mangrove roots it will be only a matter of seconds before the angler is reeling in the remains of a broken line.

boat she laughed at me and said she bet I wouldn't ever catch a fish."
With that, he turned the ignition key and shoved the throttle full ahead.

When the noise and wake of his boat subsided, I picked up my
spinning rod, unhooked the yellow bucktail, and dug around in my
tackle box for a top water plug. Either there had been only seven hungry
snook in that pod, or they had all left for safer water. But I couldn't
help wondering if perhaps that grotesque plug with its sickly blue head
and measled body had anything to do with the man's success.

There are several species of snook found in American tropical and
subtropical waters. The common snook is unquestionably the most
numerous and the largest. He is well distributed around the coast of
Florida and far up in the Gulf during the warmer months.

When winter comes and the water temperature begins to drop below
65 degrees, the only place to do any snook fishing is around the extreme
lower tip of Florida. The Keys, Florida Bay, and the Ten Thousand
Island region are the most productive areas that I know of from personal experience.

The snook is a beautiful fish to see and one well worth the time and
trouble it takes to engage him in battle. His coloration varies slightly,
depending on the duration of time he spends in certain waters. In
general, however, his long body, which is thick through the middle, is
dark, greenish brown on the top, and shades to silver on the sides and
belly. When he has spent considerable time in rivers and creeks and
around mangrove thickets, his silver sides become dull yellow in color.
His protruding lower jaw and the distinct black lateral stripe that runs
from just behind his gills to the end of the caudal peduncle make him
easy to recognize.

The average size ranges from three to ten pounds, but those weighing
twenty pounds are not uncommon, and the IGFA record was set
January 9, 1963, by Jane Haywood fishing off La Paz, Mexico. Her
record catch measured 4 feet 1½ inches in length and weighed 52
pounds 6 ounces. Half a dozen or more other records have been set in
Florida waters with weights in the 30- and 40-pound range.

Snook have been taken on very light tackle, including fly rods and
the lightest of spinning rigs, but these classes are not recommended,
because when a big snook strikes he is going to put up a fierce and often
long-lasting battle and occasionally he makes shambles of even medium-weight equipment.

The fly-fisherman should rely on salt water rigs, and those using spinning and revolving-spool tackle should go prepared with lines testing at twelve to twenty pounds. Many large snook have been netted with monofilament line of six or eight pounds, but a hundred times that many have been lost, too.

The term "stupid fish" definitely does not apply to the snook, or robalo, as he is also known. He seems to know what he is doing every minute of the time. Some excellent game fish will occasionally act as if they do not know what is troubling them once they have been hooked and they will often put up their biggest battles in an effort to shake the hooks out of their mouths without seeming to attach any significance to the line that connects them with the angler.

The snook, on the other hand, gives the impression that he immediately senses the line's significance and will do everything in his power to cut it. This he will frequently do with his razor-sharp gill covers or by making a sudden rush for the nearest barnacle-crusted piling, oyster bar, or mangrove root. It almost seems that the snook makes a thorough inspection of the area in which he plans to take up residence and has his line-breaking obstacle all staked out before he considers making a swipe at the fisherman's lure or bait.

To beat him at his game, especially if you can slow him before he carries the line completely around a snag, you would do well to use a heavy leader. This, however, can present a problem because snook are frequently caught on top water lures or bait fished close to the surface, and a heavy leader will often spoil the live action. The best method of overcoming this problem is to keep the lure or bait on the move in a series of short jerks.

This is not to suggest that snook do not strike deep-running lures. Indeed, at times of low water when the fish is lying doggo in a deep hole, and again, when he happens to be in a mood to feed on such bottom dwellers as crabs and low-swimming baitfish, he cannot be induced to strike surface lures. On these occasions, the weight of a heavy leader does not present much of a problem.

There are three primary types of snook-fishing areas. One is from bridges or piers, another is in and around the margins of islands where the mangrove trees creep out into the water on their stiltlike legs, and the third is in tidal streams. They are also caught with some degree of regularity in the open water of bays and occasionally by surf casting, but by and large the three above-mentioned locations are best.

Of the three, there is little doubt that more snook are caught from bridges and piers than from anywhere else simply because these structures are most accessible to the greatest number of fishermen; ergo, more fishermen, more fish.

In bridge fishing with either live or artificial bait, it is important to cast to the uptide side, or against the flow, so that the lure or bait is retrieved toward the pilings. The reason being, as previously mentioned, the snook likes to be close to some kind of obstacle. The most productive time when fishing from bridges and piers is in the night and especially when there is a moon. Very early morning and late afternoon are fairly good periods, and also the snook is one type of fish that becomes most active just after a full tide. An exception will be described later.

When fishing at night, a gasoline lantern is not mandatory, but it is a great help. After you have the lantern burning brightly it should be attached to a length of strong line and let down until it is about four feet above the surface. This method is also effective when angling for game fish other than snook. If there are any snook in the area they will approach the light and many times can be seen lurking in the shadow.

It is important to cast your offering so that it will either drift or be retrieved in that shadowy region just to the side of the brilliant circle of light. When a snook strikes, try to work him away from the light, because if he gets excited and carries your line around the lantern cord you are going to have more confusion than you bargained for. If you happen to be using monofilament line and it passes against the hot lantern globe, it will melt in a second.

Naturally, when bridge or pier fishing, tackle has to be heavier than when fishing from a boat because you are either going to have to walk your catch back to shore or, if the distance, number of fishermen, and potential obstacles are too great, you will have to horse him up to the span. Therefore, a rod should have more backbone than you might normally prefer. When it comes to the size of the hook, don't make the mistake of thinking too small. Remember the snook has a large mouth and he is not adverse to opening it wide. A 4/0 or 5/0 is not at all too large when using live bait. A bucktail or feathered jig should be tied on a 3/0; certainly no smaller.

In winter fishing for snook, the action starts in the vicinity of Stuart on the north and south forks of the St. Lucie River. From there it continues on down the coast, including the Keys, across Florida Bay, the southern fringes of the Everglades and around the Gulf side up as far as Fort Myers.

The author admires a snook that made the mistake of grabbing a silver spoon cast into the tangle of roots on the far side of the narrow tidal stream.

Although I have caught snook at many widely separated points in Florida and under a variety of conditions, whenever I contemplate fishing for old linesides I automatically think of the Everglades National Park. Especially do I think of the Shark River region and the Ten Thousand Islands, both of which are in that vast stretch of primordial wilderness that covers nearly a million and a half acres on the southern tip of the state.

Here is undoubtedly the largest and most primitive stretch of untamed jungle country in all of North America, and if the land developers and flood control people will just let it alone it will remain a true wonderland for ages to come.

There are two primary entrances for the snook fisherman who wants to try his luck along the fringes of the Park. One of these is from Everglades City, and the other is from Flamingo. If you are coming down the east coast take State Road 27 west from Homestead, follow it to the end and you will wind up at Flamingo. If you are trailing your own boat there are free launching ramps and if you have no boat there are plenty there to rent at a reasonable fee, and this means anything from skiffs to powerboats.

In the past few years the Park Service has added something to make a fisherman's dream come true—houseboats. A few years ago my wife and I, with another couple, decided to rent one for a week and do some serious fishing, with snook as our main objective.

On previous occasions I had fished Ponce De Leon Bay at the northern tip of Cape Sable and I had always caught so many snook around the mouth of the Shark River that I laid my reputation on the line and sold my crew on the idea of going back there by houseboat. It can be reached, of course, by running south from Naples, but to make any respectable time it is open water cruising.

When I started talking about houseboats I think Dorothy and Betty envisioned some kind of rough old barge with a shack built on top. They did a genuine double take when Bob and I ushered them aboard one of the Park Service houseboats.

"Beautiful!" was Dorothy's sole descriptive adjective when she stepped inside and found bulkhead to bulkhead carpeting, a galley with an alcohol-burning stove, ice chest, running water, head and shower.

The boat was thirty-four feet in length and powered by a 70 h.p. inboard diesel engine and carried 125 gallons of fuel. It was built to sleep six people, and with only four of us aboard there was more than enough room. Because I remembered the waters we planned to fish, I also rented a fourteen-foot skiff and took along a 7½ h.p. outboard.

With the logistics taken care of, there was nothing to do but tell the ranger station where we planned to go and how long we would be there. While this precautionary measure is not demanded, I haven't seen a boat or engine yet that is infallible, and when you are going to divest yourself of every last line of civilized communication, it is a comforting thought to know that if you don't return somewhere close to your ETA, there will be somebody out looking for you.

Since this was fundamentally an inland voyage through the heart of the Everglades, it will be exceedingly difficult for me not to wax eloquently on the fabulously beautiful and exciting country we cruised. We are, however, off on a snook-fishing trip and so I'll file the notes I made about the alligators, turtles, snakes, birds, and all the rest of the flora and fauna we passed. Instead, I'll just sketch the bare bones of the route we followed from the Flamingo Marina to the mouth of the Shark River where it empties into Ponce De Leon Bay.

With the engine purring along at slow speed, we traveled due north up Buttonwood Canal to Coot Bay. From there we could increase the speed and follow the channel markers up to the north end and slow down again for the short run up Tarpon Canal.

Popping out of the canal, we were in the big water region of the Everglades. To the north was Whitewater Bay, and while we could have gone across it, I had charted a course that called for an abrupt westward turn just after leaving the canal. This would lead us in a general north-west direction along Joe River up to Oyster Bay. It was virtually impossible for us to get lost along Joe River because we were flanked on either side by an almost solid wall of jungle.

When reaching Oyster Bay we steered just about due north. There was plenty of water as long as we stayed clear of the numerous small islands. Right at the north end the going was a little tricky because of a string of bars. We bumped bottom a couple of times, but with the throttle way back it caused no trouble. As soon as we were clear of Oyster Bay we were able to pick up the channel of Little Shark River and we followed this for a short run to the eastern tip of Shark River Island.

Should the names Little Shark River and Shark River be confusing, I will explain. Both rivers drain down from the fastness of the Ever-glades interior and the Little Shark passes to the south of Shark River Island and out into the Gulf while Shark River itself empties into Ponce De Leon Bay. This was where we wanted to go and we were there well before dark.

The reason for choosing the Bay was because, although it was the fall of the year, there is always the possibility of squalls sweeping in from the open Gulf, and the Bay is dotted with numerous islands that afford excellent protection from the wind. Houseboats are fine, but they don't react too well in high wind that often accompanies squalls.

Ahead of us lay a full five days of fishing, but I could not resist hooking the outboard on the skiff's transom immediately and making a try for at least one of the snook we had come after.

Putting my tackle box and a saltwater spinning rod aboard, I cranked the engine and moved away from the houseboat. I skirted the endless array of mangrove islands on my right that are laced with dark streams coming down out of the Everglades. Off to the west the sun was nearing the horizon in the Gulf, leaving the azure heaven to meet the glassy undulating swells of the blue counterpane that stretched away across the open water. Minutes, hours, years, and in fact, time itself suddenly seemed to be as nothing. I shut off the motor and let the boat drift silently to a stop.

Standing up, I stared almost transfixed at the shimmering surface of the water and absorbed the soft breeze that bore the faint sulphur smell of a falling tide. It might have been today, a year ago, a century ago, or a millennium. Perhaps, almost certainly, a red man such as the seafaring Calusas had stood in his dugout canoe at this exact spot and heard the ticking and snapping of barnacles and coon oysters closing as the falling water left them clinging to the exposed mangrove roots.

Earlier I stated that the near-flood stage of the tide produces the most active snook fishing. As with all angling, however, there are exceptions. When fishing for snook around mangrove islands there is no question that they are actively feeding near the flood. As a rule, at such times, they are so far back in the jungle of roots that casting for them is out of the question. Hence, the angler must wait for the ebb when they forsake their inland prowl and head back toward the channels.

Quickly threading the monofilament line through the guides on my rod, I tied on a 3-foot leader with a test of 30 pounds and a floating yellow Mirrolure and cast it toward the jungle of the nearest island. It landed with a small splash, and I let it lie there for over a minute. The place looked good, so I was not in a hurry to retrieve the lure. Instead, I gave it a little twitch and let it lie still again. If a snook was down there he might be eyeing the artificial and I did not want to take it away from him too quickly. Another twitch and there he came. He had not been under the lure where I thought he should be, but off to one side maybe ten yards away. I saw him pushing a little bow wave as he zeroed in on the bait. Possibly ever since the tide had begun to ebb he had been waiting for a small bird, a crab, or a mouse to fall from a low limb or root. My Mirrolure was just that to him.

When I realized he was coming for it I began a slow retrieve, lifting the rod tip in a series of short jerks to make the lure look alive. It has been the same since man began fishing for the fun of it. He catches a fish and then tries to recount the moment of truth when the fish clamps his jaws on the hook. The water explodes—the fish strikes like a torpedo —there is a welter of foaming confusion—and on and on.   .

Somehow, maybe it is a sixth sense, you seem to know for sure whether or not a fish is going actually to strike when you see him swimming toward your lure. I had that feeling and I was positive he would boil up out of the dark water and slap his jaws shut on the plug.

He didn't.

When he came close he rolled in a sweeping turn that took him back toward the mangrove roots. Dumbfounded, I stood there and stopped cranking the real handle, wondering what had caused him to change his mind.

Already, he was growing in size and would no doubt reach thirty or forty pounds before I returned to the houseboat. With no attempt to twitch the rod or do anything to entice him to try again, I cranked the reel and when the lure was close enough to the boat to lift out of the water there was a crash and I saw the snook with the plug cross-wise in his mouth.

I don't know what he did or how he did it. Maybe he was a little suspicious and decided to make a deep dive and come up under the plug, or maybe it was an entirely different snook. Whatever the case, he was hooked and hooked solidly. In that fleeting instant I had seen hooks all tangled in his big mouth.

Instead of turning and heading back toward the sanctuary of the mangrove roots he did something I had no idea he was going to do. He swam directly under the boat and headed for the open water of the bay. Swinging my rod around toward the stern, I pointed it down close to the water to keep the line from fouling in the outboard's lower housing. Line was screeching off my reel. I let him run for perhaps twenty or thirty yards. Why not be honest, though? I did not *let* him run. He ran, and there was nothing I could do to stop him.

Remember I said earlier that a snook knows the area in which he hangs out. Well, when I had collected my wits I saw what he had in mind now. He was headed straight toward a small oyster bar off to the side of my boat. A few more seconds and he would swing around it and pop my line as surely as if it had been drawn across the blade of a knife.

"No you don't!" I yelled. There are times when you can turn a snook and make him take a different direction. Holding the rod as far toward the bow of the boat as I could, I set the brake tighter and tighter and somehow it worked. The pressure was a bit too much for him and he had a quick change of mind. He reversed his direction and headed back toward the roots and this time I could tell he was going to pass across the bow.

I don't know how fast a snook can swim, but a wahoo and a tarpon can hit thirty-five to forty miles an hour. I would guess a snook is a bit slower, but surely he can turn up something close to twenty knots. This one was doing his best, and I was about to throw my arm out of joint as I cranked the reel handle to take up the slack line until he had passed, and then the battle was on again.

Up he came in one of the most beautiful jumps I have ever seen a fish make. The fading sun glinted off his silver sides and when he hit the water he scooted for about five yards and duplicated his first jump. I could swear I heard the hooks rattling around in his jaws while he was in the air.

The two long runs and the pressure I was putting on him began to take its toll, and when it was getting almost too dark to see I had him up beside the boat. Holding the rod tip high, I guided him into my landing net.

That was all of the fishing I needed for the day. Dorothy, Betty, and Bob had already turned the lights on in the houseboat, and instead of cranking up the outboard, I paddled back. It gave me time to admire the beautiful fish and cool it, as the saying goes.

"Have any luck?" Bob asked as I made the skiff fast to the stern. "We thought we saw you fighting a fish but we couldn't tell for sure."

"Picked up a little one just to get us started," I said.

Out comes one very angry snook to take a quick look at the fisherman who is brash enough to think he can win with such light tackle. That black mark running the length of his body has earned him the nickname of "Old Linesides."

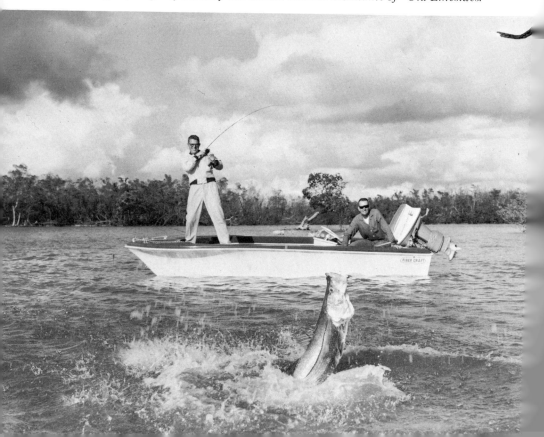

"A little one!" Betty yelped when I lifted twenty-two pounds of snook and flopped him over on the stern deck.

That was the way the trip began, and it continued for five beautiful days. Several times we caught redfish, again we hit a school of Spanish mackerel; Bob held a big tarpon for three jumps, and there were several mangrove snappers plus a few others that added to the variety. Except for the fish we wanted for the frying pan, we let most of them go as soon as we had them up beside the boat.

Because snook are generally caught in water where there are pilings, roots, and other underwater obstructions, there are far more lost than are ever brought to the gaff or net. The most important thing to do is to make him fight it out in open water.

A snook can be absolutely maddening if he wants to be. Many times, especially in clear water around bridges, one can be seen holding steady against the current, and you can cast your arm off and use every lure you have in your tackle box and often he won't even move when you pop a lure right over his head. The same holds true when using all kinds of natural bait. The answer can only be that it is not his dinnertime and he doesn't eat snacks between meals.

FLOUNDER

If you consider yourself a saltwater fisherman and have never caught a flounder, then you are not truly a "compleat" angler. Even more deplorable, you have bypassed two great phases of saltwater fishing: pitting your skill against one of the really fine members of the game-fish clan, and depriving yourself of one of the best table delicacies to come out of the sea.

My first recollection of flounders goes back to a time when I, with my parents and a couple of their friends, spent a week or ten days as guests of an old quasi hermit who had a house out on a peninsula called Beacon Beach near Panama City on the Florida panhandle.

The area I am referring to is across the channel and near the eastern tip of Shell Island. Most of that beautiful stretch of land was taken over by the government during World War II and still comprises part of the sprawling Tyndall Air Force Base. But prior to that, it was truly wild and woolly country, and about the only practical way to get there was to take a boat from the city dock at Panama, cross the bay to Redfish Point, and then follow the coastline around to Beacon Beach.

Except for his infrequent trips to town, the old hermit's only contact with the outside world was a battery-powered radio that he listened to with a pair of earphones.

It wasn't that the old man was antisocial. As a matter of fact, he and my dad had been friends for years. It was simply that the old fellow, to use his expression, did not "cotton to city life." His idea of a place to live was somewhere he could shoot his old 30–30 Winchester in any direction of a circle surrounding his house without the slightest danger to his nearest neighbor.

No one was ever quite sure just when the old gentleman moved into the vicinity, but one thing was certain—he was not a penniless beachcomber, because his house was really a place of rustic beauty. It was built entirely of cypress with a huge living room that boasted a gigantic stone fireplace.

Upstairs there was a balcony that overlooked the living room, and there were five or six spacious bedrooms opening out onto the balcony. The furniture was good and the beds were comfortable, and as long as one could accept the fact that certain primary elements of the plumbing facilities were outside and down a path, it was as nice as any beachhouse you could ask for. He had an enormous hogshead mounted at one end of the roof, which supplied all the warm water needed for washing and taking showers. Water for drinking and cooking was in the kitchen and came from a handpump connected to a deep well behind the house.

The man's only steady companion was an old hound of uncertain

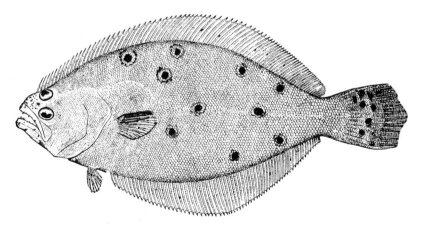

Summer Flounder

ancestry who answered to the name of Mark Anthony. If you failed to speak both his names when trying to attract his attention he would simply give you a nonchalant glance from a partly opened eye and proceed to ignore you completely. Pronounce both names, however, and he was instantly on his feet and bounding toward you with wagging tail, ready for a hike through the pines or a run along the beach.

Mark Anthony laid no claim to being a hunting dog. To him most animals that frequented the area, and there were plenty of them in those days, were simply tax-paying members of the rustic population and had the right to remain unmolested. In fact, he would occasionally be seen ambling along the beach in the company of a raccoon, and the old hermit avowed he had a black bear for a pal, too, but I was never quite sure about that.

There were only two creatures that Mark Anthony could not abide. One was the wild hog (pine rooters, as they were known), the other, any kind of snake. The hogs that occasionally wandered into the area were quickly put to rout with frenzied barking and furious attacks that would send the swine rushing pell-mell back into the fastness of the deep woods with loud squeals of terror. On the other hand, if the dog's keen nose detected a snake, Mark Anthony would set up such a commotion that there was nothing to do but get a gun and dispatch the interloping reptile.

The hermit of Beacon Beach was skilled in many phases of fishing, from surf casting to popping for speckled trout with a long cane pole. He could throw a cast net for mullet while wading in water almost up to his armpits, an act readily admitted by anyone who has ever tossed a net to be a considerable accomplishment.

When the mood struck him he would impale a dead stingray on a king-size hook and float it seaward on a chunk of driftwood on an ebbing tide. When he had payed out several hundred feet of quarter-inch Manila line, he would tie the end to a scrub oak and wait for a big shark to take his offering.

Then, when the line began to grow taut, the old man would let out a war whoop and the battle would be on. Sometimes he would sweat and struggle with his catch for hours before he could wear the shark out and pull it into shallow water. When he was sure it was exhausted, he would wade out into the water and deliver the *coup de grâce* with an ax. Then he would drag the dead shark up on the beach and bury it in the ground behind his house where he had a garden growing.

All of this, admittedly, is a long way around to get started talking about the sport of flounder fishing, but that's the way it always is with any type of fishing. There are so many things to see and do on a fishing trip that half the fun is missed if a person is so dedicated to the explicit business of catching a fish that he shuts his eyes to the rest of the world around him.

The hermit loved all methods of fishing, but flounders were his favorite and he would go after them in only one way. That was in a skiff at night and he would spear them with a strong four-pronged gig mounted on the end of a stout hickory pole about twelve feet in length. He called the sport "graining" flounders.

Spotting the flounder was accomplished with the light from a rusty kerosene lantern suspended from an improvised bowsprit. A wide metal shield was fitted over the top of the lantern so that the light would be deflected down into the water and away from the eyes of the person with the gig.

It was probably not the most sporting method of fishing, but what it lacked in that department was more than made up for in excitement, especially for a youngster with an abnormally enlarged imagination gland. Even today, many years later, I still find a certain unexplainable thrill at being out on a bay at night in a small boat. The whole world dissovles into one endless void of blackness that seems ready to swallow my boat and me.

The trip for flounders at Beacon Beach would begin just before sundown. Before it grew too dark to see, the lantern would be lighted and fitted on the bowsprit of the old rowboat. One of the men would sit or stand in the stern and quietly propel the boat along with a sculling oar while the other two would take up stations in the bow so they could keep a sharp lookout along the bottom as we floated over the shallow water.

Suddenly, there would be the whispered call: "Here's one over here!"

Instantly, there would follow the splash and swish of the gig pole and then a moment of excitement while the captured fish was hoisted flipping and flopping over the side and left slapping the bottom boards with his tail. I learned that when spotting flounders with a light at night you seldom actually see the entire fish. Rather, you see his outline and if you look closely enough you can catch a glint of at least one of his eyes.

The flounder is one of the strangest fish that inhabit salt water. When he emerges from his egg sack he begins life as an almost microscopic larva that, for all intent and purpose, resembles any of a host of other infant fish. At first, as he begins to develop, he swims about in an upright position with an eye on either side of the head. Before the flounder is hardly an inch long, however, he seems to grow weary of the conformity of swimming like conventional fish and sinks to the bottom, where he spends a large part of his time lying on his side.

No one has ever come up with a completely satisfactory answer as to just why flounders do this, but it is their way of life. Nature has an uncanny way of helping her creatures adjust to their peculiarities and she recognized countless eons ago that something had to be done if the flounder was going to be able to take full advantage of the two eyes with which it had been endowed.

Obviously, the eye that was always lying flat against the bottom would be of no value, so to compensate for this, nature arranged it so that the eye on the underside migrates to the side that points upward. When the transition of the bottom eye is complete, the flounder's face assumes a somewhat distorted look with the original upper eye being in the normal place above the jawbone and forward of the gill plates. The eye that has moved through the head comes to rest close to the side of the head and just above the normal eye and gives the impression of having been stuck on as an afterthought.

Well distributed in the Atlantic and Pacific, there are many species of flatfish that are closely related to the flounder family. They range from the giant Atlantic halibuts that have been known to weigh several hundred pounds, all the way down to the soles, also of both oceans, that average about eight inches in length.

An interesting fact of nature concerning the flatfish that defies explanation is that each species of flounder follows an almost invariable rule. According to its type, it begins early in life to lie on one particular side. For example, the winter flounder *(Pseudopleuronectes americanus)*, that ranges along the Atlantic coast as far south as Georgia, begins to rest on its left side so that the coloration and the eyes are on the right side. Such flounders, having the right side uppermost, are known as *dextral* in nature.

Conversely, the summer flounders *(Paralichthys dentatus)*, which share part of the same range in the Atlantic and all around the Gulf of Mexico, are *sinistral* in that they prefer to spend their life lying on the right side so that the eyes and color are on the left side. Only on rare occasions will a member of a particular species decide to deviate from the norm and come to rest on the wrong side.

When fishing for them, however, it does not make any difference whether the flounder in question is dextral or sinistral, he is exciting to catch, and because of his peculiar method of horizontal swimming, he can exert a sudden and abnormal amount of stress on the angler's line simply by turning broadside when he is fighting.

For the angler who finds his sport in southern salt waters, there are four primary species of flounders to be fished for, all of the order *Pleuronectiformes.* One is the winter flounder that ranges from Labrador all the way south to Georgia and is plentiful during the summer months in Chesapeake Bay. In some areas it is also known as the blackback, blueback, and black flounder. Smaller members are generally known as sand dabs.

Like other flounders, they feed on plants and small crustaceans when young. As they grow larger they switch their diet to worms, crabs, shrimp, and minnows. When mature, the winter flounder will measure between fifteen and twenty inches and weigh anywhere from two to five pounds, with an occasional one exceeding twenty pounds. Those of extra large size are generally referred to as "doormats."

Sharing almost the exact same range is the summer flounder. It differs from the winter variety in that in addition to being sinistral, with eyes and color on the left side, it has a scattering of small spots on the colored side.

The third flounder of interest is the southern flounder *(Paralichthys lethostigma).* It ranges from North Carolina southward and is common in the Gulf all the way around the coast of Texas. It is olive drab in color and lacks the spots of the summer variety. It is common in the Gulf all year long. Like the summer flounder, it also prefers to lie on its right side and has both eyes and color on the left.

The fourth species found in the southern range is the Gulf flounder *(Paralichthys albigutta).* Like the summer and southern varieties, it too is sinistral. The Gulf flounder is gray brown in color and is speckled with pale, round blotches with three primary spots forming a triangle on its side. It is the smaller of the three left-handed flounders, and despite its localized name, it shares the same range from North Carolina southward, but is most plentiful in the Gulf.

The flounders move freely from deep water to very shallow water, depending on tide, time of day, and season, and when they come to rest on a sandy or muddy bottom they immediately begin to vibrate the fins which encircle their bodies from head to tail. In a matter of seconds they have almost completely covered themselves, with the exception of the head and eyes. Here, under the covering of silt, they wait until a shrimp, crab, or small fish swims nearby. Then they "erupt" and seldom miss their target.

During the daylight hours flounders will move into deep water offshore or in channels and passes in the bay, but in warmer weather they make their way back toward the shore at night and will often conceal themselves in water not more than a foot in depth. It is during the dark hours that they are most often captured by the gig fisherman as he moves quietly along, searching the bottom with a bright light. For some reason, the approach of a light does not seem to disturb them, but noise in the boat or the sound of an engine will quickly frighten them away.

The nocturnal rod-and-reel fisherman who wishes to score on flounders would do well to make a study of the section of the coastline during the daylight hours to locate the areas where flounders are likely to be hiding at night. The best places are close to shore where there is a mud bottom. A stretch of sandy mud is also good and so is a place that is littered with small rocks and pebbles. Pass up the grassflats because such regions, along with hard-sand bottoms, are seldom favored.

After the diurnal research is complete the angler can return at night and drift or paddle very slowly over the selected areas.

When fishing for flounder it is important not to be in a rush and not to try to cover too much ground in a hurry. Slow drifting with numerous casts will always produce more of these fish than moving along at a rapid pace. The reason for this is simple. As has already been mentioned, the flounder covers himself and lies in wait for his choice of food to pass within range of his sharp eyes or sensitive nose. If the bait fails to come near enough for him to see or smell, or both, then it will be a wasted cast.

In daylight hours, drifting is still a good method, but again, the angler should have some knowledge of the type of bottom over which he is fishing. Frequently, flounders will be caught both day and night near piers, docks, and around rock jetties, probably because they find plenty of dark hiding spots in these areas. In daylight hours they may also be caught from beneath bridges and by bottom fishing in channels and passes.

In Chesapeake Bay, drift fishing from May through October is a popular method for catching flounders. The best areas are around the

Bay Bridge-Tunnel and the waters between the barrier islands and the mainland of the Eastern Shore peninsula.

Flounders are essentially a type of fish that should be angled for with natural baits such as whole small crabs or chunks of larger ones. They will also take strips of squid or mullet, shrimp, shiners, and other small minnows. They will, however, and especially at night, strike artificial lures such as small bucktails or spoons. Whether live bait, cut fish, or artificial lures are used, the important point to remember is to keep the bait moving, but slowly, along the bottom in a series of short jerks.

One of the unusual characteristics of flounders that inhabit the southern range is that they seem to pay little or no attention to roiled water. Of course, I have never fished for them in the middle of a hurricane, but I have caught them in satisfactory numbers when a hard wind has been blowing for several days and most of the other fish are lying doggo, or waiting out the weather in deep water offshore.

Still another interesting characteristic of the flounder is its chameleonlike ability to change color, depending upon the shade of the bottom on which it is resting. The underside of all flounders is flat white and not subject to change, but the pigmented side will assume the color of the bottom of the bay. Frequently, when placed in live-bait wells of skiffs which have holes in the bottom to admit the free flow of water, the captured flounder will quickly develop distinct dark spots directly over the holes. Tests have also proved that if the fish is allowed to rest on a tank bottom that has been painted with black-and-white squares, the flounder will quickly change his coloration to resemble a checkerboard pattern.

Because the average flounder is generally rated as a small fish, he will obviously provide more sport for the angler if the fishing tackle is light. Once he has taken the bait and been hooked, the fisherman had best be ready for a real battle. It is also a good idea to have a landing net handy because many a bragging-size flounder has thrown the hook just as the happy angler was about to lift him over into the boat.

As food fish, flounders rate among the best. They do, however, require a little extra attention when it comes to the stage of cleaning and dressing. They can be cooked after simply scaling and gutting, but they are much, much better if skinned. This can be accomplished with a common fish knife, but the task has been greatly simplified by any of several patented devices known as fish skinners, which are stocked by most tackle stores.

～～～～～～～～
～～～～～～～

OFFSHORE

AMBERJACK

Herb Willis stood in the stern and looked down at the line squeaking off his tight-set 4/0 reel. He was muttering some strange incantation that at one moment seemed to be a pious supplication and the next a vulgar and defamatory denunciation of everything pelagic.

"What the heck is the matter with your friend back there?" the charter-boat skipper out of Ocracoke asked in his soft North Carolina drawl, throttling back to a slow speed.

Having fished so often with Herb, I was able to make a fair translation of his *bêche-de-mer*. "He's just complaining about having a terrific strike and now he's hung up on the bottom."

The captain scratched the back of his head and chuckled softly. "W-a-ll, if you can get through to him," he said, "tell him to quit that

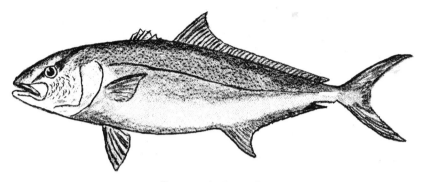

Greater Amberjack

crazy grumbling, 'cause from the looks of his rod tip bobbing like it is I'm guessing he's jest tied into a big ol' granddaddy amberjack. That big ol' fish is jest down there standing on his head and flapping his tail."

Turning part way around, Herb looked at the skipper, then at me, and back at his reel. Fingering the drag, he released the pressure, and line peeled off.

The summer weather was clear, the waves were smooth, and at the mention of amberjack I picked up my own rig, removed the feathered jig, and replaced it with a blue runner on a 6/0 hook. If the captain had guessed right, and if Herb managed to bring up an amberjack, I knew from past experience that the chances were good he would raise a whole school of these stubborn fighters.

The greater amberjack *(Seriola lalandi)* is a big and powerful game fish with numerous peculiarities. He also has a vast number of close cousins and near relatives that all come under the family *Carangidae.*

They are found in the Atlantic from North Carolina, south around the Florida Keys, and in the Gulf of Mexico. In general appearance, they resemble a huge bluefish with a blue topside, fading to bluish silver on the sides and below. They often have a subdued amber cast, and the fins are tinted with yellow. The IGFA record of 149 pounds has been standing since 1964 and was set by Peter Simons on 30-pound test line. Remains of amberjacks mutilated by sharks after being hooked testify to the fact that they grow much larger.

Herb was suddenly shouting, pumping his rod, and cranking the reel handle. "You're right! I'm not stuck on the bottom. There's a fish down there all right. You sure its an amberjack?"

"Only one way to be sure," the skipper said, picking up the gaff. "Bring him up where we can get a look at him."

Herb continued to struggle with the fish on the other end of his line, but I could tell by the fullness of his reel that he was getting close. I swung my blue runner out and it landed with a splash far off to the side. Letting the line run free for about thirty feet, I flipped the lever and adjusted the drag so that I could strip off line by hand without much effort.

The small fish flashed in the sunlit water as it began to sink, and then we saw the amberjack Herb had caught and behind his fish and off to each side were at least ten others, accompanying their hooked companion. Just as my own bait was fading from view, I saw one of the ambers make a dive for it.

Flipping the free-spooling lever, I let him grab the bait and when I hoped he had it well into his mouth, I set the drag and gave him a hefty punch. It was as if I had tied my line onto an express elevator on a nonstop trip to the ground floor.

"You better try to turn him before he goes much farther," the Tarheel skipper mused. "There's some bad rocks down there in that reef and he's probably got a special place all picked out just fit to saw your line in half."

Nodding, I fingered the drag until I was nearly positive one of two things would happen. Either he would pull the tackle out of my hands or the line would break. He stopped "falling," but he was telegraphing his displeasure by shaking his head violently. Glancing up briefly from my reel, I saw the captain reaching for Herb's line. He had the gaff poised and I could tell Herb was having a struggle to keep his big jack from going under the boat. I wanted to watch, but I was too busy for more than an occasional glance. It was during one of these moments of distraction that I noticed the other amberjacks. They were milling around behind the boat, darting first one way and then another, like spectators moving about to keep track of the progress of a sidewalk street fight.

In that respect, amberjacks are much like dolphin. When they begin their battle, however, they are unwilling to put on a surface display. Their main objective seems to be to fight their way straight toward the bottom. Certain fish seem instinctively to know their best route of escape, and whether they are actually consciously aware of it, the big jacks have two things going for them by following this *modus operandi.*

An amberjack has fought the good fight and now waits for the gaff that will swing him over the gunnel. That bit of white fluff is a lead jig that has been pushed halfway up the leader during the battle.

They have exceedingly rough edges on their mouths which make a leader important. Also, if they do reach the bottom they are almost certain to find some obstruction that will cut a line.

Do fish think? Science says no, they only react or respond to various stimuli. There are times, however, when you cannot help indulging in a bit of heresy. How, for example, would an amberjack who had never before felt the restraint of a line or, for that matter, even be aware of a line, know the quickest and best way to rid himself of his trouble? I certainly don't know, but I will never cease to wonder.

Herb's fish was broadside to the stern when the skipper socked him with the gaff and swung him over the transom. "Bound to weigh fifty pounds," Herb puffed, flexing his fingers.

"Nice one, all right," the skipper said. "But he won't quite hit twenty-five. You're just tuckered out 'cause he was stubborn. I know a charter-boat skipper up the banks a piece who has a special set of scales that weigh heavy jest so his customers will feel good."

My own amber was beginning to show about that time. I could see his tail snapping like a tomcat between rounds. He was still determined to keep staring at the bottom, and I was beginning to wonder if a tail rope might possibly be a better tool than the gaff. During a lull, two other big jacks cruised right up beside him and I was willing to swear one of them was looking inside his mouth.

"If you're up to some more fun," the skipper said, pinning another runner on Herb's hook, "you better get this back in the water while they're all stewed up and ready to play ball."

"I'll take that big fellow over there close to the surface," Herb said. "He looks like he's hungry enough to bite a rubber boot and man enough to chew it up."

If an angler ever called his shot, Herb called that one. I thought about Babe Ruth pointing so the fans would know which way to watch the ball vanish. Herb swung the bait toward the big amberjack and both had a head-on collision at the top of a swell.

In my moment of distraction while I watched that third amber make his strike, mine took that opportunity to unhorse me. He suddenly reversed his tactics and made a beeline for the boat's slow-turning propeller. For the next few seconds there was an ungodly thundering and rattling on the bottom of the hull. My amberjack had won the battle but lost the war and was now little more than shark food sinking into the depths. By odd coincidence, the contact with the wheel had not fouled my line but the runner was knocked off and began to drift downward. Another fish hit it like a torpedo, swallowed it, and rejoined the school.

Before the afternoon was half-done, we had caught a total of fifteen fish and boated four of them. Several had broken free, but the others we released without using the gaff.

Bait for amberjacks cover a wide range with blue runners, mullet, and mackerel considered prime. They are most frequently caught on live or trolled bait, but are occasionally taken while bottom fishing with cut bait. Once a school has been contacted, they will strike at almost anything tossed their way.

For the average sport angler and many experienced commerical fishermen, finding a school is a hit-and-miss proposition. I know a few charter-boat skippers who have their secret spots around wrecks and reefs where they can generally count on finding them. Depth seems to be of little concern, since they will occasionally strike a rigged ballyhoo trolled on the surface, and again, they have been caught on the bottom in water as deep as two hundred fathoms.

If you have the material on hand and are patient and, of course, if they are down there, a steady flow of chum will often bring a school to the surface to investigate. Whatever the case, most large amberjacks are blue-water fish and are not easily spooked once the school has become interested.

WAHOO

Although they are occasionally caught close to shore, the wahoo *(Acanthocybium solandri)* is essentially a blue-water fish and most frequently caught while trolling well offshore.

Known by other names, the wahoo is distributed practically worldwide in tropical and subtropical seas. In general, it resembles the king mackerel and is often mistaken for this fish. There are, of course, many differences, but for the average fisherman the most important and noticeable difference is the size and shape of the first dorsal fin. On the wahoo it is considerably larger and bows upward near the center whereas, on the king, the fin tapers swiftly toward the second dorsal. Also, the wahoo's sides are often marked with narrow, vertical bars. These are especially noticeable while the wahoo is alive and full of fight. These bars fade quickly after the fish dies. It also resembles the Spanish mackerel, but lacks the flecking of yellow spots, and the snout is considerably more pointed, while the teeth are more pronounced.

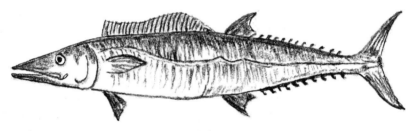

Wahoo

In the waters surrounding the eastern section of North America, they are found from the tip of Florida to as far north as Maryland and are not rare off the Virginia capes. They are also widely distributed in the Gulf of Mexico. The state record for Louisiana is a 110-pounder caught by Mrs. Homer "Bud" Moore in July 1964. The largest recorded by the IGFA is one that weighed 149 pounds and was caught by John Pirovano while fishing off Cat Cay in the Bahamas in June of 1962.

These large members of the mackerel family are noted for their extremely fast and powerful first run immediately after taking the bait. As with the name of many other fish, you just have to guess about the origin of the name *wahoo*. The most popular explanation is that it came from the expression of dismay voiced by an angler seeing the torpedo-like rush of an attacking wahoo and the resulting high-speed departure once he has taken the hook. To be completely honest, I find this a somewhat flimsy excuse for a name, since I can think of a dozen other expletory expressions of profound astonishment that might be uttered at the moment of contact with such a fish, many of which are not generally considered to be socially acceptable. As a result, I have filed the name wahoo along with my collection of other unexplained fish names.

One thing is certain, however, when it comes to the slashing attack of a wahoo, and that is that the angler is going to be startled. What he says is up to him, but of more importance is what he does. If he is fishing with medium to light tackle and the wahoo is in the thirty- or forty-pound class, he would do well to set the brake lightly and hope he has enough line to let the wahoo make his initial run before the reel is stripped. If he clamps down on the brake just as the fish is leaving, the fisherman may be reasonably certain of hearing that sickening "ping" sound as the line breaks.

As a general rule, the larger wahoo are solitary fish. Smaller ones tend to travel in schools, but these schools have increasingly fewer members as the size of the fish grows larger.

Unless you are so fortunate as to know a charter-boat skipper who is at the very top of the expert list, the chances are somewhat slim that you will set out from the dock determined to catch more than a stray wahoo and accomplish your goal. There are times, however, when a school may be spotted and then several fish may be boated. These powerful creatures will move into fairly shallow water when feeding, but they usually stick close to the edges of reefs where the drop-off is sharp and extends down for many fathoms.

Once while trolling for sails out of Fort Lauderdale, we had only two lines out. One of the rigs was baited with a ballyhoo and the other was towing a feathered jig. Both sticks were in the rod holders and the lines were clipped to outriggers.

Marsh Whitcomb was lounging on the fly bridge eating an egg salad sandwich and waxing eloquently on the beauties of the Gulf Stream, the mounds of ice cream clouds over the land, and the soft purr of his new twin engines. My wife, Dorothy, and I were trying to remember whether or not we had rolled up the car windows before leaving the dock.

Suddenly, Marsh jumped to his feet and pointed aft at some spot in

No one knows for sure just how the wahoo got his name, but once you have hooked one of these super-speedsters out on the blue water, it is not too far-fetched to believe it came from an expression of dismay uttered by a startled angler long ago.

our wake. His gesture was with the hand that held his sandwich and the immediate result was that the two slices of bread disgorged themselves of the yellow-and-white stuffing.

"That looks like a big wahoo coming up behind!" He shouted the words and then glanced briefly at what remained of his lunch.

Scrambling out of my chair, I reached for the starboard rod. "Not that one!" Marsh yelled. "He's coming up on the bally!"

Dorothy was busy dusting egg salad off her slacks as I scrambled across the cockpit and grabbed the other rod out of the holder. Unless you live a very long time and spend most of it fishing, you seldom catch enough wahoo to learn all their tricks. But one of the first facts you do learn is that your chances of boating a wahoo are increased if you are trolling a flat line. The drop-back from an outrigger is often all a wahoo needs to get rid of the hook.

"Hurry!" Marsh was almost jumping up and down with excitement. "I can see him plain as day and he's a record for sure!"

Dorothy said later that I was moving rapidly, but at that moment I felt I had no more agility than an astronaut climbing the side of a moon crater. Everything seemed to be working against me. I thought for a while that I was going to have to climb up and get the line out of the snap with my fingers, but it finally came free and I began reeling in the slack.

"He's got it!" Marsh roared.

It was a fact of which I did not need to be apprised. The wahoo left the water and pounced on the trolled bait like a cat attacking a mouse. A second later any resemblance to feline and rodent encounter vanished. The shock of the attacking fish ricocheted back up the line, nearly pulling me over the stern.

"Don't squeeze him! Don't squeeze him!" Marsh called. "Give him all the line he wants."

Fumbling with the drag, I set it to a point I hoped would provide sufficient tension without breaking the 30-pound test line.

The whole show was over almost as soon as it had begun. The wahoo —remember, Marsh said he was a record—made one long surface run and then decided to find the bottom of the Stream. I stood there watching line melt off my reel and when I knew the inevitable was about to happen, I tightened the drag, but it did nothing to slow the diving fish. Suddenly, the reel was empty and that was that.

There are anglers who can lose a big fish and toss it off with bits of homespun philosophy such as "Well, it was fun while it lasted," or "You can't win 'em all," and other allied phrases. Most of the time, I can feign that "contemplation" and "quietness" on which Izaak Walton was wont to dwell. This was not one of those times. I sat down in the fighting chair and thought dark thoughts. Dorothy and Marsh exhibited restraint and did not try to be witty. When I had grown weary of thinking my dark thoughts, I got up and put fresh line on the reel, and on the way in, Dorothy caught a beautiful sail which we released.

The car windows? We had left them down, but it made no difference anyway because it had not rained.

With the coming of warm weather, wahoo move northward in the Gulf and along the Atlantic coast. When the sky is cloudless and the weather hot, they will run deep. A period of cloudy skies and frequent rains will bring them to the surface; again they will move up with the coming of fall. When the chilly days of autumn begin, they start to vanish, and it is believed they migrate southward. At least it would seem so, because they are fairly abundant in southern waters during the winter months.

DOLPHIN

Seldom if ever does anyone fish for dolphin *(Coryphaena hippurus)* more than a few times before someone on board feels called upon to quote a few lines from the immortal pen of Lord Byron. They might not know Geoffrey Chaucer from Robert Service or Alfred Tennyson from Edgar Guest, but you can bet that somewhere along the way, if they have caught enough dolphin, they have been exposed to stanza 29 in Canto IV of "Childe Harold's Pilgrimage."

Parting day dies like the dolphin
Whom each pang imbues
With a new colour as it gasps away,
The last still loveliest,
Till—'tis gone, and all is gray.

How true these poetic lines, for if ever there can be beauty in death none can surpass that of a dying dolphin. Even in life, the dolphin is a beautiful fish. High of head, he is almost an iridescent bluish green with a dark dorsal fin that runs from the top of the head in a long smooth flow to the caudal peduncle. The body is lean and flat, yellowish on the sides, fading to a white belly. There are vertical bands that are at times dark, only to vanish completely and suddenly reappear. The tail is deeply notched and not unlike that of a bonefish.

Once caught and hauled aboard, the fish is frequently violent in his effort to disassociate himself from his unnatural abode. It is only after he begins to die that the fisherman is witness to a strange yet beautiful, and unforgettable, sight. It is as if some unseen revolving kaleidoscopic light were trained on the dolphin's body. Moving waves of color that

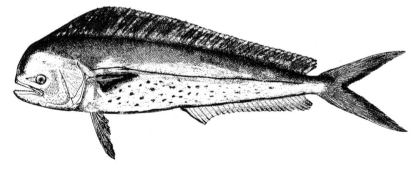

Dolphin

A good example of a bull dolphin caught off Panama City, Florida. Note the enlarged head that develops with age and size. Note, too, the grin of victory on one well-pleased angler who won the contest.

range from blue to gold to green tremble and quiver, fade to yellow and gradually subside to the gray of tarnished silver. There are many theories as to the reason for this chameleon death, but it seems surely to involve some rapid change in body chemistry as the heart falters.

Found in tropical and subtropical waters around the world, the dolphin is plentiful in the waters of, and close to, the Gulf Stream. He moves north in the summer and retreats with the beginning of fall. School dolphin range in size from two to ten pounds. There are times when large dolphin ranging from fifteen to twenty-five pounds will be found in schools, but as a general rule, the larger members are alone or in groups of two or three. The world record is 85 pounds, caught by Richard Seymour on 50-pound test line while fishing out from Spanish Wells in the Bahamas on May 29, 1968. It measured 5 feet 9 inches in length and had a girth of 37½ inches.

No matter what his size, the dolphin is one of the gamest of game fish. A large one—upward of thirty pounds and commonly referred to as a bull dolphin—is a creature to be reckoned with where speed and brute strength are concerned. Their natural food probably begins with flying fish and then includes dozens of others. The sight of a big bull dolphin exploding a school of flying fish and following the winged speedsters in their aerial hegira with bounding leaps across the surface of the waves is awe inspiring.

The flying fish, of which there are several types, does not actually fly in the manner of a bird. It was long debated by observers as to whether or not they flap their "wings" (enlarged pectoral fins). High-speed cameras settled the question in 1940 by recording numerous flights. Photographic evidence shows that the pectoral fins are extended, but held motionless in flight. The illusion of flapping wings is created at the instant a flying fish breaks the surface when he is sculling the water with his tail. Such violent motion causes the flying fish to rock slightly, but the "wings" are as rigid as those of any conventional aircraft.

Startled by the rush of a dolphin, any of a number of other predatory fish, or even the approach of a ship or boat, the flying fish thrusts its body out of the water and at the same time extends its pectoral fins. Under certain conditions they have been clocked at thirty-five miles an hour, which is considerably faster than its water speed. Rapid though the flight may be, the dolphin has frequently been observed to keep in such hot pursuit as to be ready to grab the speedster the instant he touches down. The distance of a single flight of a flying fish depends on two basic factors. One is the speed with which he leaves the water and the other is how skilled he is in taking advantage of the wind. It is possible for one to glide for a distance of a thousand feet or more, but the average flight is usually much shorter. They have also been observed to rise twenty to thirty feet into the air.

Dolphin are often caught while trolling, and the wise skipper will stear a course for floating objects including patches of seaweed. Once a school is located, it is possible to catch them in vast numbers by trolling slowly around the school, or by simply shutting down the power and casting to them. One trick that has long been known by experienced dolphin anglers is to leave one caught fish swimming about at the end of a line. The rest of the school seem to take this as an indication that there is no cause for alarm and they will remain in the vicinity for a considerable length of time.

Such willingness on the part of these game fish to strike at almost any lure tossed their way, coupled with the fact that they make excellent eating, frequently results in greedy anglers catching and killing far more dolphin than is reasonable under any condition.

Admittedly, the excitement of the "chase" is infectious, and when the angler's enthusiasm is at a fever pitch, it is not easy to stop. Such a practice, however, is nothing short of a gross waste of good material and the conservation-minded fisherman will not indulge in it, no matter how much fun he may be having.

If a fair catch has been made and still there are those on board who refuse to abstain, there is one action many skippers take to stem the tide of waste. They simply flatten the barbs on the hooks with a pair of pliers and let the spoilers have their fill. The barbless hook enables the angler to have all the excitement of the battle and still generally makes it possible to let the exhausted dolphin shake himself free at the boat's edge. Because of his frantic nature, the average dolphin, large or small, will generally kill himself by violent action if he is brought on deck. Of course, in the case of a big bull, it is virtually impossible to boat one without a gaff, which causes a mortal wound.

Dolphin fishing in southern salt waters generally begins in late spring and continues throughout the summer months. They are occasionally caught in relatively shallow water, but by and large they are, like the sailfish and marlin, deepwater species. Once a school is located, they will frequently commence what in sharks might be termed the "mob feeding pattern," where they will strike at anything, natural or artificial, tossed their way. As the craze subsides, they may become somewhat more selective and refuse to touch anything but strips of cut bait.

There are two types of anglers who actually detest dolphin. One of these is the charter-boat captain who has agreed to take his clients out to catch sails or marlin. If he has the misfortune (to his way of thinking) of running through a school of medium-size dolphin, he is certain to lose rigged trolling bait that has required considerable time to prepare for the larger quarry. Of course, his fishermen catch dolphin, but that is not what they are after. The other malcontent is the hapless party-boat skipper who finds his boatload of fishermen shouting with glee as they hook into a school of ferocious dolphin. With twenty to fifty lines over the side and half a dozen hooked dolphin running amuck through them, the captain and his crew will have a horrendous job of untangling them.

The vast majority of offshore anglers seldom fall into either of the above two categories. Rather, they consider that fortune has smiled upon them when they do locate a school of dolphin, or for that matter, manage to pick up a stray while trolling.

Bait is of secondary importance when searching for these fish. Of far more importance is knowing where to look. The best bets are seaweed rips that float on the surface like vast irregular-shaped blankets. When trolling, it is always a good bet to set a course that will cause the lures to pass close to such patches. Offshore oil rigs are another good bet and so are buoys. In fact, anything that floats is a good bet. We once spotted a huge loggerhead turtle lolling on the surface. Cutting the engine, we allowed the boat to drift down toward him and suddenly found a small school of dolphin were using him as home base. It is also well to investigate an explosion of flying fish or the disorganized scurrying of jacks on the surface.

At such times it is well to have a few buckets of chum. Some anglers I know carry along a case of the smelliest cat food they can find, just in case they happen upon a school of these eager feeders. The family cat might turn up his nose in disgust at such a fare, but it smells like fish, and the dolphin will cooperate and remain in casting distance as long as the can opener keeps working.

The selection of the proper tackle is of utmost importance if one is to enjoy to the fullest the game of dolphin fishing. In random trolling, where the possibility of encountering a large bull is to be expected, the angler would do well to be rigged for sailfish or white marlin. Again, if a pod of schoolies are encountered, put away the heavy gear and break out lighter tackle—bait casting, spinning, and even fly rods can serve well and make the taking of each fish an exciting experience. As previously mentioned, the bait is not of vital importance, and I have found the same to be true where artificials are concerned. If they are in a feeding mood—remember to chum them if they are hesitant—they will hit practically anything from a spoon, feathered jig, bucktail, or plug. I once watched one engulf a cigar stub someone had tossed overboard. If a fish ever skidded brakes, that one did. He spit it out, looked at it for an instant, and then grabbed it again and swam away.

The dolphin strikes hard and his mouth is filled with small but sharp teeth. It therefore behooves the angler to protect his bait or lure with the addition of about eighteen inches of light wire leader. Frequently, when in a feeding frenzie, they will make a grab for one bait, set the hook in their jaw, and then make a dive for a second lure.

The game of diving with scuba gear is forever increasing man's store of knowledge of fish and their behavior. Several summers ago a couple of friends and I were cruising along the Keys and while well out in the Stream, we decided to don our gear and jump overboard just for the fun of it. Suddenly a school of small dolphin ranging in weight from

A hooked dolphin is one of the gamest gamefish and, despite his size, he invariably puts on a show well worth watching. At times he will leap clear of the water, throw the lure and then grab it again before the spray stops falling.

two to five pounds spotted our drifting boat and moved in around it. We watched them for a few minutes and then one of my companions touched me on the arm and motioned for me to follow him down deeper to see something he had found. At about the twenty-foot mark we realized there was another school of dolphin swimming in lazy circles. Not one of them was less than fifteen pounds in weight. They did not seem at all concerned with our presence and we had a chance to observe them for fully ten minutes.

Back on board we discussed the double-deck school. Is this a common practice for larger schools to keep company with smaller ones? I do not know and report it only for what information it may add. I do know, however, as does almost anyone who has fished extensively for dolphin, that it is not uncommon to be catching small ones at a rapid clip and suddenly have a reel stripped by a big bruiser that suddenly appears on the scene. Later, we all three wished we had dropped down another thirty feet or so and checked to see if there was a big bull or two keeping pace with the younger members of his tribe. If I ever encounter the same situation again that is just what I intend to do.

One final note on dolphin concerns their eventual destination on the platter. The flavor will be greatly enhanced if they are bled while still alive. Some skippers and fishermen cut off the tails the instant the fish are brought over the side. True, it makes for a lot of slippery gore on the deck, but if you are fishing for the frying pan, you will be doing your dinner guests and yourself a favor if the fish is properly bled almost as soon as caught.

〰〰〰〰〰

〰〰〰〰〰

three

ALONG THE SHORE

CHANNEL BASS

Whenever I think of almost any type of fish, be it a sailfish, snook, bonefish, pompano, or what have you, some sort of device in the back side of my head goes into instant action like an **IBM** card-sorting machine. Almost before you can say "fishhook," one particular card pops up on which is recorded the minute details of a single episode concerning said fish.

It may be an incident involving a small skiff out on the flats of Florida Bay with a big thundersquall building in the southwest; a trim cabin boat far out on the blue water; a fall night on a long bridge, or some other setting. For one reason or another, each individual fish brings to mind a first and foremost venture that stands alone.

There is, however, one single fish that can put my imaginary card-

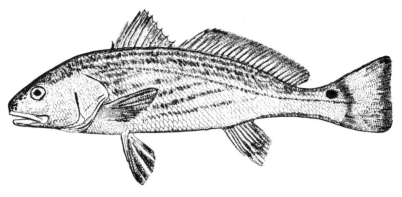

Channel Bass

sorting machine into a state of complete breakdown, and that is the channel bass. I think the reason for this is that I have fished for him over such a long period of time, and such a wide range, and under such varied conditions that it is like calling for a whole mob of different fish at the same instant.

The fish in question is actually the red drum *(Sciaenops ocellatus)*. All around the Gulf of Mexico and the coast of Florida he is known as the redfish. In the Atlantic there is a gray zone that begins along the Georgia coast and by the time you have moved on up to the Carolinas and Virginia, he is the channel bass, except for the small ones that are called puppy drums.

He represents many different localities and different methods of fishing. There are memories of days and nights on the lonely Outer Banks of North Carolina, prodding about in mangroves of the Ten Thousand Islands, skimming across the waters along Virginia's Eastern Shore, looking for big schools and seeking him out in bays and along beaches all around the Gulf.

One channel bass episode that I guess will always bring a chuckle to mind involved the girl that was a few months later to become my wife. What happened involved a redfish, and it was a study in determination.

Dorothy, for all her attributes, was not an angler. In fact, I am pretty sure her closest association with anything piscatorial was limited to restaurants and an occasional catch her father would bring back from river fishing in Tennessee and Alabama. She had never caught a fish herself and viewed my collection of tackle box lures in a highly suspicious manner. She simply did not believe any fish would be so foolish as actually to get caught on such objects. If she had been forced to admit it, I think she would have placed more validity in the workings of a Ouija board.

That misapprehension was happily dispelled shortly after we had met when I invited her to go sailing with me in a new seventeen-foot catboat I had recently bought. About halfway across Panama City's St. Andrew Bay, I spotted a school of jacks working a vast shoal of glass minnows. Just for the fun of it I clipped a double-aught drone onto the line of a light boat rod and handed her the rig, instructing her to let the tiny silver spoon trail along about a hundred feet behind the boat.

As I had expected, one of the jacks hit the spoon so hard it nearly jerked the rod out of Dorothy's hands. After she had experienced the wild darting struggle of the jack for a couple of minutes, all the while declaring she had undoubtedly hooked a monster and could never reel it in, I quite gallantly took the rod and boated the fish.

Something must have snapped in her brain right at that moment. She insisted that we make another run through the jacks and then another and another. Each time I would come to her rescue and bring in her fish. I failed to recognize it at the moment, but what she was catching was a severe case of fishing fever and to this day it has not abated one iota.

Two days later, when I called to arrange a date, she informed me in excited tones that she had something important to show me. When I arrived at her house, I half expected to see some normal female purchase such as a new dress, a record player, or maybe a kitten or puppy. I was totally unprepared for her *something important.* She had gone out to the nearest tackle store and bought a complete fishing outfit: rod, reel, spools of line, an assortment of lures, hooks, corks, sinkers, and even a tackle box.

Naturally, she did not have the faintest idea how to cast, and there followed the usual numerous backlashes and most of the other misadventures that go with learning to fish. After what I considered enough tutoring, I borrowed a skiff from a friend and took my protégée out on a likely spot at the east end of the bay, and we proceeded to catch a string of speckled trout. There were long, steady runs deep in the water. After I saw that she was getting down to the point where her reel was almost empty I offered to take over.

"Absolutely not!" was her emphatic reply. "We might as well get one thing straight right now," she continued as her rod dipped and bounced and she struggled to crank in a few badly needed yards of line, "from here on, whenever I hook a fish I either catch him or lose him, but whatever the case it's going to be my show from beginning to end."

I had been found out! Ever since that day in the sailboat I had been letting Dorothy do the work and then, under the guise of chivalry, I had pretended to come to the rescue at the moment of truth and brought the fish aboard.

Stepping back, I sat down on the center seat and watched my wife-to-be struggle with her unseen adversary. At one point when she had managed to horse the fish in fairly close to the boat I caught sight of him in the fading light of day. It was a redfish and a big one for the small freshwater tackle in which she had invested.

Just about then the fish made up his mind he had frolicked enough and putting the line over his shoulder he decided he was going to leave. Despite Dorothy's blistering thumbs, the reel slowly emptied until the spool was bare. There was one saving factor. The man at the tackle store had sold her 30-pound test line and the knot that held the line to the reel remained fast. It was obvious the fish was securely hooked and I guessed that if the knot did not weaken the line too much she might just possibly wear him down with a bare reel. Just then the unexpected happened. The reel began to break up.

There would be nothing to be gained by naming the name. Suffice to say it was one of the recognized brands and one that has performed well over the years, but this reel in particular must have been a dud. Sitting there I had a ringside seat to watch a piece of machinery self-destruct.

First the pall jammed on the level wind. That would have been trouble enough, but there was more to come. The nut that holds the handle began to come loose, and then one of the spool spindles sheered off, and finally the entire side of the reel started to break away from the crossbars. In a matter of a minute the entire piece of mechanism had fallen apart into a hopeless jumble.

"Want me to help you?" I asked.

Dorothy's only reply was a shake of her head as she resolutely grasped the line at the rod tip and began doggedly to haul in her fish hand over hand. I winced with sympathetic pain everytime I heard the wet line squeaking through her fingers. The poor fish had met his match. Foot by hard-earned foot she continued to struggle until she

Call him redfish, red drum, or puppy drum, the channel bass such as the one the author's wife has just boated is well distributed throughout the Gulf and far up the Atlantic coast.

reached the leader and at that point she lofted the angry fish over the gunnel and into the boat.

After that she sat down and began to examine the pitiful remains of her new reel. When we got back to the dock, we weighed the red on regular commercial fishermen's scales and I stared incredulously when the pointer stopped squarely on fifteen pounds. Properly handled, and providing there was not something fundamentally wrong with the reel, a fifteen-pound channel bass is not at all beyond the potential of a small freshwater reel, but they can be brutal on a hand line such as Dorothy had resorted to.

To my way of thinking, the channel bass is one of the prettier of saltwater fish. He is a reddish-copper to bronze color on the back, shading to silvery white on the sides and belly. His upper jaw protrudes over the lower, and at any age all have one or more pronounced black spots on each side of the caudal peduncle near the top and close to the tail.

He occurs on the Atlantic coast from the Florida Keys up to Massachusetts. He is also plentiful in the Gulf of Mexico. The IGFA record was set on August 5, 1949, by Zack Waters, Jr., at Cape Charles, Virginia, when he landed one that weighed 83 pounds and measured 4 feet 4 inches in length.

The channel bass is essentially a bottom feeder, with almost all available forms of mollusks and crustaceans rating high on his favorite diet. He is, however, not restricted to bottom feeding and will frequently pursue other fish such as mullet and menhaden. As his name implies, he is frequently found in channels and cuts close to shore.

In the spring the channel bass follows a northward migratory timetable that is so much the same year after year you would almost be willing to believe Old Red plots his course with a calendar and a stack of Coast and Geodetic Survey charts.

Saltwater anglers in Georgia and South Carolina begin oiling reels, checking tip-top guides, and testing the breaking strength of last year's line late in February. They know with almost certainty that the channel bass is going to be showing up in numbers in early March. For some unexplained reason known only to nature, the vanguard will be small fish; those ranging in weight from two to three pounds up to nearly ten.

The favorite spots are Jekyll and Sea islands, Georgia, as well as Bull Island and Cape Romain off South Carolina. Shortly after the first run of small fish there will be a decided lull, and then the big ones move in, usually in fantastic numbers with catches of thirty- and forty-pound fish being common. Depending on the weather and the whims and fancies of the individual waves of fish, the action will continue to be good all the way into June.

The migration continues and their next major assault on the coastal waters will be in April in the vicinity of Cape Fear, North Carolina. Again, the masses will be preceded by smaller fish with the heavyweights seeming to hang back waiting for the all clear before making their onslaught. By April the huge schools are increasing their speed and sometime around the middle of the month they are swarming along the Outer Banks in ever increasing numbers. Next comes the fast action around Ocracoke and the Cape Hatteras area, with a steady northward movement through the rest of the month with big schools at Oregon Inlet.

By the first of May they are numerous off Virginia Beach around Cape Henry Light. Another slight lull and then the Old Dominion fishermen have a big red circle drawn around the 5th of May. This is the time when the reds will have crossed the mouth to Chesapeake Bay and begun to take up residence in Magothy Bay like a swarm of hungry relatives, with the main action centered on Fishermans Island and Cape Charles Light on Smith Island. The channel bass will remain in this vicinity at the southern tip of Virginia's Eastern Shore until somewhere near the end of the month, gradually moving on up toward Chincoteague Island. As the summer progresses, the huge schools will continue northward until they reach Massachusetts, where they pass a brief summer sojourn, and then they once again turn southward and cruise back down along the coast, dragging the cold northeasters of winter behind them.

The careful reader will note what seems to be certain incongruities in the timetable set for the spring migration of channel bass, asking why it is stated that big channel bass are being caught in the month of June in South Carolina while it is plainly stated that the action reaches its peak as far north as Virginia in the early part of May. They do follow a migratory pattern that corresponds very closely to that which has been set down. There is, however, a variable concerning certain members of the species that cannot be readily explained along the Atlantic any more than it can in the Gulf. For some reason that the science of marine biology has yet to determine, certain groups of a specific type of fish will refuse to follow the rules. They seem to reach a designated point and decide this is as far as they want to go. Such strange behavior is not restricted to an individual fish, but often to large schools. They seem to like the conditions in first this place and then another and elect to hole up in those waters for the summer.

What is important is that the vast majority of channel bass do follow a timetable that varies only to a slight degree. If the stragglers were restricted to individual fish it might be logically assumed that they drop from the main school because of age, injury, or illness, but this apparently is not the case. Very little is known about the spawning habits of the red drum, and it is to be supposed that certain portions of the mass turn off along the way to cast their eggs. There is some evidence to suggest that spawning takes place in the northern end of Chesapeake Bay, and it is reasonable to assume that other reds choose other bays along their route.

The fall run of channel bass is much the same as the spring run in reverse. The wise fisherman keeps a weather eye peeled for signs of cold waves moving down the Atlantic seaboard. When the New Jersey temperature takes a nose dive, the surf fishermen in Virginia and North Carolina begin to rub their hands in glee, because it is certain that Old Spottail has set sail on his southward voyage. October and early November are the big months for the second run. This is especially true for the surf casters.

One good point to remember about surf casting for channel bass is

Noted for its wide variety and abundance of fine salt water game fish, North Carolina's Pamlico Sound rewards these two anglers with a 50-pound channel bass.

that he loves the pounding surf and the more it pounds the better he likes it—anything short of a full-blown hurricane, of course. The reason is simple. The harder the waves are pounding, the more the shallow water is roiled, which he knows causes the creatures that form his diet to be dislodged. Such conditions are not always favorable to the man on the beach with the long rod, but if you can take the elements, the chances are good that you will strike a fish bonanza.

There are several different methods of channel bass fishing along the east coast. The three most favored and the ones most likely to produce results are surf casting, trolling, and sight-hunting from a small boat.

Trolling, or blind trolling, as some anglers refer to it, is more or less self-explanatory. You simply choose a stretch of water, either inshore or off, where the fish are likely to be found and rig up with natural or artificial bait and cruise along until the hoped-for happens. Such a procedure is not quite so haphazard as it might seem if certain important conditions are carefully considered.

If, for instance, the spring or fall run along a particular stretch of coastline is in full swing, it is almost certain that the fish are there in abundance. When a bass is hooked the chances are good that he is part of a large school. If the fish are running deep, there is no way to tell whether you have caught one of the leaders at the head of the school, picked up a straggler far behind, or hooked one right out of the middle. Under these conditions you just have to take your chances.

Sight-hunting is a far more exciting way to fish for channel bass from a boat. Under optimum conditions you will choose a day when the sun is not obscured by clouds and the water is relatively calm. This time you will be looking for large schools of reds that may number anywhere from a couple of hundred fish to up to as many as a thousand. Even the small schools are not difficult to spot if you have the sun at your back or off to one side. They can be seen from a small outboard-powered boat, but a pair of Polaroid sunglasses are an absolute must for scanning bright, sunlit water. When there is an overcast I have found that glasses with a yellowish tan tint improve the definition.

Naturally, since you are trying to see something well ahead of a moving boat, the more altitude you can get the better your chances. The fly bridge of a cabin boat is an excellent vantage point, and logically a boat equipped with a tuna tower is even better.

High or low, you are searching for the same thing, and a school of surface-swimming bass will look the same from any altitude. They generally appear as a dark brown smear on the surface, but if they are a foot or so deeper and the water is unusually clear you may spot them as an almost violet-colored section moving along at a steady clip. Skates and shoals of menhaden are often mistaken for red drum schools, but it takes only a few minutes to move in and make certain. If they are channel bass and if you have moved close enough to see their silvery bodies with reddish backs flashing by your boat, you are in too close, and you had better chop the throttle instantly and let the school move on unmolested until they have had a chance to recover from the excitement and resume a normal feeding pattern.

Once the surface school is sighted, the safest practice is to approach it with utmost caution, staying well to one side or following at a discreet distance. A hundred feet off to the side of the school is closer than you should be. Twice that distance is better. This is just another good reason to consider spinning tackle when you are buying your equipment. You can get longer casts with less effort. I know plenty of skilled fishermen who still rely entirely on conventional boat and surf rods with revolving spools who have no trouble making consistently long and accurate casts, and they catch their share of fish. It is just that I do a better job with spinning tackle and for sight-hunting reds I would not consider any other.

My favorite tackle for this type of fishing is a saltwater spinning outfit consisting of an 11-foot rod with a reel that will comfortably hold 250 to 300 yards of 25-pound-test monofilament line. I also like to use about two feet of 60-pound leader with a strong swivel clip at the end. Many anglers refuse to use the heavier shock leader because they say the knot that joins the leader to the line interferes with their casting. For some reason this has never bothered me, and after all, it is a matter of personal choice.

The selection of lures is, like the use of the leader, a matter of personal preference. One of my favorites has long been a hammered metal squid with a 5/0 hook. Running a close second is a spoon about four inches in length with the same size hook. Whatever the case, don't restrict yourself to one or two lures. If a spoon does not work after a few casts, switch to a bucktail, jig, a diving plug, or even a plastic eel. Be sure the hook is honed to a needle point. The red drum has grinders in his throat and a dull hook will slip out.

The pompous character who sits back with a wordly wise look on his face and states with great authority that this certain lure or that is an absolute must is simply talking through his hat. When I hear experts expounding on the exact artificial lures for certain types of fish, I am always reminded of old Uncle Garro, that wonderful character in William Saroyan's *My Name is Aram* who had once taken a trip on a train and knew exactly what pitfalls were almost certain to await the unwary traveler.

Anyone who does a lot of fishing for a particular type of fish can make an educated guess as to what lures are best, in general terms, but beyond this it is all a bunch of hokum. Depending on the conditions, any fish that will strike an artificial lure will one day seem to go wild at the sight of one particular lure, and fish after fish will strike it. The next day you might do as well if you were throwing rocks. That is exactly why I think some kind of monument should be erected in honor of whoever the unsung hero is who invented the clip. It enables the fisherman to shift from one lure to another without a lot of fuss and bother of tying knots when the fish are there and you are in a hurry to catch them.

Fish for the channel bass at the end of a pier, on a bridge across a pass, in a small boat in a sheltered bay, around the twisted roots of mangroves, or anyway you please. My own personal choice is surf casting on a lonely beach near an inlet, be it Cape San Blas out from Port St. Joe, Florida, along the vast stretch of Texas' Padre Island, or the Outer Banks of North Carolina. Something there is about the red drum and surf casting that just seem to go together in a natural sort of way, like ice cream and applie pie, shoes and socks, or baseballs and bats.

You hike along for mile after mile close to the water's edge because the sand is firm and makes for easier walking. The endless beach is a little cosmos unto itself, the waves rolling in one after another, the sea grass whispering, ghost crabs scurrying for the sanctuary of their holes, and the sanderlings, like feathered ballet dancers tripping on slender legs, pausing now and then to probe the sand which is sucking water like a blotter with each receding wave. You keep searching the surf for just the right spot, and then comes the first cast. Somehow you know Old Red is out there waiting. You start the retrieve and then, there it is! The strike is so solid it almost jerks the rod from your hands.

Listen to that brake on your reel screech and see how the rod is determined to dip down into the water. It's up to you now, with no one around to offer advice or help. Everything you have ever learned about channel bass and fishing comes into play, and finally you see him breaking water. His head is pointed toward the open sea and he is putting every ounce of strength in his powerful body to pull you and your tackle out behind him.

That's right, use the waves to your advantage. Catch one of the big ones just as it begins to curl and you can gain a few yards of line. If you don't time it right the channel bass will—and will take advantage of the backwash to help him strip more line off your reel. Seesaw, Marjory Daw; man, this is work and no fooling about it. Your arms feel as if they are about to come loose at the wrists and elbows, and your back is beginning to ache from the endless contest.

Suddenly you see you are going to lose him to a wave of extra size, big, green, and crested with snowy foam. He's got the bit in his teeth now and is headed for the Gulf Stream, taking all your line with him. You run out into the water until you are waist deep with the rod held high. It weighs only a few ounces, but now it has turned to a bar of lead.

This is one bass that is too big and too smart. Won't he ever give up? You consider cussing, but there is no time for cussing—or crying either.

You are a prizefighter that is getting punched so hard and fast that you would be willing to sink down on the ropes and let him punch you to the canvas, but there are no ropes to lean on.

Another wave. This one smacks you full in the face and drenches you and vaguely you know that it knocked your hat off. It revives you like a bucket of cold water on a downed fighter. You forget about the weight of the rod and the ache that spreads out from your shoulders in all directions.

Gradually, almost imperceptibly at first, you feel a lessening of the strain. Cranking the reel handle furiously, you back out of the water and with each retreating step you are gaining line fast. The tide of battle has changed, and then there he is out there in the shallows. He is coming toward you now, but still struggling to get his massive head turned the other way.

Great Jehoshaphat! Was there ever a channel bass so huge. You give the drag an extra twist and fumble with stiff fingers for the hand gaff on your belt. You hold the rod high over your head and make a swipe at him, miss, and try again. This time the sharp point gets him in the jaw and you drag him up on the beach, stumble, and sit down hard before you planned to. In front of you, your record fish has given up, and you strip a few feet of line from the reel to take the strain off the rod. This is what you came for, and this is the fish you have been waiting to catch. The one you have thought about through countless thousands of casts over the years.

The fish still has the last laugh. You are the one who has to drag his vast bulk all the way back to the place where you left your car.

Often when the subject of channel bass fishing enters the conversation, the Atlantic coast angler will shuffle through a stack of photographs and say: "Oh, I know our channel bass are the same as those they call redfish over in the Gulf but they are just little fellows, like the ones we call puppy drums."

It is then important to point out at least one fact of life that has somehow eluded this eastcoaster's piscatorial research. A redfish was caught by O.L. Comish while fishing off the coast of Louisiana in September, 1963, weighing 56 pounds 8 ounces.

There is something about the human animal that drives him to strip his gears in an effort to catch the biggest fish. I cannot explain it and I go right along with the herd. Unfortunately, the biggest *Sciaenops ocellatus* are not always the best. If you are fishing for the taxidermist, the record book, and the camera, that is different, but if you are fishing for the dining-room table, take heed! Big channel bass are poor fare. The flesh is coarse and tasteless. Those in the three- to ten-pound class are excellent when cut in filets or baked whole. Ones that weigh fifteen pounds drop into the fair-eating category, and beyond that I would just as soon settle for a haunch of rhinoceros.

As with most fish, the angler using natural bait will do well to offer the channel bass the kind of food he likes to eat. Tops in the natural bait department are such tidbits as shedder crabs, fiddler crabs, bloodworms, sand bugs, clams, and strips of cut bait, including mullet or menhaden. One excellent way to get old Spottail to take the hook is to offer him a sandwich. You make it by pulling the carapace off a shedder crab and pinning it on a hook and then adding a chunk of clam. If you have trouble making the two pieces stay on the hook together, resort to sewing thread and tie them together.

One final word where channel bass and natural bait are concerned. Don't think that just because you are out after a forty- or fifty-pound fish that you have to use a chunk of bait big enough to catch a shark. Except when he is in a hurry to get from one place to another, Old Red is always eating. He is forever grubbing about on the bottom or chasing small fish and he is not impressed in the least by the size of the bait. You just want to be certain you have something out there when he comes along.

There is still another interesting way to catch redfish, should you happen to be anywhere down in that broad shallow stretch of water known as Florida Bay. As the tide begins to rise, the redfish, just like the bonefish, swims up out of the channels and begins to forage about on the mud flats, and you will often see his dorsal fin projecting above the surface. Move with caution and don't rattle things around in the skiff. Try to approach to just within casting distance and drop a piece of bait or an artificial in his path. Keep it moving slowly and the chances are good that he will pick it up. Once hooked, he will give a good account of himself and on light tackle he is a prince of a game fish.

STRIPED BASS

You can talk your head off, cast your arm off, freeze your pants off in the early spring surf, and work out formulas as involved as the

Pythagorean theorem and you still may not have much luck in catching striped bass *(Roccus saxatilis).*

No matter how involved you get, the whole subject boils down to a few basic facts. First, it is important to know that the striper is a selective feeder. When he is gorging himself on alewives, he is not likely to give a shedder crab a passing nod. The same goes for whatever type of bait he is feeding on at the moment. Second, it is necessary to have natural bait that matches what he is currently eating—or you must scramble through your tackle box for an artificial that comes close to looking and performing like the real thing. Tomorrow the same bait or lure may not be worth a hoot, simply because the striper has had his fill of mullet or eels or whatever and is hungry for something else. Then you have to do it all over again.

Also, learning the art of finding a school of feeding stripers is of utmost importance. There are always exceptions, but if you hope to get in on some fast and furious action, look for signs that will tell you where the stripers are working. In the daylight the birds—gulls, terns, and so forth—are sure to be present when the striped bass are feeding on the surface. Again, you may see bait fish jumping in frenzied attempts to escape. Even the stripers themselves will sometimes go on a brief jumping spree and thereby disclose their location.

Another very important bit of knowledge is that these fish often do the bulk of their feeding at night. Therefore, you won't have the birds working for you; you can't see either the bait or the stripers themselves. Your only recourse then is to listen for them, or know where they *might* be, or carry a rabbit foot.

Night does have one advantage. They are somewhat easier to fool and more prone to strike anything that passes near them. The same applies to fishing for these bass when they are feeding in roiled or cloudy water.

The whole problem would be quickly solved if you could simply catch one of them and open him up to disclose his stomach content, but because they are so selective when they are on an eating binge, this is a pill that is easier to prescribe than swallow. It is analogous to the newspaper editor who told the aspiring young man applying for a job: "Son, no newspaper is going to hire a reporter without experience."

The next best thing is to know as much about a striped bass as he knows about himself. In the case of some fish, this is next to impossible, but ichthyologists and just plain fishermen have been studying the striped bass for more than three hundred years, and with modern

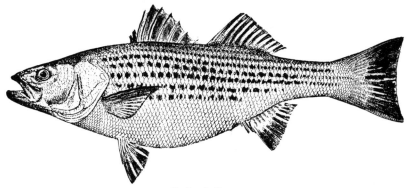

Striped Bass

tagging and other methods of observation a considerable store of knowledge has been accumulated.

Many are unaware that the striped bass is largely responsible for the first public school in the New World. It all dates back to the days of the Plymouth colonists who thought so highly of the striper as a food fish that the legislature passed laws prohibiting the use of them as fertilizer. Later, in 1670, a law was passed that all income from mackerel, herring, and the striped bass at the fisheries at Cape Cod be set aside to establish a free school. With the bass being caught in vast numbers, the money was soon available and formal education took a giant step.

As with the salmon, the striped bass is anadromous. Unlike the salmon, however, after traveling far up into freshwater streams to spawn, the striper does not die. Instead, both male and female return to salt water and repeat the process for many years. The female is approaching sexual maturity at about four years of age. In her early years she may cast only sixty-five thousand eggs at a spawning. As she grows older the number of eggs continues to increase until by the time she is fourteen years old she may lay as many as five million at a time. Some of the old "cows" that have been caught, tagged, and released, and then caught again prove that they reach an age of at least twenty-three years. Males, although not nearly as large as the females of the same age, mature in their second year.

The striped bass is primarily an Atlantic coast fish, although they are also found in the northern Gulf of Mexico. Some of the best Gulf fishing for striper is to be had in February and March as they make their way up the Apalachicola River. Those of ten pounds are fairly common and some even reach fifty pounds. In 1879 they were successfully intro- duced on the Pacific coast of North America. Also, some have become landlocked and spend their lives in freshwater lakes and reservoirs.

Along the Atlantic coast they range from the St. Johns River in north Florida all the way up to Cape Cod and beyond. The center of their range and the chief spawning grounds are in rivers emptying into Chesapeake Bay and North Carolina's Albemarle Sound. One of the best-known spawning grounds is as far from salt water as one hundred miles up the Roanoke River in North Carolina.

After spawning, the eggs drift along with the current and hatch two or three days later. The fry then spends a period of its early life in its flowing cradle of fresh water, but gradually moves downstream and eventually into its natural saltwater habitat. In southern waters spawn- ing usually begins in late March or early April.

Once seen, the striped bass is easily recognizable thereafter. It is a particularly beautiful fish with a deep body, prominent and separate fins with the anal fin slightly smaller than the second dorsal. The sides are silvery white, shading to a brownish green on the top. Generally, there are seven lateral stripes on each side and the scales are clean-cut. The lower jaw projects slightly and the trailing edge of the caudal fin is nearly vertical.

One minor variation of the head shape occurs in occasional stripers. In these comparatively rare specimens the handsome head will have a somewhat pug-nose appearance. They are, however, exactly the same fish and it is believed that the deformity of the head is due to oxygen deficiency in the embryo stage. Fishermen prize these pug-nose or pug-head bass, as they are often called, and claim that they stage a more spectacular battle than their normally formed siblings. It is thought that because of the malformation of the pug-head it is necessary for them to work harder in their pursuit of food, and thus they acquire more strength and stamina.

Unlike many other fish, the striped bass is not burdened with numer- ous names. The most notable exception to this is on the Chesapeake, and to some extent north and south, where he is generally called the rockfish. In some localities he is also known as the greenhead.

The average size ranges between two and six pounds, with fifteen- and twenty-pounders not at all uncommon. It is believed that the largest striper ever caught was taken commercially in 1891 near Eden-

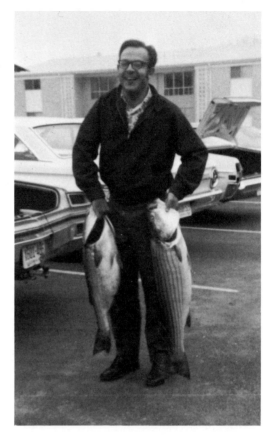

Doug Whalen of Portsmouth, Virginia, winds up a day's fishing with a pair of striped bass. That's 38 pounds of fish he's holding.

ton, North Carolina, close to the mouth of the Chowan River where it empties into the western end of Albemarle Sound. Records show that the fish weighed 125 pounds. The IGFA record lists the largest one taken on sporting tackle as a 73-pounder caught by C.B. Church in Vineyard Sound, Massachusetts, on August 17, 1913. Many records have been set in the northern reaches of their Atlantic range, but large ones are not uncommon in southern waters. One weighing 58 pounds 8 ounces was caught in 1963 by Dewey Norton in Chesapeake Bay near Gwynns Island at the mouth of the Piankatank River.

On the Atlantic coast the fishing begins in very early spring as the stripers are moving along the beaches searching for the particular bay or sound into which they plan to turn. This is the time for the surf-casting angler to swing into action. Often such excursions mean keeping a lonely and cold vigil on some stretch of sand and—oftener than not —at night. A bright moon helps, but some hearty souls will even plod along in pitch blackness with nothing to guide them save the booming surf.

As in all beach fishing, it helps to scout the area ahead of time and set up markers of driftwood that will be important landmarks only to you. What you will be looking for are cuts and tidal rips that mean lots of swift water—water that will be rushing seaward on the ebb tide and carrying with it vast numbers of bait fish that foolishly played around in the pass until the sweep of the current became too strong.

The striper knows these foolish ones will always be plentiful. Maybe it is coincidence or just happenstance, but I've always had better luck with the fast-moving waters of a spring tide nearing the ebb. Of course, that combination has to occur when the stripers are feeding close to the places you have scouted, admittedly something that does not always happen.

Night or day, when a school of stripers is located, and you are casting artificial bait, it is a waste of time to stick with one lure long if you know you are reaching the school and yet not having results. If a big bucktail fails to produce after half a dozen casts, shift to a popping plug. If the plug does not get their attention, clip on a silver spoon or metal squid and then try a plastic eel. Whatever the lure, it should be kept in motion. This does not mean simply a long cast and a steady retrieve, but rather a retrieve that causes the lure to move ahead in spurts, tilting the rod from one side to the other to produce a shift in direction. Sometimes another color of the same lure will make all the difference.

There are times when striped bass, like any other fish, simply refuse artificial lures. It is, therefore, well to have a working knowledge of the types of natural bait they prefer. Starting from the bottom and working up toward the surface, they will occasionally be feeding on clams and mussels or maybe just sea worms on that particular tide. Later on that day—or maybe several days later—they will suddenly decide, as if by popular vote, to devote their attention to a diet of crabs or shrimp. Again it may be eels, and then their appetite shifts to fatbacks (herring) or bunkers (menhaden). The next time it may be mullet, tinker mackerel, anchovies, or squid.

Whether they go in search of one particular type of food or whether they are opportunists and become temporarily addicted to whatever they happen to find is a question I have never been able to answer satisfactorily. Because they shift about so swiftly from one spot to another in such a short space of time, I am inclined to think they simply become satiated with one type of food and go streaking off in search of something different.

By late spring, the bass are done with their spawning and move back into the bays. Summer fishing for stripers is average to good, but often spotty. The next *big* season begins in early fall, and I have seen autumns on the Chesapeake when they seemed to be all over the surface of the Bay in both small and large schools. It gives one the impression they are laying in a supply of food for the winter.

Boats play an important role in fishing for stripers, because while they will frequently be within easy casting distance from the shore, there are other times when the only thing to do is to go out and look for them. Trolling is a popular method, and often one can locate a school only in this way, all the while keeping one's eyes on the surface for patches of disturbed water that suggest some kind of activity is taking place a few feet down. As previously mentioned, birds are always a big help. A lone gull may appear to be just flying along meditating on avian thoughts, but you can be fairly sure he is on active subpatrol. And right there is another enigma of the sea that never ceases to amaze me. There goes a lone bird drifting along through the air. All at once he spots a school of feeding fish and he knows he has lucked onto a free meal from the scraps that will be left behind. Before you can realize what is happening, he will be joined by a dozen, two dozen, or some-times scores of other birds. It seems almost as if he sends out an allpoints bulletin and his friends come winging in from far distant places to join the feast. They do a lot of squawking when the action starts, but sometimes the distance from which they come is little short of astounding.

The striped bass are unconcerned about the birds diving and wheel-ing overhead, but they are easily scared by the sound of a boat engine. The trick is to throttle back and make a rapid appraisal of the situation. Determine the direction in which the school is moving. If they are coming your way, move slowly out of their path and get the casting tackle ready so that you can begin tossing lures their way when they are in casting distance. If they are going away, proceed slowly after them, again until you are in range. Should you elect to make your play by trolling, it is important to circle so that the boat will stay well away from the school, but so that your line and lure will cut through its fringe. The bass do not seem to attach any importance to the fact that one of their members has become involved in some kind of a problem by striking your lure and they will keep right on feeding as long as there is no banging and clattering around in the boat.

Frequently, you will not be the only angler on the Bay with enough sagacity to have paid heed to the birds, and chances are good that one or more boats will head for the action. As a rule, most sportsmen will respect your find just as a good bird dog honors another's point. They will ease in and follow your lead of slowly circling. Now and then, lamentably, there will be the boatload of boobs who will come charging in full steam ahead and plow right through the middle of the school. That puts the lid and lock on that particular school of stripers and you might as well start looking for the birds again.

The same observance of stealth is required when the bass are staging a roundup of baitfish close to shore. Talking, even shouting, does not have any effect on fish, but let some character go splashing out into the water and once again you have lost your school. Wading certainly has its place in striped bass fishing, but there is a vast difference betweeen the cautious approach and the angler who plunges in like a three-legged hippopotamus on the run.

One of the best trolling rigs I have ever found—and this will occasionally work even when the stripers are interested in some other type of food—is a Colorado spinner with a sizable chunk of bloodworm or sea worm on the hook. In theory, the bass catches sight of the bright spinner flashing through the water and darts over for a closer look. When he is near enough, he smells the worm and decides to sample it. Such a belt-and-suspenders trick is in no way restricted to the "rocks," because there are scores of other species that will fall for the same gimmick.

Jointed plugs are good and so are hammered spoons with trailing pork rind. One of the best trolling rigs I have ever found, especially around the Chesapeake Bay Bridge and the tunnel under the Bay, consists of a three-way swivel arrangement at the end of the line. To one of the swivel rings a ten-ounce dipsey sinker is attached with about three yards of monofilament. Onto the next ring is a terminal leader of about fifteen feet. Of course, the end of the trolling line goes on the third ring of the swivel.

Line is then payed out and the boat speed adjusted until you can feel the sinker bumping along on the bottom. This gets the lure down deep, but sweeping several feet above the bottom.

There are two primary types of tackle for striped bass. When working the schools of small-to medium-sized fish, my preference is salt water spinning tackle with a 7-foot rod. I use 8-pound test monofilament with a short 20-pound test leader. A thin wire leader will do just as well, but something has to be there to protect the line from the bass's sharp teeth.

For surf casting, I am inclined to use heavier tackle, but ten to twelve pounds suits me best if monofilament is used. The size of the surf-casting hook should be fairly large. A 7/0 or 8/0 is big enough to secure a live bait fish such as small mullet, and even if you are using whole blue crabs these hooks are not too large. The striper has a big mouth and he hits hard. Crabs, by the way, are excellent bait and if you can get shedder crabs, so much the better.

Hooks do not need to be so large when using bucktail, plastic eels, or plugs. Even with a bucktail, I like a 4/0 hook. Of course, you can hold most stripers with even smaller hooks, but there is always the possibility that one of those record breakers is just over the next wave and when they go into action a small hook can come back to you as straight as an arrow.

In the Chesapeake and in Albemarle Sound the fishing for stripers begins in April and continues until the latter part of June or early July. From that point on, things settle down during the summer months, but it moves into high gear again in late September and often continues well into December.

One of the nice features about fishing for stripers in the late fall out of the Norfolk area and along the Eastern Shore is that the tourist season is over and the rates have come tumbling down. If the weather is not too raw, the Rudee Inlet area between Virginia Beach and Sand-bridge Beach is excellent.

There are two distinct types of migrations made by the stripers. One of these is the annual spring run from open water into the bays and up the rivers. The other is the north and then south migrations, they make along the coast in spring and fall.

One more tip that has special significance to the angler who fishes for old man "Rock" in the Chesapeake is this: when you happen to spot oyster fishermen working the tongs from a boat, it is well worth the effort to take note of the current and troll along the natural chumline being kicked up by the tongs. This disturbance of the bottom will turn up all manner of striped-bass food and if you troll deep the chances are good that you will find just what you are looking for—and without any help from the birds.

BLACK DRUM

The black drum *(Pogonias cromis)* would surely be eliminated way back in the semifinals if a fish beauty contest were ever held. He doesn't tailwalk or perform aerial acrobatics, once hooked, and a big one would be shunned as food by all but a family of cave dwellers on the brink of starvation.

The natural question then, after such a defamatory introduction is "Why bother to catch him?"

The answer for the angler of southern salt waters is threefold. One, he is plentiful all the way from Chesapeake Bay, south along the Atlantic coast, and from the lower west coast of Florida all the way around the Gulf of Mexico. Second, the sport fisherman just naturally takes pride in catching a big fish. Third, while the black drum does not possess the speed and agility of some of his contemporaries, the angler who catches a big one has a struggle on his hands from the first tug on

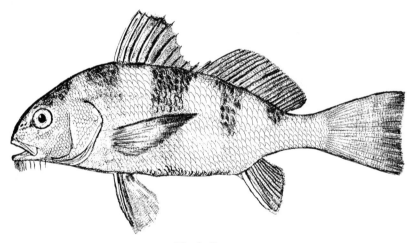

Black Drum

the line until the battle is won or lost, as the case may be.

Also, before further digression, it should be noted that while large black drum are not fancied by piscatorial gastronomes, the smaller ones of ten pounds or less provide fairly good table fare.

Those who break out the fishing tackle along the Texas coast can count on catching the black drum in plentiful numbers from January through March, and often the prime period is extended a month or so in both calendar directions, from December through April.

Those fishing the lower Atlantic coast in the Georgia and South Carolina areas will find that large drums are to be found in bays and tidal rivers in the spring. In the fall, smaller members will be plentiful for the surf caster and pier fisherman.

In Virginia, the black drum is included in the trio of game fish which the Old Dominion anglers have called the inshore "Big Three." The other two in the Chesapeake region are the cobia and the channel bass. The season for the black drum in Virginia waters begins in April and reaches a peak on the lower Eastern Shore near the middle of May.

According to IGFA records, Gary Hilton Kelly, fishing out of Willis Wharf, set the record for black drum on June 12, 1967, with a catch that weighed 98 pounds 8 ounces.

These fish are known to have been caught weighing 146 pounds, and the eleventh edition of Rube Allyn's *Dictionary of Fishes* reports one weighing 115 pounds caught in Tampa Bay, near Safety Harbor on Florida's west coast, on January 8, 1967, by Gene Perkins of East Saint

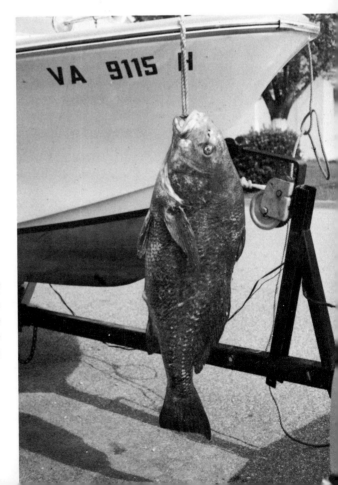

The black drum would hardly be expected to win a beauty contest, but one like this 35-pounder from the Chesapeake Bay can put up a powerful struggle.

Louis, Illinois. Another one that topped the hundred-pound mark by seven pounds was taken in a net in Virginia's Chesapeake Bay near New Point Comfort.

Unless I get busy and work at it, the first black drum I caught stands an excellent chance of being my lifetime record. It was the glorious time of year in early June when school was finally over and three full months were spread before me in a vast smorgasbord of summertime delights. To reward my sister and me for passing, my mother and father had promised to take us to Virginia Beach for a two-week vacation.

When we arrived, I helped to carry the luggage from the car to the cabin my parents had rented, but that was all the time I wasted. My tackle was not the best there was to be had, but my reel was loaded with a vast amount of new cuttyhunk and I was confident my surf stick would stand up against any monster the Atlantic sent my way. I was somewhat overgunned for the countless one- and two-pound whiting I pulled out of the surf, but it gave me an excellent opportunity to practice casting and to study the action of the waves. Before the end of the first week, I had a mental picture of every swash channel and sandbar in a north and south direction for as far as I could walk.

One of the natives had examined my rig and suggested I make a try for some of the channel bass he was sure I could catch. To back up his tutelage, he provided me with the proper terminal tackle that consisted of an improvised fish-finder rig and 7/0 hooks. He showed me how to make a clam-and-crab sandwich by securing a big meaty chunk of clam to the back of a blue crab with sewing thread and then jabbing the hook through the offering. It is a combination bait that has proved itself to be a real killer for both drum and channel bass. The top shell should be removed from the crab before the clam is attached.

It would make a nice tale to say that I promptly marched out into the surf and caught a fish on the first cast. It didn't happen that way. In fact, I lost much bait and did a lot more casting that afternoon, three days before we were to head back to Richmond. Everybody along the stretch of beach said I was too late to catch the big ones in the surf and besides they were too far out, or already in the bay where they go to spawn.

Now that I know better, I guess they were right, but there was also one old black drum plodding his way along that didn't know better either.

My first thought was that I had hung up on a submerged timber or something. That was, until the line began stripping off my reel at an unhurried, but steady pace. Standing knee-deep in the surf with white suds swirling around my knees and occasionally coming high enough to wet the seat of my pants, I realized I had a fish on the other end of the line.

Clamping down on the drag, I gave one mighty heave that, by all rights, should have snapped my venerable old rod with the frayed wrappings and grooved guides. Somehow, the rig held together while the fish decided he was going to look for the Gulf Stream.

The excitement of making contact with so much unseen power sent me into a state of mild shock. Determined not to let the fish have his way, I began to inch out deeper and deeper and I might have continued until my head was under water had my dad not come bounding out beside me.

"Loosen the drag a little," he said. "Let him have some line until you can get back closer to shore."

I followed his instructions and walked backward while that powerful cuttyhunk continued to unwind. I had never hooked onto a fish of such size and several times I secretly hoped my dad would insist on taking the rod, but he just stood by offering an occasional suggestion and watching. He was wise enough to let me finish the job I had started, but remain nearby in case he was needed.

The afternoon wore itself out and the fish wore the boy out, and the reel's gears were beginning to have serious tooth trouble. The sun went down, and my mother brought us sandwiches and a lantern and still the fish continued to contest the issue. When he was finally up in water shallow enough for us to hear him churning around in the waves, Dad ran after a garden rake he had spotted under the cabin. Not the most sophisticated gaff ever used, but nonetheless effective.

When I had the fish in shallow water, Dad socked him hard. The rake tines dug in and he dragged the still-struggling "monster" high upon the beach. My arms felt as if they had been pulled loose at the shoulders and elbows and my fingers were twisted into claws. Nothing would do, however, but we must load the fish and all the family in the car and go looking for an ice house that was still open.

"Got yourself a fair-size drum," the man said, adjusting the weights on the big scale. "I make it sixty pounds smack on the nose."

My joy was unbounded. "I'm going to stuff him." I did not have the vaguest idea how one would go about mounting a fish, but at the moment I was not concerned with such details.

The man at the plant agreed to keep him iced down because I had to take the fish back with us when we left three days later. The hot weather and the long trip to Richmond settled the stuffing question, but it was not entirely in vain because I rounded up all the youngsters in a country mile of our house and let them have a look before the old drum had to be interred.

Somehow, the sunfish, chain pickerel, and perch that inhabited the waters around Richmond were never quite the same, at least for the rest of that summer.

In recent years, Virginia has become increasingly aware of the interest in saltwater sport fishing. The Eastern Shore from Cape Charles up to Assateague and Chincoteague islands are the favorite drumming region, and statistics prove that a largely untapped source of drum fishing is to be had all over the Chesapeake.

There are many fish that will take an artificial lure as readily as natural bait. It is almost certain that anglers do occasionally catch a black drum on some form of artificial, but they are fundamentally a natural bait fish and a bottom feeder as well.

Whether angling for them in Texas, Florida, or Virginia, it is wise to offer them what they want in the way of food. Mussels, clams, shrimp, and crabs are the best baits. If you can get shedder crabs the chances are even better.

Of equal importance is knowing where to fish. It is not something that requires a lot of thought. Just go where the bait is and this means mussel and clam beds and near the mouths of tidal streams where crabs are likely to be plentiful. But, as with all fish, the drum has to swim to get from one feeding ground to another, and this means that if the angler has the proper bait on the hook the chances of catching one or more between these areas is good. It is because of this roaming instinct that the drum is a favorite of many pier fishermen.

four ~~~~~~~~~~~~~~~~~~~~~

~~~~~~~~~~~~~~~
~~~~~~~~~~~~~~

ON THE FLATS

PERMIT

You might as well make a note of it right here and now—unless you forsake family and fortune and dedicate your life to the task, you are not likely to catch a great many permit *(Trachinotus falcatus)*, even over a number of years of saltwater fishing. I used to know a man who caught a 30-pound permit one afternoon while fishing on the bonefish flats off Florida's Lower Matecumbe Key. His joy was unbounded, and as a group of us sat around a restaurant table that evening, he could talk of nothing but his fish. Before the night was over all of us could practically recite in chorus every detail of the event, including the type of bait, how it was presented, how long the fish was in sight before he paid attention, and the ebb and flow of the battle that followed, up to and including the actual boating.

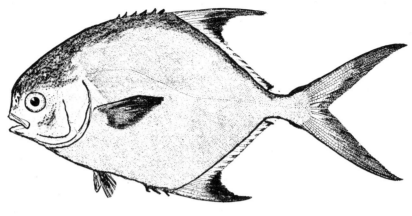

Permit

"I'll be out there before the sun tomorrow morning and catch another." If he said that one time he said it twenty.

The poor fellow was true to his vow, but he came back without another permit. "The tide was wrong," he said. "I'll get one this afternoon."

Again he failed. One time because a gull flew low over his intended quarry. Again, a shark moved in just at the wrong moment. On and on it went. The rest of us assumed his infatuation would diminish with the passage of time as one defeat followed hard on the heels of another.

But that was not to be.

He used up the rest of his vacation fishing for permit, and while he apparently saw a lot of them and came close to catching a few, he failed to score again.

He went back north and sold his business and moved to the Florida Keys. He bought a small house and a boat and did nothing but eat, sleep, and fish for permit. He wrote letters to me about his investigation of the fish. Once he even called me long distance to tell me that he had finally caught another. I heard that his wife tried to have him committed, but the court ruled that the man was completely within his rights if he wanted to quit work and fish. It finally did award her a divorce on the grounds of desertion or something like that, but the proceedings did not cause any hesitation in the man's determination to catch permit.

With the pasage of years I lost track of him, but it is entirely possible that he is out there right now squinting his eyes against the glare of sunlit water and trying to set a world's record for the most and the biggest permit. If time finally caught up with him I can imagine him boarding the barge and pointing out across the water, telling Charon to go easy with the pole because the permit are in and too much disturbance will frighten them off.

Fortunately, not everybody who catches a permit goes that far, but one thing is certain and that is that once you catch one you are a long time forgetting. I've caught a few, hooked lots more—which I lost— and seen hundreds of them. I rate them as one of the best game fish that swim.

Their range is reported to extend from Brazil to Massachusetts, but in the waters of the United States the angler stands the best chance of catching one if he fishes the lower half of Florida, and his chances are further enhanced if he concentrates his efforts in the waters surrounding the Keys. At the same time, many are caught in the Indian River area on the east coast and a record of a 42-pound 4-ounce permit was set in 1953 by R.H. Martin, fishing out of Boca Grande on the Gulf side of the state. This record stood until 1960 when F.G. Burke, Jr., caught one weighing 47 pounds 12 ounces, also at Boca Grande. This stood until Robert F. Miller topped it in March of 1965 with a 50-pounder caught in Biscayne Bay. Both Martin and Miller set their records using 12-pound line.

The permit is the largest member of the pompano family and small permit are often mistaken for the common or the round pompano. The permit has a flat body, dark on the top, as does the smaller round and common pompano. In the adult specimens the sides are bright silver. The first dorsal fin consists of six stubby spines and the second dorsal is exaggerated in length for the first few softrays for a total of seventeen to twenty-one in all. Just forward of the anal fin there are two independent short spines followed by one that begins the sixteen to nineteen softrays. The caudal fin is deeply notched and both are dark. The pelvic fins are often tinged with a bright orange color.

It is virtually impossible to set one weight as being the average. It can be said, however, that those weighing twenty pounds are frequently caught, with the above-mentioned record of fifty pounds being the current top weight. It is believed by a good number of conscientious fishermen that even larger permit will eventually be taken.

Permit are frequently found in the same areas as bonefish, but because of their greater body depth they will wait for sufficient water to cover the flats before they move onto them. The bones, on the other hand, will often be found in very shallow water.

Sometimes schools of thirty or more permit of medium size will be seen feeding on the flats. As with the bonefish, they are often spotted during their feeding periods by their dorsal fins breaking the surface, and more frequently by their entire tails sticking out in the air while they stand almost on their heads to blow crabs and worms out of their hiding places. Unlike the bonefish, permit schools do not create the areas of cloudy water known as "muds." Also, they will work on a small stretch of sand or marl for a minute or two and then dart swiftly for a considerable distance before pausing again to explore the bottom.

The large permit are seldom seen in shallow water, preferring to stick to the deeper channels that cross and crisscross the flats. The new-comer, not accustomed to looking for permit, often finds it impossible to see a fish, although he may actually be looking straight at it. This is because a permit can stop suddenly and blend with the background so that the camouflage is nearly perfect.

Well do I recall the first time I "saw" one. The guide was standing in the stern of the shallow-draft skiff and suddenly he said in a hoarse whisper, "There he is. He's a big one and I don't remember ever getting this close to one."

Glancing back at the guide, I saw him lift his index finger surreptitiously from the pole and point out across the water. It was early morning and the sun was at our backs. Hardly daring to move my head, I began to search the bottom in the direction he was pointing. I could see patches of grass, shells, sand, and dozens of little inverted cone mounds made by crabs and worms, but no matter how hard I looked I could not see anything that resembled a fish. "He's there, all right," the guide said. "You jist ain't looking in the right place."

I knew the man well enough to be sure he was not playing a joke on me, but still I simply could not see the fish he was seeing and pointing to.

"You ain't got bad eyesight or something?" he questioned. I could tell he was slightly irritated at my inability to spot the fish. "You'll come out here lots of times, and you'll never have a better chance to see one close up."

I began to feel as if I were playing the picture game where you try to find the hidden faces in a line drawing. I squinted, blinked my eyes, and followed every instruction from my guide such as "Look ten yards out from the side of the boat—just to the left of that clump of grass with empty crab shells near the piece of barnacle-crusted wood." The directions were explicit, but they were useless to my untrained eyes.

"Yon he go!" the man in the stern said. "He ain't coming back, neither." As he spoke I saw the permit. In fact, I realized I was looking directly at him when he suddenly broke and ran. It was not until he rocketed into motion that I was able to see him.

Polaroid sunglasses are a boon to the angler stalking the flats, but it still takes more than glasses to learn how to "see" a fish that can be almost invisible in the water. Sometimes the only part you see first is an eye or a fin. Only then does the camouflaged fish begin to take shape. The same is true of numerous other fish, but the permit surely must have invented the game.

While the permit's mouth is devoid of teeth, he does have grinders which he uses to crush shellfish. The most important fact about his mouth is that it might as well be made of madeira or some other equally tough wood. You simply don't fool around when a permit takes the bait, be it natural or artificial. You sock it to him hard instantly and then hit him again and again on the slim hope that you can at least drive the point of the hook in a fraction of an inch.

What's more, when he starts to run, and all the time he is on, you have to keep the line taut as a banjo string. Give him just a little slack and you've lost him.

A hooked permit will use the ruse of running like lightning, stopping suddenly, and scrubbing his mouth on the bottom in an effort to dislodge the hook. He will then make another scorching run that will make the reel drag scream in agony. Some fish do not seem to be aware of the line they are fighting. If you are unwilling to give a fish credit for that much intelligence, watch a permit run around a clump of sea fans, a coral head, or any other obstruction he can find, and try to figure out what he is up to if it isn't to cut the line.

Not only does a permit have a tough mouth and speed to spare, but he has stamina and he can go broadside in the water and become almost as immovable as King Arthur's Excalibur in the rock. If you bring in a twenty- or twenty-five pounder on light tackle in less then half an hour, you are an expert. The odds are against you accomplishing it in an hour, and if you have a really big one on you may spend several hours at the task.

Whether by himself, as the large ones often are, or swimming in a school, the permit can be exceedingly exasperating when you are trying to interest him in your bait or lure. A typical scene is a fisherman, skilled in his angling ability, standing as nearly motionless as possible and shooting one cast after another so that the bait lands precisely where he thinks it should: right in front of the permit that is standing on his head investigating the bottom with his forked tail pointed skyward.

Let's suppose the bait is a small blue crab, about three inches across the carapace, that has been carefully hooked so he will move about after sinking to the bottom. The fisherman knows that the crab is bait par excellence for any even reasonably hungry permit. The stage is set and the angler has every reason to expect his offering to be accepted.

The feeding fish moves close, the fisherman twitches his rod tip, and the movement causes the bait to jump slightly on the bottom. The permit is within inches of the bait now and the man in the skiff tenses, ready to slam the hook home with a solid wallop.

Nothing happens.

The angler waits for another permit that is jackknifing close by. He allows for the deception of the refractive properties of light passing through the water. He knows that objects are not always where they appear to be, so he gives the reel crank a turn or two and causes the bait to move directly across the path of the feeding fish.

The second permit passes by. Then a third and fourth and suddenly the school decides to move fifty yards away to investigate another dinner table. Unruffled, the angler reels in, inspects his bait, and cautiously picks up the push pole. With careful thrusts he propels his boat ahead in pursuit, letting it ghost along over the smooth surface until he is once more in the proper position for a good cast.

Repeat first scene with minor variations.

Still the angler is unruffled. He does not know why his bait is being spurned, but he has come prepared. Off comes the crab and it is replaced with a live shrimp. This, too, is ignored. Another deft cast. Another failure. The school moves on. The angler maintains his composure. He knows the fish he is stalking and he knows that if he makes one slip, even so minor as accidentally kicking the tackle box or bumping the pole against the skiff, his quarry will be gone for good.

Move, change bait again from a shrimp to a smaller crab, then a chunk of meat from the tail of an iced spiny lobster, cast again and again and continue to follow the feeding school.

This may not be the day. The angler knows the permit has excellent vision and an equally good olfactory system, but they also have a mind of their own. Today they may be feeding on sand worms, and nothing else may entice them. The tide continues to rise and the feeding school becomes increasingly difficult to locate. The fisherman lifts the lid of his tackle box ever so softly and clips on a yellow bucktail, then a white one, and then a miniature silver spoon.

Five separate stalks and several changes of baits and lures, and then a trio of lemon sharks sweeps up from a channel. The school of permit is gone for sure this time. Turning his boat around, he starts poling back across the flats.

Is the angler annoyed? Of course he is. No one likes to play a flawless game and fail to score a single point, but he also knows that the permit would not be the supreme trophy he is if he could be caught every time. As a matter of fact, the fisherman may not locate another school for several days, but he knows that sooner or later the law of averages will catch up with the fish and the next time another small crab or a carefully worked bucktail may be just exactly what the lead permit is looking for.

This is the day and the fish he is waiting for, and when it comes he will know how to set the hook and fight the battle to a successful conclusion. That will be the day that the 7-foot spinning rod with the saltwater reel filled with 10-pound test line will get its workout. The angler will have a leader of twice the line's test and he will be using a hook ranging from 2/0 to 6/0.

Permit fishing is not restricted to the flats. Often the larger ones are caught in passes or in deep channels. The ebbing tide flowing through the spans of a bridge is also a good spot, but in this case it is necessary to use tackle with more authority. If given a chance, the permit will whip around a piling like a fox running through a hollow log, and barnacles and monofilament do not mix. If he is to be landed or boated, he must be forced to fight it out in the open.

There are two basic conditions that determine the movement, and it is to be assumed, the feeding habits of the permit. One is the condition of the tide and the other is the temperature of the water. Availability and abundance of food are, of course, equally important factors. The fact that the permit is fundamentally a bottom feeder means he is not going to waste much time on barren territory. A rule of thumb is that if the area in question is known to be a favorite feeding ground for bonefish, then it is also highly likely that permit will be found in the same general range. The fact that crabs and other invertebrates comprise a large part of his diet does not rule out the fact that from time to time he varies his fare with small fish. Consequently, small shiners and other live minnows often attract a permit's attention when other bait fails, and a wider choice is open for the angler who uses artificial lures.

The permit does not like warm water, nor does he like very cold water. Armed with such knowledge, the fisherman is not going to waste his time plodding over endless miles of flats in the heat of a summer day hoping to catch sight of the permit. Instead, he will concentrate his efforts in the early morning and late afternoon, with the early morning generally much more productive because the water has cooled during the night. The cooler night hours would be considered prime time except for the fact that unless you can see a feeding school the chances are remote that one will be caught. There are few fish more easily scared than the permit and the sight of a boat's running light or a flashlight simply sends them to the safety of deep water long before you know they are in the vicinity.

The reverse is true in winter because the shallow water warms more quickly than deeper water, the flats attract the permit during the daylight hours, and the period of suitable fishing conditions is extended.

Because he is a deep-keeled fish, the permit must wait for a sufficient amount of water to cover the flats before he moves in. He will frequently spend the first few hours after dead low water cruising the intermediate zone that separates the shallows from the channels. When the flood tide has supplied a sufficient amount of water on the flats he goes to work, and this is the period when the angler should be on station and watching.

One area of fishing that should be given due consideration when in quest of the permit is along an open stretch of coast when combers are lashing the beach. Admittedly, fishing such waters along the east and west coasts of Florida is a hit-or-miss proposition, but the chances are fairly good. Fleet swimmer that he is, the permit often approaches very close to the beach to pick up sand bugs, crabs, and other small creatures that are washed out of their hiding places and caught up in the undertow that sends them tumbling seaward.

The surf caster will be aware that while the permit is often within easy casting distance, he is not going to allow himself to be caught in a shallow swash channel. In effect, he is going to leave the back door propped open. In this case, his "back door" is going to be a cut between sandbars that will provide a quick route of escape if needed. It is therefore logical to concentrate the fishing efforts near such a break in the offshore bars.

To catch a permit in the surf is definitely a bonus, but the trip need not be wasted because there is a considerable number of other worthy game fish that are ready to provide plenty of action while you are hoping for the coveted permit.

BONEFISH

There was nothing else to do, so I just sat down on the stern seat and rested my left elbow on the top of the outboard and waited. I was watching a man losing a fight and I could not help him. The wispy veil that divides comedy and tragedy was never thinner. I wanted to cry and at the same time I wanted to laugh.

Spraddle-legged in the bow of my skiff was a friend of long standing. Zack comes from the state of Washington. We had put four years in the Navy together and during that time and in the years that followed we had fished together in various parts of the country. Zack had taught me the thrill of salmon fishing up in the Puget Sound area years before. Now he had wanted to be introduced to Florida game fishing.

"If he doesn't slow down in a few seconds I'm gonna be fishing with an empty reel." As he spoke, Zack rolled the dead stub of a cigar from one side of his mouth to the other.

He was actually standing on tiptoe and holding his tackle so high over his head I got the impression he was showing it to the traffic that was moving along U.S. 1, better known as the Overseas Highway

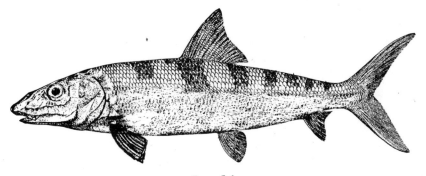

Bonefish

between the mainland of Florida and Key West. He was trying to extract every last ounce out of the rod that was bent in an almost motionless arc. If I had not been able to see the monofilament peeling off his protesting spinning-reel spool, I would have sworn he had snagged his hook on a sea fan or a piece of coral and was trying to free it by brute force.

In a last desperate effort to turn the biggest bonefish I have ever seen, Zack screwed the brake knob tighter and tighter. The reel growled louder, but the line did not slow down. Then there it was—that pinging noise a line makes when it breaks off a reel spool, followed by the whispered hiss as the knot zipped through the rod guides. Then there was nothing but a man standing there with his tackle still held over his head, as if waiting for someone to take his picture.

Slowly, joint by joint, the statue of the defeated angler began to crumble. His head dropped forward, the cigar fell out of his mouth, and the fingers on his left hand released their grip on the reel handle. One arm descended, followed by the other and he sat down and looked at the empty reel as if it were a living creature that had betrayed him in an hour of need.

"I don't think I ever wanted a fish so badly in my life," Zack spoke softly, either to the reel or to me. There was no way to tell which. "I haven't asked too much out of life," he continued, picking up his cigar stub and throwing it overboard. "Just a few things here and there. I never even wanted a million dollars, but I did want that fish."

"O, Heart of mine, we shouldn't worry so! What we've missed of calm we couldn't have, you know!"

Zack looked at me with a summer squall brewing on his craggy face. I decided the better part of valor was not to continue quoting lines from James Whitcomb Riley's poem.

"If you make one smart crack about what I said about bonefish, I'll turn this boat over and drown the both of us."

"It wouldn't do you any good," I chided. "The water's only two feet deep and we'll just wade ashore."

As the saying goes, time heals all wounds, and although I was discreet enough not to rub it in that day, I think enough time has passed to reflect on the way that particular fishing trip had begun.

Zack had found a reason to leave his business in Washington and drive all the way to Florida. There had been letters and phone calls and we had laid plans for several different types of fishing trips, some of which we had already made and there were still some to go. Part of our state-wide rambling had taken us to the Keys, and I had listed a trip or two out on the flats for bonefish as a must.

"I'll go bonefishing with you," he had said. "But that is one fish I can't generate much enthusiasm for. He's not fit to eat and it seems to me that any fish that waddles along in water not deep enough to swim in must be nuts to begin with."

My feathers had been somewhat ruffled at his scathing denunciation of one of the gamest fish ever to flip a fin, and I was determined to prove him wrong.

We had put the boat in on Lower Matecumbe Key and headed out toward Lignumvitae Bank. It was not just a random shot, I had been there several times before; the first two times with a guide who knew so much about bonefish and the ways to catch them that he could even tell what one of them was going to do before the fish himself knew. Well, that day Zack learned all about bonefish.

Once you become addicted to bonefishing it is something akin to a disease within a disease. You are in enough trouble when you get hooked on fishing in general, but once you add bonefishing to the malady, strange things begin to happen, and some men have become so enthralled that they have been willing to mortgage their houses and lots even their souls, to pursue the sport to its fullest.

Bonefish *(Albula vulpes)* are globe circling in distribution, but found only in tropical seas and known by a few other names such as grubber, macabi, raton, and banana fish. In the waters surrounding the United States they are found only in the extreme lower section of Florida, along the chain of Keys, and in Hawaii where they are called o'io. The record bonefish was caught off Zululand, South Africa, by Brian Batchelor on May 26, 1962. It weighed 19 pounds. Shy of this weight by only fourteen ounces was the one caught off Hawaii's garden island of Kauai on October 14, 1954, by William Badua. This one weighed 18 pounds 2 ounces. Those weighing twelve to fifteen pounds have been caught frequently in Florida waters and in the Bahamas. Recent IGFA records lists no less than half a dozen fifteen-pounders caught on 12-pound test line.

The bonefish or "white fox," as he is also known, because of his scientific name, is one of the truly beautiful fish of southern salt water. He has the forked tail of many pelegic speedsters, a torpedo-shaped body, silvery white on the sides and belly and bluish green on the back.

Barracuda, often found on the same flats inhabited by bonefish, are occasionally mistaken for them by anglers who have not fished for either extensively. Both have long heads, large eyes, and are similar in color and shape; but the bonefish has the distinction of having a single tall dorsal fin whereas the 'cuda has two, separated by considerable distance.

Of course, when the bonefish is near enough to be seen clearly, the confusion no longer exists. The mouths of the two fish are about as different as those of a pelican and a sparrow. The barracuda has a long bottom jaw and a mouth filled with spiked teeth. The bonefish is the reverse. He has a long upper snout, an inferior bottom jaw, and no teeth at all. Instead of teeth he has a tongue with a pebbled surface and a triple set of pebbled ridges in the top of his mouth. He uses this combination to crush the mollusks, crabs, and other shelled creatures on which he feeds.

The Florida Keys, all the way from Biscayne Bay to Key West and Dry Tortugas, is the only bonefish territory in North America. Fully 90 percent of the fishing is done on the shallow flats on either side of this string of islands and it is an all-year sport. On those rare occasions in winter when cold fronts push unusually far south and stay there long enough to drop the water temperature below 70 degrees, the bonefish

Wading the flats off the lower coast of Florida this angler has won the battle with a fine example of a bonefish. Note that the lure has been removed and this excellent game fish is just about to regain his freedom.

quits the flats and sulks in deep water. Such times are pleasantly rare, however, and winter or summer the angler will be able to find bonefish in shallow water. This may be close to shore or several miles out.

Fishing for this speed demon is far from just finding a stretch of shallow water and sitting there waiting for one of them to come along and grab your hook. A guide is recommended until the fisherman has learned enough to strike out on his own. What is more, and nobody seems to know why, just any flat will not do. The bonefish takes a liking to a certain stretch of water and if he is not fished too hard he will be there day after day.

But if you are the type who insists on going it alone right from the start, there are certain rules that must be followed. He runs on a schedule that is governed entirely by the tides, and you had better be waiting at the station when the whistle blows or you'll miss the train.

A glance at any chart of the Keys will show that the bottom, particularly on the Gulf side, is a patchwork of channels, stretches of fairly deep water, and large areas of sand or mud bars that are barely covered, often completely exposed, at low tide.

These flats are the feeding grounds of the bonefish. When the tide is low he is resting in deep water. The moment the tide begins to rise, the bonefish starts to move. It is possible actually to spot schools of them patrolling the perimeters of these bars when the water first begins to cover them.

This calls for a small boat with a very shallow draft that will enable you to get well out toward the middle of the flat as soon as there is enough water on which to float. Better still, unless the bottom is too gooey to walk on, tilt your motor, step over the side and push your boat well in toward the middle of the flat.

Once on the flat, if you have chosen well you will not have long to wait, because the bonefish already has his lunch box open and he wants to get on with his eating just as soon as there is enough water to enable him to swim. And they can, and will, swim in water that is no more than six inches deep. By the time the water is at flood, it may be two or even four feet deep, but the bonefish is not even considering waiting for that much water.

Often you will see him "finning," which means that he is literally scooting along the bottom on his belly with that tall dorsal fin out of the water. As the water gets a little deeper you will see him "tailing." This means he is hard at the business of grubbing about the bottom, practically standing on his head with his tail out of the water. Give him another foot or two of incoming tide and you will be able to spot him by "muds" or "smokes." If the bottom consists of marl, the "smoke" will be easier to see than over a sandy bottom, but even here he can still make quite a cloud. This disturbance will also pinpoint a large school working its way across the bottom in frantic quest of food.

A good way to increase your chances is to have your boat in such a position as to be uptide. Bonefish have a tendency to move into the flow of the tide, probably because they can smell food that is being swept their way.

One truism about bonefish is that they are among the most easily startled fish to be found anywhere. Make some kind of rattling noise in your boat, splash an anchor over the side, or anything like that and they are long gone. Even splashing a lure or chunk of bait too close to a single fish will cause him to shy, sending the entire school into a get-away stampede like a herd of frightened range cattle. This Chicken Little attitude is something I have pondered for years and I have yet to come up with a satisfactory answer. They are not afraid of seabirds because most of the bonefish that come up on the flats are four- to seven-pounders and much too large to be grabbed by a bird. Besides, as I have already said, they will actually wallow along in water too shallow for normal swimming. It might be suggested that they are afraid of sharks.

Not so.

Sharks often move right along with a school of bonefish and, of course, they will grab one if they have a chance, but the speedy and highly nervous bonefish knows he can outrun any shark that might start after him. They no doubt keep a wary eye out for what the shark may be doing, but they certainly show no fear of him.

Could they have a natural fear of the fisherman and his boat? I know fish are much smarter than most of us give them credit for, but wildlife in general has to have thousands of years to develop an instinct to fear certain things. Sure, a deer will bolt at the sight of a man walking through the woods, but the deer has had millennia to learn to fear predators such as wolves, bears, and panthers, and man might be any of his natural enemies as far as he knows. Why is the bonefish so ready to bolt at the sight of man? I do not know and I'm still wondering.

You now have your boat on a flat that is known to be good bonefishing ground. You are wearing Polaroid sunglasses to cut the glare on the water, and your tackle is a light rod about seven feet long with an open-face reel that will hold at least three hundreds yards of monofilament of 6 or 8-pound test. Heaven help you if you do not have a couple of spare spools already filled with the same test line. If the action gets hot and heavy you are going to lose some line, and this is no time to refill a spool. Your selection of lures is somewhat restricted. The lure should be as light as you can comfortably cast. I have an obsession when it comes to bonefish artificials and these are the Upperman bucktails. I want it to be yellow on a 1/0 hook and weigh a quarter ounce. Other bucktails, I am sure, work equally as well and so do feathered jigs in the same weight class.

Some expert fly-rod anglers are adept at taking bonefish on that type of tackle, and I have seen some thrilling performances put on by the experts of these long rods.

Whatever your choice of tackle, the important point always to keep in mind when bonefishing is to use the lightest and most delicate casting you are capable of executing. To pop a lure smack in front of the lead bonefish may prove your accuracy, but it is almost certain to scatter the school. You can generally determine the direction in which they are moving, and the skill is to drop the lure or baited hook as softly as possible well ahead of the school. Keep one eye on the fish and the other on the spot where your lure landed. When your prey is within a few feet of it, twitch the rod so that the lure will hop across the bottom in a series of short jumps. By the time it is close to the lure, move it more and more. By now you can probably see the fish fairly clearly, although there are certain light conditions when a bonefish becomes almost invisible.

Don't be in a rush to make another cast. The first two or three fish may have spotted something else more interesting and are going to ignore your lure or bait, no matter what, but there are more coming. In general, a school will have about fifteen to twenty-five fish in it. This number, by the way, may well exceed a hundred during spawning seasons.

If the fish are showing signs of passing the lure completely, then it is a good idea to reel in and get ready for another cast. Sometimes, the speed of a lure darting through the water will get one of them excited and he will start to follow. If he does, don't slow up. He could easily outrun your fastest retrieve and a sudden slowdown may make him suspicious.

If he grabs, you must let him do the hooking job. Even if you see him take the hook, wait! A sudden strike will snatch the lure out of his mouth. Almost invariably he will make a sharp turn once he grabs the lure and hook himself. One thing is certain. When a bonefish strikes, you will know it because he hits hard and you will have all the battle you bargained for once the fight begins.

If a school happens to slip up on you, avoid casting right in the middle. Instead, shoot your lure over the school and then bring it through the fish in a series of short jerks.

The natural-bait fisherman stands an excellent chance because, while the bonefish is far from being troubled by poor eyesight, he depends to a large extent on his sense of smell to guide him to his food. Prime baits are hermit crabs (out of their shell, of course), small crabs, and shrimp. Chunks of conch flesh are also excellent bait and used extensively in the Bahamas.

If you are well uptide from an approaching school and have a plentiful supply of bait you can up your chances considerably by tossing some chum in the water. This can be broken crabs or coarsely ground and chopped shrimp or conch. The flavor will draw the school your way and frequently get them so excited they will take any bucktail or feathered jig that passes close to them.

There are frequently going to be times when you see a school tailing or mudding, and after watching them for a minute or so you are able to determine that they will pass too far one side or the other to reach them with your best casting skill. This means that in order to get near enough to them you are going to have to move your boat.

Of course you should not be foolish enough to crank up the outboard, but you might be tempted to row toward the school. Forget it. Oars are much too noisy. The answer, then, is to pole the boat across the flat. If you are over reasonably solid sandy bottom and don't try to rush things, you stand a good chance of getting in range. If the bottom happens to be gooey marl, you had better have had some experience or you will lose your pole, or worse still, let it pull you overboard. I have seen this happen.

The soft marl is easy to push a pole into, but it grabs on like Chinese finger cuffs. The trick is to push and then rotate the pole as you draw it out of the mud.

Once the bonefish is hooked he is going to run, and run far. A hundred-yard dash is not at all unusual and when he is moving at twenty-five miles an hour you are well aware that line is coming off your reel spool at a frightening clip. Set the drag lightly so he is pulling about two or three pounds. Get the rod well up over your head and make it work for you. Too much braking power will result in a broken line.

If you are lucky and your bonefish does not decide to take a turn around a sea fan or sponge, you can gain some line after he has made his initial bid for freedom. The battle is far from won, because once he catches sight of the boat he is off again, and it is all to do over, and then he will break again and again.

After a while, however, he will begin to tire and you can guide him over the edge of the landing net. Of course, if he is a big one, or you want to have him mounted, or if he is your first and you just have to bring him back, fine! After you have caught a few, however, you will work your heart out on one, wear your nerves to a frazzle and then, while he is still in the net in the water, you will take the hook out of his mouth and watch him swim away. A dead bonefish in the bottom of the boat is no good to anybody.

Anyway, look over there on the far side of the flat. Isn't that another school mudding their way along? If you handle the pole right and your tackle is still in good shape, there may be time to tie into another one before the tide changes.

five ～～～～～～～～～～～～～～

～～～～～～～

～～～～～～～

BLUE WATER GLADIATORS

BILLFISH

Swordfish, White Marlin, Blue Marlin, and Sailfish

> *Nature her Bounty to his mouth confin'd*
> *Gave him a sword, but left unarmed his mind.*

This bit of Oppian verse was probably dedicated to the swordfish, but it often applies equally to other members of the billfish family.

Somehow it seems wrong just arbitrarily to group four truly regal game fish under a single heading. In southern salt water the four important billfish are the sailfish, blue marlin, white marlin, and swordfish. Of the four, the swordfish *(Xiphias gladius)* is the rarest and probably the largest. The IGFA lists the world's record as weighing 1,182 pounds and measuring 14 feet 11¼ inches. It was caught off Iquique, Chile, on May 7, 1953, by L. Marron, on heavy tackle.

100

Swordfish

The swordfish inhabits all tropical and subtropical waters of the world and is found along the Atlantic coast and in the Gulf of Mexico. The bill or sword of the swordfish is longer in relation to overall body length than that of the other three and it is considerably thicker and flatter. The body is well rounded and the dorsal fin quickly distinguishes it from either of the marlins and sailfish in that it is tall and sickle shaped, as is the tail. In the adult stage the swordfish is devoid of scales. In general, the color is brown on the back, shading to a white underside.

With the approach of summer, billfish begin a northward migration that leads them into the Gulf and well up the Atlantic coast. All use their bills as slashing weapons when feeding on school fish such as mackerel, jacks, anchovies, and others.

It has long been known that broadbill swordfish inhabit the Gulf. They have been taken on long lines by research vessels and seen "finning out" or basking on the surface with their tall dorsal and upper caudal fins exposed. It was not until July 21, 1969, that one was caught on game fish tackle. The fisherman was George M. Snellings III, fishing aboard the *Holiday,* which was skippered by Captain Bert Smith. They were fishing out of South Pass, Louisiana.

The broadbill was spotted by Snellings while the fish was "sunning" on the surface. He trolled a rigged mullet near the swordfish and the bait was taken on the first pass. The fish made four jumps and took approximately twenty minutes to bring alongside. It measured 8 feet 5 inches in length with a girth of 35 inches, and the weight was 112½ pounds. The sword, itself, measured 2 feet 11 inches.

Depth means little to the swordfish. He may spend part of his time

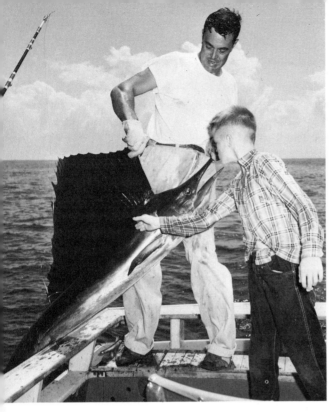

There is no mistaking the identity of a sailfish once that enormous dorsal fin is extended. The young angler off the Florida coast wants at least to touch the fish before he is released.

on or near the surface, and long lines from research vessels have proved that he also swims deep. Perhaps one of the most unusual "proofs" of the broadbill's deep-swimming propensities was demonstrated when the research submarine *Alvin* from the Woods Hole Oceanographic Institution fleet was operating at a depth of two thousand feet on the Blake Plateau off the east coast of Florida. The three men in the sub felt a sudden jolt. The underseas craft was brought to the surface by the mother ship and when it was in view, the crew saw that a swordfish had rammed the sub and driven his bill so deeply into a seam of the exterior fiber-glass hull that it was unable to break free.

Divers managed to get a line around the fish's tail, and along with the sub, it was hoisted aboard the tender. The sword, which measured 4 feet, was so deeply imbedded that it required two hours to dig it out. The swordfish weighed 198 pounds and was 8 feet long.

Stories of swordfish attacking ships and boats date far back into history. Pliny the Elder wrote, during the first century, of their attacks on ships, occasionally with such fury as actually to sink the target. Numerous wooden ships have been hauled into shallow water for careenage only to discover the bill of a swordfish deeply imbedded in the hull. At times they have struck ships with such force as to drive their swords through heavy copper sheeting and then well into stout timbers.

John Josselyn is probably the first seafarer to write of a swordfish attack on a ship in American waters. In his *Account of Two Voyages to New England,* written in 1674, he told of such an incident: "The twentieth day in the afternoon we saw a great fish called Vehuella or Sword-fish, having a long strong and sharp finn like a sword-blade on the top of his head, with which he pierced our ship and broke it off striving to get loose."

The spear on any large billfish is a dangerous weapon and especially where swordfish and marlin are concerned. Any of these fish should be treated with utmost caution at that critical moment when they have just been brought alongside. At this point a quick decision must be made —either to keep the fish or cut him free. Of course, for those new to the game the trip would not be complete without a few photos standing beside the trophy back at the dock. Thus it is perfectly logical that the fish should be kept. Then, it may be that the prize will be mounted as a present for the fisherman's wife. There are few things that the average housewife loves more than a huge stuffed fish to compliment the decor of her living-room wall.

More and more sport anglers are becoming increasingly conservation

The aquabatic sailfish will clear the water time after time until he throws the hook, or is brought alongside to be boated or released. Sails are numerous in the Gulf and Atlantic waters.

minded, and before the fish is seriously injured by gaffing or dragging him into the cockpit, he is released. To release a sail or marlin or swordfish, for that matter, it is necessary only for someone of experience to don a pair of heavy cotton gloves and take a tight grip on the spear while someone else leans over the side and cuts the leader close to the hook. The fish is then allowed to drift away until it recovers from the fight and realizes it is free. There is no need to worry about the hook. It will not interfere with the fish's feeding and it will soon rust out and cause no damage. Often the hook can simply be lifted out, which is still better. Many anglers tag their fish before releasing them, a practice that provides biologists with valuable data should the fish be caught again at a later date by another angler. A properly affixed tag is not injurious to the fish. Most oceanographic institutions will gladly supply tagging information and details of how to go about it.

Several summers ago Al Jennings, Ashley Lofler, and I were on a billfishing trip in Al's 41-foot cabin boat. We had left Destin, Florida, and run about thirty-five miles southwest toward the 100-fathom curve. The day was average for August with piles of thunderheads on the horizon, a light breeze out of the west, and a slight chop on the surface.

We were fishing four lines. Two were clipped to the outriggers and the other two were being trolled flat. On the way out we had picked up several bonito which we tossed in the ice box for a shark-fishing trip we were planning and when the Fathometer showed we had reached the curve we baited up with rigged mullet, backbones and gills removed, and the second hook extending aft of the sewn belly.

Everything was ready except the marlin. We were certain they were there because the radio was rattling every fifteen or twenty minutes with first one skipper and then another telling about a fish he had boated, tagged, or lost after a short battle. It was the usual line of chatter that serves to keep one from dozing off, or at least from going sound asleep.

"Here he comes! Here he comes! You guys snap out of it and keep those rods ready." I looked over my shoulder and saw Al on the fly bridge pointing to something that had attracted his attention off the stern.

Digging my Polaroid glasses out of my shirt pocket, I pushed my cap back and put them on, getting to my feet at the same time. The marlin was moving in behind the bait on the port outrigger rod. I saw his fins light up briefly as he made a feinting pass at the trolled mullet. Since the rod that was about to see action was on my side, I made hasty preparations to man it. It had a 10/0 reel loaded with a little over seven hundred yards of 60-pound test Dacron.

All at once the marlin's outline resembled a neon sign. It is always a fantastic sight to watch a billfish begin to glow as if he might be suddenly charged with radium. It is a phenomenon that has long puzzled anglers and one that has been debated to great extent. Some claim it is the excitement of the chase, others say it is fear of being near a boat, then there are those who are certain it has something to do with a movement of the skin, similar to the prickling of hair on the back of one's neck or getting a case of chill bumps. I don't know, and it really doesn't make a great deal of difference one way or the other, except that it is an interesting sight to observe.

The important thing at that moment off Destin was that the following fish was now recognizable as a white marlin *(Makaira albida)* and he looked to be a big one.

Glowing like a Christmas tree, he bore in on the bait. The clothespin holding the port outrigger line snapped like a cap pistol. Grabbing the rod from the holder, I siddled crabwise toward the chair. Ash had taken over my 6/0 reel and was busy cranking the line in. When it was clear, I sat down and braced myself.

When a marlin comes out and begins his famous tail-walking stunt it is a breath-taking sight that often leaves the angler's mouth gaping almost as much as that of the fish in the photo above.

There are all manner of theories about the best way to set a hook once a marlin has whacked the bait and begins to run with it. Some anglers count ten; others use the drop-back method and let the line run free for a few seconds. I have lost several and caught a few. Anyway, enough to think I have a feel for the game. I left the drag alone and waited until I felt the precise moment had come, then I socked him hard. A marlin can be hit much harder than a swordfish because his mouth is tougher.

Upsidaisy! Out came Number One fish and he rose majestically from the water in one beautiful air ballet, crashed back in amid a shower of white suds and then, *lumpo!* He made a slow cross to port, changed his mind and went starboard, and then turned broadside with the slow steady pull of a sea anchor.

"Hit him a couple of times," Ash suggested. "I think he's half asleep."

Dropping some line, I brought it up short with a jolt that should have put life into a lard can. Nothing. Absolutely nothing. The white marlin was not the least bit concerned with the hook in his jaw or the strain to which I was subjecting him.

Al had chopped the diesels to almost idle and was now hanging onto the fly bridge rail like Tarzan ready to swing from one limb to another. "That fish must be sick," he said.

The marlin continued to pull with all the enthusiasm of a chunk of seaweed, and yard by yard, I moved him in closer to the boat.

"We might as well pull him aboard and have a look," Al said, dropping down to the cockpit. "A few more like him and I'm ready to start grouper digging."

When the marlin was in the wake, he was obviously just drifting and as I began to guide him over to the port side Ash reached out for the long wire leader with a gloved hand. Al was leaning over the gunnel.

White Marlin

Just then the fish exploded. So sudden and unexpected was his action that I was barely able to hang onto the rod. The big white marlin was now wide-awake and he literally vaulted himself out of the water. Instinctively, Ash dropped the leader and ducked. Al jumped back, but not quite quickly enough.

The fish was green and as excited as a bronc in a corral full of sidewinders. He cleared the gunnel by nearly two feet, and we heard Al yell as he and the fish sailed over into the cockpit and hit the starboard side. Somewhere in the tangle of line, broken gear, and wildly thrashing fish we could see Al rolling and tumbling about and a great wash of blood was spreading over his shirt.

My first thought was that the marlin's spear had struck him full in the chest. I remembered hearing of one that had killed an angler by driving its bill straight into his heart. In the tiny confines of our seagoing slaughter pen, Ash reacted swiftly. He grabbed a shark billy that consisted of a baseball bat with a lead core and smashed it down so hard that it shattered the marlin's head, knocking both of the huge eyes out of their sockets.

Scrambling over the quivering fish, Ash and I grabbed Al, who was clutching the left side of his chest and staring down at the bright blood flowing through his fingers. Together we ripped his shirt and by the time we could unlock his clutching hands and wash the excess blood off with a wet sponge, we began to breathe normally. The wound was only a surface one, or actually, it was two wounds in one. The spear had struck him just below the left armpit, ripped a gash in the side of his chest, and cut through the side of his upper arm. When we were able to see what we were doing, we washed the blood away and staunched the flow with sterile compresses.

"You know," Al mused, while we waited for the doctor back at the emergency ward of the nearest hospital to patch him up, "I still can't get over the way that marlin acted. I honestly don't believe he knew anything was wrong with him until he realized he was right up beside the boat."

"You're just lucky," Ash said. "Three inches more toward the center and he would have driven that bayonet right through your heart."

Van Campen Heilner, who pioneered in the sport of billfishing in the Bahamas, aptly likened the marlin to the "rhinoceros of the sea" in his book *Salt Water Fishing*. Al, Ash, and I were ready to subscribe wholeheartedly to Heilner's analogy.

The blue marlin *(Makaira ampla)* is considerably larger than the white. The largest on IGFA records was taken on the Fourth of July, 1968, by Elliot J. Fishman, while fishing out of St. Thomas, Virgin Islands. Fishman's big fish weighed 845 pounds. Many marlin anglers are firmly convinced that the Caribbean does not have a secure corner on the market where record-size blue marlin are concerned. It is a perfectly valid belief, too, since thousand-pounders have been harpooned as far north as Montauk and Block Island. Also, a 664-pound blue was taken on rod and reel out of South Pass, Louisiana, in the summer of 1967. It topped the previous record of a 565-pounder set by Al Childress, Jr., three years earlier. Many very large blue marlin have been hooked and lost and many more sighted in the Gulf and along the Atlantic coast.

From the moment he takes the bait the blue marlin is a powerful fighter. Three pairs of skilled hands are none too many to bring one over the side. The photographer climbs to the flying bridge of the charter boat to look down on the big fish and busy crew.

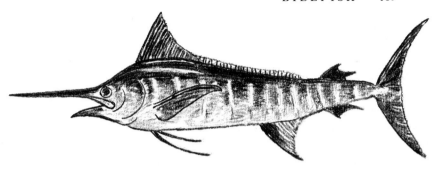

Blue Marlin

It was only a few years ago that anytime a billfish was caught in the northern Gulf, the feat rated as big news. All of that has changed now and with each passing summer, July through October being the prime months, large catches are the order of the day.

They were first discovered here in the mid-1950's when the 100-foot research vessel *Oregon* of the United States Fish and Wildlife Service began to explore systematically the fishing potentials along the 100-fathom curve which comes close to South Pass below New Orleans, runs along the coasts of Mississippi and Alabama, and bends northward to within about thirty miles of Pensacola. This 100-fathom curve is only the fringe of a really deep trench known as De Soto Canyon, a little farther south where the bottom is over half a mile down.

Sharks are frequently the curse of the billfisherman. True to his unpredictable nature, one can never be sure just when he will be around, nor in what sizes and numbers. Each year countless billfish are hooked and boated without interference from sharks. At other times the sharks border on becoming a plague, dogging the wake of a boat in prime fishing waters. One trip I recall vividly was an absolute fiasco. We were out for three nights and two full days in the Gulf near De Soto Canyon and time after time we hooked fish, including a few outstanding marlin. Every fish was cut up by the sharks, and at times they would take the trolled baits and even rip off the teasers that gurgled and churned along behind.

Time after time we would reel in all the lines and race along at full throttle with the idea of leaving the sharks behind, but the instant we put out the bait they were there. They seemed to be completely aware of what we were up to, and the prospects of a free marlin feast kept them with us.

Most charter-boat skippers keep either a rifle or shotgun on board to dispatch sharks, but firearms are akin to shutting the barn door after the horse is gone, once a shark has bitten a chunk out of a potentially record-size fish. One of the inflexible IGFA rules is that no mutilated fish may be entered in the records, and there are many billfishermen who know they would have been listed on the rolls had it not been for the rapacious jaws of an accompanying shark. A fish as big, powerful, and swift as a marlin is certainly not a part of a shark's normal diet, but once hooked he doesn't stand a chance against these hyenas of the sea.

Although, as stated, a mutilated fish cannot be entered in IGFA records, there are times when there is enough of a shark-chewed fish to enable the fisherman to make a reasonably accurate estimate of the weight. Frequently, sharks will bite great chunks out of the belly, sides, and back and still leave the spine of a large fish such as a blue marlin intact so that the tail is still attached. At such times, and solely to satisfy the angler's curiosity, it is well to know the mathematical formula by which a fish's weight can be estimated.

The procedure is to measure the fish's girth at the largest point. In the case of the marlin this would be in the section on the body near the anterior end of the dorsal fin. This measurement should be made in inches. The next step is to measure the length of the fish from the front of the mouth (point of lower jaw) to the fork of the tail. This, too, should be measured in inches.

To find the approximate weight, multiply the square of the girth by the length. Next, divide this figure by 800. The result will be a fairly close approximation of the weight in pounds.

For a quick reference, the formula is shown below:

$$\frac{Length \times Girth^2}{800} = \text{weight in pounds.}$$

One of the interesting dimorphic facts about billfish is that the female is consistently larger than the male. Accurate statistics are difficult to accumulate when dealing with such wide-ranging fish as the billfish. However, it is fairly well established that while a female blue marlin may top the thousand-pound mark, the largest male of the same age will be something of a giant if he exceeds three hundred pounds.

The smallest member of the Atlantic and Gulf billfish clan is the sailfish *(Istiophorus americanus)*. In general terms, the average sailfish weighs slightly over forty pounds while the white marlin average is closer to sixty pounds. The largest sail on IGFA records is one that weighed 141 pounds 1 ounce, and measured just an inch shy of 8½ feet.

Because of his spectacularly large dorsal fin or "sail" and his beautiful cobalt blue back, more sailfish are mounted than any of the other billfishes of southern waters. Rare, indeed, would be a restaurant specializing in seafood that did not have a mounted sailfish on the wall. Vast numbers also bedeck the walls of marinas, tackle stores, and heaven only knows how many are tucked away in homes and offices.

There are few sights on the briny equal to that of a hooked sailfish leaping and tailwalking, with that enormous fin in fully erect position. That, with the frothy suds of whitecaps curling on breaking waves, the gentle roll of the cockpit deck, and the final release of the hooked fish after he has been subdued, is the essence of billfishing memories, and they will last for a very long time.

It is true that sails and marlin are occasionally caught from fishing piers, but this is the exception rather than the rule. Hence, a boat is needed to go out and meet them where they are most numerous. Countless numbers of small billfish are subdued annually by an angler standing in the cockpit of his boat. The problem is that there is no way to tell just when a big one is going to connect with the hook. That is the time that the price paid for a good fighting chair mounted in the rear of the cockpit is going to be money well spent.

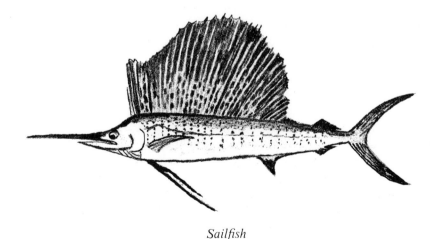

Sailfish

Next in importance is a pair of outriggers. They enable the fisherman to keep two extra sets of widely separated tackle working for him during the time he is trolling. The fishing line is generally clipped to the standing line on the outrigger with a humble clothespin. When the fish hits the lure, the line is snatched out of the clothespin jaws and the resulting slack provides the proper amount of drop-back to enable the fisherman to strip off enough line to convince the fish that he has succeeded in "killing" the bait.

A point that should be remembered is that one good billfish is enough for one boat to handle at one time. The other lines should be reeled in as quickly as possible, because billfish occasionally take it into their heads to make a community affair out of the bait-grabbing, and the results will almost certainly be utter chaos.

I was involved in just such a madhouse once while trolling on a 32-foot sports fisherman out of Fort Lauderdale. There were six of us aboard, counting the skipper and mate. For three days in a row we had gone out to blue water and tried every maneuver in the book. Other boats were returning at sundown with two or three white marlin, but all we could catch were dolphin and a varied assortment of other fish for which we were not fishing.

At about ten o'clock on the fourth morning, we were moving along at about four knots, feeling a bit sorry for ourselves and secretly wondering which one of us was the Jonah. Our four lines, two flat and two from the outriggers, were baited with three types of bait, consisting of rigged ballyhoo, mullet, and strips of bonito. Along with these we had two teaser lines bubbling, bouncing, and churning along to attract attention. Suddenly, the mate, who was up on the fly bridge steering and looking, jumped out of his chair and shouted for us to watch the starboard outrigger.

At almost the same instant I had a solid wallop on the flatline I was tending on the same side. Instinctively, I let the line fall back and the skipper was doing the same with the outrigger rod he had grabbed from the socket. Our first thought was that we were dealing with the same fish. Instead, in a matter of seconds we realized we both had made contact with different fish. Two of the other fishermen made dives for the remaining port lines, but before they could even come close to reeling in, both were struggling with hooked fish.

Three days of nothing, and then in a space of three minutes we had four white marlin leaping, tailwalking, crossing and crisscrossing all at the same time. The action that followed was akin to one of the old Mack Sennett slapstick comedies. The four of us were ducking under rods, slipping, sliding, and stumbling about on the deck while the one fishless angler was dodging to and fro like a referee caught in a football melee.

For the first few minutes we tried to make some semblance of order out of the confusion, but it was hopeless. Even the marlin started their own private war several hundred yards behind the boat. In rapid order the lines began to be braided into one single strand. Hoping to get at least one of the marlin home, the skipper and I elected to make the equivalent of sacrifice bunts by cutting our lines, but the damage was already beyond repair.

Propping my rod against the cabin, I began to see the funny side of the whole ridiculous affair. Then, considering discretion to be the better part of valor, I climbed to the flying bridge with the mate and then laughed until I nearly fell over the side. I am afraid that had I started laughing while in the middle of that cockpit brawl I would have been hit over the head by one or more of those sweating, swearing, and frustrated anglers.

It would make a nice tale to be able to report that we finally managed to boat one of the marlin, but it would not be true. The final tally showed one reel stripped down to the spool, two lines deliberately cut, and the fourth half empty when the quartet of enraged fish exerted their combined efforts at the same moment and snapped the lines.

An hour and a half later we had rerigged and we spent the remainder of the day looking for billfish to no avail. "I guess these things are bound to happen," the skipper remarked dourly, as we headed back to Fort Lauderdale, "but I never thought I would get in the middle of anything like that." He was silent for a moment and then added somewhat wistfully: "I know of a chicken farm in Arkansas that I could buy if I sold my boat and . . ." his voice dwindled away and he never finished the sentence.

There are numerous good baits for billfish and equally as many ways to rig them. Ballyhoo are excellent and so are flying fish and mullet. Some experienced anglers swear by the practice of removing the gills and packing the bait in salt for twelve hours. The theory is that it toughens the flesh and keeps it on the hook longer. Others prefer to use strictly fresh fish and change the bait more frequently, while still others go to elaborate extents, such as removing the entire backbone and sewing the limp fish on the line.

My own procedure is more simple. I break the bait's backbone in three places, thus saving a lot of fuss and bother. The triple-jointed fish waggles along with enough lifelike action to suit me, and apparently my quarry, because it has produced satisfactory results over the years.

The importance of teasers cannot be overemphasized. They can be made from almost anything that is handy: a string of empty drink cans, blocks of wood, or any unstreamlined object that will churn the water. They should be strung on a length of line and towed along about seventy-five yards behind the boat. The idea is that the disturbance they make will attract billfish to the immediate vicinity to investigate, and thus attracted, they may be prompted to strike one of the trolled baits. It should be remembered that billfish are not strictly surface feeders and often need something to attract them up from deeper water.

The proper size tackle is vital if the billfisherman is to derive his full quota of pleasure from the fish he hooks. With the great strides that have been made in saltwater spinning tackle, many anglers are boating sails and white marlin with the fixed spool. It is a safe prediction that such rigs will become increasingly popular with billfishermen as time passes, and many records that stand today on conventional "deep sea" tackle will be broken by those who favor the lighter rigs. For that matter, even the fly rod has been used to take billfish. For those not highly skilled in saltwater fly-fishing, however, a sail or marlin can make a man look pretty foolish in a hurry when such tackle is used. I have never tried it, but I know those who have done so successfully.

Looking back over the years, it is interesting to observe the gradual but steady decline in the weight of tackle used for billfish. In his fishing years, Zane Grey was an exponent of superheavy equipment, up to a 20/0 reel! In all fairness to the great novelist, he was generally in quest of the heavyweights of the billfish clan and he was not alone in the use of heavy tackle for big fish.

I shall never forget the time I tied into my first big blue. I nearly had my socks scared off and wished I could magically convert my 6/0 reel into one of those cargo winches of the twenties and thirties. I struggled with my 6/0 and then later bored everyone to tears telling about the 425-pound blue marlin I had boated with such *micro-tackle*. But then again, I guess everybody is entitled to strut like a peacock a few times in his life, and that blue did look so very big. No, big is not enough. Huge is more like it. Chances are you will even go for colossal when you tangle with your first big blue. They always look about three times their actual size when they come up in that breathtaking first jump.

The size of proper tackle must always be spoken of in general terms, for two distinct reasons. One, you have absolutely no guarantee of catching a fish that will fit nicely into a specific weight bracket. There is always the big bully traveling with small- or medium-size fish, and conversely, you may be sure that some little pipsqueak is going to come racing in after the bait just when you are all geared for something much larger. The second reason is that what might seem light tackle to one angler might be considered entirely too heavy to one with more experience.

There are, however, basic guidelines that anyone going out after billfish should consider. The following applies to revolving-spool reels. Should the marlins or sails be running under a hundred pounds, a 4/0 reel with 30-pound test line is abundantly adequate. At this point we leave the sails and white marlin behind. If the blue marlin (and perchance a sword) is in the 300-pound bracket, it is suggested that one move up to a 6/0 reel and line with a 50-pound test. When the quarry passes the 400-pound mark one will not be overgunned with a 9/0 reel and 80-pound test line. When aiming in the 500-pound or more class, a big 12/0 reel packed with 130-pound test line is admittedly a bit grandiose, but the fisherman will not be taking unfair advantage of the fish in question, and don't ever let him think it!

Stainless steel leaders ten to fifteen feet are valuable and 10/0 to 12/0 hooks are not too large for a 50-pound sail or white marlin's mouth. Naturally, they can be taken on hooks half that size, but here again, should a really big one latch on, the larger hook will be out there working for the fisherman.

The subject of the actual hooking of any billfish is of such importance that, although it has been touched on briefly a couple of times in this chapter, it is worth a trifle more attention.

If there is one warning that stands out above the rest, it is *don't strike too quickly.* Sails, marlin, and swords all usually employ their bills to stun fish they intend to eat. At times, however, they will simply run a fish down and swallow him in a single gulp without using their weapons.

The sight of a billfish boring in on one's bait is an exciting moment. If I ever reach the stage when I can observe such a happening without feeling the hair prickle on the back of my neck and discover that my tongue is stuck to the roof of my mouth, I will be through with billfishing. There may be anglers who can calmly watch such a sight and not feel a tenseness, but I don't know any of them and if I did, I would not want to go with them anyway.

Because of this built-in tension, many billfishermen lose billfish that are otherwise ready to be caught. Often it will look as if the marlin, or what have you, has actually taken the bait, and the temptation to strike back instantly is almost overpowering.

Don't!

There are many anglers who will claim the drop-back method of billfishing is old fashioned. It may be, but resisting the urge to strike too quickly will take fish nine out of ten times, so if that's being old fashioned then I'm ready to be called an old fogey.

That is one of the nice parts about having a billfish strike a line on the outrigger. Whether he hits it with his bill or grabs it in his mouth, the jolt is going to cause the line to be snatched out of the clothespin jaws resulting in a pile of loose line dropping on the water. This provides just about enough time for the bait to cease its forward motion, and there is nothing phoney about it to a billfish's way of thinking, presuming, of course, that he does go through some form of thought process.

One should learn to practice the same outrigger procedure with a flatline trolled over the stern. Count ten, repeat the alphabet from A to Z, or quote the first two stanzas of "The Shooting of Dan McGrew." Do anything to kill time, but give the fish a chance really to chomp down on the bait. Then, and only then, sock it to him!

six ～～～～～～～～～～～～～～～

～～～～～～～

～～～～～～～

THE SWIFT AND THE MANY

BLUEFISH

One summer, during the first week in June, my wife, Dorothy, and I trailed our boat from Richmond to Norfolk, Virginia, across the Chesapeake Bay Bridge and up the Eastern Shore to Chincoteague Island. The purpose of our trip was to catch bluefish.

After launching our boat, we began trolling. We covered the Narrows and Chincoteague Inlet and still by midday had not seen our first bluefish. Pulling into a quiet spot just north of Wallops Island, we broke out the thermus jug and a box of sandwiches. I had just taken the first bite when there was a slap on the surface behind my back. The trolling gear was stowed in the bow and the only piece of tackle nearby was a small freshwater spinning rig armed with a yellow bucktail.

Placing my coffee on the seat beside me, I balanced my sandwich on

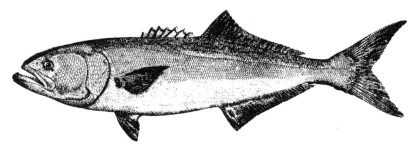

Bluefish

the rim of the cup and picked up the spinning rod. Turning around, I shot the bucktail at the spot where the bubbles on the surface were vanishing. If the lure actually touched the water I don't remember it. It seemed more as if it vanished in the mouth of a fish.

Dorothy was in the process of asking why I could not wait until after lunch before starting to fish again, when the pitiful little reel began to scream as the 4-pound monofilament line was ripped off at high speed —not just plain high speed, but super high speed. Yard after yard poured out while I fumbled with the brake and scrambled to my feet. Dorothy made a grab for my coffee cup, but the sandwich hit the floor boards and a second later it became mush beneath my feet. At the same instant a furious bluefish broke the surface and shook himself in obvious rage.

What a way to treat a friendly bluefish. Invite him to share a lunch break with you and then hit him in the mouth with a hook! If I was going to be that inhospitable, the blue chopper was going to make me pay for it.

By the time he had fifty yards stripped off the reel, I thought I had him under control. At least, he let me think I was bringing him in and again he bounced out of the water. I could swear he was glaring at me and while he was in the air I could see his jaws chewing all the hair off that bucktail. When he hit the water, he ripped off another twenty yards.

"You are standing on your sandwich," Dorothy said.

Right at the moment I was not in the mood for jokes. Here we had used up a tank of gas and now I was tied into a big blue and about to strangle on the bite of sandwich I still had not chewed.

All fish have a way of doubling in size when I have just seen them at the end of my line and I would gladly have made a deposition that this blue streak to which I was tied would not weigh an ounce under twelve pounds. Common sense told me there was no hope of getting him back and into the boat. The hook was small, the tackle was small, and the leader was nylon only a few pounds heavier than the line itself.

My blue streak sounded, broke the surface, and raced around all over the cove like one of the wild ponies of the islands. I would gain a few yards, and he would take it all away again. Over and over we contested the ownership of the line. I am a devout advocate of using light tackle, but this was carrying it a bit further than I had intended. If I set the brake too firmly I knew the line would break. If I used it lightly I was certain to wind up with a bare spool.

That sort of predicament is what game fishing is all about, but at times it is difficult to make oneself believe it. This was one of those times.

"Did you see the size of that devil?" I asked. "It's bound to top twelve pounds and I'm going to boat him if we have to stay out here all afternoon."

"Your coffee got cold and I poured it out," was Dorothy's only comment.

The battle did not last all afternoon, but it did continue for nearly thirty minutes. Even then, as I led the blue up close enough to snag with the short gaff, I almost lost him when he put on a final show of fury.

Scrambling in my tackle box, I took out the scales and gingerly placed the hook between his still-snapping jaws. As I hefted the big fish up, Dorothy squinted at the pointer. "That's the first time I ever saw a fish sweat off five pounds in a fight," she chided.

I jiggled the scales, certain they were jammed, but Dorothy was right. The fish weighed exactly seven pounds. It was still a feat to be proud of, so far as I was concerned, and somehow if he had broken free as he should have done I think I would have claimed he weighed at least twenty pounds.

The climax to that little episode came when we returned to Snug Harbor Marina and found that two other boats had brought in seventeen and twenty-two blues respectively. The weary anglers were taking pictures, rubbing sore muscles, and telling fantastic lies about the giants that broke off. One did have a fifteen-pounder, and he had the impudence to ask that I hold my fish up beside his and pose for a picture. I told him I would if he would hold his marlin tackle while I held my little spinning outfit. Fortunately, the issue was solved when the photographer found he had just snapped the last frame on his roll.

There are few, if any, saltwater game fish that can match the fury and stamina of the bluefish *(Pomatomus saltatrix)* on a pound-for-pound basis. One Old Dominion angler I know swears you can never catch bluefish on Fridays because, as he says, "That's the day the devil calls 'em all to Hades to teach 'em new meanness." Come to think of it, I don't ever remember catching old slash-jaw on a Friday, so he may be right.

The sight of a school of big blues raising havoc with a shoal of bait fish is similar to watching a gang of sharks in the midst of a feeding frenzy. They will race through the fish, chopping them to shreds and even cutting up the smaller members of their own kind. When they have eaten until their bellies are filled to the bursting point, they will slow down long enough to regurgitate all they have swallowed and then go right back to the slaughter and do it all over again.

At such times they will strike virtually any object in or on the water that represents food. Even the gulls and terns that generally join in the surface feeding sprees of most fish are not safe. They are there all right, because they know there is sure to be an abundance of free food, but the gulls do not settle and the terns do not plunge. They know that should one become incautious he may be torn to shreds by the blues. It could just be my imagination, but it seems to me the birds scream louder when they are working over a school of blues than over any other type of fish. I have seen these fish strike at paper cups, floating drink cans, half-smoked cigars, and frequently even bare hooks.

Another interesting fact concerning a large school of feeding blues is that they produce a distinct smell not unlike fresh-cut cucumbers or watermelons. I have known some expert anglers who can sniff the breeze at night and lead you straight toward a feeding school. Some say the smell results from the offal of the bait fish, but I am inclined to think it originates from the bluefish themselves. The same general odor is always present, despite the kind of bait they are slaughtering. Also, I have ground much chum over the years and to me it has never smelled like melons.

A world traveler, the bluefish is called by a wide variety of names. In southern salt waters of the United States, however, he is the bluefish from Texas, around the Gulf, and up the Atlantic coast. The only exceptions are that the smaller ones are frequently referred to as snap-

There are few, if any, salt water game fish that can match the fury and stamina of the bluefish. Doug Whalen of Portsmouth, Virginia, took this 19½-pounder off Virginia Beach.

per blues, the middle-sized ones of five to ten pounds are called choppers, and the real heavyweights are naturally known as jumbos.

The adult bluefish is in a class by himself when it comes to description. His body is fairly long, the head is large and rounded, and the bottom jaw juts forward, not in the pointed and pronounced way of the barracuda or snook, but more rounded and bulldoggish in appearance. These jaws are powerful and studded with numerous sharp teeth. They can inflict serious injury to a hand or bare foot, and even after they are boated or beached they should be handled with utmost caution until dead.

The first dorsal fin is just forward of the center of the body and consists of six or seven sharp and stubby spines. The second dorsal is more than twice the length of the first and the anal fin is almost identical to the second dorsal. The caudal fin is broad and forked. As would be expected, the basic color of the fish is blue on the topside, occasionally with a faint tinge of green. This color fades to a dull white on the belly. They are highly respected as food fish, but should be iced shortly after catching to prevent the flesh from becoming soft. Of course, no fish should be kept off ice for a long period of time, but the ill effects seem to be more pronounced in the bluefish than is the case with many other species.

Bluefish, both large and small, are plentiful in south Florida in midwinter, as well as off the coast of Louisiana in the vicinity of Grand Isle and South Pass. The northward migration along the Atlantic coast begins in early spring and by March and April they are frequently present in large numbers off the coast of Georgia and the Carolinas. By early May they have reached Virginia Beach and continue on up the Eastern Shore throughout June and July.

There is still much work to be done in tracing the migratory habits of bluefish, but it is generally considered that great shoals of them will suddenly desert the coastal waters during midsummer to go far out into the Atlantic to spawn, perhaps well into the Gulf Stream. Reasonable proof of this is exhibited when large numbers full of roe and milt will be present close to shore for a month or more, only to vanish in the middle of summer for two or three weeks. Suddenly, they are back in the same area completely empty and ravenous for food. They continue their northward pilgrimage throughout the warmer months and then return south along the same route in the fall.

One of the perplexing aspects of the migratory habits of this fish is that they may follow a regular schedule for several years in a row and suddenly there will be an entire year when they are scarce almost to the point of becoming rare. The following year, however, they are likely to return in abundance.

When they are running they are a fish for everyone, since they are caught from piers, bridges, small boats, and by surf casting. For fishing from the beaches, the late afternoon and early morning hours are the best times of the day, and occasionally they will continue to feed close in throughout the night.

It is superfluous to say "if a feeding school is sighted," because whenever a school is sighted the fish are feeding. It is true that these fish may cover long stretches in deep water and are always ready to attack a school of bait fish. It is only when the bait is either near the surface by choice or frightened up from the depths by a horde of blues that they churn the surface. At such times either lures or live bait will take fish. The only word of caution is to avoid cutting through a school, because it is almost certain to put them down. On the other hand, they seem to ignore completely a drifting boat or one that is trolling around the perimeter.

Again, schools may be located by flocks of birds. If you are out at night and your olfactory nerves are in good working order and the wind is right, you may learn to smell them.

The real test in bluefishing comes when they cannot be seen on the surface. The best chances then are to set several rigs and troll at depths ranging from ten feet all the way down to the bottom. If one rig catches a blue, all others should be quickly converted to cover the same depth. Hot weather will usually send the fish far down, and unless they have chased a school of bait to the surface that is where they are likely to be found.

Hot or cold, bluefish like swift water. They are a fast-moving fish, much like mackerel in this respect, and they have no intentions of sitting around waiting for something to happen. That means they are best found in a swift-flowing tide under a bridge where bait is likely to congregate, or in tidal rips, near jetties, and around swash channels close to the beach. A school will suddenly appear at times over reefs, wrecks, and around buoys and oil rigs. At such times the duration of their stay depends almost entirely on the abundance of bait. If it is in short supply they may remain for only a few minutes and suddenly streak off for greener pastures.

Chumming is frequently a good way to attract a school. Bunkers, mullet, sardines, anchovies, or anything handy can be put through the grinder and fed out to form a slick on the moving tide. It is the smell or taste of fish flesh in the water that attracts them, and I think they come more to investigate than to pick up the small particles. It is then that live bait of almost any type works well. The same holds true for artificials that range from popping plugs to tin squid, as well as spoons and flashy lures.

As previously mentioned, bluefish have powerful jaws and once they are hooked they immediately start chewing the lure. Some plastic lures are ruined beyond repair in the mouth of chopper and jumbo blues. The same holds true for feathered jigs and bucktails. On the other hand, they will actually break their own teeth on spoons and other metal lures.

There is an art to hooking a bluefish that often has to be practiced before it is learned. In the case of many species of fish, it is well to let them get a firm grip on the bait before setting the hook, as some will pick it up gingerly and make a short run before taking it well into their mouths. In the case of the bluefish, large or small, live bait or artificial, the surest way to hook him is to try to snatch his head off the instant he strikes. This rule applies whether you are presenting him with a streamer fly at the end of the lightest tackle or a 4-ounce tin squid hurled out with a beach stick.

The bluefish is a rough and tumble alley fighter who is not going to treat you with respect and does not look for any from you.

KINGFISH AND SPANISH MACKEREL

The Spanish mackerel and the king mackerel *(Scomberomorus maculatus* and *Scomberomorus cavalla)* are both high-speed, streamlined game fish. While they are members of the same family, they are not easily confused in physical characteristics. The Spanish mackerel is the smaller of the two, reaching a maximum weight of about twenty pounds, with one weighing seven or eight pounds considered large. They are quickly recognized by numerous golden-yellow spots on the sides.

The kingfish is considerably larger and has been known to exceed eighty pounds. Location seems to be of little importance where record size is concerned. In 1963 a King weighing 50 pounds 12 ounces was caught near the Chesapeake by Harold Johnson. Similar catches have been recorded throughout almost all their range.

Both the kingfish and Spanish mackerel are dark blue on the back, shading to silver on the sides and belly. Each has a long, spiny, first dorsal fin that begins just behind the head and extends backward to a point near the center of the body. The second dorsal fin is prominent and the tail deeply notched. Each have finlets on both top and

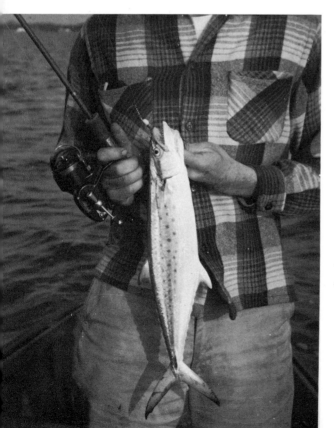

The Spanish mackerel is easily recognized by numerous golden-yellow spots on the sides. As well as being fine food fish it provides excellent sport when fished for with light tackle.

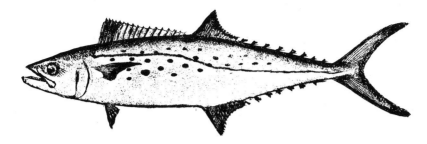

Spanish Mackerel

bottom sides aft of the second dorsal and anal fins.

Lacking swim bladders, mackerel are forced to keep on the move throughout their lives. During the winter months they inhabit tropical waters and with the coming of spring large numbers begin their northward migration. One group moves up the Atlantic coast to the Chesapeake, another moves up the western Gulf and ranges along the Texas coast, while a third section migrates along the west coast of Florida and around the northern perimeter of the Gulf to the mouth of the Mississippi. As the cool days of fall begin, they reverse their direction and head south again.

Charter-boat skippers and private fishermen keep what amounts to a "hot line" open all along the coast and maintain a daily progress report on the migration of the vast schools. When the kings are due to appear along a certain stretch of the coastline, it is virtually impossible to make reservations on commercial boats, because they have already been booked solid for weeks in advance.

As a rule, both king and Spanish mackerel travel at a depth of from five to twenty or thirty feet and when they have decided on a certain depth you had better fish for them there or miss out on the fun. Frequently a trolled lure or natural bait even ten feet below or above the school will remain fishless, while one a few feet higher or lower will stay in action almost constantly.

One of the most exciting experiences in offshore fishing is to spot a school of mackerel feeding on the surface, which they do occasionally during the daylight hours. The birds—terns, gulls, and others—will gather in abundance and keep track of the school for you as they wheel and dive, picking up the scraps of bait fish being cut to shreds by the ravenous mackerel.

When a surface-feeding school is spotted, the best method is to reel in the trolling lines and cast toward the action. If the fish are kings, the most productive tackle is medium-weight spinning gear. If they are Spanish, lighter tackle provides more excitement.

The angler who has never tangled with a twenty-pound king is invariably in for a shock, both physically and mentally. They strike hard and the instant they feel the hook, they take off on a scorching run. Two hundred and fifty yards of 12- to 18-pound monofilament is about right for medium-sized kings, and a stainless steel wire leader is almost mandatory. These large mackerel have a mouthful of sharp teeth and they can cut an unprotected line almost instantly. For the uninitiated, the reel-stripping run of a big king is a startling experience, and unless moderate braking power is used, the result can be wrecked tackle.

Doc Anderson was an M.D. with a lot more knowledge of the art of setting broken bones, curing illnesses, and of the human anatomy in general than he had about fishing tackle. Being dedicated to his profession, Doc never went anywhere without that little mysterious black bag that most medical men carry. He even had it with him that summer morning Captain Bill Strong, the good doctor, and I left Roy Walker's Boat Works at Orange Beach, Alabama, and headed south into the open water.

"Plenty of kings around," Captain Bill said when we were several miles out. "You two Izaak Waltons can give yourselves a good morning's workout if you flip a couple of jigs over the stern and see what happens."

Out came the tackle and over into the foaming wake of the 32-foot cabin cruiser went the feathered jigs. Hardly five minutes passed before I yelled "Strike!" and Captain Bill slowed the speed while I pumped in a long sleek kingfish.

"Strike!" Doc shouted while my first captive of the day was still beating a tattoo in the bottom of the fish box.

The star-drag on a reel is a complicated stack of disks hidden in the space between the plate on the handle side of the reel and the spool. The marvel of it is that they are so well constructed on most reels that they keep on working as long as they do, considering the poor maintenance that most fishermen give their tackle after a day of exposure to salt water. Now and then, however, a star-drag will either become totally inoperative all at once, or it may begin to malfunction a little at a time until the angler takes the hint and either puts the reel in the repair shop or does the job himself.

On this particular morning, Doc's star-drag just gave up the ghost about the time he had his king halfway up to the boat. It suddenly released all its braking power, and the big mackerel took full advantage and began heading back toward Alabama. Doc made a few tentative attempts to slow his fish by pressing his thumb down on the rapidly revolving spool, but finally the end of the line came and snapped off.

"There are plenty of other rigs down in the cabin," Captain Bill said. "Set yours aside and use a good one for a change."

"Nothing doing," Doc said. "I've got plenty of spare line in my tackle box and besides, I like to fish with my own gear."

Neither Captain Bill or I paid any attention to what the good doctor was doing for the next few minutes, and it was not until he had refilled his reel, tied on the necessary swivel, wire leader, and brand-new jig that I noticed anything different. He had taken a roll of adhesive tape out of the black bag and wound enough around his thumb to make it appear about three times bigger than its actual size.

"When you work with machinery it is nice to know how to improvise." Doc held up his massive white swathed thumb for me to see. "All of this tape will act as a cushion and prevent the line from rubbing a raw spot when I put pressure on it."

It seemed like a good idea, and I was reminded of the old thumbstalls that were made of leather and fitted on the crossbar of big reels before the star-drag became the accepted tackle. The angler would simply bear down on the leather pad, and when one spot became too hot for comfort it was a simple matter to slide the thumb over to a fresh and cooler spot and keep on applying the pressure.

In the old days of wading the flats after bonefish, down on the southern tip of Florida around Cape Sable, there were times when a big old boney would make such a scorching run that you were forced to dunk the reel under water to cool it off because there were no more cool spots left on the thumbstall, but that was a long time ago and the reels were smaller.

About the time I had my third king up to the gaff and the boat was just poking along at slow speed, Doc let out a yell that could have been heard all the way back to Gulf Shores.

"I've got the granddaddy of all kings out there," he shouted.

Doc may not have been an expert when it came to keeping his tackle in good repair, but he certainly did not exaggerate when he boasted

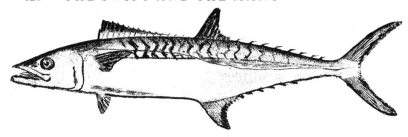

King Mackerel

about the size of the fish behind the boat. The arched rod was telling the story.

All at once the kingfish cut in his afterburner and took off for parts unknown.

"Hold him, Doc!" Captain Bill shouted as he began a slow turn that would help Doc ease the strain on his line.

Doc Anderson was a man of determination, and since the king was still on, we all felt reasonably sure he was solidly hooked.

Heaving my fish into the box, I stood behind Doc's chair to lend all the moral support possible and I involuntarily shuddered as I saw the line peeling off his reel. Even with the speed of the boat, it was obviously going to be a toss-up as to whether Doc could slow his fish first or run out of line.

Neither of these events happened.

Suddenly Doc let out a screech, stood up in the cockpit waving his right arm wildly in the air, and a second later his whole rod and reel was snatched out of his left hand and plummeted over the stern.

For the next few seconds Captain Bill and I both thought our medical friend had lost his mind. He was doing a regular war dance around the cockpit and then suddenly he threw himself across the gunwhale and plunged his right hand down into the water.

Just about then the true picture came into focus. What had happened was that as soon as the king had begun his long, fast run, Doc had pressed down hard with his taped thumb on the rapidly revolving reel spool. In a matter of seconds, the friction of the fast-moving line had generated enough heat to turn the wrapping of tape into a firmly anchored and superheated mass of gunk. When the pain had become unbearable, Doc had given up all thoughts of fishing and was concerned only with getting rid of the firebrand on his tortured thumb. After the crisis had passed, he removed the tape, opened his black bag, and doctored his burned thumb, then continued fishing, but with one of Captain Bill's more dependable rigs.

Trolling speed can frequently be a vital factor when mackerel are running deep. A wise skipper will vary the speed from three to six knots when he suspects he is over a large school. Should they begin to strike at any given speed that is the one to use.

Several springs ago a couple of friends and I had that graphically proved to us. We were fishing south of Steinhatchee on the west coast of Florida but having no luck. Herb's boat was a thing of beauty with all the refinements, including an electronic fish-finder. On the scope we could "see" a large school of fish running deep. The day before, every boat in the area had loaded up with kings, and it was perfectly logical to assume we were right over them.

We tried everything—changing lures, experimenting with different colors, adding strips of cut bait to lures, and using whole bait fish. We trolled deep, we trolled close to the surface and changed the speed from barely making headway to nearly seven knots. Nothing would provoke a strike.

Deciding to go to the extreme, I clipped on a heavy-keeled lead and was nearly bumping the bottom while my two companions took turns steering and changing lures. We knew we were over the fish and finally steadied down to a speed of about four knots. The twin diesels were purring a soft background music, trying to put one another to sleep with the monotony of the whole situation.

Suddenly Herb, who was steering, became annoyed with our lack of success. "Reel 'em in and let's go to some other spot." As he spoke he shoved the throttles ahead and within seconds we were churning along at a good twelve knots. I was cranking the reel handle rapidly and the speed of the retrieve combined with that of the boat had my feathered jig zipping through the water at a fast clip.

Then it happened.

My first thought was that I had foul-hooked a huge loggerhead turtle or struck some underwater obstruction. I shouted for Herb to slow down, and he chopped the throttles instantly. After a battle of nearly ten minutes, we caught sight of the flashing sides of a big king mackerel.

"Maybe they have at last started to get hungry," Kurt said with enthusiasm, pinning on a jig identical to the one I was using.

Again we continued to troll at about five knots and nothing happened. Once more we tried all the tricks, but not another suggestion of

Not a world record, but it is a safe bet that the young fisherman who brought this king mackerel aboard is going to remember this day for a long time to come.

a strike was forthcoming. Again we decided to look for greener pastures, but this time I did not start to reel in when the boat picked up speed. It happened again. Another solid strike and another big king brought to the surface.

That was the secret. For some reason, the kingfish were refusing to give a lure trolled at normal speed even so much as a second glance. If we had been equipped with reels filled with thin wire lines we could have trolled deep with small weights, but not having them, we were forced to use heavy trolling leads and keep the boat moving ahead rapidly, cutting the throttles only when one of us would get a strike.

It was the order of the day so far as that particular school was concerned. We would rush ahead for a few minutes, slow down long enough for the hooked fish to be played, and then back up to fast running again.

We caught all we wanted and returned to port. Everybody on the waterfront was grousing about not having caught any kings and they nearly fell overboard when they saw our bulging ice chest. The strange part about it was that on the following day things were back to normal and all the boats, including ours, caught plenty of kings trolling at a normal speed.

Whether there is a fish-finding device aboard or not, one good practice when mackerel are running deep is to keep several marker buoys handy. They can be anything from an empty plastic bleach bottle to the more sophisticated flag buoy that can be seen at a greater distance. Either type should have its own anchor line wound around it, and when a deep running school is located, the buoy is tossed overboard when a strike is made. It is a simple way to keep visual track of the school, and as it moves on, the buoys are retrieved and rewound, ready for the next time a school is located.

When macks are close to the surface, it is indeed a poor sportsman who tries to hog the action by cutting across the school. Not only does he lessen his own chances, but he puts the fish down and frequently scatters them so none of the other boats have a chance. A school feeding on the surface is easy to see and the best method is to circle them in a manner so that the lure will pass close enough, but not actually into the school. There are always plenty of outriding fish that will provide strikes and the main body will not be disturbed.

When the action is fast and furious and several boats are working the same school, they generally quickly develop a pattern. Most of the time everybody cooperates, but alas, once in a while there is the odd ball who insists on going the wrong way. He is frequently responsible for tangled lines when he cuts across another boat's wake and causes confusion. All the others who abide by the rules can only mutter dire incantations and secretly hope that Neptunus Rex will come to their rescue and jab his trident through the bottom of the offender's boat.

When it is an established fact that the migrating king and Spanish mackerel are in abundance, but for some unaccountable reason are stubborn about feeding, chumming will often get them started. The chum may be ballyhoo, menhaden, and any of a number of otherwise worthless fish. If the mackerel are around, the bits of fish flesh drifting down from the chum line will often awaken them to a feeding frenzie. Should you happen to be lucky enough to find a shrimper cleaning his nets of trash fish, move in behind and get braced for action.

Many kingfishermen keep track of the shrimp fleet in the vicinity for just this purpose. Most commercial shrimpers work at night and sleep during the day. While they are sleeping, the deckhands who do not work the nets earn their pay by cleaning them and washing the waste over the side. When a large school of mackerel have found such a bonanza, they literally go berserk. At such times the type of lure makes little or no difference. They will strike at anything, including a bare hook, that is moving through the water. When fishing in such a chum line, mackerel are frequently accompanied by other saltwater game fish, as well as sharks.

A word of warning is in order where kingfish of medium to large size are concerned. He has a large pointed mouth that is filled with needle-sharp teeth. When they are just brought over the side and still very much alive, keep your hands away from the business end or you are likely to wind up with them severely lacerated.

Both king and Spanish mackerel are widely used as food fish. The larger kings are steaked, and to my way of thinking, their flesh is most desirable when smoked. It is a matter of personal choice, of course, but I would rather have one Spanish mackerel in the freezer than half a dozen kings.

seven ～～～～～～～～～～～～～～～～～

～～～～～～～

～～～～～～～

ROUGH AND TUMBLE

TARPON

If you have the stamina of a prizefighter, gymnast, and weight lifter all rolled into one; if you don't mind wrestling with a pugnacious gladiator that is ready, willing, and able to compete in a piscatorial decathlon; if you don't mind working yourself into a lather for as much as an hour and often more; if the thought of getting knocked out of your boat, or having your tackle smashed and maybe putting up with the discomfort of a broken bone, then you probably qualify as a tarpon angler.

Pound for pound, inch for inch, and jump for jump, the tarpon *(Tarpon atlanticus)* is one of the most beautiful, one of the fastest, strongest, smartest, and most exasperating fish found in southern salt waters. If you manage to bring one out of five to gaff you rate as an

133

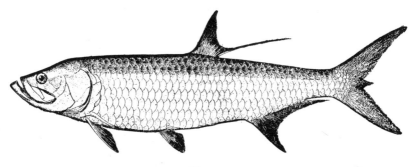

Tarpon

expert. Then, even if you do get him up to the gaff, you will probably let him go, because he is not fit to eat and there is no point in dragging him back to the dock, unless you want to have him mounted or enter him in a big tarpon contest that may be in progress in your particular locale.

So, then you say, anyone who deliberately fishes for tarpon must be out of his mind. You are absolutely right! The problem is that catching a tarpon is like eating salted peanuts; you can't just catch *one* and let it go at that. You keep going back for another and another and after a while you become addicted to the game. I seriously believe that the tarpon fisherman just does not want to admit that any fish is smart enough to outwit him so consistently.

Tarpon spend their winters in the Caribbean and around south Florida. Each spring they begin a mass migration that sends vast numbers into the entire Gulf of Mexico. At the same time another group starts moving up the Atlantic coast.

Chesapeake Bay is about the northern terminus for tarpon in worthwhile numbers, but there are always some that apparently enjoy longer ocean voyages, and they provide the exception to the rule. They have been found as far north as Cape Cod and on rare occasions off Nova Scotia.

Like most other fish, the tarpon is known by a number of pseudonyms that include *sabalo, tarpum,* and *savanilla.* In Louisiana, where they are plentiful in summer, the French name of *grande écaille* is often heard. It means large scales, which a tarpon certainly has. His most popular sobriquet is *silver king.*

One look at the tarpon, and it is not difficult to understand the reason for the nickname of silver king. The back is greenish black that shades quickly to silvery white on the sides and belly. On large adults the scales measure nearly three inches in diameter and form an armor plating over the body. The eyes are also large and set well forward near the top of the head.

The single dorsal fin, which is located midway on the back, has no true spines as in many fish. It consists of fifteen or sixteen rays, with the final ray elongated into a whiplike filament that may measure over a foot in length. It is a curiosity that apparently serves no purpose. Ichthyologists and just plain fishermen have pondered the reason for this long streamer, with some suggesting that it may assist the tarpon in falling on either the right or left side after a jump. High-speed action film of jumping tarpon tends to discredit this theory, since the streamer seems to flop from one side to the other with no consistent pattern.

The caudal fin is large and deeply notched, but not so lunate as with the tunas and other fast-swimming fishes. It is this large tail of the

A beautiful portrait of a tarpon that has just been hooked. If you look closely you can spot the bait fish that has been knocked halfway up the leader.

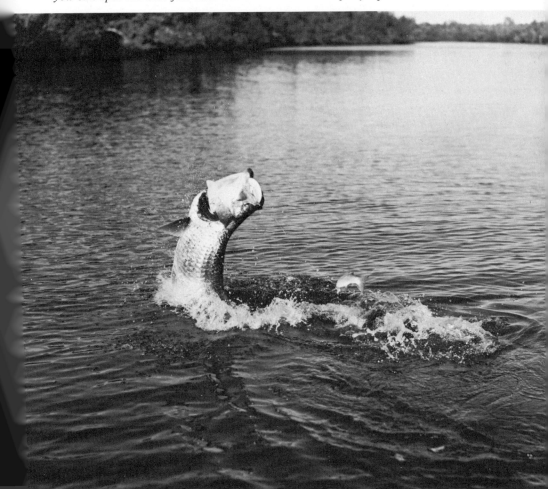

tarpon that enables it to make long runs at high speed and send the heavy body up in eight- to ten-foot vertical jumps, and horizontal leaps of twice that distance.

The design of the silver king's mouth is unusual, for several reasons. Not only is it enormous when fully extended, but the bottom jaw extends well forward and closes upward in such a manner as to give it a bulldog appearance. The teeth are minute and in the form of grinders, rather than true teeth. But it is not the size and shape of a tarpon's mouth that concerns the fisherman. What does concern, or frustrate, him is the extreme hardness that has earned this fish the reputation of having a mouth made of cast iron.

Not only is the inside of the mouth so tough that few strikes result in a solidly hooked fish, but unless a stainless steel or heavy-test monofilament leader is used, the scissorlike action of the jaws will cut the line with all the ease of a pair of wire cutters.

Countless are the number of fishermen who have had a tarpon strike a baited hook, feathered jig, or other lure and they have managed to hold onto their fish for five and even as many as ten gill-rattling jumps, only to have the tarpon seemingly grow tired of the game and literally spit the hook out and swim away as if nothing had happened.

There are occasions when a desperate situation can have such ludicrous overtones as actually to become comic—but only with the passage of a sufficient interval of time. Many anglers have had tarpon cast the hooks out of their mouths with such force as to send the missiles whistling past the angler's head or imbedding themselves in the gunnel of the boat.

I will not divulge the name of a fishing friend of mine who had a decidedly unpleasant experience with such a plug-throwing tarpon. For, while the physical wound has long since healed, this angler has never been able to manage more than a grim smile when he is reminded of the time he had his bad day on the briny. Just for the sake of anonymity we shall call him Harry.

It began one morning at a spot along the west coast of Florida when the tarpon season was reaching its peak. Harry drove down a long, sand-rutted road to the bay's edge, launched his aluminum car-top skiff, and attached a small outboard to the transom. The sun was just peeping through the pines when Harry approached the stretch of shallow water near a pass. Almost before he had reached the target range he caught sight of a school of tarpon moving his way. Quickly shutting off the outboard, he unlimbered his medium-weight rod and made a 5½-inch, red-and-white plug fast to the end of a 2-foot wire leader.

As often happens, a big tarpon, which Harry claims would have weighed at least a hundred pounds, made a rush for the artificial the second it splashed on the water. It is essential to mention at this point that the plug was fitted with three sets of needle-sharp gang hooks and they were large ones.

The silver king rolled on the surface as he engulfed the lure and then headed down. Well versed in tarpon fishing, Harry waited for two or three seconds and then he struck with considerable force.

Instantly, the tarpon made a short run and then erupted in a beautiful jump that lifted him five or six feet into the air. No sooner had he hit the water than he was out again. After a scorching run toward the pass he surfaced and began gobbling air. Harry put a stop to that by exerting several heavy tugs with his rod, sending the tarpon into a third jump.

It was at the apex of this third jump that Harry really leaned back on the rod with all his might. Even today he is not sure whether it was the force with which the tarpon threw the lure or the elasticity of his tightly stretched line that caused the plug to fly through the air with such speed. Harry saw it coming and instinctively turned to shield his face and bent over to present a smaller target. Whether the tarpon intended it that way or not is unimportant, but his aim was as true as that of little David with his sling. The plug landed with a solid wallop against the fatty portion of poor Harry's posterior extremity.

The sting of pain caused by the hook points entering his flesh threw Harry off balance and he stumbled backward and sat down hard on the stern seat of his boat. The result was that two of the big hooks were driven in beyond the barbs.

With a howl of pain Harry stood up and clutched at the lure, but a few experimental tugs convinced him that the hooks were stuck fast. Just how deeply he did not know, but what he was positive of was that every time he twisted around to try to see the unwelcome appendage on the seat of his pants the pain increased.

His first thought was to remove his pants, but such a plan was quickly abandoned when he lowered them to the point where they were affixed to his flesh. Next, he took a pair of wire cutters from his tackle box and tried to cut the hooks loose from the plug. It would not work. The shanks of the hooks were much too tough for the jaws of his wire cutters. All he could do was to cut the leader free from the plug.

With a sense of painful desperation settling over him, he tossed the rod and reel into the bow of his boat and started the outboard. He knew he would have to get back to town and medical aid as quickly as possible. The motor ran smoothly, but hapless Harry's trial was not nearly over.

It was obvious he could not sit down, so he resorted to kneeling in front of the stern seat, steering with one hand and bracing himself with the other. By the time he reached the beach near where he had left his car the pain had grown to a steady throb and his knees were raw from so much kneeling.

Ramming the boat ashore, he tossed the anchor up onto the sand and waddled like a strawberry picker over to his car, with every step sending new waves of pain through the afflicted portion of his anatomy. Even as he opened the car door he realized the task of driving the car was going to present more problems than had faced him in the boat.

"I had never given much thought to automotive design," Harry related dourly, "but I suddenly became decidedly aware that they were built in such a manner that the driver be seated behind the wheel so that at least one of his feet be available to operate the accelerator and the brake."

With the certain knowledge that walking back to the highway was out of the question and knowing that he could not endure the pain of sitting on the hook-studded plug, Harry knew that he must think of something, and the quicker the better.

His spirits at the lowest possible ebb, he sagged against the side of his car and pondered his peculiar predicament. Just at that point his native resourcefulness and ingenuity came to his rescue.

Painfully making his way back down to his boat, he took out one of the buoyant seat cushions, and with his pocket knife, cut a hole in the center. Placing the square doughnut of a cushion in the driver's seat, he cautiously positioned himself in such a manner as to cause the plug to protrude down into the hole. Thus ensconced, he proceeded to drive out to the main highway and straight to the emergency entrance of the nearest hospital.

Minor surgery removed the hooks. The reason I know all the details of this story is because Harry called me to ask me to go get his boat for him. The nurse in the emergency room invoked Harry's ire when she admonished him to be more careful about sitting on dangerous objects. When he tried to explain that it was a tarpon that had thrown the plug at him she said something about hearing all sorts of excuses, but his was unique.

Fortunately, not all fishing for tarpon is as involved as it was that time. Harry, by the way, is still loyal to the sport and he has caught some big ones since then. Those who know him well enough to get away with it call him "iron pants" and swear he has a pair of metal plates sewn in the seat of his fishing trousers.

Tarpon spawning occurs in February and March, and one large female will cast several million eggs. When first hatched the larvae are thin, ribbonlike little creatures, so different in appearance from the adult that for many years marine biologists did not know they were embryonic tarpon. For years they even had them listed under an entirely different classification.

Shortly after this larval stage, they change into tiny replicas of the adult. They begin life by feeding on plankton and gradually progress

For the angler who believes in using a cargo wench to land a big fish, take a look at the small bait-casting tackle that subdued this tarpon. The lighter the tackle, the greater the contest between man and fish.

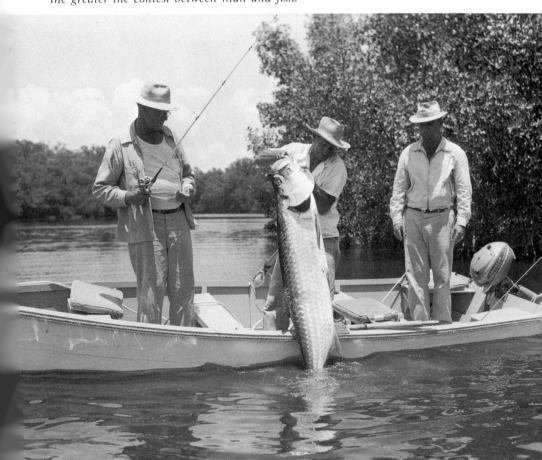

until they include the larvae of crabs and aquatic insects in their diet. As growth continues they capture tiny minnows, crabs, and other small aquatic creatures. By the time they are six inches in length they are ready to tackle anything they can catch and swallow.

It is after the spawning period, a large part of which occurs in Florida Bay, that the tarpon begin their annual summer migration to the north. An unexplained fact, however, is that some remain in the Florida Keys and undoubtedly all around the southern tip of the state. The natives refer to them as "yard tarpon" or "dock tarpon."

There is no standard-size rod and reel for tarpon, for the simple reason that the fish come in such a wide variety of sizes. Small ones in the canals beside Everglades roads are fished for with light fly rods, spinning tackle, and bait-casting rigs that are normally used only on fresh water for small to medium fish. It is axiomatic that the larger the tarpon, the heavier the tackle should be. Some very large tarpon have been landed on comparatively light tackle, and conversely, some medium-size tarpon have made shambles of heavy gear.

My personal choice for what might conceivably be termed an *all-around tarpon rig* begins with a tubular glass spinning rod about seven feet in length and with enough stiffness or backbone to sink the hook when the time to strike occurs. The reel is a medium-size open face with a spool capable of holding about 225 yards of 15-pound test monofilament line. Properly used, such a combination will handle tarpon in the fifty- to one hundred-pound range and is not too light for even larger ones.

As previously mentioned, a stainless steel leader or heavy monofilament is an absolute must, whether natural bait or artificials are used. The size of hooks can range anywhere from 5/0 to 9/0, but the size is secondary to the sharpness of the point. I keep a finger-size hook hone in my tackle box and work a needle-sharp point on every hook I plan to use for the silver king. If I have a strike and hold him even for one or two jumps, I do not make a second cast until I have redressed the points.

Natural bait for tarpon covers a fairly wide range with live pinfish, sardines, and mullet leading the list. Under certain conditions, blue crabs, either halves or whole, are as good or better than the above. Close behind come large live shrimp, bunkers, and needlefish. Often a filet of mullet or a small squid will attract attention.

Artificial lures cover an even wider range, beginning with saltwater flies and continuing on to large bait-casting plugs, spoons, feathered jigs, and bucktails. There is much scientific evidence to substantiate the theory that fish are color blind. There is nothing to be gained here by taking issue with the piscatorial ophthalmologists. It has been my observation, however, that lures that are yellow or a combination of red and white tend to excite tarpon during daylight hours. At night color seems to be of little or no significance, but this may simply be that colors need light to become colors in the first place.

Tarpon are known to exceed three hundred pounds in weight, but the IGFA record stands at 283 pounds. This giant silver king was caught in Lake Maracaibo, Venezuela, on March 19, 1956, by Mario Salazar, and for those who insist on cargo winches for tarpon tackle, it is interesting to note that Salazar was using only 30-pound test line. His bait was a mullet on a 9/0 hook.

The battle between man and fish was extensive, with the tarpon towing Salazar's small boat for two miles during the course of the fight. Near the final stages of the struggle Salazar managed to maneuver his boat in close to the shore where he jumped over into the shallow water to continue the contest. During the beaching the tarpon thrashed so violently that he hit one man attempting to help and knocked him six feet through the air, breaking two ribs and inflicting bruises on the man's arm and leg.

In general, there are two best times to catch tarpon. One is early morning and the other is from late afternoon well into the night. There have been many of them caught when the sun is high in the sky, but the chances are not as good as at the other times.

Tarpon are truly the big game fish for everybody, since they can be caught from bridges, piers, small boats, large boats, and even surf casting from the beach. At times they can be spotted in schools feeding on surface-swimming bait fish and again they are prone to seek out deep holes.

My choice location is almost any pass, especially on a falling tide. Along the Keys and on Florida Bay they spread out over the flats on high tides, and if you can position yourself in the path of an approaching school and cast ahead of it your chances are good. Tarpon also have a habit of lying almost motionless in the still water around mangrove-flanked channels. Here they provide exciting sport, but if you hook a real jumper he may wind up shaking free after he has left your line in an unfathomable tangle. At times they will seemingly make a game of swimming around and actually leaping over the limbs and roots.

It is difficult to single out any one location and say it is the best place for tarpon fishing. At one period the Louisiana anglers may be jumping their *grandes écailles* with nearly every cast. Again, the hottest action may be along the coast of Texas, off the coast of South Carolina, Cape Hatteras, or Virginia Beach. South Florida unquestionably has a genuine corner on the market, so far as the length of the season is concerned.

Anywhere between May and September, Boca Grande Pass, just north of Fort Myers, is one of the most popular tarpon fishing spots to be found. The water surges through this pass at a swift speed on certain tides. In places it is only several hundred yards wide and the hottest fishing area is only about a mile in length from beginning to end. It is tricky fishing, and the angler, if new to the pass, is well advised to hire a guide and his boat, especially until he has had time to absorb some of the facts concerning the methods of fishing as well as the conditions peculiar to the area.

These guides, many of whom have headquarters on Gasparilla Island, know the waters of the pass practically foot by foot, and almost to a man, they will insist you fish their way. They favor fairly heavy tackle, which they furnish, and you get a morning and afternoon trip for one price.

Their procedure is to drift with the current, and when the first of two deep holes is being approached, they will tell you how much line to pay out, and when you, and likely a fellow angler, hook a fish the other lines are called in promptly. Sinkers are attached to the terminal end of the tackle by light threads and are broken off almost the instant a tarpon strikes. Considering the countless thousands of tarpon that have been hooked in Boca Grande Pass, the number of lead sinkers on the bottom must be fantastic.

The fish may be a 50-pounder, or one weighing three times as much. The guides have generally had a few unpleasant experiences with big tarpon jumping aboard. As a result, they put the engine in gear and begin to move away. It may not be more than fifty yards, but it gives them an opportunity to steer clear if they see trouble about to develop.

When the tarpon is boated, released, or lost, all lines go back in the water and it is usually only a matter of minutes before the action starts all over again. By ten o'clock in the morning the guide calls a halt to the fishing and heads back for the dock. There is seldom any complaining from the paying passengers, because it is almost certain they are looking forward to a rest. Late that same afternoon it is back to the boat and out on the pass for a repeat of the morning activity.

Tarpon are unusual fish in many ways, with some seemingly strange habits. On frequent occasions they will be seen rolling on the surface. The first thought often is that they are chopping into a school of bait fish. Frequently, however, this is not the case. Instead, they are breathing air and it is known that they gulp air which enters a lunglike bladder. They will do this when the oxygen content is lower than usual in the water and it is a habit they practice if solidly hooked and exhausted from fighting.

Essentially a warm-water fish, there is frequently at least one deviate that likes to break the rules. I met such an example one chilly March afternoon when my wife and I were casting for speckled trout off the north end of Honeymoon Island on the west coast of Florida. I was using light spinning tackle with 4-pound test line. My lure was a small

With so many big tarpon rolling on the surface only a few yards away from the boat it is logical to assume the fisherman is almost certain to catch at least one. Don't be too sure. Tarpon will frequently roll like this on the surface to gulp air which they store in a lung-like bladder.

yellow bucktail tied directly to the line. The trout had cooperated nicely and just about the time we decided to crank up and head for home I spotted the unmistakable fin of a tarpon moving along a course that would bring him close to our boat.

I knew it was too early in the season for tarpon, but there he was. For a minute or so Dorothy and I watched and then, just to see what would happen, I made a long cast that landed directly in his path.

Beginning the retrieve with slow, short jerks, I saw the fin vanish, and suddenly the water boiled. Cold water, a tiny lure, and 4-pound line on the lightest of tackle, everything was wrong, but I had hooked a tarpon. Out he came in a spectacular jump and we could see he was nearly five feet in length. When he crashed back in, he set a course due south. I already had the brake set almost as tight as I dared, but I screwed it down a bit more and horsed back on the rod. The tarpon jumped again and the reel began to squeal. Two big jumps and he still had not cut the line. It was hard to believe.

In all, he made five jumps and had taken every inch of line from my reel spool. Naturally, he broke off, but it was an interesting and somewhat puzzling way to wind up an otherwise excellent fishing trip.

One of the most serious mistakes an angler can make is to attempt to boat a green tarpon, one that is still full of fight when he is brought alongside. This warning is naturally more important to the small-boat fisherman than to someone in a larger craft. There are times when one will allow himself to be led quickly to the side of the boat, only to go into a frenzy just as he is about to be gaffed. Bones have been broken, tackle destroyed, and people have even been killed. The safest course is to let the tarpon fight until he has worn himself out completely.

Sometimes they do not even have to be hooked to jump into a boat. A good example occurred in the summer of 1970 when two men were sailing a 14-foot boat just south of Sarasota. Suddenly a large tarpon leaped out of the water, slammed against the sail, and fell thrashing into the cockpit, knocking one of the sailors overboard. The boom swung across and almost knocked the second man over the side. All the while the tarpon was banging and plunging around in the boat. Fearing that a shark might have been chasing the tarpon, the man in the water wasted little time in getting back aboard. Just about then the big silver king gave a mighty lunge and cast himself back into the Gulf and swam away, leaving behind a few scales and two bewildered sailors.

Whether large, small, or in between, the tarpon is never a dull fish

to tangle with. If you think you have caught enough to have learned
all their tricks—just wait. The next one, or the one after that, will have
a surprise waiting for you.

COBIA

The cobia *(Rachycentron canadus)* probably has more local names
than any other species of fish that is found in abundance over such a
wide range. It would be a simple matter to tick off at least a dozen and
a half other names, besides ling. Some of the more popular are crab-
eater, lemonfish, and cabio. This extensive list is doubly peculiar when
it is realized that the cobia is in a family by itself *(Rachycentridae)* with

*This jumping tarpon is still a safe distance from the boat, but they often land
aboard. If it happens to be a big one it is time to clear the deck for action. There
are few sights in fishing that can equal the thrill of seeing a leaping silver king
trying to throw the hook.*

no close relatives to clutter the picture and add to the confusion, as is the case with so many other game fish found in southern salt waters.

Wherever you catch him and whatever name you elect to call him, the cobia is one of the best game fish to be found anywhere. He does, however, refuse to follow the rules, except those he sets for himself. One day you can see one or more lolling about near the surface close to a patch of floating sea grass or timber. You can cast your arm off and try every kind of artificial and natural bait, and he will just hang there without giving your offerings a second glance. Encounter the same situation a day later, and the fish will attack furiously the second your bait touches the water. At other times he will be sulking in deep water or practically on the bottom.

Neither will he follow the rules when it comes to a standard *modus operandi* in fighting. On very rare occasions he seems to give up as soon as he is hooked and allows himself to be led up to the boat like an old cow being brought back from the pasture. Far more often, he will literally go wild and fight with maniacal fury. At times he does his scrapping right on the surface with leaps that hurl up his big brownish black bulk flashing in the sunlight. The very next cobia may decide to sound as soon as he is hooked and do his best to run all the line off your reel as he rips along the bottom like a runaway submarine.

I have caught them at numerous locations along the Atlantic and Gulf coasts, but one of the zaniest encounters came a few summers ago about a half mile offshore near the little community of Crystal Beach, Florida. At that time there were several dozen peculiar structures known as bird racks built in open water along the Gulf from Clearwater to somewhere north of New Port Richey.

Not everybody knew just why the racks were there. Some were convinced they had been built by the Audubon Society, or some other

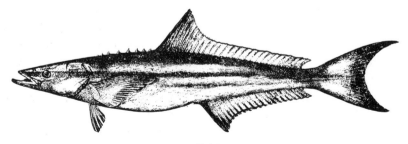

Cobia

dedicated group, to give weary pelicans, gulls, and cormorants a place to rest. The real truth was that those platforms were there for a strictly commercial reason, the collection of guano.

They were big flat platforms about twenty feet square and mounted on a dozen or so palm logs that had been driven into the bottom. The platform itself was about fifteen feet above the surface at high tide, and once every few weeks barges would be towed alongside while a crew of men with shovels scraped the platforms clean of the deposits left by the birds. From the barges, the guano went to the fertilizer factory.

Local fishermen knew the platforms as good places to catch a supply of bait on their way out to deeper water in quest of larger fish. On this particular day, I had stopped by the one near Crystal Beach and baited a light casting rig with bits of bacon on a number 8 hook. It generally required about twenty minutes to boat enough of the little pinfish to put an ample supply in the live-bait well.

On light tackle, pinfish are, by the way, about as sporting as bream or other popular freshwater sunfish. I had boated about three or four of the shiners to use for tarpon and suddenly there was a jolt on the end of my line. Just one quick bump and that was all. A minute later I was lifting the head of a fish out of the water. It had been cut off as cleanly behind the gills as if it had been placed on a bait board and chopped with a sharp knife.

My curiosity aroused, I tossed the head over the side, rebaited the tiny hook, and made another cast. Immediately I was fast onto another shiner and again I started reeling in. For the second time there was a quick jolt and I had another fish head to remove from the hook.

My first guess was that it was a barracuda, so cleanly had the bait fish been decapitated. When the third and fourth shiner were removed in a like manner, I decided something had to be done. I switched to my tarpon rig and pinned on one of the shiners from my bait well, hooking it through the top lip with a 4/0 Sproat hook, and cast it up under the shadow of the platform where the others had been attacked. After the bait had landed and begun to swim around in circles, I saw a swirl close to the big red-and-white cork and then nothing. I could tell quickly by the lack of action that the bait had been taken off the hook.

Reeling in, I found I had another fish head and the riddle was still not solved. Taking out one of my few remaining shiners, I put the hook through the back just under the dorsal fin and again cast under the platform. This proved to be the trick my unseen bait robber was not expecting, and the cork vanished underwater. Heaving back on the rod, I felt the hook go home in the jaws of what I could instantly tell was at least a big fish. What, I still did not know, but after an initial tug-of-war I found out. I was able to lead the fish straight toward the boat. I was fairly well convinced at that point that I had hooked a small shark. I was, however, still wondering about the cleanness of the cut the fish had made on all the other pinfish. The bite had definitely been like that of a barracuda, but what was being reeled in so docilely was certainly not that fish.

When I had him near enough to the boat, I reached for my short-handled gaff, and as I looked down at the dark creature below the surface I began to have serious doubts that it was a shark. The shape was all wrong.

Getting the gaff in position I was about to jab it home when the fish suddenly came to life, and at that moment I realized I had hooked a cobia and he was as green as any fish I have ever seen. If a fish ever did a double take, this cobia did. He rolled slightly as I reached for him with the gaff and then, in a wild explosion and churn of water that almost tossed me over the side, he headed back for the shelter of the bird rack.

His sudden maneuver caught me off guard and before I could tighten down on the drag, he had made a couple of turns around one of the pilings and short roped himself so snugly that all he could do was spin and thrash about some seven or eight feet below the surface.

Realizing that the fish was caught, for all practical purposes, I began to experiment with ways of getting him in the boat. At first I pulled the boat up against the piling and began to pass my rod around from one side to the other, unwinding my trapped fish, hoping all the while the line could withstand the abrasive barnacles that coated the log.

I unwound him all right. The cobia seemed to have been waiting until I had removed all the turns, because at the very second when I was about to take hold of the reel handle, he took off again. This time he carried my tarpon rod with him. I saw it hit the bottom in a little cloud of roiled sand and almost at the same instant the cobia did another maypole dance around still another piling.

For a few minutes I toyed with the idea of trying to snag the rod with a gang hook from one of the plugs in my tackle box. It was a hot day, however, so I changed my mind and removed my wrist watch, shoes, and various pocket articles and dived overboard. I swam down and retrieved the rod and then scrambled back aboard. I moved the boat under the platform and repeated the process of unwinding the cobia by passing the rod around and around the second piling on which he had trapped himself. This time, on the final turn, I made sure that I had a vicelike grip on the rod and it was well that I did, for the cobia, sensing he was free, again made another explosive rush, heading for open water.

Trouble was still with me because at that point I had my skiff completely under the bird rack and I was forced to lean out over the transom to keep the rod from banging against the cluster of pilings. From the way he was peeling line off my reel I was fairly well certain that I did not have time to maneuver the boat out into the open and still maintain a grip on my tackle.

Heedless of my predicament, the cobia was headed straight out toward the Gulf and twice, when I tightened the drag on my reel, he leaped clear of the surface. After another fifteen minutes had passed I had worn him down to the point where I could finally move the boat out into open water and still maintain the proper tension on the line. When I led him back to the boat for the final time, I once more picked up the gaff. I had no doubt that the fish was done for and would be in the boat within the minute, but this was no ordinary cobia. He had fought like a tiger, and from the time I first hooked him until he was ready to be hoisted aboard, I was convinced that he was securely hooked.

That was what I *thought.*

As I was leaning over the gunnel, the cobia did a slow roll to his right side and practically spit the hook right back into my face. An instant later I was sitting there pondering how the hook had managed to stay so firmly imbedded in his mouth for all that time and then virtually fall out right at the last moment.

Fortunately, all cobia fishing is not so involved. Most of the time, when an angler is lucky enough to hook one, there is a good hard fight and either the fisherman or the fish emerges the winner.

One interesting footnote to my bird-rack cobia is that an IGFA record catch was made in the same area by Roy English on April 25, 1962, using light tackle with a 20-pound test line. The fish weighed 91 pounds! The important difference was that English brought his back, while I clowned around, going swimming, unwinding my fish, and being sprinkled with dry guano.

When they are in an eating mood, cobia make real hogs of themselves. Tests made at the Michael Lerner Marine Museum at Bimini showed that captive cobia will gain about fifteen pounds per year if supplied with all the fish they want to eat. In fact, one specimen that was kept at the museum for five years continued to gain until he reached a weight of one hundred and forty pounds, and when he died it was believed that he had literally eaten himself to death.

The angler who fishes southern salt waters is in prime cobia country, and most of the IGFA records are listed from Chesapeake Bay, down along the Atlantic coast and into the Gulf. The official all-tackle record is a 102-pounder caught by J. E. Stansbury off Cape Charles, Virginia, on July 3, 1938, in the area known as the "Cabbage Patch." The Chesapeake also has produced a 99-pounder, and another one weighing 97 pounds was taken from Oregon Inlet, North Carolina.

There really is no way of telling just how big cobia actually grow. The largest I have ever heard of being caught is not listed in the IGFA records, but Rube Allyn's *Dictionary of Fishes,* eleventh edition, records one that weighed 149 pounds 12 ounces and measured 6 feet 3 inches in length. That giant was reportedly caught by Garnett L. Caudell while fishing from the M/V *Friendship* off Grand Isle, Louisiana, on May 15, 1965. Rube and I were good friends for many years and I know from personal experience that he was meticulous when it came to the business of accuracy in listing record catches.

Perhaps right in the middle of a chapter on cobia fishing may indeed seem an odd place to pen a few words of eulogy about a good friend and one of the truly great sportsmen who spent a considerable portion of his life on southern salt waters. However, knowing Rube as I did, I strongly suspect he would have no objection, unless it might be to choose a chapter on bonefish, tarpon, snook, or some other fish. Still, I think this chapter is best because the cobia is a singular species, and that fact alone has much in common with Rube Allyn.

My first meeting with him was in the late summer of 1952. It came about as a result of a complimentary paragraph or two that he had written in his daily waterfront column in the *St. Petersburg Times* about one of my fishing tales that had currently appeared in a national magazine. As one is wont to do under such conditions, I gave him a call and expressed my appreciation for his kind words. He responded by inviting me to visit him with an eye toward planning a fishing trip.

Rube Allyn was far more than just another fishing editor for a daily newspaper. To his countless thousands of readers he was an institution unto himself. He was intensely interested in anything pertaining to the waterfront and especially if it had to do with fish and fishing.

One of Rube's creations was a fictional character known as John's Pass Sadie. It is only fair to add that those of us who knew Rube just assumed she was a fictional character because we never met the lady. She served Rube well, however, as a foil when he wanted to add a bit of preposterous spice to his daily column without letting the yarn be directly attributable to his own observations. On the other hand, maybe she was real, but I rather suspect she was to Rube what Huckleberry Finn was to Mark Twain.

Another popular feature from Rube was his "Best Bet." It told the local fishermen who followed his column where certain fish were most likely to be biting best on each day of the paper's publication. Because the *Times* is a morning paper, many anglers in the area would wait for its delivery before shoving off on a fishing trip.

Early in his outdoor writing career, Rube sensed that fishermen were forever wondering about the names, habits, and other biographical data concerning various types of fish they caught. With that thought in mind, he began to accumulate a vast storehouse of information about every fish he saw and caught and about others that had been caught in far-flung outposts. The result was the publication of his *Dictionary of Fishes*. It was something every fisherman had been looking for, and as a result it was an immediate success.

In May of 1957 he left his desk at the *Times* in the capable hands of Red Marston to devote full time to developing a specialty publishing house known as the Great Outdoors Publishing Co., in St. Petersburg, Florida. When he had the business going the way he wanted it, he sold a portion, with an eye toward devoting more time to fishing, boating, and allied sports.

Accidental death is difficult if not impossible to predict. In fiction the matador falls before the enraged bull, the mountain climber plunges from a precipice, the test pilot goes down in a blaze of glory, and Paul Bunyan simply vanished into the hills with his blue ox, Babe, at his side.

In true life the accidental finish often comes in a much more mundane manner, and so it was with Rube Allyn. He was riding his bicycle when he was hit by a motorist, and that was the end for a man whose life had been filled with high adventure.

According to his wishes, Rube's friends buried him at sea, far out in the depths of the Gulf of Mexico that had been so much a part of his life. Rube lived the life he had wanted and made a success of it. He left behind him so many written words about angling that it would be virtually impossible to make an even reasonable count. His study and practical research has added immensely to man's store of piscatorial knowledge. Most important of all, however, is the fact that those who knew the one and only Rube, either personally or through the medium of the printed word, were not just made more proficient fishermen, but decidedly better sportsmen.

This is far too little to say about such a man, but if Rube were looking over my shoulder he would most likely suggest that I get on with the cobia fishing.

Some of the best of this fishing in its entire range is along the northern coast of the Gulf. Many anglers are so addicted to the sport of fishing for cobia that they wait for the first run as tribes of Indians once waited for migrating herds of buffalo.

The spring run of cobia begins in northwest Florida around mid-April and lasts until late May. A couple of years ago I was on a trip to Mobile and stopped for gasoline at a station in the town of Port St. Joe. Noticing the fishing tackle in the back of my station wagon, the attendant said: "Betcha headed up to Panama to get in on the ling fishing. A pal of mine up at Millville was just down here and he says the tackle stores are almost sold out, so many folks have come in for the run. They say it's gonna be the biggest in years."

As I moved along the coast from Panama City, Laguna, Destin, Fort Walton, and on along to Pensacola, I became increasingly aware of the accuracy of the attendant's information. Piers were literally teaming with fishermen, small boats were patrolling the coastline, with real and improvised tuna towers for lookouts, to spot the schools of westward-bound ling—you just have to call them *ling* along Florida's panhandle or risk a lynching party.

The "run," as they refer to the annual migration, comes in waves of one school after another. They approach the shore so closely that Jeeps and other vehicles with four-wheel drive are out on the snow white sand in numbers. The pier and surf fishermen don't particularly like the boats cruising close to shore, because they claim the sound of the engines scatters the schools and sends them out into deep water. It does not make much difference, though, because for about six or seven weeks the action is fast and furious and some of the anglers are so enthralled with the cobia that they will not bother to go fishing after the heavy run is over until the same time a year later.

When matched with some of the more glamorous saltwater fishes, the cobia would not get many votes in a beauty contest. To be perfectly honest, he is a bit on the ugly side. He has a large catfish-type head with a protruding lower jaw that gives the impression of a bully wandering around looking for a fight. His color is dark brown to almost black on the upper side, shading to a lighter color on the underside. His thick body is covered with a sheath of minute scales. The fins are black and the first dorsal consists of a series of short, stiff spines.

Despite his pugnacious countenance, the cobia is a true game fish when you have him on the end of a line. He makes good eating, too, if properly prepared. It is important that he be bled while still alive if he is slated for the dinner table. He is also excellent smoked.

In some respects, certainly not in looks, the cobia are much like barracuda. They are capable of high speed when they decide to move and they swim great distances, as evidenced by their extensive northward migration in summer. Like the barracuda, however, they will often spend hours, if not days, suspended almost motionless in one general area.

The cobia has a handful of other names including the lemonfish, ling, and crab-eater. They are plentiful throughout the Gulf and up the Atlantic coast with the world's record weighing 99 pounds caught in the Chesapeake Bay.

Favorite hangouts are either under or around clumps of floating seaweed, large pieces of driftwood, around buoys, sunken wrecks, offshore structures, pilings, and even anchored ships.

Frequently they will lie close to the surface, and one of the most productive methods of fishing for them is to spot them first. This is not to imply that cobia do not move about in open water, because they certainly do. It just means that if you see a resting cobia your chances of catching him are enhanced. Along the northern Gulf coast the offshore oil rigs are dependable hangouts. One of my favorite cobia fishing areas along the Louisiana coast is near the Tenneco oil platforms off Cameron.

Small live bait such as pinfish is excellent, but they also will strike on shrimp, strips of cut mullet, and squid. Small blue crabs are another choice food of cobia and their propensity for this diet has led to their being known in some localities as crabeaters. There are times when they can be maddeningly choosy as to what kind of bait they will accept. Once while a friend and I were trolling for bluefish off Kitty Hawk, North Carolina, we passed close to what we took to be a hatch cover that had probably washed overboard from some freighter.

Shutting off the engine, my eagle-eyed companion began reeling in rapidly. "Big cobia over there by that hatch cover," he said. "Get your casting rig ready and we'll have some fun."

Standing up and shading my eyes against the sun, I looked toward the large piece of flotsom. There was a cobia there all right, just lolling about in the shade with only his head protruding into the sunlit water.

"He ought to be just ready for a nice fat bunker," my friend said, pinning the small fish onto the end of his saltwater spinning tackle.

Out went the first cast and it was nearly perfect, landing only a couple of feet in front of the big cobia. Splash went the bait fish and immediately it began to dance around in a series of didoes guaranteed to whet the appetite of even a well-fed cobia. Nothing happened. The antics of the small fish, plus the movement of the tide, began to carry the bait away and the cobia just twisted around slightly like someone settling into a more comfortable sleeping position.

Again the offering was presented, and still the cobia paid it not the slightest heed. By that time I had my own spinning rod ready and I decided to try a strip of cut bait. In my eagerness to cast accurately, I succeeded in landing the strip of bait squarely on top of the hatch cover.

"That's sure to attract his attention," my friend said with enthusiasm. "He undoubtedly felt the thump and if you just pull it off slowly I'll bet you my hat he'll grab it as soon as it hits the water."

I won a hat. Nothing happened.

When we had drifted away too far for casting, we cranked up the engine and moved back into position. The cobia was still there and we spent fifteen minutes more trying to entice him. At that point we went into the old tackle box scramble. Out came everything—yellow bucktail, deep-running plugs, spoons, and metal squids. Nothing, absolutely nothing, would work.

"I've had it!" I said in disgust. "Let's get back to trolling before the whole day is gone."

With spinning tackle put away, we went back to our trolling rigs and my friend clipped a big feathered jig on just before he started the engine. "If we can't catch him, I'm going to scare him to death," he said.

Shoving the throttle ahead, he made a large circle at high speed and skimmed right by the hatch cover. You guessed it. The cobia rushed out into the wake and slapped his jaws shut on the jig. When we got back to the dock and put him on the scales we found he weighed forty-eight pounds and measured exactly 4 feet in length. Not a record by a long shot, but plenty of fish to catch all in one bundle. Your guess is as good as mine as to why he took so long to make up his mind. Maybe he just was not hungry and decided to vent his rage on us for disturbing his solitude.

On and on the stories could go about the business of catching cobia, and each one would be different from the other. Maybe it is because you can never be quite sure what a cobia is going to do next that makes him such an interesting game fish.

eight ~~~~~~~~~~~~~~~~~~~~~~~~~

~~~~~~~~~~

~~~~~~~~~~

THE ANGLER AFLOAT

CHARTER BOATS

It is often amusing and occasionally annoying to watch the newcomer to the saltwater fishing scene strolling along the dockside of a modern marina observing the fleet of charter boats that have just returned from a day's fishing. If the sight of big blue-water battlers such as marlin, sails, and dolphin being weighed and photographed excites a latent urge to cast himself in the role of a big-game fisherman, the person will not walk far before he begins to wonder how much it would cost him to hire one of the boats and sally forth on a similar trip.

A few more boats farther along the dock and the newcomer spots a man washing down the cockpit or tidying up the mooring lines. He moves over in a casual sort of way and after a few perfunctory platitudes gets around to the business of asking how much it will cost him

156

to go out and spend the day catching a few fish. The answer is often likely to involve a sum of money considerably out of proportion to what the man had expected.

On the average, the newcomer will say thanks and weigh the quoted price against the entertainment he anticipates, deciding whether or not to pursue the subject further. If he feels his pocketbook can stand it, he will then see if the boat will be available the next day or so. If, on the other hand, the cash outlay will put too much of a dent in his vacation budget, he will let the matter drop.

Either of such reactions is perfectly acceptable to the charter-boat operator because he, too, is a businessman and is not offended if the potential customer simply does not feel he can afford the price. Occasionally, however, there is the inevitable crank who has no idea of the business and instantly chooses to believe that the charter boatman has

Equipped with tuna towers above the flying bridges, two good examples of modern charter boats are underway for a day of fishing on the blue water. The tuna tower is a lookout platform that gives the skipper or the mate the necessary elevation to spot big game fish at a much greater distance than would be possible from the bridge or deck.

him pegged as a sucker and is out to fleece him of his resources.

Such unpleasant characters will often resort to abusive language and let the man on the boat, as well as everyone in earshot of his loud mouth, know that just because he is a tourist he is not going to be "taken" by some local yokel seeking to make a fool of him. Every charter-boat skipper has from time to time been irritated by an encounter with such people, who wander through life hoping to get something for nothing and then become irate when their utopian dreams fail to materialize.

I am deliberately refraining from quoting any price range, for several very good reasons. The first of these is because what might be a reasonable price this year might be entirely different next year, just as the cost of any other commodity or service seldom remains constant for very long. Secondly, there are such unknown factors as the type of charter boat and the season of the year. Furthermore, what might be a reasonable price for a boat operating out of one port is likely to be different in another port a hundred miles away.

As one who fishes over a wide range, I frequently find myself a self-appointed advocate of the charter-boat skipper, although I have no vested interest in the charter-boat business. Over the years, however, I have shelled out many a hard-earned dollar to employ their service. I can say, too, that with very few exceptions it has been money well spent in the pursuit of a sport I enjoy.

My strongest argument in pleading the case of those in the business of charter boating generally involves comparison with the cost of entertainment in other fields. For example, the man who howls at what he considers an exorbitant price charged for spending the day on a charter boat has only to compare it to what he would pay for a single night's entertainment in any of several large cities. That same man who spends an expensive night on the town and unflinchingly pays the tab may feel he is being played for a sucker when he seeks to charter a boat. If, on the other hand, he were to put himself in the charter-boat captain's position, and consider all the facts, he would quickly see the reason for the price that may be charged.

The skippers of charter boats are a breed unto themselves. Almost without exception, they know their trade, they have a considerable amount of money invested in their boat and equipment, and they earn every dollar they take in.

To begin with, the skipper does not become a licensed captain overnight. Of even greater importance, a man does not become an expert fishing guide simply by closing up his grocery store or quitting his job at the bank and declaring himself a professional fisherman.

Almost to a man, they have spent a considerable number of years in various phases of fishing. Some have begun as deckhands on commercial fishing boats, and others have served long apprenticeships as mates on charter and head boats. Not only have they had to learn practically everything there is to know about fishing, but they have had to learn seamanship, become skilled in the operation and repair of boat engines, and especially today, they must be thoroughly versed in radio, depth finders, and numerous other electronic devices that are part and parcel of the modern charter boat.

Somewhere along the way, during his apprenticeship, the man who is determined to become a charter-boat captain has to manage to save up enough money to buy and equip a boat, or at least be able to make a sizable down payment on one.

Even after he has done all this, the bout is still not yet won. He must next set out to earn a reputation, and there is no college or university that passes out diplomas proving that the new Captain John Smith will consistently be able to take people out on the blue water and catch fish. There is inevitably a number of lean years to live through before the word begins to spread that Captain so-and-so is the man to go with if you want to catch a sailfish or a tuna or what-have-you.

When he does "arrive," the charter-boat skipper is generally booked up solidly for several months in advance. But there are still perils to be considered. Adverse weather conditions may put him out of business. He may lose his boat and all his gear, which is frequently still mortgaged up to the gunnels. At best, there is no business until the threat of the storm has passed.

There are, however, compensations. Most charter-boat skippers are truly dedicated to the sport of fishing. They are doing what they like best to do and if they have the determination to stick with it long enough they can earn a decent living as independent businessmen doing what they want to do.

After they reach the status of "expert" and find themselves reasonably well booked in advance, most skippers give free rein to their individualistic natures that put them in this line of work in the first place. If the paying angler refuses to act like a sportsman, or makes himself too obstreperous, the charter boatman is likely to squint at the horizon and mumble something about the weather and return to port.

Considering the scores of skippers I have known over the years, I think I am aware of their three most disliked types of customers. The first, and most serious because of the potential danger, is the angler who is convinced that heavy drinking is an integral part of any well-organized fishing trip. Not only does he spoil the fun for others on board, but he is likely to fall overboard and if conditions are such that he cannot be rescued, the loss reflects seriously on the captain.

The second objectionable customer is the fish hog. He is the type who feels that to get his money's worth he has to fill not only the ice chest but half the cockpit and then catch a few more just for good measure. In this case, the skipper has ways of dealing with such nonsporting anglers. He knows the best grounds and he can also circle too close or too far away from a school, in order to reduce the quantity of the catch.

It is not that such men are overly dedicated to conservation and they are not trying to keep from working. It is just that there is a limit to everything and when a party has gone out and accomplished its mission there is no reasonable excuse for overdoing it.

The third miscreant is the fisherman who tries to pack the boat, often so that the total cost of the trip will be divided by a large number of anglers. Here, the size of the fishable deck or cockpit space is generally the determining factor. In the average thirty- to forty-foot sports-fisherman there are two or four fighting chairs. In trolling for big game, two lines can quickly become a handful should two big fish latch on at the same time. With experienced fishermen, four can be comfortably accommodated, but they have to be ready to get the extra lines out of the water in a hurry if one really big fish is beginning his battle.

Two or three anglers are a comfortable party; five or six can go along if they are willing to take turns. Any number beyond that is a crowd and actually illegal by Coast Guard regulations on certain boats not equipped to handle more than six passengers.

There are many boats for hire that can take a considerable number of passengers, but they generally fall into the classification of party or head boats. The acceptable number, however, is a problem that can easily be resolved well in advance of the trip. If the skipper sets a limit, it is usually because he has a perfectly valid reason.

Next behind the three most objectionable types is the know-it-all angler. He is the man who thinks he knows more about fishing than anyone else. He ignores suggestions concerning bait and lure, tells the skipper how fast or slowly to troll and just where to go. There are exceptions, and once in a while the paying angler does know what he is talking about. As a rule, however, when dealing with this sort, the skipper and mate will adopt a "so what" attitude. When they see their advice is unwanted, they will often let the wise guy call the shots. After all, it is his money and if he wants to play captain and risk a fishless day, who cares?

Occasionally there is misunderstanding about the ownership of the catch. Some skippers adjust their rates with the agreement that they will keep the majority of the day's catch. An even greater number sell only their services as guides, and the fisherman can do whatever he pleases with his catch. Once again this is a subject that should be clearly understood by both parties before the trip begins.

Just what constitutes a charter boat? Basically, a charter boat is one that is for hire to a specified number of people, with fishing being the primary objective. In size it may range from a small open craft, designed to take one or two fishermen a short way off shore for several hours, to one with a cabin and limited facilities such as an ice chest, head, and maybe a couple of bunks, or it may be even more deluxe with accommodations to go far offshore for several days.

Generally speaking, the average charter boat is somewhere in between the small open boat and the far-ranging cruise boats. The captain usually has plenty of fishing equipment on board, but there are no rules that say you cannot bring your own. The boat is inspected at regular intervals by the Coast Guard and is required to carry all the important equipment such as life preservers, fire extinguishers, and other safety devices.

The skipper usually supplies ice for the fish box and the necessary bait. With exceptions, he does not guarantee that you will catch fish. Remember, however, that he depends largely on word-of-mouth advertising to stay in business and he is just as anxious to make a good trip of it as the paying customer. Too many fishless days can damage his reputation and eventually his pocketbook. But don't expect him to be a miracle worker. There are days when the fish simply will not cooperate for anyone.

How does one go about selecting the best charter boat in the fleet at any given marina? We are a nation of glitter lovers. If this were not so, the neon-sign business, makers of costume jewelry, and most of the automotive industry would not be nearly so prosperous. This is not to say that the man with a fancy boat replete with chrome railings and polished mahogany decks is not just as good a guide as the owner of the less ostentatious boat tied up in the next slip. It is all a matter of the skipper's individual taste.

Of course, the surest way to pick the best boat is to find the skippers who are booked up well in advance. If you have only a few days to spend on the coast such knowledge is of little value at the moment, but it is good to store away for future use. Frequently it is a good idea to ask if the skipper has a small party coming up that might agree to taking on another passenger to share the expense. As a matter of fact, many boats are booked on just such a contingency, so it does no harm to ask.

Most charter-boat skippers invite prospective clients to step aboard and look around. This is your chance to reach some important conclusion, providing you keep your eyes open and know what you are looking for. It may be because of the years spent in the Navy, but two of the first things I look for are cleanliness and a reasonable sense of order. Worn-out lures with rusted hooks hanging from nails on the bulkhead, out-of-date navigational charts, wads of dirty clothes stuffed under bunks, and a compass with discolored and barely legible cards give me the heebie-jeebies. The same is true if the boat and its head have a generally unclean smell. Spit and polish are not particularly important to me, but a dirty, cluttered boat suggests a careless attitude on the part of its owner. The Coast Guard can keep a governing hand on whether or not the fire extinguishers and running lights are in good working order and the fuel tanks are properly vented, and other such things as are required by law, but it cannot tell a man to clean up, unless a potential fire or other hazard exists.

It is my belief that a boat must be in shipshape condition at all times. Things can happen with awful suddenness when an unexpected blow makes up, and I don't relish risking my neck with a skipper who is content to rely on an album filled with photos of fabulous catches while his boat resembles an aquatic pig sty. I do not expect a boat just returning from a full day of fishing to be ready for an admiral's inspection. There is, however, a big difference between a boat that has not had time to clean up and one that is dirty from constant lack of care.

If you are a newcomer to a certain port there is another investigative procedure that is frequently well worth the time it takes. That is to ask around in tackle stores and marine supply houses. As a rule, each of these has its own favorite skipper and will give you his card showing the name of the boat, with the captain's name and telephone number. If a certain name keeps cropping up at first one place and then another, it is a good bet you have found a winner.

PARTY BOATS

Most sport fishermen who have been at the game long enough naturally become somewhat selective in the type of fish they seek to catch. Over the years they have had time to experiment with and analyze a large number of species, types of tackle, and methods of angling for the specific fish that appeal to them most. During this period of development they have also decided on the types of fishing that appeal to them least.

Party boats come in many shapes and sizes. The Double Eagle II *out of Clearwater, Florida, is one of a fleet of several with the catamaran-type hull design. Like most modern party boats, she has ship-to-shore radio and numerous other pieces of electronic equipment designed for safety and speed in finding the best fishing grounds far offshore.*

Regrettably, many seasoned saltwater fishermen assume a sort of supercilious attitude toward those who find pleasure in boarding a party, or "head" boat as they are frequently known, and going out on the Gulf or Atlantic for a day of bottom fishing. These fishermen will almost invariably make such statements as:

"Anybody that wants to go out with a gang of people who don't know how to fish and don't know what they are catching when they do must be nuts!"

"There is nothing selective or creative about head boat fishing. You just let down a baited hook and pull up whatever happens to bite."

"Anybody can catch fish on a party boat if they don't care what they are catching."

On and on it goes, but it is worth taking the time to look more closely at such criticism.

In general most people are gregarious. They enjoy being around other people. Proof of this is seen in the stadiums that are filled to capacity with spectators watching baseball, football, auto races, and so forth. Of course, there are many people who go out on party or head boats who do not know how to fish and are unable to tell a red snapper from a black sea bass. Still, I don't know anyone who was born with a skill at fishing anymore than I know anyone who was born knowing how to play golf. Nor do I know anybody who entered the world with the knowledge of fish identification.

There is also a vast number of people with an inherent yen to go fishing, but they simply have never had an opportunity to do so. Even for the "sometime" fisherman who has never caught anything larger than a catfish or a sunfish, the sight of a fifty-pound grouper or a thirty-pound red snapper coming over the gunnel is a genuine thrill. And after all, isn't that what it's all about? The refinements and specialization will come in due course.

As for the part about anybody being able to catch fish on a party boat, to that I take off my hat to the party-boat skipper and his mate and those boys who scramble about through the crowd baiting hooks, taking off fish, and untangling lines. It is to their ever-lasting credit that this know-how makes it possible for the uninitiated to catch fish.

Then, too, there is the ever-present question of money. Unfortunately, not everybody can afford to own his own boat or spend the required amount for a charter boat.

To my way of thinking, there should be no snobbishness where fishing is concerned. Of one thing I am certain, the fish down there could not care less who is on the other end of the line when he gets a hook caught in his jaw. What is of more importance, some of the most avid and accomplished fishermen I know today caught their first salt-water fish while dangling a line over the rail of a party boat. It gave them the chance to become exposed to the fishing fever.

Most fishermen try to measure any form of fishing by three cardinal rules: first, it must be a method that provides the angler with the fun for which the sport is intended; second, the fish must have a fighting chance; and third, the method should be one that produces results.

Let's suppose, however, that you are a complete novice when it comes to saltwater fishing, but you think you would like to go out on a party boat and see what it is all about. Where do you go? What do you look for? What is it going to cost? What about tackle and bait? Are all boats the same? What are you likely to catch?

Obviously, the first question tends to answer itself. Most any port from Chesapeake Bay to the southern tip of Texas has its own fleet of party boats. Generally, they are found berthed in public marinas. Many are diesel powered and fifty feet or greater in length. As in most other successful forms of businesses, there are the excellent, the good, the mediocre, and regrettably, there are a few bad ones scattered about here and there.

Picking the best is a mixture of luck and at least a sketchy knowledge of the subject. There are some fairly dependable guidelines to look for. Make a trip to the marina of your choice, whether it be Norfolk, Charleston, Miami, Biloxi, or any of the scores of other resort areas along the way. If time permits, be on hand when the boats come in at five or six in the afternoon, a day or two before you plan to go out. The word spreads rapidly, and the crowd of regulars who are always on hand to watch the unloading of the day's catch generally congregate when first one boat and then another is easing into its slip.

The boats that draw the largest crowds usually deserve their reputa-tions. So far as safety is concerned, there is not much to worry about. Party boats are common carriers and most are of sufficient size to carry forty to sixty and occasionally more passengers. Because they are oper-ating out of United States ports they are rigidly inspected by the Coast Guard, and those boys know what to look for where safety is concerned. No party boat stays in business unless it is as safe as a boat can be.

Some of the boats operate on half-day trips from 7 A.M. until noon and from 1 P.M. until late afternoon. Others go out farther and spend the whole day. Naturally the all-day boats charge more than those that make two trips in a single day. In any case they are infinitely less expensive than charter boats.

One of the important features to look for is cleanliness. Again, as with charter boats, one with trash and loose gear scattered about the deck or one that shows signs of needing a good scrubbing often represents the attitude of the skipper and his crew. This observation refers to the condition of the boat when it is ready to leave in the morning. Do not be too critical when it has just returned to port with several hundred pounds of fish in the box and a large number of sunburned and tired fishermen tossing candy bar wrappers and drink cans all over the deck.

You can almost be certain that bait will be furnished free, but don't be surprised if you find you have to rent a rod and reel—and buy it if you drop it overboard. This is only fair, because tackle is expensive and if there were not some control the boat owner would soon go out of business. If you have your own rod and reel, most skippers will be glad for you to bring it along because, considering the wear and tear, they are barely breaking even by renting the tackle to you at the small price they charge for the added accommodation.

The answer to what you may expect to catch must necessarily be somewhat vague because much depends on what part of the coast you are fishing, the season of the year, and the depth of water. Sometimes it may be grouper, red snapper, kingfish, cobia, black sea bass, and occasionally such scrappers as dolphin, amberjack, and other even more exotic species. Frequently, somebody will latch onto a shark and it generally means trouble for the rest of the fishermen and especially the crew, who have to go through the process of untangling a dozen or more lines the shark has managed to wend his way through and around until he either breaks off or is hauled to the surface and dispatched with a lead-tipped "persuader."

In the northern part of the Gulf, the red snapper is one of the highly prized fish that is caught with pleasing frequency from the decks of party boats. Not only is the red snapper an excellent food fish, but he is also a powerful fighter. As the name implies, they are red in color and generally caught in water of seventeen fathoms and often considerably deeper.

They travel in large schools, feeding several feet off the bottom, and the standard bait is frozen squid, pinfish, or common cut bait. Those weighing somewhere around the ten-pound mark are considered small and those ranging from twenty to thirty pounds are of medium weight. Now and then a party-boat fisherman may win the jackpot by hauling up an even larger one. Commercial fishermen catch them in vast numbers in the lower Gulf, especially on the Campeche Banks.

Other heavyweights that are plentifully available to the party-boat fishermen in the Gulf are the red and black groupers. Like the snapper, they feed close to the bottom and what is bait for one works equally well for the other.

Party boats working out of Texas ports may concentrate on one or more types, depending on the season. This same practice is true along the Louisiana coast. Because of the shorter winters and wider range of bottom conditions, party boats operating out of south Florida ports naturally produce a wider variety of fish.

As one moves up the Atlantic coast, the types of fish regularly caught by the anglers on party boats include the black sea bass, groupers, porgies, and grunts.

Because of its size, Chesapeake Bay makes it possible for party boats to catch large numbers of fish without venturing outside. Some, however, make regular trips far offshore in quest of different game.

One of the interesting aspects of party-boat fishing is that with so many lines in the water, someone is forever bringing up a fish of a type radically different from the standard fare. If some member of the boat crew, or sometimes one of the passengers, fails to identify it with a degree of assurance, it is sometimes given a special place in the ice chest and turned over to the nearest marine biological laboratory when the boat returns to port. On occasions, even the experts are stumped.

Man's knowledge of the creatures that inhabit the sea is forever increasing; but even in this enlightened age, the silent depths far offshore remain an enigmatic world filled with strange forms of life.

For the newcomer to the fishing game, almost any fish other than those which come aboard with regularity is of intense interest. Just the opportunity to examine at close range such creatures as an octopus or a triggerfish is an unforgettable experience. While aquariums, with their wide and varied collections, are excellent places to visit and observe many of the creatures of the sea, the deck of a party boat gives the viewer an entirely different and frequently more rewarding perspective.

When the boat is nearing the selected fishing area, the skipper will begin to slow down while he studies the bottom, the color of the water, and the drift of the current. Along about this time, he will pass the word for the anglers to get their tackle ready. But, if you want to be a good sport, don't let your line over the side until the engines are stopped and the skipper gives the "start fishing" signal. Jumping the gun often gets the whole show off on the wrong foot when the early bird finds his line has become entangled with the propeller. It is the best way I know to become unpopular with the crew and all the other passengers.

There are other rules of etiquette to be followed, too. The usual procedure is for all the lines to go down at about the same time, and it isn't long before there's the shout of: "I've got a whale!" or "What in the world is this?" or "I must be stuck on the bottom." Amid all the excitement, fish begin coming over the side and from that point on the mate and his helper are busy as two bees in a tar bucket. They help the novices get their fish off, rebait the hooks, and put the fish on the proper stringer in the ice chest. Sooner or later, somebody hooks something big and fast and this is where good and bad manners begin to manifest themselves. If you see that by leaving your line over the side the big fish is going to create a tangle, reel in quickly. Naturally, there will be a few who either don't understand the importance of giving the big fellow the right of way or are too stubborn to cooperate. It just means less fishing time for everybody if the lines become snarled and have to be untangled.

Most party boats today are well equipped with ship-to-shore radio telephones, electronic fish-finding devices, and a host of other refinements unheard of a few years ago. As a rule they even have lunch counters and large comfortable cabins where a passenger can take a rest if he grows weary of fishing.

Most party boats have it plainly stated on their signs as to whether or not the passenger is allowed to keep his catch on return to dock. If there is any question, ask before you go out. Most boats do allow the fisherman to keep his catch and often there is a wholesale fish truck waiting at the dock to buy at the current market price from anyone who wants to sell. Many party-boat regulars more than pay for their day's fishing trip and still save a few for the frying pan.

To be sure, there are more refined methods of saltwater fishing, but a day on a party boat can be a lot of fun and excitement.

SMALL BOAT HANDLING

Boats have been, are, and always will be an important adjunct to saltwater fishing. Ever since early man first sat astride his floating log and paddled out beyond the breakers, fishermen have found boats of all descriptions essential to getting to where the fish are, rather than waiting for the fish to come to them.

With the steady advancement in hull design and nearly foolproof engines, boating is far safer than driving an automobile. Nevertheless, boating accidents continue to increase. This, of course, is due mainly to the fact that so many more people are taking to the water in boats. Like it or not, the overwhelming majority of these accidents are the fault of the boat operator.

Fully 90 percent of all fishing boats are those that fall into the general classification of small boats. This means open boats powered by outboards. The remaining 10 percent covers everything from the larger cabin boats to sailboats.

If the average person had the inclination to fly an airplane, he would first invest in a reasonable period of actual training under a competent instructor's guidance. Coupled with this he would spend a considerable amount of time in the study of flying. After this period of apprentice-

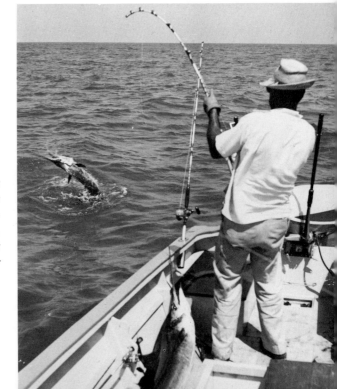

Small boats, such as this one powered by an outboard, are becoming increasingly popular with the off-shore angler. In this photo one sailfish is already boated while another breaks the surface.

ship, he would be granted a license to solo and would then continue to practice and study.

By some strange, illogical line of reasoning, or rather a lack of reasoning, the same man will unhesitatingly park his car at the nearest boat livery, pay whatever the rental fee happens to be, and strike out for open water with all the assurance of an experienced sea captain.

The average person seems to just naturally assume he is capable of handling a powerboat as soon as he climbs aboard. The wonder of it is that in the majority of cases the rank landlubber will be able to make his trip without getting into serious trouble. Of course, he may run aground on a sandbar, bump into a piling, and do some damage to the boat's trim, violate a few rules of the road and of common decency, have a few close calls without even being aware of the danger, and he may even run out of gas, but even then chances are good that someone will come along and tow him back to the dock.

Establishments that rent boats on salt water come under the jurisdiction of the Coast Guard and are subject to inspection to be sure the boats are equipped with fundamental safety devices. By and large, the Coast Guard does a good job of checking, too, but with the vast numbers of liveries it would take ten times the available number of personnel to be certain that all rental boats are seaworthy. Then there is the fleet of privately owned boats that grows larger each year.

As difficult as it is for many people to accept, the sea is as much alien territory to man as is the air. Of the two, the sea is usually a far more forgiving mistress. She will let the dunderhead make one mistake after another and get away with it. Sooner or later, however, her patience will reach the breaking point, and when that time comes, watch out! There is often no chance for a second try.

Having lived on and around boats most of my life, I have made my share of mistakes and I have occasionally had strong reservations as to whether or not I would ever reach land again. In looking back over the predicaments I have found myself in from time to time, I believe I can honestly say that in the overwhelming majority of cases, the fault was mine. Either I failed to have the proper equipment aboard or I attempted to tax a boat beyond its possible limits. Then there are the times when I neglected to pay proper heed to the weather or when I was just too cocksure of my own ability.

Where safe boating is concerned, it would be almost impossible to say *this* comes first and *that* comes second. A man might make a fetish of equipping his boat with every known safety device and then fall overboard and drown simply because he did not know how to move about properly in his boat.

One of the strangest paradoxes concerning a man and his boat is that he will frequently spend a small fortune to buy the best boat and motor available and scrimp like a pauper when it comes to fitting it out with the basic safety equipment. The most common faults are inefficient or worn-out lifesaving devices. Just because a life jacket or buoyant cushion was in good shape a couple of years ago does not mean it will remain that way forever. They suffer from dry rot, exposure to the elements, and simply deterioration from age.

You may operate a boat for years on end and never have need of a fire extinguisher. If the time does come when you suddenly find yourself with a fire on board, you had better hope your extinguisher is of the proper type, within easy reach, correctly filled, and in good operating condition. It could mean the difference between a little scorched paint and the loss of a boat, or even your life.

While on the subject of the possibility of fire, never under any conditions should gasoline be on board any boat in glass containers. Even a cupful of spilled gasoline can turn an otherwise shipshape boat into a raging inferno. Break a gallon jug and there is only one thing to do if a spark sets off the contents. You jump overboard and start swimming and just hope you can make it to the beach.

For an open outboard skiff, a bilge pump may seem to be an unnecessary luxury. It is, until you run into a squall and find your bilge filling to a dangerous level. In an emergency even an empty coffee can or a bait bucket can probably save the day. Admittedly, modern hull designs of many open boats incorporate self-draining bottoms, thus virtually eliminating this hazard.

With today's engines becoming more and more foolproof, a pair of oars seem almost passé. They are just something else to bother with until that one time when you need them. On any small boat a paddle is essential while moving about in cramped quarters.

Of course you will have running lights on your boat, but when was the last time you inspected the wiring and bulbs to see that they were operational? A flashlight can be a big help in signaling, finding channel markers, and changing a sparkplug after dark.

The cost of a whistle or horn is practically negligible, but it can more than pay for itself in fog, darkness, or when you need help from a passing boat. The same applies to some of the excellent flares and smoke signals that are available in most boating stores.

Overcrowding is one of the common causes of small-boat accidents. There is no hard-and-fast rule, but a crowded boat is dangerous. Five or six passengers might be okay in a sixteen-foot boat under ideal conditions. But let a sudden blow come up and your freeboard seems to lower with each passing minute.

People fall out of boats. Of course, safety rules dictate that no one should stand up in a boat, or sit on the gunnel, but the fact is they do, and unless you are a real Captain Bligh there is not much you can do about controlling your passengers. Suppose, however, you are clipping along at say fifteen or twenty knots and someone tumbles over the side. Would you know what to do instantly, without having to think.

Of course, the experienced boatsman would turn the boat in the direction of the man overboard, thus kicking the stern of the boat away so there would be no danger of the propeller striking the person in the water.

The next two overboard steps must be taken almost simultaneously. One is to reduce the speed, but don't kill the engine because it might be difficult to restart just when it is most needed. The second act is to throw some flotation gear such as a lifejacket or buoyant cushion toward the person. Even a styrofoam ice chest or a paddle will serve as something for him to hang onto. Of course, be careful not to hit the person in the water. Even a nonswimmer will almost always be able to thrash about a few feet to reach some floating object.

Far too often the boat operator will attempt rescue by leaping in behind the person who has fallen overboard. Ninety-nine times out of a hundred this only compounds the accident and frequently results in two drownings where none would have happened if the operator had stayed with his boat and circled to the downwind side to avoid letting the current, waves, or wind force the boat over the person being rescued. When close enough to make contact with a paddle, length of line, or hands, the engine should be stopped.

Under no conditions should a man-overboard accident be treated in a lighthearted manner. It could be far more serious than it first appears. Even the best of swimmers could be suffering from a cramp, his clothing could be too heavy and dragging him down, and there is always the possibility of shock.

With the exception of a severe fire on board, there is rarely a reason to abandon ship. Most modern boats will remain on the surface even if stove in to the point of swamping. Of course, a large outboard still attached to the transom will drag a boat to the bottom, but one of medium size may only cause it to stand in a vertical position. Admittedly, clinging onto the bobbing bow of a nearly submerged boat leaves a lot to be desired so far as comfort is concerned, but it is a far better object than nothing at all. Of more importance is the fact that two or three shipwrecked sailors clinging to even part of a boat is a much better target to spot by rescue parties than a scattering of lone swimmers trying to reach shore with only their heads above water. The rule is, stay with the boat. The beach may appear to be only a short distance away, but it is generally much farther than it seems.

Weather is one of the most frequent causes of boating mishaps. If small craft warnings are flying and you are determined to go fishing, go ahead. It is wise, however, to check before you leave port and be certain your insurance premiums are paid up to date.

Even with today's excellent forecasting of weather and frequent reports on radio and television, there is always the chance of getting caught in a squall. If such storms are visible when you leave the harbor, it is up to you whether you go out or wait for a better day. On the other hand, if you shy away from angling just because there are clouds in the sky, the chances are you will not get in much fishing. The important thing is to know how to cope with a squall when it does come along.

Almost without exception you will have anywhere from fifteen minutes to an hour of warning before a squall hits. Generally, you will see rain falling from a dense mass of cumulus clouds, the wind will begin to freshen, and the surface will develop a chop. Chances are good the squall will miss you by a country mile, but it may be zeroed in on you.

The fishing may be so hot right about then that you are inclined to ignore the signs nature has provided for you. You may be listening to a siren song. Better to play it smart and start making a few preparations while you still have time. Don a life preserver and see that everyone else in the boat does the same. Get the engine running in neutral, collect and store loose gear, and if at anchor, be certain it has not become fouled so that it cannot be raised in a hurry if the need arises.

Bear in mind that you are generally safer inside a sheltered bay and still safer in the lee of an island, but watch out for shallow water! Two of the worst places to be in a sudden squall is in a pass or along an exposed beach. Far too often the small-boat skipper waits until a storm is almost on top of him and then he tries to outrun it through a pass. In such narrows you are likely to be confronted with a sweeping tide going one way, waves going another and wind racing along over the top. Equally dangerous is to be close enough to an outside beach where waves can build with frightening suddenness that may swamp your boat and cause it to broach to in the shallows.

It is far safer to be in open water with plenty of room to maneuver. Distribute the weight evenly, point the bow into the wind, and use just enough power to maintain headway. Occasionally, but it takes practice, it is safer and drier to quarter into the sea rather than to hit it head on. This is often true of a boat with a "V" hull.

As in all cases where weather is concerned, the chances are that you will be caught in open water by a squall that is headed seaward. This will mean that you must head for shore if you are to keep your bow pointed into the wind. The rule still stands, but because of the offshore direction of the wind, the combers that would otherwise be rolling shoreward are almost certain to be flattened out and you may find yourself in a stretch of relatively calm water due to the sheltering effect of the land mass, be it an island or open stretch of coastline. A word of caution, however. Remember that sudden wind shifts are commonplace in squalls and what seemed to be millpond water may suddenly become a tempest. The weatherwise skipper of the small boat caught in such a situation will not be lulled into a sense of false security. Go ahead and take advantage of the sheltered water, but refrain from moving in too close. If you do and that possible wind shift does occur, you are in for real trouble.

No matter how dependable an engine is and no matter how well it is maintained, it is still a piece of machinery and subject to failing right at the time you need it most. There is only one smart move at such a time and that is to get the anchor over the bow and hope it is heavy enough to hold. Even a small anchor is likely to hold if, and this is a big if, you have plenty of anchor line. A short line that will just barely enable the anchor to touch bottom is virtually useless in heavy weather. For the anchor line to have the proper scope, it should be about five times the depth of the water. Of utmost importance is to snub the anchor line around the bow post after you have the proper scope. This will keep the bow of the boat headed into the wind.

Suppose, however, that you find yourself in water too deep for your anchor line. Ideally, under such conditions, you would replace the metal anchor with a sea anchor which would open like an umbrella as the boat is forced backward. To expect the small-boat owner to keep a sea anchor aboard is approaching the ridiculous in the list of safety devices. A fairly good substitute for a real sea anchor can generally be made from material usually carried on a small boat. An empty tackle box with the lid open and lashed to a paddle is helpful and so would be a bait bucket or ice chest. A convertible canvas top with its metal frame makes a highly satisfactory sea anchor. A friend of mine once successfully rode out a bad blow by tying his small anchor to his fish box and making this fast to the end of his anchor line. All that is needed is something that will create a drag in the water and keep the bow pointed toward the wind.

Another Lorelei that has been the downfall of many small-boat skippers is an offshore wind. You head out through the pass, and the open expanse of the Gulf or Atlantic is delightfully smooth. The kings are farther out than you expected them to be, so you keep on heading seaward in search of them. You stray too far, run out of gas, or the engine quits. The water is too deep to anchor and the wind keeps blowing. What do you do then? The answer is very simple. You keep on drifting out to sea and hope someone will come along and tow you back. There are few places in the world more lonely than being out of sight of land in a small boat that has lost its power.

Did you remember to carry along some spare food and a jug of drinking water? Let's hope you did, because the chances are you will be needing them.

Right here is a good place to pause and suggest another safety precaution the average saltwater angler makes a habit of neglecting. Leave word with someone you know, whether it be your wife, your next-door neighbor, the motel manager, or Uncle John, approximately where you intend to go. If you are expected back before midnight and are not on hand for bacon and eggs in the morning, at least someone ashore will be able to suggest where the search should begin.

Small boats are high on the list of this nation's forms of recreation. Because we are nomadic by nature, a large percentage of these boats are trailed along behind the family car. Buying the proper type of trailer for a particular boat is of utmost importance, but it is another item that the otherwise cautious boat owner often ignores. If you don't know the manager of a marina that you can depend on, there is a simple solution. Write to the manufacturer of your boat. Tell him the make, model, length, and size of motor, and he will be glad to tell you just what you need for proper performance on the highway and the launching ramp.

After you are properly fitted out, remember that a trailer is a piece of machinery and as such cannot be expected to run forever without a reasonable amount of preventive maintenance. The wheel bearings should be properly lubricated, the tires should carry the recommended air pressure, brake and tail light and turn signal wiring should be carefully inspected, and safety chains checked for rust-damaged links. Also, when pulling a trailer, the driver should remember the extra length that demands more room for turning, changing lanes, and passing other cars. He should also be cautious to allow more time for stopping because of the additional weight of the boat and trailer.

The fisherman, whether he trails his own boat or rents one at the place he plans to fish, would be doing himself a favor if he invested in a few United States Coast and Geodetic charts. The cost of these charts is nominal and their value inestimable, both from the standpoint of finding the best fishing and learning the area to lessen the danger of running aground, or taking the wrong channel. The angler who plans to fish southern salt waters should write to the United States Department of Commerce, Environmental Science Services Administration, Coast and Geodetic Survey, Washington, D.C., and request a copy of "Nautical Chart Catalog No. 1," which lists all charts available for the Atlantic and Gulf coasts. Specific charts can be ordered from the Coast and Geodetic Survey headquarters and can generally be purchased from authorized dealers in the area where you plan to fish. The United States Coast and Geodetic Survey team deserve a tip of the ol' fishing cap for the remarkable job done in constantly updating and improving these coastal charts.

For those who wish instruction on the fundamentals of safe boating, there are always courses being conducted by the United States Power Squadrons and the United States Coast Guard Auxiliary in numerous cities. One of the best books available on the subject is Charles Chapman's *Piloting, Seamanship and Small Boat Handling.* It covers, in plain language, practically every facet of boating safety, including how to tie important knots, buoy and channel marker identification, rules of the road, safety, navigation, use of compass and charts, and countless other related subjects. Chapman's book is to the small-boat operator what Nathaniel Bowditch's *American Practical Navigator* is to the sea captain.

nine ~~~~~~~~~~~~~~~~~~

~~~~~~~~
~~~~~~~~

ON SOLID AND NOT-SO-SOLID FOOTING

BRIDGE AND PIER FISHING

It often comes as somewhat of a shock to the saltwater angler when he learns that statistics prove the vast majority of game fish are caught from piers and bridges.

The reason is really quite simple when one stops to realize the logic behind such a statement. There are literally countless thousands of bridges and a vast number of piers that provide almost unlimited space for an untold number of anglers. All are readily available to the motorist, and access to many piers and most bridges involves no cost. Also, something that is especially important to many people, bridges and piers provide a solid, nonmoving platform from which to fish.

All the above reasons would be of little attraction were it not for the basic fact that both bridges and piers span passes or reach out into deep

177

The Caldwell pier at Port Aransas, Texas, reaches 800 feet out into the Gulf of Mexico. It is typical of many such structures that spike the coastline from the Chesapeake Bay to the Rio Grande. All afford the angler a steady platform to fish for "the big ones" that prefer deep water.

water where fish congregate. Consequently, if the average angler has at his disposal a place that is easily reached, costs little or nothing, and produces good results, then that is where he is going to do most of his fishing.

Of the two structures, the bridge wins hands down in attracting the largest number of fishermen, for the basic reason that there are far more bridges than there are piers. It would be virtually impossible to say which of the two structures produces the most fish per fisherman, since in the case of bridges there is no way to keep an accurate count of how many people use them. On the other hand, most well-run piers have caretakers or concessions operators who maintain records. In the latter case, the number of anglers per month and per year is known, and frequently reasonably accurate records are kept on the numbers and types of fish that are caught.

Except for the legions of "sometime" fishermen who just happen to stop off and dangle a line over the railing for an hour or so when they are en route from one place to another, pier and bridge fishermen are a breed unto themselves.

Most of the regulars know their particular bridge or pier as well as, and often better than, the boat fisherman or surf caster knows his favorite stretch of water. They know well in advance just what the stage of the tide will be at any given hour today, tomorrow, or a week from now. They know which fish are most likely to be caught at any season, they have made a study of the baits that produce the best results, and they even have their own spot on the structure.

Naturally, certain bridges have to be declared off limits to fishermen because of the safety factor that must be considered. Frequently, however, the "No Fishing From The Bridge" signs go unheeded to a large extent and often law-enforcement officers will blink at the outlaws unless there is a genuine hazard involved. Happily, the departments of transportation in many southern states are becoming increasingly aware of the recreation value of bridges and are constructing them in such a manner as to afford the fisherman safe catwalks or suitable guardrails to protect him from the flow of automotive traffic.

Before leaving the subject of bridge fishing safety, however, I would be remiss if I failed to emphasize the fact that most "No Fishing" signs found on certain bridges have not been put there by caprice, but for a decided reason, and failure to heed them is not only a violation of the law, but occasionally results in serious or fatal accidents.

Bridges along coastal roads often span passes that connect bays with open water and are natural routes followed by numerous types of fish that alternately enter and leave these bays with the changing of the tide. The result is that there are frequently more dense concentrations of desirable fish passing beneath the bridge than will be found in open water on either side.

Another important element to be considered in favor of bridge fishing is that whatever the type of structure built in salt water, no sooner has the first footing or piling been put in place than it becomes home base for a variety of sea life that constitutes food for larger fish. Barnacles and certain types of algae and an endless array of crustaceans are quick to take up residence on solid underwater objects. Bait fish find protection in and around such construction, and in the logical sequence of events, the larger fish come there to feed.

For some reason no one has ever been able to explain satisfactorily, many game fish that will frighten at the slightest disturbance, such as the careless handling of an oar in a boat, will completely ignore the rumble and vibration of heavy bridge traffic.

Fishing from piers has long been a favorite method with countless numbers of anglers. One of the most unusual piers to be found anywhere is out almost in the middle of Chesapeake Bay. For anyone who is aware of the enormity of Chesapeake Bay and has not seen this unique pier, the natural question is: How is it possible to have a pier out in such a vast expanse of open water?

The answer is found by crossing the 17.6 mile Chesapeake Bay Bridge-Tunnel on U.S. 13 that connects the Virginia Beach and Norfolk areas with the Eastern Shore. The pier projects from the bridge out near the middle of the Bay almost within casting distance of one of the world's busiest seaways. The variety of fish caught from this pier is extensive, and it is an unusual experience to be standing on solid footing so far from the mainland.

In years gone by, piers projecting out into the Gulf and Atlantic were few and far between. As the popularity of coastal vacations has grown, so have the number of piers. Today, there hardly exists a tourist-oriented stretch of resort beach that does not boast at least one pier, and sometimes several, built for the express purpose of providing the angler with an avenue out to deep water. Some are municipally owned and may be used by the public without charge. Others have been built with private capital and a fee is charged for their use. In some cases it is a

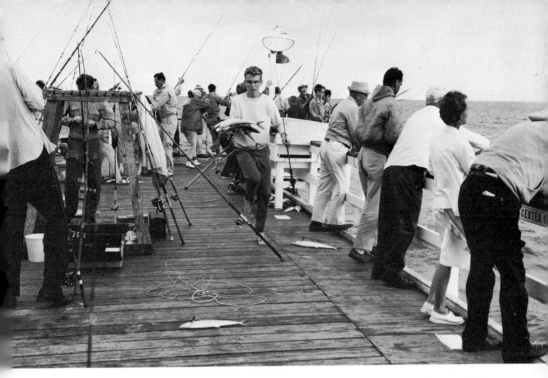

Pier fishing is one of the most popular forms of salt water angling. The young man in the center is in a hurry to put his catch on ice and get back to his place while the school is still running.

combination of both, where municipalities regain a percentage of their expenditure by leasing tackle, bait, and food concessions to private interests.

In any case, fishing piers generally are well worth the small fees charged for their use. Almost all the large piers are well-organized establishments that are equipped to handle an angler's needs. Generally, there is a bait and tackle shop. In these concessions the fisherman can buy a bucket of live shrimp, pinfish, or any of several types of frozen bait. He can also purchase replacements for broken or lost tackle or, for that matter, he can walk out on the pier empty handed and rent everything he needs.

Pier fishing is the perfect answer for some people who could not otherwise enjoy the sport. Sometimes they are prevented by age, or physical infirmity, and then there are those hapless individuals who get seasick everytime they set foot on any kind of boat. This, however, is not to suggest that piers are populated only by the aged and handicapped. This type of fishing just happens to appeal to some people more than any other form. Often it provides an opportunity for them to get in a few hours fishing that they would otherwise be unable to do. It is not uncommon to see a baby enjoying a quiet, fresh-air snooze in his carriage while mom and pop crank reel handles.

As with any other form of fishing, pier luck depends to a large extent on the types of fish that are currently running in a given locality. If the bluefish, channel bass, or snook are in a feeding mood, then that's the big fish catch of the day. Again, it may be a time for tarpon, kingfish, or Spanish mackerel. The dependable standbys are croaker, drum, flounder, sheepshead, speckled trout, as well as the inevitable "unusual" fish of the day.

Now and then you will find somebody fishing with the old-fashioned hand line, which he dangles over the railing. For the most part, though, pier fishermen use rods and reels, and generally speaking, they use tackle that is a bit on the heavy side. Lines that test twenty and thirty pounds are not uncommon, and some optimistic anglers go even heavier. The use of large plastic floats are popular with pier fishermen, and sometimes where there is an offshore wind, they use penny balloons to carry their lines far out beyond the end of the pier. The balloons act as floats and generally burst once a fish is hooked and the battle begins.

In a way, pier fishermen are similar to party-boat regulars, but on a stationary platform. They get to know one another, and as a rule are helpful to any newcomer who needs advice and suggestions. When someone hooks onto something big almost everybody nearby shows a courteous spirit and reels in his line so the busy angler will have plenty of elbow room and also won't get tangled in other lines and thus risk losing his prize fish of the day.

Let somebody haul up a strange-looking fish or an unusually large specimen and the word spreads like a jungle telegraph. It isn't long before others find some excuse to reel in and stop fishing for a few minutes, and while they give their legs a little exercise they naturally stop by to observe the "special" catch.

Of course, it has been known for a long while that fishermen across the board are a friendly group. There is one fellow who makes himself decidedly unpopular on any pier or bridge, however, and he is the person who has not learned the overhead casting technique. This "side-winder" is generally given wide berth and if he persists in his dangerous practice he may even be asked to leave until he learns a safer method of casting.

On the whole, both bridge and pier fishing are good and they are growing more popular each year.

SURF FISHING

There is something strangely enchanting about surf fishing that stirs a primitive urge in me. Maybe it is the aloneness of wandering along a deserted beach, watching the sea with its ever-changing moods, feeling the clean breeze that has been washed as it blows across countless miles of open water. Perhaps it is the belief that here on this very beach, or one just like it thousands of miles away, man first began to fish in salt water.

It is intriguing to pause now and then, when I watch the combers rolling in across a submerged bar, to feel the sand sucking out from beneath my feet and hear the chortle of tiny wave-rolled shells and wonder what Stone Age man thought about the sea. He doubtlessly knew there were fine food fish there in abundance because he could see them, but for a very long while they must have seemed almost as unobtainable as the stars that sprinkled the heavens at night.

He had probably already learned to kill land animals with clubs and

There is a strange enchantment to surf fishing that is unmatched by any other form of angling. Always, there is the ever-changing sea, the sand sucking from beneath your feet, and the question of whether or not the fish you are seeking is just beyond the next foam-crested wave.

rocks and spears. In all likelihood he had figured out how to trap freshwater fish by driving them into weirs he had woven from grass and vines and how to gig them with a wooden grain.

Certainly, from time to time early man was able to capture a fish of the surf when it became stranded on a bar or trapped in a shallow slough by a swiftly falling tide. By and large, however, he must have pondered a better and more dependable method of catching two or three of the big fish to provide him and his family with food.

The skill or brute force he used to capture the land animals seldom worked on the fish that cruised the surf. If he and his fellow hunters rushed into the surf, throwing rocks and flailing the surface with sticks, the fish quickly darted out to the safety of deep water and kept on swimming in their relentless search for food.

In time he finally came to the realization that in order to outwit the fish he would catch, he must first learn why they came close to the shore. As a result, he was forced to make a study of the fish.

Today, so much of man's knowledge is written and readily accessible that occasionally it seems inconceivable to realize the vast span of time early man must have been forced to devote to learning the rudimentary skills necessary to accomplish the most basic chores.

It is logical to assume that after he could not solve the piscatorial conundrum by standing on the beach, he climbed to the top of a tall tree or sand dune so that the glare of the sun on the water would not blind him. Gradually a pattern must have begun to take shape. From his lofty perch he could see that the big fish were swimming in close to the beach and feeding on schools of minnows that remained in the limited shelter of the shallow water. He saw, too, that some of the larger fish fed on clams and other forms of shell life and others ate worms that lived in the sand close to shore.

With the solution to part of his puzzle, he still had a long way to go. He could collect the bait he had discovered the fish were seeking, but what was he going to do with it? Tie it onto a long thin vine or strip of rawhide and toss it out where the big fish were feeding? It is almost certain he tried this and he must have been overjoyed when a fish swallowed the crab, sandbug, or glob of clam flesh. He could even feel the tug as the hungry fish tried to swim away with the bait, but when it realized the tidbit was tied to the vine that led to the shore, the fish simply let it drop from his jaws or regurgitated if he had already swallowed it.

Man was getting closer, but he still needed something to hold the fish once it had taken the bait. The process of inventing the first suitable hook must have been maddeningly slow in developing and it can only be guesswork as to how many unworkable methods were tried without success. Archaeological finds prove, however, that man was not to be outdone, and eventually he hit upon a workable solution.

He found that by sharpening each end of a short stick and cutting a groove around the center he could tie his line around the depression, cover the two ends with suitable bait, and wait for a fish to swallow his offering. This was no hook to be pulled back on as soon as he felt the first tug. He must have had to exercise extreme patience and let the hungry fish carry the bait until he swallowed it. It was a hit-or-miss proposition, but if things went right and the prehistoric fisherman waited long enough, the fish would swallow the bait, gorge and all. Then was the time to strike. A sudden hard jerk on the line and the improvised hook would turn sideways and stick in the fish's gullet.

Man was then on his way to becoming an expert at surf fishing. The gorge was improved upon by making it of stone and bone and shell, and finally someone thought of carving a crude hook similar to that which is used today. And so it went through the Bronze Age, and the Iron Age and eventually to the tackle store.

No wonder man likes to fish. It took him long enough to learn just to fashion the rudimentary tackle he needed. It would seem, then, with his vast store of knowledge to draw upon and the fantastic change from the crude gorge and rawhide line to modern tackle, that all man would have to do would be simply to walk down to the seashore, cast a baited hook, and immediately reel in a fish. Alas, that is not exactly how it works.

The osprey, the tern, the pelican, and all the other seabirds know how to go about their brand of fishing from the moment they leave the nest. Unlike the birds, man's skill at fishing must be acquired by trial and error. In a sense, he must start at the bottom and learn the ways of the fish he wants to catch, as did his forebears of the dim past.

For the angler who wants to surf fish in southern salt water there is a vast stretch of coastline to choose from. There are nearly three thousand miles of beach that fronts on the Atlantic and the Gulf from the northern part of Virginia's Eastern Shore to the southern tip of Texas. Multiply that figure by ten to get the actual coastline when both sides of islands and the perimeters of bays are measured. But the true surf fisherman is concerned only with that three-thousand-mile stretch of sand that is constantly pounded by the waves from open sea.

The list of fish that are caught with regularity from the surf is entirely too long to waste time enumerating. Even a seasoned surf fisherman who has made a serious study of beach fishing and tried his luck at a hundred or more stop-offs would be hard pressed to say which fish are the most popular. This, because it depends to a large extent on what part of the coast he is fishing and the time of the year and even more, what type of fish he wants to catch.

Certainly high on any such list would be the striped bass, channel bass, the pompano, the drum, and on and on it could go, including mackerel, tarpon, ladyfish, sea trout, and a host of others.

In general, the surf fisherman uses a type of tackle that is often quite different from that used when fishing from a bridge, a small skiff in a sheltered bay, or far out on the blue water in the fighting chair of a charter boat. There is a basic type of tackle that affords the fisherman a better chance of catching certain kinds of surf-running fish than there would be if he tried his luck with another style of angling equipment. Fundamentally, he needs a rod of sufficient length and with enough action to heave a lure or glob of bait a considerable distance out into the water, but that too must also have enough backbone to stand up to, for example, the powerful struggle of a large drum. Again, if he is fishing for pompano or trout he will want a considerably lighter stick. The strength of the line and the size of the reel must be fairly well matched to the rod.

One of the most popular conceptions of the surf fisherman is someone wearing chest-high waders, a sou'wester, web belt strung with an assortment of gear, including a bag for tackle, another for bait, and a short-handled gaff. This apparition that appears as a cross between a deep-sea diver and an astronaut ready for a moon walk is armed with a huge twelve-foot rod and at least a 9/0 reel.

On some stretches of coastline this stereotype surf fisherman will be found, but in southern waters and especially during the warmer months, the average surf caster is much less encumbered. Frequently he just rolls up his pants, which seldom does any good because he is going to get wave sloshed anyway, and wades in. One reason for this lessening of formal attire is that surf-casting tackle has improved so much in recent years.

Actually, with spinning tackle that is capable of shooting a lure or

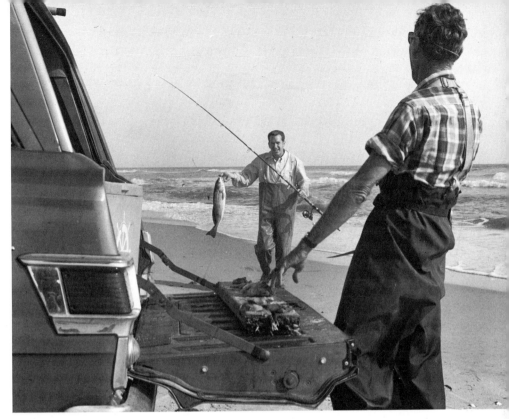

Surf fishing is one of the most popular forms of angling. This obviously pleased "surfer" has gotten the show started well with a channel bass that is a fine size for the table.

bait so far with so little effort, it is almost unnecessary in many cases to even get your feet wet. You can stand on the beach and toss out farther than you used to be able to do in water up to your armpits. For some reason, however, surf fishermen can't seem to keep out of the water.

Anglers who do insist on those chest-high waders should take a safety precaution that is well worth the few dollars it costs, and this is the wearing of a life belt. The same is true when wearing hip boots. Some stretches of coast line are as flat as a street, but the best surf-fishing waters are scarred with drop-offs and deep holes. If the surf is running high and one's britches or boots get full of water, there can be real trouble. The belts such as many water skiers use are good and so is the pneumatic type that can be instantly inflated with carbon dioxide cartridges. There will always be the rugged individual who will scoff at such precautions, but it is almost certain he has never taken a knockdown and tried to fight an undertow with his hip boots full of water.

My personal choice of what might be termed a good all-around surf-casting rig is an 11-foot fiber-glass rod with an open-face spinning reel that will hold at least 225 yards of 15- or 20-pound monofilament. For those who have not fished salt water extensively and are planning to invest in a good glass rod, the guides are one of the most important items to consider, especially the one on the tip. Plated rings will do the job they are designed for and are unquestionably cheaper, but the plating will eventually crack and peel. The result is a frayed line. The tip guide is the one that receives the most wear as the line is constantly being dragged through it under pressure with casts and retrieves. Agate guides have been long favored but carbaloy is most commonly used on good rods today.

If one is not sold on spinning tackle, then he will do well to consider the stouter rod with a revolving-spool reel. A good choice is a wide-spool squidding reel that will hold a couple of hundred yards of braided line of 30-pound test or heavier. The reel should be the type with a free-running lever and a star-drag.

Surf casting or fishing from the beach can be as relaxing or as vigorous as the individual personally cares to make it. The two extremes are often seen along the same littoral scene. One angler may be seated in an aluminum folding chair, contentedly puffing on his old briar pipe while he keeps a wary eye on his surf rod that stands upright in a beach rod holder. His more energetic counterpart will be walking rapidly along the surf's edge, casting frequently as far out into the water as his skill and equipment will allow. At times he may be seen wading waist-deep to toss his lure just that many extra yards farther into deeper water.

Whether he sits still and waits for the fish to come to him or rushes along trying various spots, both fishermen stand a good chance of making a catch if they know and are willing to follow a few rules of the game. And, as with all other forms of the sport, surf fishing does have certain fundamental rules.

Assuming one has equipped himself with a suitable rod and reel and has an assortment of lures in his tackle box, and also presupposing he has become fairly proficient in casting with the long stick, the next and most important point is knowing how to read the water.

The successful surf caster will, like his prehistoric forebear, often stroll along an unfamiliar stretch of beach for half a mile or more before deciding to make a cast. He will have learned to look for certain signs on the surface of the water that suggest where fish are most likely to be found. The action of the waves is one of the first and most important. Waves that break far out from the beach and continue shoreward as steady foaming combers indicate a gradual shelving or even sloping of the bottom. At times and under certain conditions, this type of water can be productive, but under normal circumstances there are almost bound to be better spots a little farther along the beach. The stretches of shoreline where the bottom is gouged and irregular with gullies, deep holes, swash channels, and cuts through submerged offshore sandbars are the locations where game fish are likely to be most active.

Granted, the experienced surf fisherman knows what places to look for and how to find them, but what about the neophyte? There are two answers and the first is the surest, but it takes time and planning. It is also a method many experienced surfers use when contemplating a trip along an unfamiliar stretch of beach.

A United States Coast and Geodetic Survey chart of the area should be purchased and a trip made to the beach when the tide is at its lowest point of ebb. At such times it is a simple matter to spot the offshore sandbars and cuts through them. Gullies and swash channels will also be obvious. While the water at the moment may be so shallow as to seem unimportant, it should be remembered that most of these places will be covered with several additional feet of water when the tide is at flood. These places should be marked on the chart and notations made of storm-tossed objects, such as a large chunk of driftwood or even trees on the shore, as they will be useful as checkpoints for triangulation or dead reckoning. These checkpoints are needed for best results because a shoreline is entirely different in appearance at the two extremes of the tide.

If, however, one is ready to fish and the tide is right, there is still another way to find the likely locations to be frequented by game fish. White water breaking offshore and then flattening out dark and smooth before reaching the beach indicates the presence of gullies or swash channels. Breaking waves that have stretches of smooth water at first one place and then another betray a series of cuts through the sandbars. One should imagine the offshore sandbars as a range of small hills with passes through which the big fish travel into the deep channels near shore.

One of the most popular misconceptions held by the newcomer to surf fishing is that he should try for the longest possible cast. This is not always the case, and it often means that the fisherman has outdone himself and landed his bait on the top of a barren shallow bar far from shore.

It should always be kept in mind that large fish approach the beach for one basic reason and that is to find schools of minnows, colonies of sand bugs, sea worms, and certain shellfish that are not available in the deep water far out.

The consistently successful surf fisherman is forever on the lookout for concentrated activity of terns, gulls, pelicans, and other seabirds. When a flock is spotted diving and wheeling over a stretch of water close to the beach it is an absolute certainty that some form of bait is below them. Birds don't make repeated dives into the water for the fun of it. For them, fishing is a deadly serious business and if the tide is right it is almost certain that the bait fish are being harried and driven to the surface by larger fish below. Casting into such a busy area is a good way to get the action started in a hurry.

The condition of the tide plays such an important part in surf fishing that it cannot be overemphasized. Large fish do not actually want to come in close to shore, because of the constant threat of stranding themselves. They do come in close, however, when the tide is right, because that is often the best time for most productive feeding. But they are forever on the alert for a change in the water.

Over the years I have found that the two hours before high tide and the hour or hour and a half that follows the flood are often the periods most productive. If the tide is at flood just around daybreak and again at sunset, so much the better. If a thorough study of the beach has been made and one likes to fish at night, his chances are also excellent. Darkness gives the fish a feeling of security.

There is always an exception to any rule when it comes to fishing, and one that comes to mind happened some years back when a fellow fisherman and I were on a sailing trip along the west coast of Florida. We were youngsters at the time and our tackle was more or less anything we happened to have.

We had beached our boat at the south end of Caladesi Island, which thank heavens has now been purchased by the state and is being preserved as an unspoiled park. In those days and at a young age we had been impressed with tales of pirate treasure that was supposed to be buried on the island. We spent the morning searching and by noon we were hot, tired, and somewhat disillusioned. To make up for our lost labor, we took our two freshwater bait-casting rods and started to hike along the beach at almost flat low water. Suddenly, in a swash channel that was not more than two feet deep, we spotted one of the largest schools of redfish I have ever seen.

We started casting with battered old plugs, and the reds started striking. Every cast, and I do mean every cast, produced one or more strikes. At times they would straighten out the hoooks and get free and at others so many fish would be fighting for the plugs that none were hooked. The action lasted for about an hour and might have continued for the rest of the afternoon had we been left any line on our reels. When the show was over we had a total of five big redfish.

Why were they within twenty or thirty yards of the shore in a shallow channel in the middle of a bright sunlit day at low water? You tell me, because I certainly don't have the answer. My only guess is that they were ravenously hungry and we just happened to be at the right place at the right time.

The best natural bait for surf fishing is generally practically under your feet. Sand bugs, sand worms, crabs, shrimp, and live minnows are always good. The same is true of the flesh of shellfish, cut mullet,and chunks of squid. When using cut bait it must be fresh. Carry along an ice chest with containers of nontoxic ice substitutes which you have frozen the night before. They last many times longer than ice and eliminate the problem of emptying water out of your ice chest every so often. They come in several sizes and can be used over and over again. Any good tackle store has them under several brand names.

Artificial lures may be anything in your tackle box, and this statement is not made in an effort to take the easy way out of answering a direct question. If I planned to cover a lot of ground and did not want to be encumbered by anything larger than a small tackle box, I would first include a spare spool of line, some extra leader material, and then I would concentrate on filling the rest of the space with a variety of spoons, surface and deep-running plugs, bucktails, feathered jigs, metal squid, and rubber eels. Of course I would also find room for some spare sinkers, swivels, and an assortment of hooks and metal clips. If there was any space left I would toss in a small jar of pork rind just to add an extra teaser for some of the artificials.

When a school of feeding surf fish keep refusing one kind of lure, I don't waste time whipping a dead horse. I change quickly to something different and keep on changing until I hit the winning combination.

I suppose if I had to come down to an absolute final choice of a few lures I could carry in my shirt pockets, they would be several spoons and an equal number of bucktails. The spoons simulate darting minnows and the bucktails can be mistaken for shrimp or any number of other creatures that represent food for a hungry fish.

All told, I think the importance of knowing when and where to fish the surf is much more vital than exactly the right tackle and type of clothes to wear.

KILLERS, 'CUDAS, AND GOOD GUYS

SHARKS

The shark is the most cussed and discussed creature encountered by anglers who fish southern salt waters. There is also more misinformation available on the subject than there is concerning any other form of sea life that swims.

The key word where sharks are concerned is *unpredictable*. The experienced marine biologist and the serious fisherman interested in making a study of the fish he seeks are continuously confounded by the ever-changing characteristics of sharks. The chief dispensers of misinformation, who have had limited experience and have done some reading on the subject, unfortunately far outnumber the more reliable sources of knowledge, and the fisherman who is genuinely anxious to learn is misled far more often than he is properly informed.

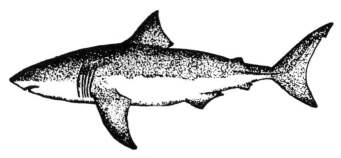

White Shark

One good example of this misinformation is the widely held belief that anyone who deliberately sets out to catch a shark is undoubtedly some kind of a demented soul or exhibitionist. The IGFA, however, has included six species of sharks on its list of game fish. They are the blue, mako, white, porbeagle, thresher, and tiger.

Actually a shark is not a fish in the exact sense of the word. A fish is a vertebrate with a skeleton of true bones. The shark, on the other hand, has a cartilaginous skeleton, or a gristlelike substitute for bones. If a fish and a shark are buried and left for a sufficient length of time, disintegration would dispose of all parts with the exception of the bones and teeth. If exhumed, the fish skeleton would be found, but all that would be left of the shark would be the teeth. There are other differences, but the absence of bones is one of the most pronounced between sharks and true fish.

The shark has been swimming throughout the seas of the world for several hundred million years. He was around to watch the rise and fall of the dinosaurs and has remained virtually unchanged with the passage of time. He is probably one of the most perfectly designed of all living creatures.

One of the most interesting parts of a shark's anatomy is his teeth. Behind the front rows in both top and lower jaws are reserve teeth. If one or more is broken off in feeding or fighting, it is quickly replaced by another that is imbedded in the inside surface of the jaws. There is apparently no end to the number of replacement teeth that are available to a shark.

For the angler who is interested in sport fishing for sharks, one of the most blatant aspects of the creature's unpredictableness is his feeding pattern. One day he will unhesitatingly strike at anything from a bloody

Catching a big shark such as this ten-foot gravid female is not a sport for the light tackle enthusiast. It requires heavy gear, and there are times when the excitement reaches the danger level.

chunk of bonito bait to an empty tin can. The next day he is likely to ignore anything and everything that is tossed his way. At times he will swim alongside a boat or circle one at anchor. Again, he will appear to be so shy that even the slow approach of a drifting skiff will send him scurrying for far places.

It is a fairly well-established fact, however, that sharks are always hungry. At times, especially when encouraged by other feeding sharks, they will gorge themselves until their bellies are distended. Should the food supply be plentiful, as when a commerical boat's nets are being ravaged, engorged sharks will often regurgitate everything in their stomachs and rejoin the feast. This ability to vomit at will is the factor that enables a shark to fill its belly with an assortment of undigestable objects such as bottles, cans, chunks of wood and metal, and even old inner tubes and rubber boots. When the accumulation of junk becomes excessive, the shark gets rid of it and is ready to start eating again.

He employs at least three senses to lead him to food. The first is a highly developed olfactory system that enables him to smell food at almost unbelievable distances. The second is his eyesight, which he uses when he is near food or something that he considers to be edible. The third, and least understood, is vibration.

Extensive studies have been made, and are still in progress, in an effort to gain more knowledge of this acute sensitivity to vibrations. That this sense exists is certain, and the number of anglers who have had record marlin, tuna, and other game fish mutilated by sharks is legion.

It is believed, but not positively proved, that a hooked or wounded fish emits some either high- or low-frequency sound waves that travel great distances through the water. A foraging shark will "tune in" on this distress message and home in on the source to investigate. When he is near the target, he begins to depend on his eyes to lead him to food.

The subject of how well a shark can see is one that has been argued and debated for many years. Dr. Perry Gilbert of Cornell University and editor of *Sharks and Survival** has done a prodigious amount of detailed and highly scientific work on the subject of sharks, especially their eyes. In his concluding statements in "The Visual Apparatus of Sharks" in the above-mentioned book, Dr. Gilbert states: "While the eyes are not necessarily their most important sense organs, vision has undoubtedly played an important role in the survival of this successful group of fishes over a period of many millions of years."

There is a widespread belief that sharks have poor eyesight but it has been my own observation that they are able to see well in clear water,

Sharks and Survival, edited by Perry W. Gilbert, published by D.C. Heath & Co., Boston, Mass., under arrangement with the American Institute of Biological Sciences, 1963.

All that is left of a red snapper after making contact with the jaws of a passing shark. When sharks move in over the snapper grounds there is nothing to do but weigh anchor and find a different location.

and because they will frequently strike at unbaited lures in the waning hours of twilight and early dawn, I suspect they have remarkably good eyesight even in poor light. I am also convinced they can distinguish certain colors. Red and yellow seem to excite them more than blue and green. This conclusion has been reached after a considerable number of experiments carried out by casting lures of various colors toward sharks swimming in clear water over light-colored bottom such as marl or sand.

A shark's sense of smell is little short of phenomenal when the scent of food is in the water. There have, however, been countless times when fish have been clean hooked—that is, squarely in the jaw with no blood connected with the hooking—and sharks have moved in and mutilated the fish while it was battling.

There is a preponderance of evidence to substantiate the fact that a shark can, from a considerable distance, sense when a fish is in a semicaptive position. This may be directly related to a shark's sense of hearing or highly sensitive nerve fibers along the length of his body. It is reasonable to assume that human swimmers are occasionally attacked by sharks because these sensory organs have been agitated. Thus, the time-honored admonishment for a person swimming in the proximity of sharks to move through the water with as little disturbance as possible.

It is also possible that a shark may be so constituted that it is able to sense fear and is thus drawn to an area by this sense for closer investigation. It is a reasonably well established fact that dogs and other higher types of animals are more prone to attack and bite humans who are afraid than those who are not fearful or, at least, are able to control their emotions so as to appear unafraid.

There is also the hotly debated subject of which sharks rate the title of man-eaters and which do not.

This question is confused by the fact that when a human is attacked by a shark he seldom has the knowledge or the inclination at the moment to identify properly the shark he is encountering. There are, of course, certain sharks with such unmistakable physical characteristics as to facilitate almost positive identification. The hammerhead, with his broad horizontal head, is a good example, and so is the thresher with his exaggerated upper caudal lobe. Often the type shark making an attack can be identified with certainty by a study of the teeth marks on the victim and occasionally by teeth that are broken off and remain in the victim's flesh.

On rare occasions, qualified observers are on hand to witness the attack and make a positive identification, and in still fewer incidences the attacking shark has been killed and dragged ashore.

But for the most part, the victim simply knows that he was attacked by a shark. One widely published marine biologist once summed up the problem by stating that there were only two types of dangerous sharks and those were the big ones and the little ones. While his remark seems somewhat facetious, it is substantiated by fact. Sharks as small as two and a half feet in length have been known to attack humans and inflict injury.

The white shark *(Carcharodon carcharias)* is unquestionably a man-eater, as are certain others. Conversely, the nurse shark *(Squalus cirratus)* that frequents shallow waters was long considered to be a creature with a somewhat oafish disposition and about as harmless as a milk cow. Several recent attacks by the nurse shark have tended to disprove this belief.

There are approximately three hundred species of sharks between the two extremes that may or may not be considered dangerous. It should always be borne in mind that a shark is a wild animal and frequently a powerful one well equipped to inflict serious injury. The angler who hooks one either by accident or intent should keep this uppermost in mind.

Large sharks, anything over seven or eight feet in length, and small boats are occasionally a dangerous combination. It is wise to treat any large fish with caution when he is near the boat, but sharks will frequently attack with savage fury once they connect the boat with their restraint. It is not uncommon for them to rush the boat and slash it with their teeth and at times even to grab the lower housing of an outboard engine and shake it with all the determination of a terrier killing a rat. Numerous are the accounts of enraged sharks grabbing motors even with the propeller spinning.

One of the most frightening experiences to which I was exposed occurred while bonefishing on Florida Bay. The shark appeared on the scene while I was battling what I will always believe might have been a record-size bonefish. The general shape, coloration, and elongated upper caudal lobe led me to believe it was a tiger shark.

The shark caught the bonefish on the end of my line and instead of being content with robbing me of my prize, he continued to cruise around my 12-foot skiff. I was positive he was somewhat longer than my boat. Disgruntled, I foolishly decided to try to catch the shark by putting a large glob of bait on a 10/0 hook and tossing it at him. He struck and I set the hook. He could easily have made one determined run and stripped all the line from my inferior rig and ended the episode then and there. Instead, he put up a brief fight against the rod and then attacked the skiff. Even after he had made a shambles of my tackle and broken the line, he refused to leave.

He had obviously come to associate my skiff with the hook in his jaw and he struck the boat with such force as to knock me off my feet. While I was attempting to start the outboard, he struck again, this time splitting one of the seams and ripping a gash in the gunnel. I strongly suspect that had I not been able to get the engine running as quickly as I did he would have swamped the boat and probably torn me apart in his rage.

Never under any conditions should an attempt be made to remove a hook from a shark's mouth with bare hands. Even an apparently dead shark will snap its jaws shut and the result could be severe. One angler I know beached a large white shark and let it lie there in the afternoon sun for two hours before he attempted to retrieve the hook. The shark revived, closed his jaws on the man's arm, and before he could extricate himself and reach medical aid he came near dying from shock and loss of blood.

The best way to remove the hook is to wedge the shark's jaws open with a heavy piece of timber. A still safer method is to forget the hook and cut the leader with a pair of wire cutters. The loss of a hook is a small price to pay in exchange for a nonmutilated hand.

Many head-boat skippers will flatly refuse to allow a shark to remain on a line once it has been hooked. As soon as they determine that the catch is a shark they will, often against strenuous protest from the angler, simply cut the line. Their seeming stubbornnesss is not without a solid foundation in experience. There are two basic reasons. One of these is that once hooked, the shark will often swim in and around all the other lines, hopelessly tangling them, delaying further fishing, and often resulting in a large amount of extra work for the crew and frequently the loss of much tackle. The second objection to bringing a shark on a deck crowded with fishermen is the distinct possibility that someone may be seriously injured.

The operators of public piers many times invoke the same ruling. Other pier owners restrict shark fishermen to the late night hours when the majority of the conventional anglers have called it a day and gone home to dream about the big one that got away. Shark fishing clubs have become increasingly popular in recent years, with rules and bylaws restricting the size reel, test of line, and methods of fishing. They also wisely provide for the proper disposal of a shark once it has been caught. Several hundred pounds of rotting shark flesh left lying on the beach is not only thoughtless on the part of the angler, but forbidden by ordinances in most communities.

Where do you go to catch a shark? The answer is simple. There is not a body of salt water, including many rivers and creeks, that is not at one time or another visited by foraging sharks. Ironically, certain chambers of commerce in Atlantic and Gulf resort towns will extoll the virtues of the unsurpassed fishing in their area and at the same time stoutly maintain that sharks are either nonexistent or present in such limited numbers as to constitute a rarity. While such an attitude is completely understandable from the viewpoint of tourist promotion, it simply is not the truth. Rather, it is axiomatic that the larger the fish population, the greater the number of sharks.

Another myth concerning sharks is their relationship with porpoises. The popular belief, as pointed out in the chapter on porpoises, is that if a herd of porpoise are frequenting a particular stretch of coastline the waters are sure to be free of sharks. Instead, the reverse of this is generally true. The porpoise and sharks are enemies, but only when the shark presents a threat to the porpoise herd.

In reality, the porpoise adopts a sort of armed truce with sharks. As long as the shark does not molest these mammals or make an attempt to eat one of the young, the porpoise pay little heed to sharks in the vicinity. The shark knows the porpoise's wasteful feeding habits and capitalizes on them by following behind a group of feeding porpoise at a discreet distance, contentedly picking up the scraps. Some of the largest sharks I have caught over the years have been those following closely behind feeding porpoise.

One aspect of shark anatomy that the angler should understand concerns the absence of the swim bladder common in most fishes. Lacking this built-in flotation equipment that enables a fish to remain virtually motionless in one spot for a length of time, the shark must constantly be on the move. Once he stops swimming he will begin to sink to the bottom. It is by swimming that he maintains a steady flow of water over his gills, thus supplying his body with the necessary oxygen needed for survival.

As with all rules, there is an apparent exception to the one that says a shark must swim constantly. They are occasionally observed to be stationary. This is true only if there is a sufficient flow of water passing around them to keep the gills supplied without forward motion. Water flowing swiftly through a pass or in the vicinity of jetties when the tidal flow is strong are good examples of where sharks will be found occasionally holding a stationary position. Closer observation, however, will show that he is actually swimming. What he is doing is taking advantage of the flow of water and swimming against it only fast enough to remain in one place while he keeps a lookout for any food that may pass within his reach.

There are so many different ways to fish for sharks that to list them all would be prohibitive in a single chapter. It can be an expensive hobby or one that costs only a few dollars for simple, but effective, rigs.

By and large, most shark fishing is done from bridges and piers for two reasons. The first is that the structure provides a stable platform, and the second, because bridges generally span narrow passes that require all fish to pass under to get from one body of water to another. Also, such structures are natural attractions for hoards of small fish which, in turn, draw larger fish, constituting a more densely populated feeding ground for the hungry shark.

With the shark's reputation of being something akin to a seagoing garbage can that will eat practically anything tossed his way, the question of bait seldom presents a problem. The degree of freshness is of little concern either, because sharks will gobble up with apparent relish chunks of rotting flesh that would turn the stomachs of conventional fish and fishermen alike. The one form of flesh that will almost invariably be shunned by them is that of decayed sharks.

No one knows why this is so, but some years ago this fact was brought to the attention of the Navy, Air Force, and War Shipping Administration. The three departments were particularly desirous of finding something that would act as a repellant to protect humans from shark attack. Armed with the knowledge that sharks will shy away from the bodies of those that are in a state of decay, the research teams began a systematic study to learn the chemical composition of such flesh. Analysis disclosed that the flesh contains a large portion of ammonium acetate. Through a long involved process of laboratory and field tests, it was finally decided that copper acetate would provide the protection needed. The chemical was crystalized and mixed with nigrosine dye packed into cakes, and given the name "Shark Chaser." It became standard equipment issued to vast numbers of servicemen who were confronted with possible survival in water.

While "Shark Chaser" would divert sharks under certain conditions, it was eventually scrapped. It probably served a useful purpose from a psychological standpoint for a downed airman or a shipwrecked sailor, but in reality it was no more effective against voracious sharks than an asafetida bag in warding off disease.

The fact still remains that of all forms of bait, trash, and garbage that a shark will swallow, tainted shark flesh is the least likely to be accepted. Conversely, ravenous sharks, those in a feeding frenzy which is known as the "mob feeding pattern," will unhesitatingly eat one another and even slash at and devour their own trailing entrails.

The favorite baits of most shark fishermen are such fish as bonito, chunks cut from stingrays, mullet, and numerous other types of fish flesh. Over the years I have had more consistent luck with bonito and I suspect this is because it is a blood- and strong-scented fish.

If fishing from a boat of suitable size, chumming is one of the surest methods of attracting sharks to the area in which you wish to fish. Ground bunkers (menhaden), pinfish, and fish scraps may be prepared in advance or the grinding job may be done from a hopper mounted on the stern. When the boat is anchored in a likely spot, the chum may be ladled over the side so as to form a slick that will spread out several hundred yards with the tide. Sooner or later foraging sharks are sure to pick up the scent and come to investigate its source. They will frequently make their presence known by the sight of a dorsal fin slicing the surface, but don't depend on visual contact before putting a baited hook over the side. Often as not a shark, by swimming well below the surface, will fail to betray his whereabouts, but it is a safe bet that he will move in very close, and where one shark is attracted there are sure to be others following.

IGFA rules permit the use of fish chum, but if you are interested in catching a recordable record, you must forego the use of chum composed of blood, animal flesh, or fowl, as this is forbidden.

When using chum it is logical to pick a spot near the mouth of a pass when the tide is flowing rapidly. This will spread the scent over a wider area in a shorter space of time. Whether the tide is coming in or going out makes little difference, because as long as a shark has enough water to maneuver in he doesn't care in which direction he is headed. He is just as likely to be cruising in the deep channels of a sheltered bay as he is to be waiting outside. The importance of fishing the passes is that he is more likely to be nearby, because this is the natural route he will follow.

The time is important to some extent, with the night generally producing better results than the diurnal hours. Especially is this so when fishing is done from bridges, piers, and from the beach. Sharks definitely come closer to shore at night. This is why the danger of shark attack on swimmers is greater at night than in the daylight hours.

The question of the proper tackle covers a wide range from saltwater fly rods to the heaviest rigs available. I have caught sharks on practically all types of tackle. Common sense naturally should be used. A big shark hooked on light tackle usually means the angler is going to visit the nearest tackle store the next day and buy a new supply of line. Conversely, a small shark snagged on heavy tackle is going to be about as exciting to catch as a rubber boot.

For those solely interested in collecting a set of shark jaws, or having their picture taken beside a large beast of the sea, the tackle may be primitive in its simplicity. It need consist of nothing more elaborate than a large seven-inch hook with a chain leader, a hundred feet of quarter-inch nylon line, and a pair of thick gloves. The hook is amply baited, the line made fast to a piling, railing, or bitt on the stern of the

The saltwater angler who thinks sharks are lacking in their ability to put up a fast and furious battle just has not made contact with enough sharks. This six-foot dusky required one hour and twenty minutes to bring alongside with medium tackle and it was fight, fight, fight all the way.

boat. After twenty feet have been let out, the line should be tied to the solid point with a piece of weak string to prevent all the line from drifting out. An embellishment, consisting of a balloon, may be added to the rig, which will serve as a float to keep the bait off the bottom. Not that the shark is opposed to picking up a piece of food he finds on the bottom, but the float prevents the hook from fouling on rocks or some other obstruction and permits it to drift with the current.

When the big moment arrives, the shark will let his presence be known by slowly swimming away. When he begins to tug, the string will snap and the angler should be ready to toss a free-running turn of the line around the piling or bitt. This permits the shark to swim unrestrained for a dozen yards or more before the line is snubbed, thus setting the hook with a solid jolt. The fisherman should wear his gloves, because he is going to need them.

From that point on, the fight may take the form of a tug-of-war, or you may have hooked a shark that is in the mood for a genuine fight that could go on for well over an hour. One such battle I remember began shortly after dark at the end of Lower Matecumbe Key and lasted until the morning hours. There were several of us participating in the struggle, and when we had the shark in shallow water and had determined that he was a mako that would weigh somewhere around five hundred pounds, we were all too exhausted to get him out of the water, especially since the one gasoline lantern we had was practically out of fuel and we would soon be working in the dark. Someone produced a .357 magnum revolver and we put six slugs squarely in the top of the monster's head. We shackled the hook chain to a longer length, which we made fast to a massive chunk of concrete left over from Henry Flagler's ill-fated railroad. It was our intention to return the following morning and drag the shark ashore, photograph him, and remove the jaws, which I wanted as a trophy.

After breakfast we trudged back to the spot, but no shark. The extra length of chain was still there along with numerous fresh footprints in the sand. Whoever had stolen the shark had at least had the courtesy to leave the chain and they even replaced the shackle bolt. Why anyone —and of necessity there had to be several people—would want to make off with a dead shark that belonged to someone else is a mystery to me. It did not make much difference, however, because we caught an even larger mako at the same spot that night.

One friend of mine, along with several of his shark-fishing friends, came near wrecking the old pier at Palm Beach, Florida, a short while before a hurricane blew it down. They were using the same kind of tackle, but they tied the end of the line to the railing. When the shark felt the hook, he took off for the Gulf Stream and carried a large part of the railing with him, much to the excitement of bystanders and the chagrin of the pier owner.

The shark angler can seldom be certain what size shark he is going to tie into, and if he is interested in those of the larger size he would do well to rig himself accordingly. For the big bruisers, my favorite tackle is a 9/0 reel loaded with 400 yards of eighty-pound test Dacron line and a 7½-foot glass rod with roller tip-top. To this, I add a 5-foot length of steel leader and a 12/0 hook.

There are numerous variations in the size of the reel, length of rod, test and length of line, length of leader, hook size, and so on. When I am fairly sure, something one can never be positive of, that the sharks are going to be running smaller, I drop back to a 4/0 reel, scaling the rest of the tackle accordingly. Also, there is plenty of excitement waiting for the angler who uses saltwater spinning tackle.

When trolling for sharks with a flat line, it is frequently possible to see one following the bait for a considerable distance before he makes up his mind to take it. At such times he will generally make his presence known as his dorsal fin cleaves the surface in a zigzag path behind the boat.

When he moves in and slaps his jaws shut, it is wise to use the drop-back method. Flip the free-running lever and let him have time to get the bait well inside his mouth. To strike quickly often results in a lost shark because he probably has the bait between his teeth and the hook will bounce off.

Allowing the line to drop back for fifty to a hundred feet gives him time to draw the bait inside his mouth, and the chances are far greater of the hook being more positively set.

One of the most frequently asked questions is: How large do sharks grow? It is a question that defies an answer. To date the largest one taken on rod and reel is the 2,664-pound white shark taken by Alfred Dean in April of 1959 off Australia. It measured 16 feet, 10 inches in length and had a girth of 9½ feet. Many shark fishermen have hooked larger ones, and confirmed sightings of even much larger ones are numerous.

The largest shark alive is undoubtedly the whale shark. In 1912 a 38-foot specimen weighing 26,594 pounds was caught off Knight's Key, Florida. Some have been observed to exceed sixty feet in length. The whale shark is a true shark in every sense of the word and is in no way related to the whale. It is, however, harmless to man since its diet consists of tiny fish.

The largest dangerous shark I have ever seen was off the northern Gulf coast of Florida, out from Panama City. At the time, I had been invited to go out on a commercial shark-fishing boat and we had stopped because of mechanical trouble. While repairs were being made, we sighted a shark rising up beneath the sixty-foot trawler, and it even bumped the bottom of the hull with its dorsal fin. The creature was at least thirty feet in length and when he was directly beneath, his pectoral fins were visible on either side of the boat. This behemoth remained in the vicinity for nearly an hour.

I was in the company of a crew of men making a living catching sharks, and it was the unanimous opinion of these experts at identifying

Never trust a shark, even if he appears to have lost all his fight. This one "came alive" in the cockpit and broke the ice chest and two chairs before he was quelled with a baseball bat.

different species that this giant beneath us was a white shark. If the one caught by Alfred Dean weighed over a ton and a half, it is logical to assume the one we saw would have exceeded three tons in weight, and probably a great deal more.

Despite the low esteem in which sharks are held by many saltwater anglers, the popularity of hunting them for sport is growing steadily. Once the fisherman recognizes the challenge of matching wit and brawn with a creature as savage as a shark, he frequently becomes addicted to the game.

One of the most popular myths and one that occasionally makes the shark fisherman unpopular, is that baiting a hook for them has the effect of drawing sharks close to swimming beaches. Complaints such as this frequently originate from uninformed sources in tourist-oriented waterfront areas. It is comparable to the fable of the ostrich hiding its head in the sand to escape danger. The bald-faced fact is that the sharks are already present.

Many of us who have made a study of the subject have frequently flown along various stretches of coastline in light planes. When the water is clear and the surface conditions favorable, we have often been astounded to see literally hundreds of sharks moving along over the sandy bottom within easy swimming distance from popular beach resorts where human bathers were frolicking in the breakers.

A shark hook baited with the bloody carcass of a bonito offers no more inducement to a shark than a stringer full of speckled trout hanging over the side of a skiff. The one exception to this observation is chumming for sharks. This should never be practiced in the proximity of swimming beaches. The reason for this is that chum spreads over a wide area and definitely invites sharks to come to investigate.

BARRACUDA

Most fish, I love. Why, I don't know. Maybe just because they are fish and I am an angler. A few fish I am not fond of—as with some food and some people, they are just ho-hum types. There is one fish I utterly despise, yet in my loathing I find an ambivalence that is akin to admiration. To hate and admire at the same time is entirely possible.

The one fish in salt water that I detest is the barracuda. Over the years I have indulged in all manner of do-it-yourself analysis, trying to find a logical reason for my abnormal dislike for this single member of the fish family. It is not entirely fear, although I will admit I have on infrequent occasions been frightened by, once bitten by, and been a witness to, some bloody deeds by the barracuda. It is not that they occasionally rob hooked fish before they can be netted. There are other fish that do this. It is not that they have an offensive odor (this is especially true in the case of the large ones). Few fish smell like a bouquet of flowers.

I have tried to reason with myself, but it just happens that the barracuda is one fish I do not like. For that matter, I abhor rats and I am not overly fond of crows. That does not mean, however, that I do not admire the skill and resourcefulness of these creatures. The same is true of the barracuda. Once, while I was discussing it with a friend, he suggested that perhaps one of my long-ago ancestors was chewed up by a barracuda and thus the reason for my dislike.

The great barracuda *(Sphyraena barracuda)* is found around the world in warm seas and is plentiful along the Atlantic coast up to North Carolina and throughout the Gulf of Mexico. They will move in close to shore as long as the water is above 70 degrees, but let it drop below this and you will have to look for him well offshore in deep water. As a rule, a barracuda of twenty pounds is considered to be a large one, although they grow considerably larger. The IGFA record was set in August of 1932 at West End, Bahamas, when C.E. Benet caught a 5½-footer that weighed 103 pounds, 4 ounces. Many larger ones have been reported, but Benet's record has stood the test of time.

Many anglers, on seeing a barracuda for the first time, have likened him to the northern pike. It is a fair comparison, but with several distinct exceptions. The pike has only one top fin located well aft, the 'cuda has this, as well as a first dorsal fin near the center of the back, consisting of five spines. The head, eyes, and undershot bottom jaws are

Barracuda

similar except that each is somewhat more exaggerated in the barracuda.

The "Tiger of the Sea," as the barracuda is often called, is a long slender fish. It is dark on the back, silver on the sides, with short vertical stripes reaching part way down. At times there is a slight rust color over the entire fish. The underside is white. There is frequently a scattering of dark, irregular spots or splotches on the sides, and the notched tail is always dark.

As with the shark, the 'cuda is interesting first because of his danger to man and second because of his prowess as a true game fish. Make no mistake about it, the barracuda is a dangerous fish, and there are numerous records of ones of moderate size attacking humans, in some cases fatally. Unlike certain sharks that actually devour people occasionally, the barracuda is more prone to make a sudden, slashing attack and then leave his bloody victim. Under similar conditions, the shark might be expected to continue the attack.

In all fairness to the 'cuda, it is generally believed that when he infrequently attacks humans in the water it is more by accident and misidentification than an intentional desire to feed on a creature so large. They will frequently loll almost absolutely motionless in the water for long periods, only to dart suddenly forward like a launched torpedo to slash at something that represents food. If that something happens to be a hand or a foot dangling over the side of a boat, or the flash of a belt buckle or skin diver's mask, it makes little difference to the human that the fish simply made a mistake.

Once in Cuba a number of years ago I saw a barracuda cut a boy's foot off while the boy was sitting on a low dock with his bare feet dangling in the water. In all likelihood the fish spotted the foot, mistook it for a fish, and cut it off.

The jaws and teeth of a barracuda combine to make a formidable weapon of offense. The anterior teeth are like canine fangs, long, pointed, and extremely sharp. Behind these are the smaller teeth used for cutting and still farther back are the dull grinders. The bite of a barracuda is almost surgically clean as opposed to the ragged, tearing bite of the average shark.

In 1665, when the Sieur de Rochefort published his *Natural History of the Antilles,* he mentioned the barracuda as follows:

> Amonge the monsters greedy and desirous of human flesh, which are found on the coasts of the islands [West Indies] the Becune [barracuda] is one of the most formidable. It is a fish which has the figure of a pike, and which grows to six or eight feet in length and has a girth in proportion. When it has perceived its prey, it launches itself in fury, like a bloodthirsty dog, at the men it has perceived in the water. Furthermore it is able to carry away a part of that which it has been able to catch, and its teeth have so much venom that the smallest bite becomes mortal if one does not have recourse at that very instant to some powerful remedy in order to abate and turn aside the force of the poison.

As with the moray, the barracuda was long suspected of having venomous fangs, a fact which is untrue in either case. Because of the deep puncture wounds such creatures are capable of inflicting, it is understandable that severe infection often accompanies their bites.

The flesh of the 'cuda has long been suspect of being toxic and sometimes to the extent of being fatal to humans. There was a time a while back when science pooh-poohed the belief, but more recent investigation has caused a reversal in that thinking. Although it is illegal to sell barracuda for food in many places, a great many of them are eaten and usually without harmful consequences. It is now known, however, that certain of these fish are, in fact, highly toxic. The exact reason is not clear, but it is suspected that it is caused by the barracuda eating large numbers of puffers and other poisonous fish to such an extent that the poison accumulates in the flesh and is thus dangerous to man.

A barracuda usually has a perfectly horrid smell that apparently comes from the slime on his body, and if only for this fact alone I would not eat one, large or small. I must admit that the cleaned flesh smells just like that of any other fish. Another belief is that its flesh becomes toxic when it swims and feeds in water where certain poisonous plants are present. With all the fine dependable seafood found in southern salt waters, I see no reason to tempt fate with a fish of such questionable qualities.

Nevertheless, there are numerous fine game fish that fall short of the mark as good table fare, but it does not in anyway diminish their sporting qualities, and so it is with the barracuda.

Many are hooked while trolling offshore for other fish. At times they are plentiful and again you may not see one for weeks on end. If there is any tried and sure method of trolling strictly for barracuda I don't know about it. The only trick worth mentioning is that if you see one following along behind a trolled lure, which they occasionally do, watch him for a minute or so. If he is reluctant to strike, shove the throttle ahead quickly. This will often cause the 'cuda to suspect he is about to lose a free meal and prod him into instant action.

The surest way to fish for barracudas is to hunt for them. They can almost always be found around old wrecks in either deep or shallow water. On medium-light tackle they can fight like a demon possessed and are willing to take almost any bait, from a whole mullet or ballyhoo to a chunk of cut bait—even including part of another barracuda. There is nothing unusual about a fish eating one of its own kind, since most are piscivorous and could not care less if the quarry happens to be a brother or distant cousin. The 'cuda's main concerns are whether or not he can catch his prey and either swallow it whole or cut it into bite-size chunks, rarely a problem because of his speed, coupled with powerful jaws and exceedingly sharp teeth.

Sight fishing for barracuda is popular on the bonefish flats around the Florida Keys. It takes a trained eye to spot them at times, since when lying motionless in clear shallow water they can become so nearly invisible as to betray their presence only by the shadow they cast and the dark outline of their tail. At other times, they hold their color and are easy to spot.

Occasionally when you are rigged for bones, barracuda can make a perfect nuisance of themselves. Unless your line is protected with about a foot of #7 wire leader, you are almost certain to have to devote considerable time replacing terminal tackle. Barracuda can slice through synthetic leader material as if it were made of straw, if they manage to get it between their cutter teeth. Again, they can be maddeningly perverse, especially if you say, "All right, I'll rig for 'cudas and forget about bonefish." At such times they are just as likely to refuse to cooperate, either shying away from the boat like frightened rabbits or stubbornly refusing to pay the slightest attention to lures cast in their direction.

I am convinced that every fish has a particularly vulnerable spot somewhere in his makeup, although I hasten to add that I do not know all of them, and what may work like a charm one day is likely to have the reverse effect a day or so later. In general, however, a 'cuda seems to have an obsession for catching something he thinks is about to escape him.

This peculiarity can frequently be capitalized on when sight casting to a barracuda. To do this, shoot the lure well beyond the target you have spotted and commence a slow zig-zag retrieve. You can be certain the barracuda has seen the lure and has been watching it since it hit the water, although he may appear to be totally uninterested. When the lure is close to, or even past him, make a decided increase in the speed of the retrieve. Such a change of pace seems to excite the fish and he will chase it. Don't worry about reeling too fast—you couldn't make the lure outrun him even if you tried. It is hard to believe that a motionless fish can generate such fantastic speed so quickly. It often seems they are launched from some unseen catapult.

Another way to "wake up" a 'cuda is to use a popping plug. Give it a quick snap so that it churns the surface, let it float for a moment, and pop it again. Such a disturbance has been the undoing of many barracuda. Maybe it whets their curiosity or maybe they become irritated at the lure for disturbing their tranquillity. On numerous occasions I have tried both of the above methods with the same fish without any response, only to have him spring into action just about the time I was ready to move on.

Hooking a barracuda in reasonably shallow water on an artificial lure

The barracuda is a dangerous fish and often called the Tiger of the Sea. *His jaws and teeth combine to make a formidable weapon of offense. He will often loll motionless for long periods waiting for food to come his way. Large barracudas are known to exceed a hundred pounds in weight. Even a small one will put up a rough-and-tumble fight when hooked.*

is bound to stir the adrenal glands of the most lethargic angler ever to crank a reel handle. Once the 'cuda realizes he has made a mistake— and this requires only a fraction of a second—he seems to go insane. There is no set pattern to his method of fighting unless it is motion in high gear. At times he will leap straight out of the water and land on the run. Again, he will streak away like a bolt of lightning, jump in a long horizontal leap, turn, and come back toward you and then, just about the time you are convinced he is going to share your boat, he will reverse his direction and take up the slack line so quickly it will all but take the rod out of your hands.

Fishing the bonefish flats gives one an excellent chance to study the habits of the barracuda. As the tide starts to ebb, you can see them moving away toward the channels. At times they will continue out toward deep water and at others they will just hole up and wait for the next tide. They often spend a large part of their time in passes, and we used to fish for them from the bridges down in the Keys. Occasionally they became almost permanent residents, with what at least appears to be the same fish taking up station under a bridge about sundown day after day.

What they do in the gin-clear waters of the flats along the Keys is a reasonably good example of their habits up both sides of the coast. They are to be found wherever the fishing is good and the water is not cold. Sunken wrecks, rock piles, submerged timber, and other underwater obstructions are good places to look for the 'cuda.

Many anglers like to wade the shallows when fishing for them. I have done it that way many times, but the more I know about sharks, the less am I inclined to go stalking about in knee-to-waist-deep water, especially with a string of fish hooked to my belt. Except for surf casting, I will admit that I am boat oriented. I have heard numerous stories about wading anglers being chased out of the water by large barracuda. I am willing to admit the fish may have made menacing moves in their direction and I honestly do not doubt that they would attack, if they thought they could snatch a couple of dangling fish. The phrase that bothers me when listening to these yarns is "chased out of the water." A champion Olympic sprinter would look as if he were crawling compared to the potential speed of a barracuda. It would be physically impossible for a man to run fast enough through water to escape a 'cuda that might have singled him out as a target. This is not always so where a shark is concerned because a shark will frequently make menacing rushes, only to haul up short, reconsider, and make another attack. I think I would be more inclined to use the term "*frightened* out of the water" by the presence of a big 'cuda.

If you want to bring a large barracuda aboard a boat or even up on a dock, it is wise to be sure he is dead before you get close to his business end. I once saw a bait boy severely bitten when he attempted to put one in the ice chest. Other anglers have been injured by the bite of a 'cuda out of water.

The only time I have ever had a barracuda draw blood from me was the result of my own foolishness. It was a ridiculous predicament to find oneself in, but it was a number of years before I could actually see the funny side of it. It happened one day when my wife and I, with Col. O.E. Henderson, were fishing for jacks off the south end of Anclote Key. I shot a long cast up under the old Coast Guard dock and a three-foot barracuda hit the plug. After a spectacular battle, I brought him alongside the boat and gaffed him in the belly.

With the gaff in my right hand, I lifted the big fish out of the water and stupidly attempted to remove the plug with my left hand. The barracuda was not nearly ready to call it quits and he promptly grabbed my fingers between his jaws. So there I stood with blood dripping and not the faintest idea what to do. I could not pull my left hand free and dared not turn loose the gaff handle with my right hand because I was certain the weight of the 'cuda would slice off at least one finger.

Seeing what I was involved in, Dorothy dropped her tackle and grabbed a towel from the engine box. Ripping it in half she used the two pieces to protect her own fingers as she attempted to pull the jaws apart. She was not strong enough and to make matters worse, the 'cuda began to twist about, driving the teeth deeper into my fingers. O.E. bounded over the top of the cuddy cabin, pulled out his sheath knife, and for a frightening moment I thought he was going to settle my problem by amputation.

Instead, he did exactly the right thing by slipping the knife into the 'cuda's mouth at the jaw hinge and, using the blade as a lever, he pried those jaws apart just enough to enable me to get my bloody hand free. Even then, with the 'cuda on the deck and the gaff in his belly, he refused to release his grip on the knife blade until he was dead.

When fishing for small 'cudas with bait-casting or spinning tackle, it is a good idea to try them with an assortment of plugs, spoons, feathered jigs, and bucktails. If all of these fail to produce the action you are looking for, an added inducement may be a strip of fresh fish flesh on a spoon or simply a flat strip of fish belly on a single or double hook. No matter what type of tackle is used and despite the size of the barracuda, it is important to separate the lure or bait from the line with a length of stainless steel wire. Naturally, the size of the wire leader should correspond to the size tackle. A #2 or #3 wire is good for light tackle, while heavier leader is necessary when after bigger fish. Hook size should range from 2/0 to 5/0.

One thing about the 'cuda that can be depended on is that once he strikes, his jaws are clamped shut, so get ready for action. He may have a number of undesirable characteristics about him, but when it comes to a knockdown, drag-out fight, the barracuda has few equals.

PORPOISE

Rare indeed is the saltwater angler who has not at one time or another come in close contact with one or more porpoises. Their arrival around a boat, along the rocks of a jetty, or their sweep through a pass will likely put a temporary stop to all fishing, but the opportunity to observe closely one of the sea's most interesting creatures is well worth the slight disturbance they may cause.

Right away one of the questions to be raised where these creatures are concerned is whether they should be known and referred to as porpoises or dolphins. It is an argument that has been going on for countless years and it is a fairly safe bet that it will never be fully resolved. Outstanding marine biologists who have spent a lifetime studying them are fairly equally divided on the question.

Aristotle, Plutarch, and both Pliny the Elder and Younger wrote of them and referred to them as dolphins. Some marine biologists are inclined to say that those with the rounded noses are porpoise and those with beaks should be called dolphins. For the sake of simplicity, I personally prefer to call them all porpoises and for what I consider to be a perfectly valid reason—because there is a worldwide important food and game fish known as the dolphin *(Coryphaena hippurus)*.

The porpoise of the family *Delphinidae* and of the order *Cetacea* is

Bottlenose porpoises are in no sense fish. They are warm-blooded mammals that give birth to their young alive and nurse them under water. Most of their lives are spent in pursuit of fish and swimming just for the fun of swimming.

in no sense a fish. Instead, it is a true warm-blooded, air-breathing mammal, the female of which conceives, gives birth, and nurses its young much the same as all other mammals, with the exception that the young are born and nursed under water.

Today science is almost universally agreed that the porpoise has an IQ second only to that of man. Serious studies currently underway are even producing evidence that leads to the suspicion that the reverse of this may be true.

The skeptic will, with all justification, scoff at such a belief, pointing out that the porpoise never erected a building, wrote a book, carved a statue, painted a picture, organized a city, received pay for a day's work, or built a highway. On the other hand, they do not engage in wars, they do not pollute their world, which is seven times the size of man's, they do not suffer from overpopulation, and most of their lives are spent in the joyous pursuit of gathering a bountiful supply of food and frolicking about their vast aquatic domain. They have a decided sense of humor and will unhesitatingly come to one another's aid when the need arises.

The porpoise most commonly seen by man is the bottlenose porpoise *(Tursiops truncatus)*. This is the one that provides spectators with exciting and almost unbelievable aquatic acrobatic performances at such marine attractions as Marineland of Florida, the Miami Seaquarium, and numerous other public aquariums. It is also the one that gained television and movie fame in the "Flipper" series.

The bottlenose is also popularly known because it frequents bays and shallow water close to the coast. Its range is far reaching and it is numerous all along the Atlantic seacoast and throughout the Gulf. The size of an average adult bottlenose is about eight feet in length, and one of that size will weigh about three hundred pounds. Some have been known to grow to twelve and even fourteen feet in length, but these are relatively rare.

Man has known the porpoise, or dolphin if you prefer, for thousands of years, and from the earliest times it was suspected that they were a highly unusual creature of the sea. Aristotle wrote that ". . . when taken out of water it gives a squeak and moans in the air." Pliny the Elder said: ". . . for a voice they have a moan like a human being."

Down through the ages seafarers have told many tales about the friendship of the porpoise for man. Chief among these have been stories of how a porpoise or a herd of them have protected people from sharks, aided exhausted swimmers to reach shore, and how they have frequently been seen pushing dead human bodies up onto the beach.

It was not until the early 1940's that serious study was begun on these creatures. The first successful birth of a baby porpoise in captivity took place at Marineland in 1947. Since then, it has happened many times and each year. With the discovery that porpoises could be satisfactorily maintained in captivity, science began to dust off the old stories and wonder just how true some of them might be.

Marine biologists and others interested in animal behavior watched in wonder when they observed the bottlenose porpoises at Marineland who would, of their own free will, engage in simple games with those who stood around the edges of the tanks and watched. A rubber ball would be tossed into the tank and the porpoise would dart up under it and toss it back ashore. Just how much could these huge creatures of the sea be taught? No one knew. Marineland decided to find out and they enlisted the services of a former circus-animal trainer named Adolf Frohn. The accomplishments of Frohn are now almost legend. Not only could he teach porpoise to play simple ball games, but he found that as soon as the porpoise understood what his trainer wanted him to do, he would learn the "trick" in an unbelieveably short space of time.

One of the first steps the anatomical scientists wanted to study was the porpoise's brain. In the past two or three decades some startling discoveries have been made. Always before, it was generally conceded that the chimpanzee more closely approached man's IQ than any other living animal. When they began to dissect the brain of the porpoise, however, the chimp made a decidedly poor showing.

Even more startling was the discovery that the porpoise possesses a brain that might even be superior to lordly man. They found that the brain weight of the average 300-pound bottlenose porpoise was 3.5 pounds while that of the average man was only 3.1 pounds and that of the chimpanzee was .75 pounds. Not content simply to record brain weight, they began to analyze the brain in ratio to the size of the creature, man included. Interest quickly grew.

In brain-to-total-weight tests, it showed that the average-size porpoises rated 2.1; man, 1.17, and only .70 for the chimp. What was more, tests began to show that the porpoise is capable of almost computerlike reasoning and his hearing far exceeds the range audible to man. It can detect and analyze the lowest audible pitch up to at least 170,000 cycles per second, which is about ten times beyond man's sound range.

The birth of a porpoise is a story that is too interesting to pass without mention. After mating, which generally takes place in spring, the gestation period lasts for a full year. The expectant mother senses that her "time" is near and enlists the aid of another female in the herd. The baby is born tail first and for a very important reason. Should there happen to be a difficult delivery, the baby would drown if it appeared head first.

Just prior to and during the process of birth, the nursemaid porpoise stays close beside the female and the instant the youngster, which is about three and a half feet in length and weighs approximately thirty pounds, emerges, both mother porpoise and her assistant quickly shove the baby to the surface so it can take its first breath of air. Until the youngster has begun to develop skill in swimming and diving, he must be pushed to the surface for a breath of air about every half minute.

When he nurses, nature has seen to it that the job takes only a few seconds. He swims to the underside of his mother and nudges her mammary glands. These are equipped with a special set of muscles that squirt a strong jet of milk rich in protein and fat into the baby's mouth. It takes only a matter of a few seconds, but this nursing process must be repeated several times per hour.

Naturally, the mother porpoise must spend part of her time in quest of food, and while she is away in pursuit of fish, the nursemaid remains with the baby, keeping it from straying away or forgetting that it must rise frequently to the surface for air. When the mother has satisfied her appetite, she returns to the pup and the baby sitter takes a break.

Surf bathers are often frightened and beat a hasty retreat for the beach when a herd of porpoise swims in close to the crowd. They see one or more triangular fins breaking the surface and somebody yells "Shark!" Once a person has learned, it is simple to tell the difference between a shark and a porpoise. The porpoise rolls to the surface, snatches a breath, and is back underwater in a second or two. When the shark swims close to the surface, his dorsal fin cleaves the water in a steady course. It should be remembered that sharks do not spend a great amount of time close to the surface unless that is where the food happens to be at the moment.

When bathers realize that the creatures out there are porpoises and not sharks, everybody breathes a sigh of relief and dives back into the waves confident that there would never be a shark around if there are porpoises in the vicinity. There is the belief that porpoises and sharks are deadly enemies and the porpoise would not permit a shark to be anywhere around under any conditions.

Don't put your money on it.

As a matter of fact, there are frequently one or more sharks following along in the wake of a porpoise herd. They know the porpoise is an excellent hunter and frequently he is somewhat wasteful when in pursuit of a school of mullet, herring, or other fish. The shark follows along and picks up the scraps that consist of injured fish and parts that have dropped from the porpoise jaws. As long as the shark trails along behind at a discrete distance, the porpoise pays no attention.

If, however, the shark begins to interfere with the porpoises' feeding, and especially if there are young in the herd, the shark had better be ready to beat a rapid retreat. Sharks will, if the opportunity presents itself, eat young porpoise. It makes no difference how great the size or what his species may be, no shark is a match for a herd of angry porpoise. They attack in numbers and literally butt the shark to death.

Several years ago a friend and I were sailing along the Gulf coast of Florida and when we were off Caladesi Island we decided to anchor for a while. It was an early summer morning and the surface of the water was exceptionally smooth. Suddenly a terrific disturbance began to erupt between our boat and the beach. Climbing up onto the roof of the cabin, we discovered that we had a ringside seat to a life-and-death struggle between a hammerhead shark that must have measured fourteen feet in length and a herd of bottlenose porpoises.

The reason for the battle could only be guesswork. A fourteen-foot hammerhead shark is a vicious and powerful animal, and it may have been that he had grabbed a porpoise pup or possibly the herd just did not want the killer hanging around.

The important fact was that we were able to see clearly just how the porpoise fought the shark. There were about ten of them and they were swimming around the shark in a fast-moving circle like a band of Indians attacking a wagon train. Every thirty seconds or so one of the porpoises would leave the circle and bore in on the shark at a terrific rate of speed. The shark would try to dodge, but the porpoise that was making the attack at the moment never missed. They would hit him so hard with their snouts and the tops of their heads that at times they would almost bend the shark double.

When he would try to make a break through the ring of circling porpoise, several of them would hit him almost simultaneously, thus holding him in the same approximate position. Once in a while, my friend and I were able to see small clouds of blood in the clear water, suggesting that the hammerhead had brought his powerful jaws into play and slashed several of his attackers.

The battle continued for nearly ten minutes, and suddenly the shark seemed to make one desperate bid for escape by leaping almost clear of the water. When he splashed back in, it was obvious that he was mortally wounded. He drifted down and lay in a twisted position on the bottom. For the next few minutes the victors circled, with first one and then another diving to nudge the carcass as if to make sure the shark was dead. When they were convinced, they turned out toward the open Gulf, rolling and puffing as if nothing had happened.

The method porpoises employ to kill a shark is unique of itself. While they have strong jaws and a mouth full of teeth, they know their denture is virtually worthless against the tough hide of a shark. So, instead of fighting with their jaws, as most animals do, they depend on their bulk and speed to do the job. When they attack a shark, they strike him with the nose and head in a sort of rolling punch and they seem to know that the quickest way to kill a shark is to rupture his internal organs. When a 300-pound porpoise hits a shark at a speed of perhaps twenty miles per hour, it is not long before the shark is battered to a pulp.

Legion are the stories of porpoise that have come to the rescue of humans. They have helped exhausted swimmers stay afloat and even supported them until they reached shallow water. They have fended off threatening sharks, and as previously mentioned, have rolled dead bodies ashore. Frequently they will help members of their own kind: one porpoise pup was found being carried along near the surface by two adults. When collected, it was estimated that the little porpoise had been dead for two or three days.

When my mother was in her teens, she was rowing a small skiff in a quiet lagoon along the northwest coast of Florida near Panama City. As she moved along, she noticed the tall dorsal fin of an extra large shark drawing closer and closer to her boat. She began rowing faster, but her boat's speed was no match for the oncoming shark. Suddenly a large herd of porpoise came in from another direction and completely surrounded her skiff, swimming so close that she had trouble rowing without bumping the oars against their glistening backs. The porpoise made no effort to attack the shark, but they stayed around my mother's boat until she reached the dock.

In his book *Airmen Against the Sea,* Dr. George Llano relates an incident, with now humorous overtones, that took place during World War II. A bomber had ditched at sea and six airmen had managed to escape on a rubber raft. They knew their position well and were aware that they were close to a Japanese-held island. As they paddled along under cover of darkness, they were studiously trying to avoid getting any closer than possible to the enemy-held island. During the course of the voyage, a porpoise appeared on the scene and sensing their plight, decided to give them a helping hand by pushing them straight toward the island they were attempting to stay away from.

So determined was the "helpful" porpoise that the airmen had to fight him off with their paddles in order to continue their trip to less hostile shores. Despite their appreciation of the porpoise's assistance, they could not help wonder whose side the big mammal was on.

Porpoise in general have a sense of humor that cannot be disputed. They have been known to swim up quietly behind sea birds resting on the water and nip at their tail feathers. Once I saw a big brown pelican resting peacefully on the surface of the bay. Suddenly a bottlenose porpoise came up under him and flipped him into the air with his snout. The pelican took off and flew a few yards away and landed. Instantly, the porpoise upended the bird again. After the stunt was performed for the third time, the indignant pelican got himself airborne and with laborious pounding wings, vanished toward the far end of the bay, probably somewhat peeved at himself for overeating. I had tossed him half a dozen large pinfish and his crop was fairly bulging. He was almost certainly outraged at the crude form of humor exhibited by the playful porpoise.

The porpoise then returned to my boat and began to swim around it. Thinking that perhaps he was hungry, I tossed the remainder of my dead pinfish supply toward him every time he came up to breathe. Once or twice he nudged them, but refused to eat them. My only conclusion was that he just did not have anything else to do at the moment and had decided to tantalize the poor pelican. Of course he could not change his expression if he wanted to, but the built-it grin suggested he was having fun.

Scattered about the waters of the world there are nearly fifty different species of porpoise. They differ in size and appearance, but all are true mammals and anatomically the same. All must breathe air, and to accomplish this they have a single nostril or blowhole located near the tops of their heads. Adults do not have to breathe as often as the very young porpoises, that every few minutes must rise to the surface and take a fresh breath that may range anywhere from four to ten quarts of air, depending on the size of their lungs and the length of time they plan to remain submerged.

While large whales, such as the sperm, have frequently been observed remaining underwater for an hour or more, the porpoise, with a much smaller lung capacity, cannot come close to matching this record. Winthrop N. Kellogg, in his book *Porpoise and Sonar,* states that the bottlenose porpoise can exist for only slightly over seven minutes without replenishing his air. Others, who now have studied them believe the porpoise can remain submerged for as long as fifteen minutes.

The blowhole, about an inch in diameter, is a highly specialized breathing device equipped with a double set of valves that open the moment the porpoise's head is free of the water and closes automatically once it is covered. By this method they never take water into their lungs or even get strangled in extremely rough seas. Their temperature is approximately that of humans, 98.6° Fahrenheit. They can be removed from the water and transported great distances as long as they are placed so that body weight does not impair the function of internal organs. The body must be kept moist with wet blankets and they must not be allowed to become chilled or overheated.

With humans, as well as with most other mammals, breathing is an automatic function of the body. With the porpoise, however, it is an act of which the creature must be constantly aware, just the same as a human skin-diver must gauge his time underwater and be prepared to surface when he feels the need to replenish the supply of air in his lungs. With this thought in mind, one is prone to ask: How then is a porpoise able to sleep?

It is an interesting question. In aquariums where the surface of the water is practically motionless I have seen porpoises suspended in an almost vertical position with only the tops of their heads, where the blowhole is located, above the surface. At such times they appeared to be sleeping. The tank, however, is an abnormal environment and it is generally concluded by scientists who have made extensive studies of cetaceans that the only sleep they get is in the form of catnaps. In storm tossed waves they probably have to go for exceedingly long periods with no sleep at all.

In bays, harbors, and along the coastline, porpoise normally travel in groups of three or four to several dozen. At times much larger numbers are seen swimming together. In 1940, while I was aboard the U.S.S. *Indianapolis,* I along with the entire ship's company, saw the greatest concentration of porpoise that I have ever heard of from any source.

When the sighting occurred, we were in the Pacific in early fall only a few degrees north of the equator and less than two hundred miles west of the mainland. The bridge lookouts sighted a stretch of disturbed water dead ahead. After those of us on the navigation bridge watched it for several minutes through glasses, we realized it was a fantastically enormous herd of porpoise that stretched from one horizon to the other.

The captain of the *Indianapolis* had the boatswain pipe all hands on deck to witness the phenomenon. With the ship proceeding at about ten knots, we began to cut through this vast shoal of southbound swimming mammals. No one aboard was able to make positive identification, but it was the general consensus of opinion that they were the common porpoise *(Delphinus delphis).* From the bridge we could see at least fifty miles, and even through the most powerful glasses aboard we could not see the end of the herd in either direction.

Knowing our own speed, we were able to estimate that the countless millions of porpoise we were seeing were just loafing along at about six or seven knots. It took us fully twenty minutes to pass through the line. There were no fish visible during the time and nothing to indicate the porpoise were feeding. We could only guess that it was a mass migration.

The top speed of a swimming porpoise is a subject that has, as have other aspects of this unusual creature, been debated down through the ages. Pliny the Elder said they were the swiftest of all animals, even including birds. More recent observers have estimated their speed as high as seventy-five miles an hour. Frequent observations by naval personnel have been reported in which they swear they have seen porpoise preceding ships that were steaming at speeds close to forty knots.

Some of the high speeds claimed for the porpoise have actually been partly true. It is known that on occasions they will place themselves in the bow wave thrown up by a rapidly moving ship and ride along on the wave much as a man on a surfboard will ride a breaker. Thus, the person witnessing such a sight could honestly be misled to believe the porpoise was actually swimming ahead of the ship. The United States Navy has conducted extensive studies in an effort to determine the best speed a porpoise of any type is capable of making. The conclusion is that a porpoise may be able to swim somewhere between fifteen and twenty knots.

Like most creatures, it is believed that porpoise had their origin in the sea and were content to remain there for a very long while. Perhaps back in the Devonian period, the predecessors of the modern porpoise found themselves confronted with shrinking seas, and out of necessity learned to live partly out of water for a while and then eventually became totally terrestrial, with flippers and tail flukes developing into true legs. Then, about fifty million years ago, they began to return to the sea. It is not known what form they took during their tenure on dry land, but evidence of this is found in the finger bones in their flippers.

A full-grown porpoise of perhaps three hundred pounds will consume about fifteen or twenty pounds of fish in order to remain in good physical condition. Normally, they feed only on live fish which they are able to catch. In captivity, however, they will consent to adjust their diet to include dead fish as long as those being offered are in strictly fresh condition. Porpoise trainers at aquariums have long used fresh fish as rewards when those they are teaching to do tricks have performed properly. Trainers have also found that individual porpoise develop a preference for certain types of fish and will be more willing to go through their lessons if rewarded with their choice.

While the porpoise has no vocal cords, he is capable of producing a wide variety of sounds that include clicks, barks, rasps, whistles, chirps, tweets, and mews; not forgetting the moans mentioned by both Aristotle and Pliny. These sounds are created by forcing air through the nasal passage and out the blowhole. The sounds are made for two basic reasons: one, to converse with one another, and two, for echolocation.

The porpoise has a highly developed echo-ranging sense that is remarkably similar to the electronic devices employed in modern ships. Like the bat, an active porpoise is constantly emitting blasts of high-frequency sound pulses, the echoes of which keep him informed as to how far he is from underwater obstructions. Basically, this is the same principal used in sonar and Fathometer devices.

With sonar the known factor is the speed at which sound waves travel through water. When a sound wave strikes a solid object, such as the hull of a ship, a fish, or the bottom of the sea, an echo is immediately returned and the time lapse is mechanically computed. Mechanical computation such as this is one of the marvels of science, since there are so many factors to be considered, i.e., the temperature of the water, the saline content of the water, the speed of the locator, and the speed of the target if the target happens to be moving, such as a ship underway or a swimming fish.

With an average condition when the water is of normal salinity and approximately 82° Fahrenheit, sound travels at 5,063 feet per second. Factors such as this must be computed in the porpoise brain in fractions of a second, and although extensive experiments have been made to outwit him, the porpoise sonar is virtually foolproof, so much so that man's electronic equipment seems clumsy by comparison. The porpoise's equipment is so accurate that he can tell instantly in totally black water whether the fish the experimenter is dropping in the water at the far end of the tank is a spot or a mullet. As proof of this, he will wait until the fish of his choice is dropped, whereupon he will immediately swim the length of the tank to take it.

As previously mentioned, tales dating back nearly two thousand years have repeatedly told of the porpoise attempting to make friends with and be helpful to man. Pliny the Younger related a story of a porpoise that became friendly with a group of people and even let a boy ride on his back, not only once, but time after time. Plutarch summed up man's early feeling toward the porpoise when he wrote: "To the dolphin alone, beyond all others, nature has granted what the best philosophers seek: friendship for no advantage. Though it has no need at all of any man, yet it is a genial friend to all and has helped many."

Graphic and recent proof of Plutarch's observation is the well-documented story of the famous porpoise named by the people of New Zealand, in the early part of the twentieth century, Pelorus Jack. No one knows why he decided to make friends with the human race, but ships making the passage along Cook Strait between the two main islands of New Zealand were regularly escorted by this celebrated porpoise. This was in the days before radar, sonar, and depth-finding devices, and ship captains had to con their vessels along the treacherous channel with lead line, guesswork, and plenty of luck. If the captain had made the passage before and noticed that Pelorus Jack was preceding his ship, he would simply follow the rolling fin of the porpoise that had elected himself to the duty of ship pilot. He always stuck to the center of the channel and never ventured into shallow water as long as he was "leading" a ship.

On one occasion, a passenger decided it might be fun to see if he could hit the porpoise with a rifle bullet. His action was stopped by the crew, and the New Zealand Government made it a crime for anyone else who decided to indulge in such irresponsible gun play.

Accidentally, Jack was struck by the prow of a ship and he was seen floundering away after the accident. Everyone thought he had been killed, but after an absence of nearly a year, he was once more back on his regular job, much to the delight of shipmasters, crews, and passengers who had come to love him.

As if to update Pliny's story about the porpoise that enjoyed frolicking with surf bathers, another New Zealand porpoise appeared in the waters of the seaside town of Opononi in 1956. It made daily visits to the resort and played with the bathers for as much as six hours each day. It played games with beach balls tossed by its human friends and allowed children to ride on its back. This cogenial porpoise came to a sad end when it was injured during some underwater blasting and finally stranded itself on some rocks where it died.

The town of Opononi, which had given an abbreviation of its name to the cetacean, went into mourning. Stores were closed and flags were flown at half-mast. Opo was buried with honors by the town and the grave is still maintained.

Dr. John C. Lilly, author of *Man and Dolphin,* along with dozens of other scientists believes that communication between man and porpoises is possible. Dr. Lilly has found that they make what he calls "humanoid emmissions" and in his book he says: "Within the next decade or two the human species will establish communication with another species: nonhuman, alien, possibly extraterrestrial, more probably marine . . ."

Also intensely interested in the porpoise is the United States Navy. Many are being used in its Man-in-the-Sea program and the Sealab project off the coast of California.

Oddly enough, man today knows more about outer space than he does about the vast ocean areas that cover the planet Earth. If, as many believe, lines of communication can be established with the porpoise, he may help bridge the vast void between water and land, and when this happens another, and perhaps even greater, *giant leap for mankind* will have been taken.

eleven 〰〰〰〰〰〰〰〰〰

〰〰〰〰〰

〰〰〰〰〰

THIRTY THOUSAND MILES OF FISHING

VIRGINIA

When I was still young, my father's work demanded that the family move from Florida, where I was born, to Virginia. I had already become fascinated with saltwater fishing, and it was not without reluctance that I thought we were bidding farewell to my favorite sport. How wrong can one be!

As soon as we were settled in our new home, my dad and I began to investigate some of the freshwater fishing in the James and Chickahominy rivers and other streams and ponds around Richmond. It was not long before we ferreted out some productive spots and began to catch a few fish from time to time. One of the laudable features of youth is its adaptability to change, and I was quite well satisfied with what we caught. I could not help but notice, however, that every time my dad caught a bass or a pickerel or a sunfish he would make some comparative reference to a snook, a Spanish mackerel, or a pompano.

One Friday afternoon he came home from work with a quart ice cream container and I was naturally interested. Handing it to me he told me to look inside. Removing the lid I was confused to discover the contents was considerably different from what I had logically guessed. It was filled to the brim with damp grass and several dozen long red worms.

They were entirely different from the common garden variety of angleworms or wigglers, as we called them. These were much less active, in fact they seemed to be rather sluggish. My dad told me he had stopped off at a tackle store down on Main Street and bought them and then he announced that we would go saltwater fishing.

Out came the tackle and the next morning before the sun was up we were on the road, driving in a northeasterly direction through the little town of Mechanicsville, on across the Pamunkey River, then the Mattaponi, until we reached a place called Brays Fork. There we turned off on a much smaller road and traveled southeast until we reached an even smaller settlement known as Center Cross. After this it was only two bumpy miles to Bowlers Wharf on the right bank of the Rappahannock River.

Hooray and hallelujah! At last we were back on salt water. It surely was not the Gulf of Mexico or the Atlantic Ocean, but it was brackish enough so that there were barnacles on the pilings and there was that certain smell that is always a part of tidal water.

There was a man there who ran a general store and rented rowboats for a dollar a day. Loading the tackle and quart of bloodworms aboard, we went out on the broad expanse of the Rappahannock to fish for croaker. My dad had been busy asking around about saltwater fishing and his informants back in Richmond had told him the croaker were really biting on bloodworms and the best place to go after them was Bowlers Wharf.

I don't know whether to attribute the success of the trip to expert advice, beginner's luck, or a combination of both, but before midafternoon both of us were actually weary of catching fish. There are those who maintain the croaker (the man at the general store called them *hardheads*) is not a game fish, but a three- or four-pounder can put up a real battle on light tackle. So, if he is fun to catch, who cares whether or not he is listed in the hall of fame? We returned sunburned, happy, exhausted, and with a gunny sack full of fish. They naturally had to be scaled and cleaned and a large portion distributed to neighbors and friends before we could call it a day.

My dad was pleased with the results of the fishing trip for more than the reason that we had had good luck. A genealogical shaking of the family tree reveals it has been deeply rooted in the Old Dominion for several centuries. An interesting fact that was brought to light in the tracing of the family history was that one of my forebears was killed in action during the American Revolution. That alone is certainly not unique, but the part that intrigues me is that he had the same full name as mine, my dad's, my grandfather's, and so on back. This early Thomas William Helm was a lieutenant under Brigadier General Daniel Morgan and he met his demise during the Battle of Cowpens when Morgan's army defeated the British under Colonel Tarleton in South Carolina in January of 1781.

The Battle of Cowpens is a far cry from catching that boatload of croakers on the Rappahannock, but by doing so my dad had scored a minor victory by proving to me that his native state had good saltwater fishing, along with its many other virtues. Admittedly, it was not an auspicious beginning for some of the angling that was to follow, but it was a step in the right direction.

While Virginia has only 112 miles of Atlantic coastline, it boasts that enormous body of water known as Chesapeake Bay, with 3,315 miles of shoreline. Anyone who doubts the magnitude of the Chesapeake has only to spend a couple of months ramming around this body of water as I did one summer in a sharpie. It will cause him to come away knowing why it is often called an inland sea instead of just a bay.

The Chesapeake is 195 miles in length and ranges in width from 3 to 22 miles. Its borders are generally shallow, but it is full of deep holes. One sounding in the bay has disclosed a depth of 174 feet.

A wide variety of fish are caught in Virginia waters. They range all the way from marlin, tarpon, and tuna down to flounder, trout, and white perch. Some of the world's best striped bass fishing (the natives call them rockfish) is in Virginia waters, and it has been estimated that at least 50 percent of the Atlantic stripers are spawned in the rivers flowing into the Chesapeake.

The inshore "big three" of Virginia are the black drum, channel bass, and cobia. The IGFA lists the world's record cobia as having been caught off Cape Charles. It weighed 102 pounds. It also lists the record

The Chesapeake Bay is frequently referred to as an "inland sea" and not without good reason because it is long and wide. It is also filled with many varieties of game fish. In the background of the above photo can be seen the fishing pier that extends out from one of the man-made islands that is part of the Bay Bridge-Tunnel that links the Norfolk area with the Eastern Shore.

black drum, weighing 98 pounds 8 ounces, caught out of Willis Wharf on the Eastern Shore in 1967, and the world's record for channel bass was set in 1949 at Cape Charles. The weight of this fish was 83 pounds. With all those record catches there is little wonder that Virginians indulge in a bit of discreet bragging about their "Big Three."

Added to the above there are at least a dozen other fine game fish taken from the Chesapeake and offshore waters. Included are the bluefish, kingfish, sheepshead, tautogs, and others.

One of the happiest years of my life was spent shortly after I had gone through my session with the Japanese in the Pacific. When I was discharged from the Navy my wife and I decided to take a sabbatical and strike out for Virginia. We really did not care where we stopped, just so long as it was close to the Chesapeake. After considerable searching we finally settled in a lonely little cabin on the Rappahannock. From there, we ranged far and wide, and if a man and wife ever fished more, I don't know who they are.

Saltwater fishing in Virginia covers a wide spectrum beginning, if you will, on the tidal reaches of the main rivers, including the Potomac,

Rappahannock, York, and James. Then there is fishing in the bay itself, with special attention given to the inshore side of the Eastern Shore. There is also surf fishing and today there are plenty of charter boats that will take you well offshore toward the Gulf Stream to look for the blue-water fish. To these methods you can add bridge and pier fishing.

It used to be that unless you were coming down from Maryland, the only way to get to the Eastern Shore was by ferry or some other kind of boat. All of that has changed now with the Chesapeake Bay Bridge-Tunnel. This 17.6-mile-long crossing over and under the bay between Virginia Beach and Cape Charles on the Eastern Shore is a unique trip in itself. It is a combination of two bridges, four man-made islands, and

This photo of the Chesapeake Bay Bridge-Tunnel was taken from the Eastern Shore of Virginia, northern terminus of the Bridge-Tunnel. The mainland of Virginia is the far horizon with the Atlantic Ocean on the left. Vital segments in the 17.6 mile long crossing that spans the mouth of the Bay are two bridges over the waterways used by pleasure and fishing craft; 12.2 miles of trestled roadways, 4 man-made islands and 2 tunnels.

two mile-long tunnels that lie submerged a hundred feet below the surface.

Each of the islands covers eight acres of land protected by huge rocks, and the fishing around them is growing better each year. Of special interest to the angler making this crossing is the 625-foot-long pier. There is no charge for its use, and because it is about three and a half miles out in the bay, it produces some unusual fishing. It is built out from one of the islands and very close to Thimble Shoal Channel, which is the main route followed by ocean-going ships bound for and leaving Hampton Roads.

Leaving the Norfolk area on this route across the mouth of Chesapeake Bay, the first point of natural land you reach is Fishermans Island, and the name sets the stage for what you are seeking. You then head due north across another superhighway bridge for the Cape Charles area, which is the southern tip of the Eastern Shore.

This section of Virginia is quite unlike the rest of the state, probably because it was for so long difficult to reach. The first settlers on the Eastern Shore in 1614 kept the Indian name of Accawmacke (spelled Accamack today), which means *the land beyond the waters.* Even the names of the islands are provocative, as are those of the inlets and passes. Some give lasting proof that the red man held a strong foothold there for a very long while, as witness names such as Great and Little Machipongo inlets and Onancock. Some of the towns bear names that are commonplace and easy to understand like Oyster, Eastville, and Willis Wharf. Again, you cannot help but speculate about Modest Town and Temperanceville.

If your piscatorial meanderings lead you toward the northern end of the Eastern Shore in late July you are in for an interesting and exciting event known as the Wild Pony Roundup of Chincoteague Island. The wild ponies are descendants of Spanish horses that survived shipwrecks. They spend the year grazing along the salt marshes of Assateague Island and on the last Wednesday and Thursday of the month they are rounded up and forced to swim across the inlet to Chincoteague, where they are put up for auction. It is quite a sight to see the "cowboys" hazing the herds by boats as they make the swim. Those that are not bought are chased back across the inlet and left alone for another year. I guess it is perfectly all right if you enjoy seeing a large number of frightened animals driven into the water, but there are other forms of sport more appealing to me.

Much depends on the weather, but the season for the drums begins in April when the front runners of the main school start to arrive. In May and early June they begin to show up en masse. By then the saltwater angler would do well to station himself at almost any point along the Eastern Shore.

Like the cobia, the black drum will never win any high honors in a beauty contest, but he is a real fighter. He heads for the Chesapeake with two objectives: one is to spawn and the other is to lard on the pounds as he feeds along the bottom on clams, oysters, and mussels. The wise angler knows this and baits his hooks with the flesh of such bivalves, or crabs, or other bottom-dwellers.

One of the wildest black-drum fishing trips I can remember was when a group of us were fishing on the south side of the channel between Cobb Island and the marshy expanse of Wreck Island. It was an early spring day and it seemed every drum in the Atlantic had decided to move in all at once. We had five boats in our little flotilla and we all started catching drum almost at the same instant.

We were using blue crabs for bait and drift fishing with the baited hooks bumping along the bottom. The boats were small open skiffs with two men to each and we were close enough to call to one another. What a scramble it was to see everybody rocking this way and that and shouting "Mine is bound to go over a hundred pounds!" and "Hi! Lookahere! I caught one without putting any bait on the hook!" There were other statements, too, well spiked with expletives that are part of the jargon of anglers who have suddenly come upon a large number of hungry fish. Izaak Walton, wont to frequently dwell on the "peace and patience" of fishermen, may conceivably have never been confronted with such a situation.

One of the stalwarts that day fell overboard and refused to let go his rod and reel. It looked for a while as if the 40-pound drum on the other end was determined to drag the fisherman out into the deep water of Southeast Channel, and he might have done so had not the other man in the boat managed to catch the back of his companion's jacket collar with a gaff and get him back to the shallow flats.

Just about the time the drum begin their invasion of Virginia's Eastern Shore waters, the spring run of channel bass elects to add to the confusion by moving in. Some natives of the Old Dominion call them red drum, which is really the proper name, but it does cause a certain amount of confusion for the angler who becomes disenchanted with local names for the same fish. It is doubtful, however, that Congress will take any action on this problem in the near future.

The favorite bait of the channel bass is blue crab, especially when the crabs are in the shedding stage. Since the black drum and the channel bass are in the same waters at the same time, the angler who likes to play both ends against the middle baits his hook with a clam-and-crab sandwich. It is made by attaching a chunk of clam to the back of a shedder crab, from which the loose shell has been removed. It is a bit like wearing a belt and suspenders at the same time, but it works wonders. If a drum comes along he is attracted by the clam, although he is also fond of crabs, and if a channel bass happens by he makes a dive for the crab.

Both fish roam the fringes of the outer islands during most of the run, but if a northeaster begins to beat the water to a churning froth, they cooperate with the fisherman by moving inside to the more sheltered waters on the bay side of the Eastern Shore, and the action continues unabated.

Sleek, trim, and fast, a skipjack sweeps along on a starboard tack across the waters of the Chesapeake Bay. Skipjacks are unique commercial fishing boats often used to dredge oysters from the bottom. When such work is in progress the sports fisherman will often find an abundance of game fish have moved in to reap the harvest of bottom-dwelling creatures that have been dislodged and are drifting with the tide.

The fall run of channel bass usually produces larger fish than the spring run. It is time then to switch to mullet or spot for bait. It is then that some really big ones are caught from ocean piers. Labor Day is the time when most of the tourists pack up and go back to wherever they came from, and the serious angler has the bass in vast numbers pretty much to himself. If he is the venturesome sort he may want to move south from Virginia Beach down along the coast toward North Carolina, with the whole Atlantic Ocean spread out before him.

Summer on the Chesapeake means cobia fishing at its very best. The nice thing about the cobia is that he ranges all over the "inland sea," from the Potomac down the western side to Hampton Roads, in the middle of the Bay, and all along the Eastern Shore. He comes here in June to spawn and arrives by the countless thousands. Live eels are one of the favored baits in Virginia waters, but almost as good are small fish and live shrimp.

During the time my wife and I lived beside the Rappahannock, we fished for them off from Gwynn Island at the mouth of the Piankatank River and later up at Windmill Point to the north. Of course, when you are thinking of these fish you will always keep in mind the record 102-pounder that was taken across the bay near Cape Charles.

Because cobia come big in the Chesapeake you will want to set out after them with medium tackle. Remember, however, that wherever there are cobia there are sure to be other scrappers such as spot, croaker, and flounder, so it is wise to include at least one set of light tackle to fill in the gaps.

No account of Virginia fishing would be anywhere near complete without a fair share of attention being paid to one of the fiercest battlers, and to my way of thinking, one of the prettiest fish that swims in salt water.

Stripers, or to use the Virginia name, rockfish, are anadromous like the salmon and return to fresh water to spawn. Some are present in the Chesapeake throughout the year, but the real fun begins in early March and continues on well into April. This is the time that the bragging-size striped bass begin to swing in close to shore near Virginia Beach, as they make their way into the Bay and on across to the numerous rivers on the western side.

When the action gets going around Virginia Beach, the surf fishermen don their waders and hip boots and pull on an extra wool shirt. Pier fishing springs into life, too, and when the rocks are running close to shore they will take just about any kind of lure or bait you toss their way. Metal squid are good, as are big feathered jigs, strips of cut mullet, shedder crabs, bloodworms, and just about anything fresh and fishy.

During the summer they are well up in the rivers and by early fall they are done with their spawning and begin their return to the ocean. One night in the middle of September, Dorothy and I were sitting on the front porch of our little cabin watching the vanishing flashes of an electrical storm that had made its way down the Rappahannock late that afternoon. Suddenly, there was a disturbance on the otherwise still surface of the river. The tide was at the flood stage and we could actually hear fish flopping about on the sandy beach.

Picking up a flashlight we went outside to investigate. To our astonishment we found hundreds of little flat minnows, silver in color and almost as flat and round as a silver dollar. I had seen them before; the native fishermen called them drumheads, apt, if not scientific.

My first thought was that we were about to witness something akin to a fish jubilee, such as periodically occurs in Alabama's Mobile Bay when vast numbers of fish, shrimp, and crabs desert the water and cast themselves ashore. Snapping off the flashlight we listened and swatted mosquitoes and gradually we became aware there was an even greater disturbance in the water some distance from the beach. Every minute or so another wave of the little silver minnows would come rushing out of the water and flip about on the sand.

It soon became obvious that some larger fish were driving them shoreward and in their hegira they were facing certain death by grounding themselves. I guessed there must be a large school of ravenous bluefish harassing the minnows. I knew there was only one way to find out.

Handing the flashlight to my wife, I admonished her to shade the beam if she found reason to turn it on. I did not want to frighten whatever it was out there with a strong light along an otherwise dark shoreline.

Hurrying back into the house, I grabbed a bait-casting rod and clipped a 4/0 hook on the snap swivel. Back on the beach I picked up one of the live drumheads and cast it out into the darkness as far as I could. It was not far enough. I could tell it was short of the main center of activity. Reeling in, I redoubled my effort, but the splash it made when it landed was still too close to the beach.

Without bothering to take off my shoes or roll up my pants I waded out into the dark water, knee deep at first and finally out until I was up to my waist. One cast after another and then bang! Something was headed back toward the Chesapeake and trying to drag me along behind.

The mosquitoes were having a feast and I was reasonably well convinced I was going to lose all my line—I knew I was going to have a blister on my thumb. Rod tip held high, I began backing slowly toward the beach, giving line only when I could not hold my thumb on the spool for another second.

It probably did not take more than ten minutes, but it seemed as though half the night passed before I dragged a big and furious striped bass onto the sand. By that time there were so many of the small fish on the beach that it was impossible to take a step without standing on three or four of them.

When Dorothy saw the striper I had caught she was literally torn between two fires. She desperately wanted to go out and catch one herself, but she said she would not wade out in that black water if the fish were made of pure gold. It was a reluctance I shared, but not to that extent, so out I went again. The second striper took the bait on the first cast, and I did not have as much trouble getting him to the beach.

My third fish must have been a giant, or maybe my thumb had simply taken all it could take. Whatever the case, the line stripped off in a steady rush while I cracked my knuckles trying to stop the spinning reel handle. Then it was all over. The line broke right at the point it was tied to the spool.

That was it for the night. One of the stripers weighed nine pounds and the other just a bit over seven. Before I could replace the line the action had ceased.

"I have never heard of so many fish on the beach," Dorothy said, sweeping the light along the sand. "We are certainly going to have a fine smelling camp tomorrow unless you get busy with a rake and a shovel."

Right at the moment I was too tired and mosquito bitten to care. What I was more intrigued by was the reason for the obviously large number of stripers that far up the river at that season of the year.

The next morning just about sunup we were awakened to the raucous squawking and cawing of several hundred crows. They had found the littered beach and called in all their relatives. Before we had finished breakfast the beach was clean and all the crows were gone. I can guess that while we were sleeping the raccoons and oppossums, which were plentiful in the area, had taken their share.

We had explored the mystery, taken two nice fish, and nature had relieved me of a chore I dreaded. I have never seen anything like it before or since, but it is just that kind of excitement that gives fishermen the reputation for treasuring truth so dearly that they are prone to use it sparingly.

But, what are you going to do under such conditions? Jump in the car and race to the nearest hamlet, wake up the community, send for a movie crew, and have everything thoroughly documented and attested to? No. You are going to try to find out what is causing the excitement and then keep telling the tale for as long as you live.

With so much fishing in the Chesapeake and rivers and through the islands of the Eastern Shore, it is almost easy to forget the blue-water fishing that is also an important part of saltwater angling in the Old Dominion. But it is there all right, and party and charter boats do a lively business from Norfolk, Hampton, and ports along the Eastern Shore.

The continental shelf slopes gently from the coast, and while there are many lumps and wrecks only a few miles offshore that provide excellent fishing for a wide variety of fish, the big game is considerably farther out.

Rich in plankton, the Labrador Current pours southward and about forty miles offshore it strikes the Gulf Stream. It is no place for the game fisherman during the winter months, but beginning in late spring vast numbers of marlin, both blue and white, begin to show. Along with them are the dolphin, wahoo, and others. Their abundance annually lures countless Virginians out onto the Atlantic.

NORTH CAROLINA

Unspoiled beaches, waters filled with a variety and abundance of saltwater fishes, and a land steeped in history are found in the state of North Carolina.

Summer is the "tourist season" when inland people migrate like the lemmings to its beautiful seacoast. And why not? Here they find superb fishing, swimming beaches, and points of interest that range from a trip to the top of a lighthouse to watching the nightly outdoor drama "The

Lost Colony," a play of such popularity that it is well into its third decade of summer-long performances. For the aviation buff there is Kill Devil Hill. Here, in 1903, Orville and Wilbur Wright gave wings to man on a powered flight that did not quite cover the distance of the wingspan of some of our jets of today.

The summer season in North Carolina, however, is little more than a figure of speech to the fisherman. His season generally begins on New Year's Day and continues around the calendar until the sixth day after Christmas. About the only differences he will notice will be the variations in the type of clothing he will find most comfortable, the variety of fish waiting to be caught, and the reduction in accommodation rates after Labor Day.

When I used the term "unspoiled beaches" at the beginning, I was not repeating the words of some dedicated chamber of commerce promoter, nor was I talking through my old fishing hat. As a matter of fact,

The Outer Banks of North Carolina offer the surf fisherman some of the best fishing to be found anywhere. The treacherous shoals of Cape Hatteras are known as the "Graveyard of the Atlantic" and not without good cause. Scattered from one end to the other, sometimes well offshore and again half-buried in the dry sand of the beach, are countless skeletons of long-dead ships.

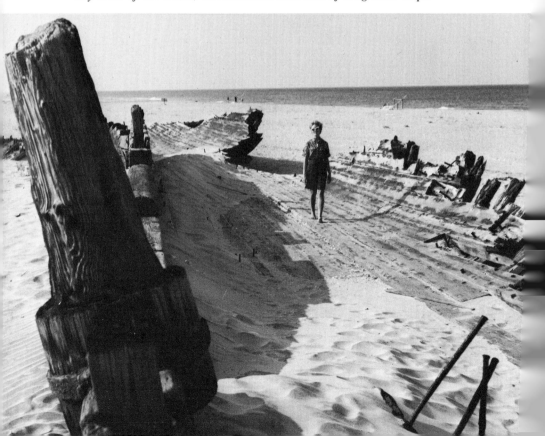

North Carolina has a bit over three hundred miles of shoreline actually pounded by the waves from the open Atlantic, and to keep the angler busy when the "outside" weather gets a little too rambunctious there is a whopping big 3,375 miles of "inside" tidal coastline. This includes the waters of Albemarle and Pamlico sounds, plus sheltered bays and rivers along the coast. That, my friend, adds up to a lot of fishable water.

The entire eastern coast of North Carolina is shielded from the fury of the open Atlantic by a series of islands that bend far out into the ocean. The north end of the state begins with a wavering stretch of sand dunes that shield the slightly brackish water of Currituck Sound, which, by the way, produces some of the best large-mouth bass fishing to be found anywhere along the eastern states.

If you are traveling south with saltwater fishing in mind, you will follow U.S. Highway 158 all the way down the western side of Currituck Sound to Powells Point where the highway bends sharply to the east and crosses the water to Bodie Island. It is just after you again head south with the Atlantic on your left and Albemarle Sound on the right that you will almost certainly stop for at least a brief visit at the National Memorial to the Wright brothers.

Moving on down the length of Bodie Island to Whalebone Junction you will be tempted to swing right on an excellent highway that will carry you across narrow Roanoke Sound to Roanoke Island, up to the town of Manteo and then three miles farther on to the site of Sir Walter Raleigh's ill-fated attempts to establish the first English colony in America. Here on August 18, 1587, Virginia Dare was born, the first child of English parentage to be born in the New World. Fort Raleigh, as it is now known, was designated a National Historic Site in 1941.

Back across Roanoke Sound you will continue south along Bodie Island to Oregon Inlet that separates Bodie from Hatteras and provides the first doorway for the waters of the Atlantic to rush into Pamlico Sound. The temptation to stop and start fishing right there at Oregon Inlet will be almost too strong to resist, but if you can abstain for a while longer lets continue south along Hatteras Island. For about the next forty miles you will be well out into the Atlantic and as you drive along you will be pleasantly comforted with the knowledge that the long, thin island is a National Seashore area. It is as primitive today as it was thousands of years ago and wise legislation has decreed that it will remain so. Of course, it is not just one long unbroken stretch of roadway

The Cape Hatteras lighthouse is 208 feet high, the tallest of any on the American coast. Its beacon is visible 20 miles at sea and warns shipping of the dangerous Diamond Shoals. The nearness to the Gulf Stream means superb fishing.

along the sand dunes. Here and there, miles apart, are small seacoast villages with such names as Rodanthe, Waves, Salvo, and Avon, with occasional fishing piers that reach out into the ocean.

After those aforementioned forty miles have rolled up on your odometer, you will arrive at Cape Hatteras and the 208-foot-tall barber pole lighthouse of the same name. It is the tallest lighthouse on the American coast, with a beacon that is visible twenty miles at sea to warn shipping of the treacherous Diamond Shoals, part of the famed Graveyard of the Atlantic. Interesting, too, is the fact that through an arrangement between the Cape Hatteras National Seashore and the United States Coast Guard, you can visit the lighthouse and look far out into the Atlantic to the east and across Pamlico Sound to the mainland of North Carolina to the west.

But your ocean voyage on wheels is not yet finished. There is a free ferry that will carry you across Hatteras Inlet to Ocracoke Island. About an additional fifteen miles of driving in a southwest direction will take you to the town of Ocracoke, where you will find a campground,

Coast Guard station, and the Ocracoke lighthouse.

Here it is, tucked just inside the sheltered waters at the end of the island, that Captain Edward Teach, better known as the pirate Black-beard, holed up after his raids on shipping along the Atlantic coast and the Caribbean. It was here, too, that the fierce old sea rover fought his last and fatal duel in 1718 when he crossed swords with Lieutenant Maynard. When the sailors under Maynard's command subdued the pirate crew, the young lieutenant had Blackbeard's head removed and tied to the bowsprit of his sloop. Thus he sailed proudly back to Virginia to collect a reward from the governor and bring to a close another chapter in pirate history.

Ocracoke is only the midway point in the string of barrier islands that fringe the North Carolina coast, but it is as far as you can go by car. From there on you can launch your boat and continue on down the sheltered waters on the inside of Portsmouth Island to Swash Inlet and thence to Cape Lookout at the south end of Core Bank. For that matter, the string of islands extends to Cape Fear lighthouse off the southern tip of Smith Island. But, unless you are willing to undertake and are equipped for much boat travel, your best bet might be to take the toll ferry at Ocracoke across to Cedar Island and continue by car to the southern end of the state, stopping, of course, at numerous good fishing locations.

Chances are that on your way down from Kill Devil Hill you will have seen so many interesting places to fish that you will turn around and head back up the Outer Banks to give some of them a whirl.

I think the people who live in the few villages along the Outer Banks are some of the most interesting I have ever met. If, however, you are expecting a lot of hurly-burly and "Oh, we are so delighted to see you," as is part and parcel of many popular fishing and boating resorts, you had best revise your thinking. This is not to suggest in the least that the natives are unfriendly. They and their predecessors, however, have lived a harsh life in an even harsher land that dates back for several centuries. They have not needed the tourist dollar in all that time and they feel confident they can still survive if they never see another tourist.

Many of the old-timers speak with a bit of an accent that is faintly tinged with the British clip. A good number are descendants of survivors of English ships that foundered on the shoals years ago. Some were "wreckers," who risked their lives in whaleboats to salvage cargo from ships that were breaking up in fierce storms. In the process they also saved the lives of otherwise doomed people.

Stop in quaint old-world villages built among the dunes, spotted here and there with gnarled oaks that shade winding streets and small stores, and you will know you are among fishermen and men of the sea. If you visit a small combination hardware and tackle store and ask how the channel bass (you would do well to call them *drum*) are hitting or something about the bluefish, don't look for an exuberant oration on how you can expect to catch half the ocean's population without half trying. More likely you will be answered with a brief "pretty fair," or "just so-so," and don't be surprised if you are told not to waste your time, or even advised to try another location thirty or forty miles distant.

Bear in mind that these people are not running a carnival concession, and one of the worst mistakes the outsider can make is to try to give the impression that he knows everything about their brand of fishing. Conversely, if these Outer Bankmen sense you are genuinely interested in learning some of the peculiarities of their own special fishing conditions they can and will save you a world of time and false starts.

Such an attitude has long ago endeared the true natives of this coastline to my heart.

Channel bass are one of the prime targets of the angler who fishes the Outer Banks. The season for these fish, and we are talking about big ones in the 40- and 50-pound class, as well as the smaller ones, actually begins in late March and runs on through the month of June. They are practically nonexistent on the outside during the summer months, but there is a southbound run along about mid-September, and under normal conditions the fall season will remain good well into December.

Of equal importance, so far as the sport fisherman is concerned, is the striped bass. Albemarle Sound is rated as having a striped bass population second only to Chesapeake Bay. Hot spots are the mouths of the numerous rivers emptying into the sound as well as in the sound itself. Good small-boat fishing is to be found on both sides of Roanoke Island. My choice of headquarters for striped bass fishing is Manns Harbor. If you are coming from the inland, such as Raleigh or Durham, just pick up Route 64 and follow it almost due east until you reach Manns Harbor. There you will find plenty of boats and other necessary accommodations.

Before writing off the fall and spring months, it is important to mention the piers that are scattered along the Atlantic side of the Outer Banks. Most are privately owned and available to the public at a reasonable fee. The important point is that you get your money's worth on these piers and the variety of fish caught from them is considerable. In November of 1967 Joseph J. Menzaco set an International Game Fish Association world record in the 20-pound-line class when he landed a 21½-pound bluefish while fishing from a pier at Kitty Hawk. The piers are well equipped with bait, tackle, lunch counters, and practically everything the angler will need—including fish.

While on the subject of IGFA record catches, in addition to the aforementioned bluefish the state of North Carolina is high on the list with numerous record catches of weakfish, black drum, cobia, and channel bass, with an 810-pound blue marlin caught off Hatteras in June of 1962 by Gary Stukes.

If you are part of that vast army of fishermen who head for North Carolina to spend your summer vacation, you have two choices and

The wind-rippled sand of massive dunes created with stands of sea oats. It might be anywhere from Virginia's Eastern Shore to Padre Island off the coast of Texas.

much depends on whether you like bay fishing or want to head out toward the Gulf Stream. If it is small boats and smooth water you want, then look to Pamlico and Albemarle sounds. You can rent boats or launch your own at places such as Manns Harbor on the mainland across from Roanoke Island or any of a number of villages along the Outer Banks all the way down Hatteras Island and Ocracoke. The fish you will be after primarily will be such scrappers as Spanish mackerel, flounders, spot, bluefish, and whiting. Don't expect record-size blues, such as those that cruise the Atlantic in the colder months, but a school of 2- and 3-pound bluefish can provide the light-tackle angler with plenty of excitement.

For those who favor the open Atlantic, the best solution is to make reservations for a trip out on a charter boat. Starting at the lower end of the state, boats of this type can be found anywhere from towns along the Cape Fear River near New Hanover and Wilmington all the way down to Southport. They will take you out on the open ocean past Cape Fear. Moving north toward Morehead City you will find other boats that fish the vicinity of Cape Lookout. North of there we will presume you have made your trip down the Outer Banks by car and will try your luck from the northern end beginning with boats leaving through Oregon Inlet. Farther south it will be Cape Hatteras and Ocracoke Inlet. By the way, the Gulf Stream flows very close to Cape Hatteras. In general, it ranges anywhere from twelve to thirty miles from shore, which is the closest it comes to land anywhere between Florida and Cape Cod.

Whether you go all the way out to the Stream or fish the waters between, you are in an area where the variety of fish reads like a piscatorial *Who's Who.* Bluefish, bonito, cobia, croaker, grouper, dolphin, sailfish, kingfish, Spanish mackerel, tarpon, sea bass, and wahoo are just a few to be mentioned. And who knows but what you may be the one to top that 810-pound blue marlin. It is here, too, that productive tuna fishing begins.

In this "Graveyard of the Atlantic" the bottom is strewn with the rusting and broken hulks of so many ships that no accurate count could ever be made. You can bet, however, that your charter-boat skipper has several favorites staked out in his mind and marked on his charts and if he knows what he is doing, which 99 percent of them do, it is practically impossible not to catch fish and in goodly numbers.

One word of caution is in order here when it comes to venturing out far from shore in your own boat. Unless you are an expert and your boat is of sufficient seaworthiness, DON'T TRY IT. Off Cape Hatteras is one of the places where the Labrador Current and the Gulf Stream collide, and while it provides just what the big game fish are looking for, it can also quite suddenly produce some wild water that will put your seamanship to the acid test.

The charter-boat fishermen can actually "smell" bad weather and they know when to get going and when to stay put. Far better to spend a few extra dollars and feel reasonably certain of a fun-filled trip with a lot of fish in the box than to add your boat to the broken bones of ships that got into trouble and are forever asleep in the deep.

While on the subject of fishing along the Outer Banks, there is another admonishment that will be heeded by many and ignored by others. All along the stretch of islands there are numerous beautiful campsites. There are few restrictions and if you elect to be a loner you can pull off the highway at some deserted spot and set up your own fishing headquarters. However, unless your transportation is in the four-wheel drive class or is a beach buggy with large tires and low pressure, watch out! Getting stuck in beach sand is not my idea of a way to begin or end a fishing trip.

One afternoon as I rolled merrily along the highway between the towns of Salvo and Avon, I noticed a recent model car sitting in a peculiar position beside the road. It was a late summer day and hot as the hinges on the front gate of Tophet. My first impulse was to pass on by, but the sight of a man, woman, and three children ranging in age from nine to fourteen scrambling around the car changed my mind.

Selecting a firm shoulder of the road, I left the air-conditioned comfort of my station wagon and crossed the highway to where the five members of an obviously abject family were working at the Sisyphean task of trying to extract their car from the clutching sugar sand. The engine was near the boiling point and the car was so deeply imbedded that the rear wheels were totally out of sight. Around it were boards, pieces of driftwood, great wads of seaweed, and the car's jack, all apparently unsuccessfully tried and tossed to one side. The five people, especially the man and woman, appeared on the verge of complete exhaustion.

"We've done everything," the man said as I walked near, "and all of it's been wrong."

I had an Army surplus trench shovel in my wagon, but one look at the foundered car convinced me that even that would just prolong the agony and nothing would be accomplished.

"If we only hadn't decided to stop and let the children go for a swim," the woman lamented almost in tears. "My husband has a very important business call to make at seven o'clock and if he misses it he will be in serious trouble with his company."

"The best I can offer is to take all of you back to the nearest town," I said.

The offer was quickly accepted and while I was helping to transfer a couple of suitcases to my car I happened to look down the highway and, wonder of wonders, a huge wrecker was plodding its way northward. Flagging down the truck, I pointed to the disabled car in the sand.

"Shouldn't take mor'n ten minutes to get 'em out," the driver said cheerfully. "Lucky I happened along. I been down at Hatteras all day working on my boat."

Such coincidences are rare and not to be depended on. It is only fair to mention that the treacherousness of driving a conventional car onto the soft sand of a beach is not restricted to the Outer Banks of North Carolina. It can and does happen continuously all the way along the coastline of any state with sandy beaches. Numerous are the cases of overheated engines, lost tempers, wasted time, and occasional heart attacks.

Even with the help of a second car to assist, the problem is not easily resolved and often results in the good Samaritan getting stuck also. There are many tricks that sometimes help, such as letting about half of the air out of the rear tires, jacking the car up by placing the jack base on a wide board to keep it from sinking, and putting planks under the wheels, then shifting into low gear and either backing or proceeding at a cautious pace. In the long run, the only answer is to stay out of the sand no matter how inviting and harmless it looks.

Many of the towns along the Outer Banks have garages where beach buggies may be rented by the day or week at a reasonable price. Thus equipped you can roll along the highway until you find a stretch that seems to be just what you are looking for and then roll fearlessly onto the sand. Another valuable piece of equipment is a tent that can be quickly erected without a lot of fuss and bother. It makes a nice retreat from the blistering sun or periods of bad weather. Just be certain to replace those regulation tent stakes with ones at least three times as long. Otherwise, in a stout breeze they are almost certain to pull out of the sand.

Some of the most delightful combination fishing and camping trips my wife and I have ever enjoyed have been along the Outer Banks. With the beach buggy snugged in beside a twisted live oak, and canvas awning stretched out from the side to guyed poles, it is pretty near heaven to sit there in canvas chairs and watch the mantle of night unfold from far out across the Atlantic. Close by, in a cluster of wax myrtle and yaupon, a family of raccoons begins to organize for a night's hunting. The myrtle berries ripen in the fall and you remember that the old-timers used to gather them to make candles.

While you sit there listening to the wind and the surf thudding against the beach, you can almost hear the ghosts of the Outer Banks beginning to move about. Perhaps they are the crew of that old skeleton of a long-dead ship you found half buried in the sand. Again, if you listen carefully you can hear the *chunk, chunk, chunk* of some of Blackbeard's pirates digging a hole with their shovels to hide a box of jewels and coins. But most of all, you listen for the change in the sound of the waves that will tell you when the tide is approaching the flood stage.

Before the sun went down you remembered to set up some driftwood markers to pinpoint the location of the most likely looking swash channels, and there is just enough time to swallow a quick cup of coffee, get the bait out of the ice chest, and see if this is the night to catch that record-size channel bass. Inwardly you know you will have just as much fun with several smaller ones. Think how happy the raccoon family will be when you return and toss the heads and backbones over into the myrtle thicket.

Of course you will roam the beach until the wee hours of the morning and wear your arms out casting and reeling in and you will promise yourself that you will sleep until noon, but you won't. Just about the time you are halfway into dreamland the piercing sun will boil up out of the Atlantic, set fire to the waves, and the day will be alive.

Never mind. As you watch a freighter riding up the Gulf Stream bound for New Bedford or London you will promise yourself a nap in the afternoon. But, sure as fate, some brother angler will come by about that time and tell you how many bluefish he caught last night down near the lighthouse or the inlet and so you let the nap go by the board while you move your rolling camp to this location.

SOUTH CAROLINA

The time was 4:30 in the morning. The date was April 12, 1861. The place was Charleston Harbor, South Carolina. It would have been a good morning to row a skiff out to the flats and fish for speckled trout with cane poles, cork bobbers, and live minnows. Instead, the predawn stillness was shattered with the thunder of cannon fire.

President Davis of the Confederacy had issued orders to General P.G.T. Beauregard to demand that Major Robert Anderson surrender Fort Sumter. Major Anderson refused and General Beauregard commanded nineteen batteries to open fire. On Sunday afternoon two days later, Major Anderson surrendered the fort to General Beauregard. It was not a weekend for fishing in Charleston Harbor. America's bloodiest war had begun.

Well over a century has passed since that fateful April weekend, but the coastline of South Carolina is remarkably unchanged. The native South Carolinians had known the beautiful stretch of island-studded coastline since the first band of about one hundred fifty people went ashore at Albemarle Point on the Ashley River. This landing near Charleston in 1670 was the beginning of the first English settlement in South Carolina. The early pioneers and the generations that followed them knew that excellent fishing was waiting for the angler at almost any location along the coast.

The odd part about it is that during the more than three centuries of civilization, saltwater fishing in South Carolina was for a long time considered almost entirely in the province of commercial fishermen. It has been only in the recent past that the state awakened to the fact that sport fishing was steadily becoming one of its most valuable assets.

The actual coastline facing the Atlantic is only 187 miles in length, the tidal shoreline is far greater with a total of 2,876 miles. All the fish that are permanent residents of Virginia, North Carolina, Georgia, and a large number of the Florida fishes are found in abundance in South Carolina waters. Nobody tried to keep this bounty a secret. It was just one of those natural resources that long went unnoticed by the general angling public.

In a report prepared for the state in 1965 by John Kretschmer, it was pointed out that South Carolina's saltwater sport fisheries were only beginning really to develop, but the needs and demands of saltwater anglers were increasing rapidly. The door was commencing to open. In

1969 another comprehensive report was prepared under the direction of Charles M. Bearden, division chief of the South Carolina Wildlife Resources Department. In this report, Bearden estimated that in the previous year $15 million was spent by South Carolina anglers directly on saltwater sport fishing. He reiterated that the needs of saltwater anglers were growing at a rapid pace all along the coast.

As many a United States Marine who has gone through training at Parris Island near the town of Beaufort will testify, there is plenty of good fishing in the southern part of the state. There are a few fair to good boat landings on U.S. 278 that lead out to Hilton Head Island and U.S. 21 to Hunting Island State Park. Party and charter boats operate out of both Beaufort and Hilton Head.

On either of these islands the angler has the choice of fishing the sheltered waters on the inside or venturing out into the Atlantic either by boat or with surf casting rod from the beach. One of the largest bays at the southern end of the state is St. Helena Sound. It separates Hunting Island and Edisto Beach State Park. The sound is about eight miles wide where it meets the ocean and several rivers empty into it. In order to reach this excellent fishing area, those who are based in Charleston will go west on U.S. 17 to the town of Osborn where they turn south on State Road 174 for about twenty-five miles. This road passes through some of the real wilderness of southern South Carolina, beautiful Old South countryside, and terminates on the Atlantic beach. Here also is an excellent pier.

Charleston is, of course, the principal seacoast city in the state, and charter boats are to be found in sufficient numbers in the harbor, principally at the municipal yacht basin and Shem Creek near Mt. Pleasant. Another good charter- and party-boat anchorage is at Georgetown on Winyah Bay. This bay, with its islands, channels, and flats is also a good spot for small-boat fishing.

While not nearly so numerous as in other states, the charter- and party-boat fishing fleet is growing and the skippers are, by and large, men who know their trade well. North of Georgetown the two main boating centers are Murrells Inlet and Little River. Both are right on U.S. 17, which parallels the coast from Pawleys Island up to North Carolina.

Also along this same stretch of beach are at least a dozen piers, including one owned by the state at Myrtle Beach. A recent count was made at this pier, and the score showed it played host to fifty thousand anglers in just one year. Multiply that by the total number of piers and it is evident that this type of fishing is a popular form of angling along the South Carolina coast. The season begins in late spring and continues until cold weather sets in, generally in mid-October.

The fish most often caught from the piers include croaker, flounder, whiting, pompano, drum, trout, sheepshead, spot, bluefish, and channel bass. At times the action becomes fast and furious when tarpon, Spanish and king mackerels, and cobia move within the range of the pier fisherman's line.

Bridge fishing is another popular method of angling in the state. Because of the numerous inlets and rivers that make their way to the Atlantic, bridges are plentiful. In some cases it is well to check with the state Fish and Game Department to ascertain whether or not you are fishing in fresh or salt water. This, of course, applies to many other states, and at times you can fish on one side of the bridge and probably have no need for a fishing license because it is designated as salt water. On the other side you may be required to have a freshwater fishing license.

One of our most memorable trips was a short while back when Dorothy and I, with another couple, spent nearly two weeks in the national forest recreation campsites from Bull Bay north a few miles to the south fork of the Santee River bridge. It was early fall and I had a twofold reason for choosing this region. The first was that I knew it to be highly fishable so far as salt water was concerned. The second dated back a few years to a time when I was on the editorial staff of a national magazine.

One day, with the usual stack of mail addressed to the editor was a brown manila envelope with the return address of a well-known northern prison. Inside was a neatly typed fiction story about life in the Santee River swamp country. The story had no byline, but in the upper left-hand corner was the writer's prison number.

Several of us read the story and found ourselves engrossed in a hauntingly beautiful tale of exciting adventure. There was no way to tell for sure whether the nameless writer had simply chosen the region with the same caprice as Stephen Foster chose the Swannee River as the setting for his song "Old Folks At Home" or whether he had actually lived in the area and was writing from first-hand knowledge. It did not really matter, since the story was so well plotted and highly readable. The next step was to send the author a check for his story, but no one in the magazine's bookkeeping department had ever been called upon to make a check out to a number.

A letter was written to the prison and sent along with the check, asking the prison warden for some information about the inmate. The reply was polite, but curt. No information could, or would, be released. The "number" sent us another story and another and another. We were never able to find the faintest clue to his identity.

Now I could not resist the urge to put a light skiff in the water and travel back into the Santee swamp country. About ten miles west of Route 17 the river forks, and from that junction on upstream we were in some of the wildest and most exciting country I have ever seen. I found it rivaled only by parts of the Everglades and the bayou country of Louisiana that I have explored.

The Santee from Lake Marion to the coast is sixty miles long, and the primordial basin known as the Santee Swamp covers hundreds of square miles. There are people living in the region: herders who "run hogs." The semidomesticated breed of wild swine are known locally as razorbacks and rooters. Now and then we would catch a glimpse of some of these hogs, but we did not see one human being except when we passed under the bridge where Route 41 crosses the river.

As we pushed our way up the ocher-colored stream, the sound of the small outboard seemed to violate the dignity of a land strangely remote from today's world. We traveled as far as time and our gasoline supply would permit. At night we stretched jungle hammocks between trees, and seldom has a campfire seemed so important. The time was deep enough into autumn so that insects did not present a problem, but all around us we could hear sounds of wildlife. At one point, about two in the morning when the fire had dwindled to glowing orbs and sleep had finally settled over our camp, we were nearly frightened out of our wits.

The excitement began with the heavy rattling and cracking of the brush around us, and suddenly there were squeals and snorts from heavy-bodied shadowy creatures racing through our campsite. With hammocks swinging wildly, we grabbed flashlights and guns and halfway expected we were being attacked by "monsters from the black lagoon."

Of course, they were only wild hogs, but the effect on our nerves was the same as if the raid had been composed of a pack of wolves. We beat on pots and pans and shouted and tried to get the fire going, and then almost as quickly as they had come, the drove was gone.

We liked the trip back down the Santee much better because we were able to drift with the current in places and again we would run the outboard just a bit over the idling speed. All about us were forests that had never been molested by ax and saw. Pines, gums, live oaks with long streamers of Spanish moss mingled with one another. On several occasions, while drifting and watching the ever-changing array of bird-life, turtles, and water snakes, we caught sight of deer and watched them go bounding off with their white flags flashing through the underbrush. The size of some of the trees, especially the cypress, was unbelievable.

It is estimated by government research that South Carolina and Georgia contain some of the largest cypress trees to be found anywhere. One in Seminole County, Florida, has a diameter of over seventeen feet and is estimated to be three thousand five hundred years old. Drifting along and marveling at the arboreal giants we passed from time to time, it was almost eerie to realize they had been standing as silent gray sentinels since the coming of Christ and perhaps even before. To such old behemoths the founding of that first English colony in 1670 must seem as only yesterday in the state's history.

When the trip was done and we were back near the coast, I had satisfied myself of one thing. The "number" who wrote of the Santee Swamp had surely lived back in there long enough to have learned every smell and sound and he probably could have vanished in the fastness while you were looking at him. I wondered more than once during our trip if he were perhaps free now and back there, watching us. Somehow, I found myself hoping he was, maybe gathering additional material for other tales.

Any saltwater fisherman knows that his chances of catching more and a wider variety of fish are increased if he fishes in the vicinity of a sunken wreck or some kind of underwater obstruction that forms a natural reef. In this age when the disposal of nondecomposable litter is becoming an ever-increasing problem, the construction of artificial reefs is often tantamount to killing two birds with one stone, or to give the hackneyed adage more piscatorial flavor, it might be paraphrased to read *catching two fish with one hook.*

A scientifically constructed artificial reef is not an oceanic dump heap. Only certain types of material are suitable, and if properly planned, it will in no way tread on the toe of ecology. In fact, it has the reverse effect by providing sanctuaries that improve conditions just as wildlife preserves offer safe havens for terrestrial creatures as well as nesting grounds for birds.

Several states have pioneered in the construction of artificial reefs, and South Carolina Wildlife Resources Commission has, with assistance from several federal agencies including the United States Bureau of Sport Fisheries and Wildlife and the United States Bureau of Outdoor Recreation, taken important steps in reef building.

Among the types of junk ideally suited for such construction are old automobile bodies, slabs of concrete pavement, large pipes of the type that may have served their usefulness as water mains, rubber tires, hulls of metal boats, discarded machinery, and other material of a similar nature. Left ashore, such rubbish is often difficult to dispose of and generally results in unsightly areas of litter. Barged offshore and dumped in suitable locations, it is almost instantly transformed into highly desirable accommodations for a vast array of sea creatures.

Drops, or artificial reefs, reasonably close to shore, attract such game fish as cobia, channel bass, drum, sheepshead, and trout. Those farther offshore provide a gathering place for amberjack, barracuda, bluefish, mackerel, and many others.

As a safeguard to navigation, it is important that artificial reefs be accurately marked and their location shown on United States Coast and Geodetic charts. Naturally, well-planned drops are in water sufficiently deep so as not to present obstructions that might be struck by shipping. They frequently do result in fouled anchors, and thus the importance of accurate charting.

South Carolina has constructed numerous artificial reefs, with some of the best being found off Murrells Inlet, Georgetown, Charleston, as well as Fripp and Hilton Head Islands. There are others and many more in the planning and actual construction stages. It is a costly undertaking to transport suitable amounts of junk to specific offshore locations, but the improvement in the fishing is well worth the expenditure.

GEORGIA

The coast of Georgia resembles the pieces of a giant jigsaw puzzle scattered helter-skelter in the form of little islands, middle-size islands, and several big islands. The result is about a hundred miles of Atlantic beach and well over two thousand miles of tidal shoreline.

One of the most delightful and intriguing combination fishing and camping ventures I have ever had the privilege of enjoying was a boat trip on the Intracoastal Waterway along the Georgia coast. It was the middle of spring and the weather could not possibly have been more cooperative, with balmy days and cool nights. By pushing we could have covered the route in two or three days. Our objective, however, was not to see how fast we could do it, but rather how much we could find to attract our attention. As a result, we indulged ourselves in three full weeks of rambling along through a waterland contrast.

At times we would move ahead at full throttle for five or ten miles and then stop for the night. Occasionally, when we found what seemed to be an island idyll, we would moor and set up more than a temporary camp.

From St. Marys River to the south where we had started, north to our destination of Savannah, we were alternately within hailing distance of civilization and as far away as if we were in a remote stretch of the Malay archipelago. Unlike most other coastal states, Georgia does not have a major highway within sight of the Atlantic. There are, however, numerous roads, some very good, leading down to the coast.

Much like the lower half of South Carolina, the coastline of Georgia is not overly tourist oriented. There are places scattered about where the fisherman traveling by automobile can turn off a north-south highway and reach salt water in a short while. But don't expect the endless parade of neon-lighted signs that beckon the traveler to pull into the next parking lot and dive into the ocean before the engine cools.

The first quarter of our trip northward was along Cumberland Sound behind the big and lonely island of the same name. We found this to be truly southern wilderness country. At places the nearest approach to anything that might resemble the coast was vast marshes of rank grass and twisted bushes. Again, the land rose, and seemingly endless forests of pines and live oaks took over. It was a region where we found it is important to pay close attention to the chart and compass. Not pressed for time, we took interesting detours when the tide was right and made our way around the back side of the numerous small islands.

All along the coast we found numerous tidal creeks and rivers emptying into the bays and inlets, and it was a real challenge to move slowly through waters uncharted except by those living back in the hammocks or on the many bluffs. Even before we saw the first sign of civilization, we often were aware that at least some other human had been there before. Some of these signs were little more than a row of stakes driven into the bottom and flagged with bits of white cloth, no doubt put there to indicate the best passage to a cabin or small settlement.

One typical example was Harrietts Bluff. We came to this by winding our way up Crooked River from the sound. This delightful spot can also be reached by car when traveling along U.S.17 by turning just north of the town of Kingsland and heading east. A launching ramp is there and generally bait to be had, but no fleets of sleek charter boats and party boats are waiting to rush you out onto the broad Atlantic. As in most Georgia towns, the people are genuinely friendly, and it is a good place to replenish your water supply and talk over the local fishing conditions with whoever happens to be around at the time.

Moving north on our trip, we came to the first large bay, St. Andrew Sound, at the mouth of the Satilla River. Here is a place where remote beach camping is possible on the beautiful stretch of sand along the outer coast of Cumberland Island.

The sound offers excellent fishing, but facilities are virtually nonexistent until one crosses to Jekyll Island to the north. Here, the line of contrast is so sharply drawn as to be startling. In a few short miles we had parted the curtain separating true wilderness from up-to-the-minute vacation-style modern civilization.

Brunswick is one of Georgia's two important seaports, but for the saltwater fisherman it is important because it is the gateway to three of the state's most tourist-minded islands.

Once the islands were the exclusive retreats of millionaires, and the way was barred to the general public. Today, the picture is completely changed, and while these resort islands boast numerous and unexcelled tourist accommodations, they have not suffered the fate of so many southern coastal resorts by becoming overcommercialized. All are connected to the mainland with first-class highways leading seaward from Brunswick.

Important to the angler is the fact that in and around Brunswick, as well as on the three vacation islands, there are numerous facilities that pertain to the sport of saltwater fishing. There are charter and party boats, small boat rentals, as well as launching ramps, fuel, and bait. Also, guides are available, and for the newcomer to the Georgia coast these men can be well worth the reasonable fee they charge for their services. For those interested in surf fishing, the islands offer a vast expanse of picturesque and productive shoreline.

Continuing northward along the Intracoastal Waterway, we found that we were once more back in primitive country largely devoid of the amenities of civilization. We found a few exceptions, but they were infrequent except in the area of South Newport, which can be reached by car on U.S. 17 and Interstate 95. Good stopovers are to be found at Shellman Bluff and Harris Neck. From either of these two locations it is only a short run to Sapelo Sound. After leaving the Sound, facilities were again spotty and far between until Savannah was reached.

Throughout the entire trip those of us who explored the Georgia coast found excellent fishing all along the way. The types of fish and methods of fishing for them are much the same in Georgia as in South and North Carolina. Inshore, the speckled trout and channel bass are the most plentiful of the game fishes, with sheepshead and flounder running a close second. In season—spring, summer, and fall—there is the migration of Spanish mackerel, bluefish, and tarpon in reasonable numbers.

Offshore, also in season, the blue water angler can expect to catch king mackerel, snapper, grouper, as well as the ever-present chance of tying into a sailfish, dolphin, and other followers of the Gulf Stream.

During the three-week trip that we made several years ago we happened, just by luck, to reach Ossabaw Sound at precisely the same time as a vast school of striped bass. Quite unintentionally, we hooked a couple of them out in the sound and this whetted our appetite. As a result, we decided to spend a few days in the area, and the longer we fished the more stripers we found. There was no question but that they were moving up into the brackish water of the Ogeechee River and probably the Little Ogeechee. Because of the abundant action around the mouth of the larger of the two rivers, we did not bother to investigate the possibilities anywhere else. It was one of those all too rare incidences when we were catching all the fish, and big ones at that, that we could possibly handle, so it seemed a waste of time and energy to look elsewhere.

In the time we spent in and around Ossabaw Sound and the mouth of the Ogeechee we must have boated nearly a hundred stripers and released all but half a dozen. By the time we had exhausted ourselves, we had depleted our supply of lines and lures and were reduced to knotting and respooling bits and pieces of line in order to keep the show on the road.

The owner of the tackle store in Savannah, where we stopped to replenish our supply, said the story had been the same in the Wassaw Sound at about the same time.

In Georgia you don't just hop out of your car and go saltwater fishing whenever the notion strikes you, but for those willing to slow down and look for some interesting water it can be a rewarding experience.

FLORIDA

Statistics collected by the Florida Department of Transportation and other state agencies have established that out of the twenty-some-odd million tourists that annually visit the state, approximately one-fourth come with the primary objective of fishing. Of this number, a high percentage arrive with their sights set on saltwater angling, while innumerable others find themselves irresistibly attracted to the sport by exposure during their visit.

No matter where one happens to stop in Florida he is less than seventy-five miles from the coast and most of the time in traveling he is much closer. That is one factor. Another is that the almost year-round warm weather is conducive to various forms of activities on the littoral scene. Then, once on the coast one cannot move about without seeing others fishing and actually catching fish, all of which leads to a monkey-see, monkey-do attitude. Added to the above reasons is the vitally important fact that practically every city, town and village along the coasts are fish-minded. Countless thousands of residents derive their livelihood by making it possible for others to go fishing.

All about are establishments devoted to the business of catering to the angler. Drive over a bridge spanning a bay or river estuary and generally one is invited by signs to stop and rent a boat and motor, rent fishing tackle, and buy live bait. Public and privately operated piers bristle along the coastline like the quills on a porcupine. Signs point the way to marinas where charter and party boats are waiting to hurry one out to deep water to catch fish. Tackle stores are plentiful and eager to cash in on the lucrative market; many large drug, hardware, and department stores have special sections set aside to supply the experienced or tyro angler with virtually every piece of equipment he may require.

Many of the finest restaurants in Florida's coastal towns bear names that indicate their specialization in piscatory cuisine. Once inside, one is handed a menu decorated with pictures of fish and fishing scenes with special pages devoted to a wide assortment of seafood delicacies. Always, the emphasis is on the freshness of the dish, often to the extent that the diner half wonders if perhaps the chef isn't dangling a baited line out the kitchen window.

In short, those who visit the Florida coast and fail to go fishing can rarely complain that the opportunity did not present itself. Without question, sport fishing is one of the foremost attractions the Sunshine State has to offer and is not overlooked by the permanent residents. The statistics, again, indicate that there are more saltwater sport fishermen per capita in Florida and Hawaii than in any of the other states in the union.

Florida's geography alone lends itself to extensive and varied saltwater fishing. Except for Alaska, it has the longest coast line. The 447-mile-long peninsula boasts 580 miles of open coastline on the Atlantic side and 770 miles on the Gulf for a total of 1,350 miles. The tidal coastline, which takes into consideration the perimeters of bays, estuaries, and all sides of islands, swells to 8,426 miles of fishable salt water.

This extensive coastline, the moderate winters, the wide variety of game fish, and the numerous accommodations necessary to fishing have combined to make Florida the undisputed saltwater angling capital of the nation.

It would indeed be difficult, if not actually impossible, to make a mark along one section of the Florida coast and say this is the best fishing area. Before such a bold statement could be made, several questions would have to be answered. Among these would be: What season of the year is one talking about? What type of fishing is desired? What style of fishing is most appealing—surf casting, bridge, pier, small-boat, or offshore fishing in larger boats? Is the proximity to major cities an important adjunct to one's nonfishing hours, or would the tranquillity of small villages in out-of-the-way places be more enjoyable.

Many serious saltwater anglers are admittedly metropolitan oriented. They may be the finest of companions and the truest sportsmen while actually fishing, but when the trip is done they like a change of pace. Anglers of this ilk actually need to be near a big city and would be bored to distraction if their only diversion was sitting around on a dock swapping yarns with other fishermen or utilizing a period of inclement weather to catch up on their reading.

At the other end of the fish hook is the angler who goes off on a jaunt to get away from the hurly-burly of urban life. To him, a week spent in fishing means a time to dispense with the mores of society that demand the daily shave, the polish on his shoes and that abomination of the human male attire known as the necktie.

Between the two extremes there exists a broad gray zone where the sportsman angler likes to mix a little of both during his time spent on the coast. I have friends who fit into each category. It would indeed be a drab and monotonous world if we were all cut out of the same pattern.

Personally, my only requirements of what I consider a good fishing companion is that he enjoy the game of angling and conduct himself in a sportsmanlike manner. Unfortunately, there exists a percentage of those who call themselves sportsmen who are not in any way worthy of the title. One of my chief complaints is the angler who automatically relegates his guide to the realm of abject serfdom, squawks about the high prices charged, blames it on the guide if the fish don't bite, and orders him around like a slave.

Then there is the character who abuses what the rest of us consider a privilege. He acts as if he were honoring the bay or the ocean with his presence and defiles or destroys any and everything in reach. I once had the misfortune of fishing with a man who pulled a revolver out of his tackle box and shot a porpoise that was keeping us company. Fortunately, that time it was my boat and I set an instant course back for port. Needless to say we have never again been fishing together.

Another type I will fish with only once is the game hog. Even now I can recall with a bitter taste in my mouth the day I went fishing with one on a north Florida bay. Almost by the time we reached the trout flats we realized we were in for one of those rare days when practically every cast produced a speckled battler. After we had put a reasonable catch in the ice chest, I began releasing those I caught thereafter. My companion upbraided me for my folly and continued to boat every fish he could until the bottom of the boat was literally covered.

Finally, I put my own tackle away and just sat there watching and wondering. That time it was not my boat and I had no alternative but to become increasingly disgusted at the wanton slaughter. Had the man been a commerical fisherman whose livelihood depended on his luck, it would have been a different story.

When the tide finally changed and the trout quit feeding, we started home. The glutton viewed the layer of dead fish with a warped satisfaction, then finally decided to clean up his boat by tossing them overboard after we had tied up at the dock. "Bet you'll never see another day like this," he gloated. He had no idea how prophetic were his words.

Fortunately, those in the angling fraternity who have an utter disregard for conservation and the basic rules of fair play are relatively few, just as in other sports. Those few, however, are a pox and a scourge and garner nothing beyond their own inane satisfaction.

But getting back to the true sportsman who likes to rough it all the way, and the one who likes to mix his forms of recreation, Florida has a place, in fact an abundance of places, for both elements.

Those entering the state from the north by highway will likely follow either Interstate 75 which terminates on the Gulf Coast or Interstate 95 which sticks close to the Atlantic coast with the Miami area as its terminus. Those entering from the west will generally follow Interstate 10 which passes through Pensacola on the western end of the panhandle, as the northwestern part of Florida is known. The saltwater angler, however, will generally leave the Interstate Highway at Pensacola and

It was here in Apalachicola on the Northwest coast of Florida that Dr. John Gorrie patented his process for the artificial manufacture of ice in 1851. For a very long while this panhandle section of the state was not recognized for the excellent sport fishing it offered. Today, the stretch of Gulf coast from Apalachicola westward to Pensacola is called the "Miracle Strip" and has become a mecca for big game fishing and an abundance of inshore fishing.

find U.S. 98 a highway much more to his liking, since it skirts the Gulf. Most of this route is right on the water's edge and passes through such important fishing towns as Fort Walton, Destin, Panama City, Port St. Joe, and Apalachicola. It was in Apalachicola in 1851 that Dr. John Gorrie patented the process for making artificial ice, something he had developed six years earlier to cool the rooms of his feverish patients.

This stretch of Florida's panhandle is not tropical except during the summer months. Even in winter it seldom feels the extreme cold, but it does often get too chilly for many fishermen. The natives know where to go—back up the tidal creeks and sheltered arms of bays. Those with the proper size boats and a disregard for cold wind occasionally venture out on the open Gulf for a bit of snapper and grouper digging.

For a very long time the panhandle was just a place for people, including those who enjoy saltwater fishing, to visit in the summer. They would arrive just after school vacation began from Tennessee, Alabama, and parts of Georgia. There they would frolic in the surf, marvel at the whitest sand on earth along Panama City Beach, get sunburned, and catch a few fish. Come Labor Day the tourists retreated, slamming the door behind them, and the natives were once again in control of their land.

It would be difficult, if not impossible, to say just when charter and party boats got their start along the northwest coast of Florida. It was more of a gradual development that began to evolve when the commercial fishermen started to realize that they could load up a boat with paying passengers and take them out for a day's fishing. They also discovered that for a small investment in some rough-and-ready tackle they could increase the day's revenue by renting it to some of the customers. The most important fact was that due to the rapid shoaling along that section of the coast, the fishing could begin in a short while after leaving the dock.

In the beginning, the red snapper was the king of fish from Pensacola to Panama City. The summer vacation fishermen loved it, and for that matter, they still do. What was so strange was the very long time required before the commercial fishermen along the "Miracle Strip" realized they were passing up the motherload of sport fishing while they catered to the bottom bouncers who reveled in their daily catch of snapper and grouper. There was some trolling for bonito and mackerel, but nothing serious for an unbelievably long time. On rare occasions someone would catch a dolphin or hook a sailfish, but they were just

The mutton snapper is a strong fighter and frequents waters not nearly so deep as the red snapper it resembles. The mutton snapper, like the smaller lane snapper has a black spot on both sides of the body just above the lateral line. It is an excellent food fish.

considered strays.

Along in the mid-1950's the United States Fish and Wildlife Service began to explore the 100-fathom curve with long-line fishing. The research vessel *Oregon* made a study of the coast. One phase of the researchers' investigation showed that the Gulf Stream, in its head-on collision with the Mississippi River, was deflected and part of it swung to the east. About seventy-seven miles southwest of Panama City they found a 488-fathom-deep depression called De Soto Canyon. The northern horn of the canyon points right toward Pensacola. From that deep hole the bottom continues up a steep slope toward the entire 100-mile-long sweep of the coast from Pensacola to Panama City. The vessel was looking for tuna and in the unexcited way of serious scientists they announced that billfish, such as the white and blue marlins, the swordfish and sails, were to be had if anyone was interested.

Still the sport fishermen dragged their feet. Of course, as always, there were a few who pioneered and brought back big billfish now and then, but it was still nearly five years before the stampede began.

Just take a look at the Miracle Strip today. Pensacola, Fort Walton, Destin, and Panama City are the important points to consider when planning a trip out on the Gulf. Fleets of charter boats as sharp and trim as any that ever graced the waters around Miami are there, and they are generally booked far in advance. The floodgates finally opened, and blue marlin in the four- and five-hundred-pound class are no longer big news. Just a few years earlier the sporting editors of the panhandle newspapers would have been taking pictures from all angles. Now they have become downright blasé. It is difficult to get excited about something that happens day after day. The sport fishing season has now been extended so that Memorial and Labor Days are just two holidays that come along between April and November.

The countryside due south of Tallahassee to Tarpon Springs is the longest stretch of Florida coastline that has to date resisted the modernization of the land developer. It, too, is the big missing link in the nation's Intracoastal Waterway which deadends at the fishing town of Carrabelle and does not resume again until one nears the Greek sponge-fishing town of Tarpon Springs, nearly three humdred miles farther south.

Here and there at infrequent intervals are occasional paved secondary roads and half a dozen state roads that turn off the southbound U.S. 19 and meander down through wilderness country to small villages. In many places the coastline is beautiful in a primitive way, but it is not an area to be causually invaded by boat. The only charts available from the United States Coast & Geodetic Survey are the general sailing charts Nos. 1258 through 1261. The four are fine for open-water travel,

Charter and party boats return to Destin after a day on the Gulf. Until a few years ago Destin was just a sleepy little fishing village on Florida's panhandle. It still is no booming metropolis, but its fame has grown steadily since it was discovered that big game fishing was to be had in abundance only a short way out into the Gulf.

but they give only a smattering of details concerning this coastline.

The fishing is often superb at such points as Steinhatchee, Swannee, near the mouth of Stephen Foster's famous river, Yankeetown, and several others. Facilities are virtually nonexistent along most of the coast, and in the event of a boating mishap the angler is quite likely to find himself confronted with anywhere from five to fifteen miles of desolate swamp country separating him from the nearest comforts of civilization.

Cedar Key is the most important town along this section of the coast and a visit to it is well worth the time and extra travel. The most direct approach for the southbound traveler is to turn off U.S. 19 at Otter Creek onto State Road 24. At the town of Cedar Key the angler will find himself in the Florida of yesterday. It was here that a Bavarian immigrant bought up vast tracts of land and cut down cedar trees by the countless thousands to make pencils by the billions that bore his name of Eberhard Faber.

Cedar Key, settled in 1842 by Judge Agustus Steele as a summer vacation retreat, has had more than its share of devastating hurricanes that found themselves bottled up in the northeast corner of the Gulf and thundered ashore along that stretch of the coast.

Out on Sea Horse Key there is a lighthouse kept for many years by Mr. and Mrs. A.D. Folks. The legend is strong that the high bluff on the island was once the lookout point for the pirate Jean Laffite when his ships were in the area.

The town of Cedar Key reached its peak of importance in the 1880's when timber, fish, stone crabs, and sponges were being exported. It seems impossible today to realize that during its zenith the town had a population of over five thousand people. Hurricanes and accompanying tidal waves have erased many of the once bustling community's landmarks. Many reminders of the past are preserved in a small Cedar Key State Museum.

Cedar Key was destined to flourish once more with the completion of the Cross-Florida barge canal that was to have its Gulf terminus across Waccasassa at Yankeetown. The dream crumbled quickly, however, when in January of 1970 President Richard Nixon issued a work-stoppage order to the United States Corps of Engineers after an expenditure over the preceeding years of $50 million. The presidential decision to abandon the controversial canal met with bitter opposition in some quarters and was loudly cheered by a multitude of Florida

Along the waterfront at Cedar Key on the west coast of Florida. Once important for the cedar wood used by Eberhard Faber in the manufacture of pencils. Now, a delightful little Gulf coast village where many of the residents think in terms of fishing.

residents who had long been warning of the serious ecological damage the completion of the canal would cause.

Meanwhile, Cedar Key dozes in the warm Florida sunlight, commercial fishermen continue to dry their nets on weathered frames, and the occasional saltwater sporting angler enjoys the excellent fishing and secretly hopes not too many people will discover his hideaway on this remote point along the Gulf coast. This is especially so in the winter when trout and redfish move into Homosassa, Crystal, and other rivers in large numbers.

Dropping south from Cedar Key and Yankeetown the coastline continues much the same with important fishing points at Crystal Bay, Homosassa Bay, Bayport, Weeki Wachee Springs, and the towns of Aripeka and Hudson.

Hudson has long been a peaceful little Florida town well known for its good fishing for speckled trout, mackerel, and a number of other important game fish. No one, however, expected it would produce big tuna, but that is just what happened in May of 1970.

Bluefin are the heavyweights of the American tuna and they have been known to frequent the Gulf in reasonably interesting numbers, especially around Louisiana's South Pass. They are also plentiful in the Florida Straits, but tuna fishing is just one claim to fame Florida's west coast cannot boast.

Nevertheless, on Monday morning, May 11, 1970, a 525-pound genuine bluefin tuna was hauled ashore. It was speared by skin divers. The action began the previous evening when the tall dorsal fin was sighted in one of the town's man-made canals. It was first thought to be a shark, but when the team of skin divers, one armed with a bow and arrow, arrived, the true identity was recognized. The spears and arrows found their target, but it was 2 A.M. Monday morning before it was beached. Frank Hoff, ichthyologist from the St. Petersburg Marine Laboratory, was summoned, and after a detailed examination he announced it was definitely a bluefin tuna, probably about fourteen years old.

It can only be guessed that the big bluefin had strayed from the rest of its tribe and followed a school of mackerel or some other fish into the canal where it was captured.

Beginning at New Port Richey, the Florida of yesteryear gives way quite suddenly to the urbanized Florida of today and tomorrow. Tarpon Springs was made famous for years by the Greeks, who put the town on the map with their thriving sponge-fishing industry. Here, along with the colorful sponge docks, are numerous charter and party boats as well as a liberal sprinkling of small-boat liveries and launching ramps. The angler will not have to look far for tackle stores.

Dunedin and Clearwater rub shoulders, and each has its own busy municipal marina with the one at Clearwater catering to countless thousands of both winter and summer tourists. The angling accommodations continue unabated all the way down to the southern tip of St. Petersburg, with the big city of Tampa across the bay.

The real hotspots along Florida's "Sun Coast" are Tarpon Springs, Clearwater Beach, Johns Pass, and Pass-a-Grille on St. Petersburg Beach. All have an abundance of boats of all sizes. At the tip end of this peninsula within a peninsula is Fort De Soto Park built on Mullet Key and a cluster of smaller islands guarding the north side of the entrance to Tampa Bay. The focal point is the ruins of the fort itself, which was built in 1898. The park, which is open daily to the public, has over three miles of open beach with a thousand-foot pier reaching out into deep water.

Moving south from St. Petersburg on U.S. 19 one crosses Tampa Bay on the towering Sunshine Skyway bridge and 15-mile-long causeway. When one considers that both sides are fishable, it provides thirty miles of top-notch open-water fishing for the angler who has only to pull off the highway and string his tackle. The regulars count on mackerel, both kings and Spanish, speckled trout, cobia, snook, grouper, and plenty of tarpon in season.

On the southside of the causeway one can turn west at Bradenton and travel across another causeway out to Anna Maria Island and fish his way south along it and Longboat Key all the way down to Sarasota. From there on, it is another fifteen miles of the same type of barrier islands protecting the mainland to Venice. Is the fishing good? Statistics show that the little fishing village of Cortez just west of Bradenton annually ships over five million pounds of fish. Naturally, a large percentage of this haul is fish caught by the commercial fishermen, but Cortez is only one small village, and the entire stretch from Tarpon Springs all the way south is probably the most fish-minded (sport-angling, that is) stretch of coastline to be found anywhere on earth. Head boats, charter boats, bridges, piers, small-boats' causeways, surf fishing—you name it and it's there.

It is not that the fishing is any better along this stretch than it is north of Tarpon Springs. It is just that there are all of the accouterments needed for the sport in such profusion, with a vast array of hostelries and places to eat that run the gammut from the lowliest hamburger stand to the finest restaurants.

Part of the tarpon fishing fleet at Boca Grande on the west coast of Florida. From this tranquil mooring it is only a few minutes' run out to the famous Boca Grande Pass. There the tranquility gives way to rough-and-tumble fishing for the Silver King.

Just a few miles south of Venice is Charlotte Harbor, which is a big bay that sprawls all over the landscape from the Peace River up in the northeast corner and back around and up the Caloosahatchie River on the north side of Fort Myers. Sheltering this body of water from the open Gulf is a string of islands with Big Pine and other small islands scattered hither and thither.

On the northern end is Gasparilla Island that terminates at Boca Grande Pass where the tarpon fishermen gather in spring and early summer to catch the silverkings that are present in astronomical numbers. A road goes all the way down to the famous pass. Heading seaward on the highway out of Fort Myers one winds up on Sanibel and Captiva Islands. Sanibel is just a small slice of heaven for the dedicated conchologist. There is something about the shelving of the Gulf out from Sanibel that causes the waves to cast ashore a wide array of seashells and toss them up in abundance. And while the waves are busy littering the beach with shells, anglers are busy surf casting for a wide variety of fish.

Naples is called the gateway to the Ten Thousand Islands, and a boat can be taken from there, and heading south, one will discover some of the most unusual fishing to be found anywhere in the world. Before leaving Naples it is almost mandatory that a few hours be spent fishing from the big pier that juts out into the Gulf.

The Tamiami Trail (still U.S. 41) runs into State Road 29 which will lead to Everglades City on Chokoloskee Bay. Everglades City is a far cry from a booming metropolis. All told, it is home for well under a thousand people, but everything is geared for sport fishing. Admittedly, facilities are limited, but there is the Everglades Rod and Gun Lodge which is excellent and so is Ted Smallwood's Dock. Charter boats are plentiful in winter and smaller craft can be had at any time.

Of course, if one enjoys getting lost, he should not hesitate to swing right out into that maze of islands. Should he get stuck on a bar or take the wrong channel and find himself a very long way from nowhere he can practice his wilderness survival tactics. This is right up in the northwest finger of the Everglades National Park, and there is a ranger station there. Eventually one of the rangers will find him and lead him back to civilization.

If, on the other hand, one is more interested in a clean-cut and highly productive fishing trip with a hot shower "and quiet sleep and a sweet dream when the long trek's over," he should hire a guide! There are plenty of them in Everglades City, and they can turn a world of trouble into one of excellent fishing.

The guides and the other good folk that dwell in Everglades City don't exactly aestivate during the warm months, but they more or less consider their domain as having been especially designed for fall, winter, and early spring fishing. They are entirely right, too, but that does not mean that one can't go fishing and catch plenty of fish on the Fourth of July. It's just that he won't get the enthusiastic response from the townspeople in the summer that he will in the winter.

I know this to be a fact because I have fished the area during the summer months and caught snook, speckled trout, sheepshead, redfish, mangrove snapper, Spanish mackerel, grouper, and many other species. I will have to admit that the insects and frequent squalls are not to be taken lightly and if one has a choice, he should throw in with the natives and wait for the cooler weather.

Winter or summer, however, the Ten Thousands are intriguing to the saltwater angler. Here and there he will find an island with a bit of a beach, especially on the outer islands, and here and there, too, is a patch of high ground. For the most part, however, the islands are virtually impenetrable tangles of mangrove trees that stand on long stiltlike roots right to the water's edge. Some are just little baby islands while others are fairly large. They are separated from one another by mud and sand bars, oyster bars, shallow water, and deep channels.

From Everglades City south and around the tip of Florida's mainland there is nothing but wilderness coastline with the vast reaches of the enigmatic Everglades on one side and the open Gulf on the other. A boat is the only means of transportation, and for those venturesome souls who really want to get away from it all, this is the place. Don't, repeat *Don't,* expect to find any facilities along the way, for the simple reason that there are none. Except for the fact that the United States Coast and Geodetic Survey teams have charted the area, the coast is exactly like it was when the early Spanish explorers stood on the decks of their ships and stared in wonder at the vast jungle.

For those of us who want to see more than a few fragments of our natural wonders and true wilderness areas preserved, the Everglades

Jetty fishing is a popular and productive method of fishing all the way from Virginia to Texas. The massive rocks provide shelter for countless forms of natural bait and the adjacent deep water is frequented by larger fish. If the sun gets too warm, just open an umbrella and you have your own little cave by the sea.

should be left alone. Those of us who call ourselves conservationists do not stand a chance of holding onto what is left, however, unless we work at it.

Where the preservation of our natural resources is concerned, the time is past to sit by and say "let George do it," because George is too busy looking after himself. This does not mean I am against progress, be it sprawling jetports, superhighways, or atomic power plants. I will, however, shout until I am blue in the face when the developers run roughshod over nature in the name of progress. If we don't all shout loud and long we are going to find ourselves in the very near future with nothing but a few sterile parks, or worse still, nothing.

Continuing the voyage around the tip of Florida's mainland, the next and only inroad of civilization is the National Park headquarters of Flamingo. Here, with a million and a half acres of primordial jungle surrounding it, is a delightful resort right on the edge of Florida Bay. Except by boat it can be reached only by following State Road 27 out of Homestead to the east.

Flamingo is up to the minute in every respect with a modern motel, swimming pools, well-kept lawns, excellent marina for both large and small boats, beautiful dining room, gift and tackle shop, launching ramp, ice, groceries, and all the rest. It is in no way a tourist trap. Instead, the entire area is built for the enjoyment of the visitors and operates under a concession contract with the National Park Service. There is a fleet of small boats for the angler who wants to go it alone, and there are guides for the more cautious. Well-equipped charter boats also make their headquarters there.

Key West is at the tip end of the Florida Keys and is the southernmost city of the continental United States. It is a small island a mile and a half wide and four miles long. It has gained the reputation of being a fisherman's paradise. Such is no idle boast, either, for the waters surrounding it contain no less than six hundred varieties of fish. The yearly average temperature is 77 degrees and rain is practically nonexistent in the winter months.

At Key West one can try his luck from the beaches, piers, docks, and bridges or go out on the turquoise water in a small boat. Charter boats can even be taken across the treacherous channels to the Dry Tortugas and the ruins of old Fort Jefferson, where Dr. Samuel A. Mudd spent his years of island banishment, after being found guilty of setting the bone in John Wilkes Booth's leg that was broken when he jumped from

President Lincoln's box after the assassination at the Ford Theatre.

The Dry Tortugas has virtually nothing to offer except some of the finest fishing in the world way out near the middle of the lower Gulf. The water is so clear that it seems almost nonexistent, as if one's boat were suspended over coral- and grass-strewn bottom with nothing separating it but the air. The water is there all right and it becomes obvious when one watches a large black ray lift from the bottom and glide silently from one hiding spot to another. Then, along comes a shark, sinister as he circles the boat, seemingly daring one to jump overboard. A school of amberjack dart by and the shark hangs around a while longer knowing that if one is hooked he will have a free meal coming.

A trip to the Dry Tortugas can be taken just for the fun of it, not discounting the idea of fishing around a cluster of islands that seem to have been cut adrift from the Keys and floated out to sea all by themselves.

Back at Key West, one will eventually begin the 165-mile drive up the length of the island string to Miami. Every key is the same, every key is different. Large or small, crossed by U.S. 1 or lying off to the side, each has its own niche in history and it is literally impossible to find one where the fishing is poor.

The names of the islands are enough to set one's imagination aglow. In most cases five people can be asked where the names originated, and different answers will be received. For who on earth today could say, with any proof to back it up, why they have names such as Happy Jack, Tarpon Belly, Hardup, Sugarloaf, Saddlebunch, Teakettle, Friend, and Knockemdown Keys. Some, of course, are easier to understand, i.e., Fat Deer, Duck, Sandfly and Raccoon Keys, but I have never been able to get even a remotely sensible answer to the reason for naming one of the shallow spots Old Sweat Bank. Also, apparently in desperation, the early settlers named one No Name Key.

Between Key West and Miami one will cross 42 bridges with the shortest 37 feet long and the longest just a bit shy of 7 miles. All about, on the beach, in the air, and in the water, it is a world to watch and wonder. Gulls, terns, and pelicans soar, beat their wings for altitude and drop like a rock to pick up a careless fish. Higher still the man-o'-war birds drift on motionless black wings, waiting, watching. They let the other birds do the fishing and then frighten them with a power dive, catching the captured fish before it falls back into the water.

Sandpipers toe-dance along the fringe of water, nervously grabbing

Bridge after bridge after bridge linking miles of islands is the story of the highway to Key West. If you like odd names, stop along the way at islands with names such as Happy Jack, Tarpon Belly, Hardup, Sugarloaf, Teakettle, and Knockemdown. They are all there and more, too. The best fishing season along the Florida Keys officially begins on January 1 and ends December 31.

a morsel here and there, forever on the move and then suddenly bursting into flight. Herons and cranes stalk the shallows on stilts, solemn, sedate, and preoccupied with their avian meditation, but pausing now and then to uncoil their crooked necks to spear an eel or fish that foolishly tarried in their path.

On the beach, fiddler crabs move along, ducking into holes or crouching behind bits of grass. Occasionally a ghost crab, a veritable giant compared to the fiddlers he resembles, breaks his perfect camouflage at one's feet and races sideways to vanish in a hole as big around as a half dollar.

Suddenly, the water explodes a few yards out from the beach and mullet are casting themselves into the air, their newly minted silver sides glistening in the sunlight. Why? One would have to be a mullet to know for sure. Maybe they just jumped because the urge struck them all at once. Maybe, too, if the sun is right and one is wearing Polaroid glasses, one can see a yard-long barracuda hanging motionless over the vanilla sand of the bottom with his jaws chopping, barking silently at the mullet he startled.

It is a place to fish early in the morning or at midday, or when polished red trunks of the gumbo limbo cast long shadows across the tufts of harsh grass and hard-packed sand. The angler can fish from the beach or pole the flats looking for "muds" that disclose the location of feeding bonefish, or maybe have it out with a permit so big it covers the forward floorboards of the skiff, if the lucky fisherman has skill enough to hold onto it.

Night comes on, and the angler can take up station on a bridge rebutment and fish the passes for tarpon, tripletail, trout, snook, or mackerel, and once in a while a shark will cruise by and tear up his tackle. All the while the gasoline lantern floods his little stronghold with a steady white light and casts eerie shadows. Nearby there may be a massive chunk of concrete with the rusting, twisted length of what was long ago a railroad—an impossible railroad that everybody said could not be built. But it was built under the guiding hand of Henry Flagler. He was already in his seventies when he decided to construct a roadbed that would leave the mainland and extend along the string of islands all the way to Key West. On the morning of January 22, 1912, a great black locomotive hissed and sneezed its way to a standstill in Key West with a string of passenger cars loaded with dignitaries.

It opened the Keys to the rest of the World and was hailed as one of the greatest engineering feats of all time. Then came the Labor Day hurricane of 1935 that destroyed it. The storm held the reputation of being the most violent ever to strike the continent of North America until Camille devastated the Mississippi coast in 1969. The railroad was left a mass of twisted steel and tumbled cement, hundreds of people lost their lives, and some of the islands were completely washed away. The barometer dropped to 26.35 inches, the lowest ever recorded in the western hemisphere. A study of the force necessary to bend the steel rail into pretzel shapes proved that the wind undoubtedly exceeded two hundred miles per hour in sustained gusts. Now, sheepshead with their black-and-white convict stripes feed on the barnacles that grow on the footings of Flagler's railroad, and a barracuda takes up station nearby. Listen beyond the hiss of the lantern and the slop of the waves, and sometimes you can hear the chanting of old Flagler's gandy dancers laying the rails.

Up at the top of the Keys out from Key Largo is one of the most unusual state parks in the nation. It is the John Pennekamp Coral Reef, dedicated in 1960. It covers approximately 115 square miles of ocean. Hook and line fishing is permitted, but the main attraction is a chance for the person interested in sea life in a completely natural state to go out on the surface of the park and look.

The park has a shore base adjacent to the highway where boats may be rented or launched. There are also camping, picnicking, and swimming areas designated, and weather conditions permitting, a concessionaire runs glass-bottomed boats out to the reefs and over the various sunken ships and boats. Those interested in scuba diving and snorkeling find themselves in an unlimited wonderland of the world beneath the waves. Everywhere there are colorful tropical fish, at least forty types of coral, forests, and gardens of sea ferns, and even a submerged 400-pound bronze statue of Christ standing on a concrete base. It was made in Italy by the sculptor Guido Galletti and presented to the park by the Underwater Society of America. It is titled Christ of the Deep.

The John Pennekamp Coral Reef Park is under state jurisdiction. It is an ideal place for the angler to study the actions and habits of the fish he seeks to catch. With so much other excellent fishing in all directions, many of us prefer to put our tackle aside in this particular area and watch rather than disturb the countless forms of sea life.

The saltwater angler who locates in the Miami to Palm Beach area, as millions do each year, is not likely to find much in the way of wilderness beaches and the Florida of yesteryear. This is all well and good, if that is what he wants, because, as mentioned earlier, a man does not necessarily have to be an explorer to enjoy fishing. Practically everything he needs in the way of modern civilization is on one side of him and the vast open reaches of the Atlantic Ocean are on the other.

When one realizes the extent of the population right in the Miami area alone, it seems next to impossible that one can go out in the sheltered waters of Biscayne Bay and actually catch fish. For that matter, it is not even necessary to take a boat. There is good fishing to be had from the banks of half a dozen causeways, especially around the bridges that link Miami with the beaches. It is not at all unusual to see a man dressed in office attire casting for snook or pompano while he waits for an appointment he has out on the beach or over in the city. In a matter of minutes he can put his tackle back in the trunk of his car and devote his attention to his briefcase.

Charter boats, head boats, and small-boat liveries are everywhere along the waterfront in abundance. The nearness to the Gulf Stream means that fishing generally begins within a few minutes after breaking out into open water. On the return of the fishermen in the late afternoon the crowds that gather at the marinas gawk in wonder as the mates unload the day's catch of dolphin, wahoo, king mackerel, amberjack, sailfish, blue and white marlin. The sight of such an array of fish is contagious, and many a dedicated saltwater angler of today was nothing more than a goggle-eyed landlubber before he made the fatal mistake of watching the boats come in.

Fort Lauderdale, Stuart, and Palm Beach are big game headquarters, with sailfish being the most sought-after quarry. Farther north the Melbourne and Cocoa Beach areas are renowned for large speckled trout and numbers of other inshore fish.

The security restrictions of the John F. Kennedy Space Center on Cape Canaveral have dulled the fishing activity around Titusville, but it is only a short way north or south to get back in business. To the north there are fishing piers at Fernandino Beach, Flagler Beach, St. Augustine, the site of the oldest permanent settlement in the United States, and at Daytona. Some are free and others charge a moderate fee. Party and charter boats are to be had at a number of spots along U.S. A1A all the way up to the Georgia line.

ALABAMA AND MISSISSIPPI

Alabama and Mississippi have less shoreline than any of the other states included in this book. Because the coasts of both states are on the same parallel and rub shoulders with one another, they offer much the same saltwater fishing.

It is possible that the relative chambers of commerce and tourist bureaus may take umbrage at this pairing of the two states, but fish are quite heedless of legal boundaries and could not care less whether they are in either Mississippi or Alabama waters, just so long as the conditions and available food supply are to their liking, which they are. The redfish, speckled trout, flounder, and scores of others are just as happy darting about in the waters surrounding Alabama's Dauphin Island as they are around Mississippi's Horn Island.

The Alabama-bound angler with a yen to get away from it all would do well to consider spending some time at Gulf Shores State Park. If he is headed west along U.S. 98 he will turn due south on State Road 59 at the town of Foley. When he reaches the Gulf he will find excellent campsites and nearly forty miles of scenic road that stretches both east and west, with Perdido Bay on the east and the remains of old Fort Morgan at the western end of the peninsula. Near the fort, which was built about 1700, is still another fine recreation area maintained by the state.

Generally around the first of April fishermen all along the northern part of the Gulf get down to the serious business of cobia fishing. Later that month and in May the attention turns to king and Spanish mackerel and by the beginning of summer they are present in large numbers. Bluefish arrive shortly after the mackerel. Throughout the summer and well into the fall the fishing along the coast, around the islands, in Perdido and Grand bays is varied and good. Whiting, speckled and silver trout, redfish, and sheepshead are the dependable standbys.

Summer is vacation time for countless thousands of tourists along the coast of Alabama, and during this period party boats do big business taking daily loads of passengers out on the Gulf. The chief quarry for the party-boat fisherman is red snapper and grouper. The red snapper is a deep-water fish, and because the bottom shoals sharply, this deep water nearby cuts down on travel time and most of the day can be spent in fishing.

Summer also means that the billfish and other blue-water denizens are in residence, and the charter-boat business is growing steadily. Mobile is the only large city near the coast in Alabama and it is generally the place the average tourist seeks out. After a period of orientation, those who are interested in fishing begin to explore the shoreline of Mobile Bay and find that there are a reasonable number of towns and coastal villages that are fish minded.

This bay is one of the largest along the northern Gulf coast, covering approximately 297 square miles. It is 27 nautical miles in length and 20 miles wide. At its northern end four rivers, the Appalachee, Blackley, Mobile, and Tensaw flow into it. The average depth is slightly less then ten feet, reaching a maximum depth of sixty feet near the Gulf entrance close to Fort Morgan. The Intracoastal Waterway runs due east and west across the lower end from Bon Secour Bay on the east to the bridge that connects Dauphin Island with the mainland.

Fairhope, a major fishing town, is located on the east side of the bay.

On the west side the best bet is to drive south on State Road 163, which parallels the bay and winds up at the toll bridge leading across to Dauphin Island. The small toll charge is well worth the trip to this island, with old Fort Gaines across the pass from Fort Morgan. For the surf caster there is about fifteen miles of beach fronting on the Gulf, and the island forms a barrier that stimulates small-boat fishing in the inshore side.

During all the years I have lived in the South and fished over a wide area of it, I often heard references to something known as an *Alabama Fish Jubilee.*

"You just ain't never seed nuthin' like it," an old-timer from Foley once told me. "Shucks, when I was a young'n my folks lived just south of Fairhope and when one of them jubilees would come along the word would spread like wildfire. Many's the time when me an' my paw and a couple of my brothers would hitch up the horses and load our big old Hoover wagon plum to runnin' over with fish and crabs. Man alive! For the next couple days me an' my folks an' most everbody else 'round would eat so much fish we'd dang nigh grow scales. 'Course," he concluded wistfully, " 'twern't no ice to be had, lessen you could pay, so what we couldn't eat or put up by smokin' had to be buried out in the garden patch but it shore was good for makin' them collard greens grow. I reckon it's twiced as good as cow manure."

On and on, year after year, I continued to hear what seemed logically to fall in the category of "fish tales." You soon learn, however, that most strange stories about fishing, providing you hear them enough times and from different people, generally have a reasonably solid nucleus of truth in them.

What happens in a fish jubilee? I must have asked the question a hundred times over a period of years. Always the basic answer was the same. For some reason the entire fish population of a particular section of the bay suddenly begins to leave the water and to swim up onto the beach.

Were the fish that participated in jubilees in good condition or did they show signs of some disease or contamination that might prompt such abnormal behavior? Another question I asked on numerous occasions. Again the answers were remarkably consistent. The general feeling of those who had witnessed these phenomena is that the fish are just as active and edible as any that might have been caught on hook and line or hauled ashore in a seine.

Why do the fish act this way? Still another oft-repeated question. Some of the answers smacked of fancy, others bore signs of logic. Those with a scientific bent and an investigative mind suggested that it was caused by a sudden chemical change in the water. Then there are those who are convinced that a jubilee occurs when too many fish begin to populate a certain area. When I put the question of *why* to the old man in Foley, he leaned back in his porch rocker and touched a match to the bowl of his pipe.

"Never have been able to rightly know," he mused. "Me and a lot of folks has studied over it for a long, long time. 'Course, it might be that some big critters from way out in the Gulf come in tryin' to ketch 'em. Maybe they's so big and ugly lookin' it just scares the daylights out'n them fishes and crabs and they figures they got some sorter chance makin' out on the beach 'til whatever's after 'em gets filled up and swims away." He leaned over and rested his elbows on the porch bannister and looked reflectively at his pipe. "Maybe the Good Lawd just reckons to give his chillun a feast ever so often. I spect if He could make tucker fall outter the sky for all them starvin' people back in the old days He still shore can shoo a mess o' fish up on the beach whenever He is a mind to."

With the passage of time I finally arrived at the conclusion that the Alabama fish jubilees were no joke. They do, in fact, occur and have been occurring for at least a hundred years. The *Mobile Press-Register* has kept an active file on the phenomena for a number of years and the times, dates, extent, location, and other data have been recorded.

I have never had the privilege of being on the scene at the beginning of one of the jubilees, but I did come so close to being a witness several years ago that I almost felt I was a part of it. I was returning from New Orleans to my home in Florida and satisfactorily mismanaged my departure so that it was well after midnight when I passed through Mobile. It was August and the tourist season was still in full swing. Motels all along the way were displaying their "no vacancy" signs and I decided that my best bet would be to take advantage of the slack traffic period and continue driving until I reached some suitable lodging, perhaps between Pensacola and Panama City. Having always been nocturnal by nature, the prospects of catching six or seven hours of sleep in an air-conditioned room while the rest of the world was out enjoying the daylight hours was enticing. After driving through the tunnel I turned south on Route 98 on the east side of the bay. It was around two in the morning when I passed through the town of Daphne, and I was surprised to notice so much activity. By the time I had moved on to the next town, which was Montrose, I noticed that here, too, the whole populace seemed to be up and stirring.

Pulling into a service station I had my tank filled and asked the station attendant what was going on.

"Another jubilee," the man said with a yawn. "People have been coming in for the past several hours with fish, shrimp, and crabs by the tub and basketful. A guy was in here just before you pulled in with two big gunny sacks packed full, and he had two peach baskets stuffed with crabs in the trunk of his car."

Excited by the thought I might at last have an opportunity to observe a real jubilee in action, I asked the attendant for directions to the beach. As he was telling me how to get to the center of the activity, a man in a pickup truck pulled in.

"Well," he said, walking over to the Coke machine. "I guess that about does it for this time. Hope I can stay awake 'til I get these up to Mobile. Market's good I hear."

Walking over to the truck, I lifted the canvas cover and saw that the body was packed with hundreds of pounds of fish. When I explained that I wanted to take pictures of the jubilee in action the truck driver shook his head.

"Not much chance of that now," he said. "Tide changed about an hour ago and the show's practically over. It'll most likely be in the paper today or tomorrow. Saw a couple of newspaper people down there taking pictures, but the beach is picked pretty clean by now."

Annoyed that I had come so close and was now getting in on the tail end of things, I rehearsed the directions with the station attendant and left as quickly as possible. I followed the *turn rights* and *turn lefts* and finally arrived. There was still a considerable number of people moving about on the waterfront with flashlights and gasoline lanterns, but most of them were leaving or preparing to do so. Two small boys clad in wet dungarees and slapping at mosquitoes were manfully struggling to drag a huge zinc washtub toward a car. They looked so weary I offered to give them a hand.

"Pop and Uncle Ed got twice as many," they said proudly. "If you want to get yourself a mess just go over that way where you see that old busted-up boat. There was plenty of flounders and crabs still flopping about when we passed." As they spoke they pointed over their shoulder into the darkness. Sweeping the beach in front of me with my flashlight, I walked along until I found the "busted-up boat," and as the two had said, there were a number of flounders, numerous shrimp, and several dozen crabs. The flounders and shrimp were nearly dead or already so and the crabs were beginning to move back toward the bay. I picked up several of the flatfish and could tell they were as fresh as if they had just been caught. The crabs seemed to be suffering no ill effects and threatened my flashlight beam with upraised claws as they sidled toward the water.

I remained on the scene until the first rays of sunlight began and during that time I managed to talk with half a dozen people who had been reaping the harvest of stranded fish. All were agreed that it had been one of the best jubilees that had come along in several years.

Having heard stories about the "fish jubilees" in Mobile Bay for years and finally actually been on the scene at the close of one, I was now fully convinced that they were indeed a fact. My next move was to turn my attention to learning the scientific reason.

Investigation, with the assistance of several marine biologists who have made a study of the subject, reveals that a combination of meteorological and oceanographic factors must be in coincidence. It is certain that these factors occur in numerous bodies of salt water on frequent occasions, but the reason Mobile Bay has gained its reputation is partly because of the formation of the proximity of an unusual land mass bordering the region of the bay where the jubilees are most numerous.

This area is on the upper east side of the bay between the towns of Daphne to the north and Point Clear to the south; approximately twelve miles of beachfront. Along this stretch there are bluffs which range from a few feet to a hundred feet in elevation. This high ground apparently has a distinct bearing when related to the combination of conditions that must be present to cause a jubilee.

In general, the phenomenon manifests itself mainly during the months of June, July, August, and September, with August being the most likely month. On rare occasions a summer will pass without a jubilee. In other years the incident occurs as many as ten times and occasionally two or more jubilees may take place simultaneously, eight or ten miles apart.

Further investigation proves that the most likely time of the day is between midnight and sunrise. On occasions they have been known to continue all night, but the average duration of a single jubilee is about two hours.

They occur most frequently on a rising tide, although there have been exceptions. The wind direction is of utmost significance because when the wind is from the east it is sufficiently strong to move the surface water along the eastern shore out toward the middle of the Bay. As this surface water is driven away, it is replaced by the water with a higher salt content from the deeper part of the ship channel. At the same time, bottom debris swept into the Bay by the Tensaw River is prone to rot more rapidly in the warmer months, resulting in a form of eutrophication and a subsequent lowering of the oxygen content in the water. During the daylight hours water plants are producing oxygen and using carbon dioxide, but this process is reversed at night with the result that the oxygen content of the water is still further decreased.

Conditions are nearly perfect for a jubilee when the time is late at night, water plants are not producing oxygen, the decaying debris is using large quantities of oxygen, the incoming tide is pushing highly saline water shoreward, and the east wind is driving the surface water out. Fish, crabs, shrimp, and other demersal animals move ahead of the tide until they reach the beach. By then they are in dire need of oxygen which has been markedly reduced by the above conditions. In desperation, they forsake the water and drive themselves ashore. A change in the wind direction and almost always a change in the tide will terminate the jubilee, but during this period of extreme oxygen deprivation the fish act in a highly abnormal manner and are easily taken by humans and other terrestrial creatures.

The jubilee is but one interesting facet of fishing in this region.

Always an important stretch of coastline from a commercial fishing standpoint, Mississippi was rapidly developing into a genuine mecca for the sport fisherman. As with all the Gulf coast, hurricanes have been something that the residents eventually learn to live with. Some have been small blows and others have been worse, but few since the hurricane that devastated Galveston in September of 1900 have caused such utter destruction as did Camille when she struck the Mississippi coast on Sunday, August 17, 1969. The National Hurricane Center in Miami rated Camille as "the greatest recorded storm ever to hit a populated area in the Western Hemisphere."

After a night of horror, Monday morning dawned on a ravaged land. Largely because of plenty of advance warning, the human death toll was relatively light. Three ocean-going freighters were washed ashore and a 600,000-gallon oil storage tank was torn from its foundation and carried along on the crest of the storm waves for more than three miles. A year later, with the coast still in shambles, but rebuilding, the final tally showed 144 dead and about three dozen more still missing.

Beautiful homes, some of which had weathered countless storms for a century or more, and moss-hung live oaks that had been standing for three times as long were ripped asunder and scattered over the countryside. Sharing the same fate were countless new motels and other tourist facilities that had offered a welcome haven to the saltwater angler and other tourists.

For one who had for years watched the steady growth and development of the Mississippi coast, with its modern marinas and excellent boating facilities, a trip along U.S. 90 a year after the storm was one of almost disbelief. Fragments of concrete footings that had formerly been the foundations of large motels showed here and there through mountains of sand washed up from the beach. Bare pilings jutted up from the now calm waters, stark and ugly grave markers to show where bustling marinas had been.

Broken seawalls and massive chunks of highway pavement littered the beach front, and countless FOR SALE signs bore mute testimony of people who had forsaken the coast, unwilling ever again to risk their lives and fortunes in sight of salt water.

Although the marinas and other boating facilities were literally swept away with the storm, many of the charter and party boats were saved. Weatherwise and aware of their vulnerability, skippers heeded the early warnings and took their boats to safer moorings farther inland along the rivers. When the storm had passed and they returned to the Gulf, the biggest problem was finding suitable mooring. Second only to this was the sudden lack of accommodations to provide them with passengers from whom they could continue making a living.

Hurricane Camille is now a creature of the past, and gradually the devastated coastline is being repopulated by people convinced that "it can't happen again." Bulldozers are grinding away at the rubble, and draglines and pile drivers are restoring the marinas. It is a slow and painstaking task, for often it is more difficult to rebuild than to start from the beginning. The boats cannot operate until lodging is available for the potential customers, and it does not make sense to build motels if there is no attraction.

Fortunately, the attraction is still there. Hurricanes, for all their fury expended on the coast, have little or no effect on the fishing potential a short way offshore. The sailfish, mackerel, dolphin, and all the rest of the saltwater battlers have not changed their habits, nor will they do so simply because of a storm that ripped the land apart.

Offshore the only major change in the Sound is Ship Island, that was cut in half by the storm tides, and the rearrangement of nearby Cat Island. In a sense, here, in Camille's wake, is a brand new fishing territory, restored in many ways to its original state. The angler with a trailer will find numerous places to launch his boat and cruise the waters of Mississippi Sound. In summer he can try his luck with the tarpon on the grassflats and in the channels around Cat, Ship, Horn, Round, and Petit Bois islands. Summer is also the time to fish here for cobia, mackerel, and bluefish. When October rolls around, speckled trout and redfish congregate in vast schools in bayous.

At this writing the newcomer to the coast of Mississippi may justifiably be dismayed at the shambles left by the great hurricane of 1969. As one who has spent many years fishing the saltwaters of both the Atlantic and Gulf coasts, I have seen many sections seemingly devastated beyond repair rebound with amazing rapidity and I strongly suspect that in far less time than now seems possible, sport fishermen will again be planning trips to include this highly productive coast. What is more, I would be willing to bet the new Biloxis, Gulfports, and other towns along the coast will return with even better facilities.

LOUISIANA

Today the way most people visit a state for the first time is to land at a major airport, step off a train, or drive in on a superhighway. My first trip to Louisiana was by a somewhat different mode of transportation. I came by water.

New Orleans, of course, is one of the great seaports and thousands of people visit Louisiana for the first time by ship. I should hasten to add that while I came by water, my entrance was down the top of the boot via the Mississippi River.

My roots are deeply planted in the Bayou State. My maternal great-grandparents left England in 1855 and arrived in New Orleans with their son and daughter just in time for the great yellow fever plague that killed people by the countless thousands. When the fever had run its course, a seven-year-old boy named Thomas Spencer and his little sister, Emma, took one another by the hand and began a long trek into a new world, leaving their parents behind in unmarked graves. Theirs was a strange and beautiful odyssey, but this is a book about saltwater fishing, and I was going to tell you how I discovered the state of Louisiana has a real *lagniappe* where saltwater fishing is concerned.

I arrived in the Pelican State on a towboat. By a devious route the venture had its beginning one summer afternoon in Florida when my wife, Dorothy, and I were visiting with our good friends and fishing companions, the late Don Eddy and his wife, Doris. Don will long be remembered for his travel articles in such top magazines as *Reader's Digest* and the now defunct *American Magazine*.

"How would you like to take a trip down the Mississippi River?" he asked as he went about the task of winding a spool of line on a new reel he had just bought.

Don was first a writer and second a fisherman, or was it the other way around? It does not make any real difference, because if he was going to write a travel story about any part of North America he first made a careful study of the region to ascertain what the fishing possibilities were in the selected area at the time he planned to go. He cared not one whit whether it was fresh or salt water. His only requirement was that the place have a good fishing reputation.

"A trip down the Mississippi?" I repeated. "What would we use for a boat, a canoe or a Huck Finn raft or what?"

"Son," he said, fixing me with his John Barrymore stare. "You know I only travel in style. We will go on a towboat. The only requirement is that you carry your camera and take about a million pictures for which, of course, you will be richly rewarded by *American*."

"What, may I ask, is a towboat?"

"I *thought* you would say yes." Don grinned and handed me his reel. He picked up the telephone and called Sumner Blossom, his personal friend and top editor at *American*.

"Tom says he's red hot for the idea of that Mississippi trip," he told Blossom. "Go ahead with the plans for the towboat and we will be in Memphis next Monday morning. Tom will take his Speed Graphic, two Rollies, a 35mm, and he may even carry along his Brownie in case all else fails. By the way," he added, "we'll be taking our wives along, so be good enough to alert the towing company to make room for them, too."

If I recall correctly, that was Thursday afternoon, and as Don had told editor Blossom, the four of us were in Memphis at the Holiday Inn that weekend, waiting to board the towboat Monday morning.

A lighter took us out from the Memphis waterfront through a fog so thick you could almost wad it up like snowballs. A couple of whistle toots, a jingle of bells, and suddenly we were tying up alongside a beautiful, powerful motor vessel owned by the Chotin Towing Corporation. Her name was the *Jos. Chotin,* after the founder of the multimillion-dollar concern.

Two staterooms had been reserved for us, and when Dorothy and I stepped inside ours we looked around in dumb amazement at the spacious room paneled in fine Honduran mahogany and furnished with the accouterments of home, including two beds with crisp white linen, and a private bath.

The trip down the river was one long, twisting, turning, happy adventure and a bit on the fantastic side when I realized that Captain J.B. Kleinpeter, the vessel's master, was guiding a string of barges with an overall length of 1,106 feet around curves and sandbars that would have tried the patience of a man in a rowboat. Towboats, by the way, push their barges in front of them rather than drag them along as a tug will do. To this day I have not heard a logical explanation of why they call them towboats.

You don't really sense the deep solitude of the swamp country of Louisiana until you get near the "bottom," which is river jargon for that stretch between Baton Rouge and New Orleans.

"Captain J.B. says we'll have some time to kill when the towboat's in drydock at Harvey," Don said on our last afternoon of the trip down river. "Of course, while we're in New Orleans we'll have to do the French Quarter and see all the important places so our wives won't feel they are missing out on the sights, but I've a friend who is going to take us on a fast trip down to the Gulf and when we get there I am going to introduce you to some of the finest fishing you ever heard of, I mean *ever* heard of, anywhere!"

Very early the morning after the French Quarter, Don's friend Syd Rodman picked us up in his station wagon, which we loaded with a wide assortment of rods and reels, tackle boxes, and other fishing paraphernalia. We left New Orleans and took U.S. 90 across the delta country to the village of Raceland and then southeast on State Road One along Bayou Lafourche. This stream leads from the town of Donaldsonville on the Mississippi all the way down to the Gulf.

If I imagined myself in swamp country as we traveled across to Raceland, I had to start revising my thinking as we followed State Road One south toward the Gulf.With every turn of the car's wheels we found ourselves slipping deeper and deeper into some of the wildest and most forsaken country to be found anywhere in the United States, with the possible exception of the middle of the Everglades. I got the impression time had simply stopped here about a million years ago.

"What would happen if we should have a breakdown on this road?" I asked.

"Nothing at all," Syd chuckled. "We'd just sit here and wait for somebody to come along and give us a lift. Folks around these parts are mighty helpful to one another. But you will notice, if you care to open the glove compartment, that I carry half a dozen bottles of insect repellant."

When we were about three miles from the coast, the road made an abrupt turn to the east, and suddenly the smell of the swamp was gone and there was the cool clean air blowing in off the Gulf. One more sharp turn put us on the bridge across Caminada Pass and instantly we were on Grand Isle.

You do not have to be a fisherman to become enamored with the

Grand Isle, Louisiana, has a charm all its own and is steeped in history. It is also headquarters for some of the best fishing to be found along the northern Gulf coast.

charm of this quaint island. For one thing, there is the sudden change of scenery from the stillness of the marsh country to the clean, wide openness of an almost tropical island.Then, too, there is a strange admixture of yesteryear and right-this-minute. Houses that have stood the ravages of time and hurricanes for over a century live in peaceful harmony with modern hostelry. Weather-beaten shrimp boats rub gunnels with sleek charter boats of the sport fisherman class. A boy in overalls will be sculling an oyster skiff along on the still waters of Barataria Bay, while overhead a helicopter swishes along on its way out to one of the countless offshore oil-drilling platforms.

Grand Isle is about eight miles long and a mile wide, so it is obvious that it did not receive its name because of its size. But, then again, the dictionary does not restrict the adjective "grand" to size alone. I rather think those who gave the island its name were thinking more of magnificence, imposing appearance, or sublimity. Whatever the reason for the name, I was soon to discover that it was a grand place to fish.

Just as the Florida Keys, the Outer Banks of North Carolina, and Texas' Padre Island are steeped in the rugged history of piracy, so is Grand Isle. Everybody on the island is aware of the greatest Gulf pirate of them all, the illustrious Frenchman Jean Laffite. This handsome, dark-eyed young scalawag who was the scourge of British shipping in the early eighteen hundreds was undoubtedly one of the most successful gentlemen who sailed under the Jolly Roger. Prodding along the upper Gulf coast, he discovered Barataria Bay. Grand Isle and Grand Terre Islands were the gateway to what Laffite considered to be the perfect place to take life easy during his shipping forays.

Many of today's inhabitants of Grand Isle are direct descendants of Laffite's crew and they take pride in their heritage. They are a polyglot mixture of French, Portuguese, Spanish, and Filipino descent, and the old-timers still speak French-Spanish patois with a nuance from the Cajun jargon heard regularly in other Louisiana parishes.

As soon as we could get the equipment transferred from the station wagon to a trim 32-foot cabin boat skippered by a giant of a man known as Captain Max, we tossed off the lines and got underway. It was a quick trip along the back side of the island and out of Barataria Bay through the pass to the Gulf. On our port we could see the ruins of Fort Livingston. It was one of a ring of forts that had been built to protect New Orleans after the British threatened the city in the early years of the nineteenth century.

"Those old ruins are just crawlin' with ghosts and goblins of every type you can imagine," Captain Max said seriously, jerking his thumb toward Grand Terre Island. "Do crazy things, too," he continued. "One night I was over there all by myself trying to get a net I had lost. I built myself a fire 'round midnight and pulled off my boots while I was getting ready to take me a little nap. When I woke up my boots were gone and where do you reckon I found 'em?"

"Probably dragged off in the brush by raccoons or wild hogs," Syd chuckled.

"Dern funny critters if that's what did it," Captain Max said, wagging his head slowly. "They were sittin' square up on one of them busted down old walls toe to toe and packed full of wet sand."

While we had been loading the tackle aboard back at the dock, Captain Max had explained that we would troll out into the Gulf for a couple of miles and then get down to some serious fishing around one of the oil rigs. Almost before we were through the pass Syd was fast onto a tarpon. The silverking was a big one and he made about five beautiful jumps before Syd could get him under control.

"Too bad it ain't a couple of weeks from now," Captain Max said, as he watched Syd working up a good sweat on his first fish. "Each summer we hold a big tarpon rodeo here at Grand Isle and folks come by the hundreds. If it was going on right now you might have a winner on your hands with that tackle you're using."

"I'll be back," Syd puffed. "I haven't missed one in ten years and maybe catching this one is a good omen. Last summer there were four of us on board and everybody caught two or three each, and I didn't even get a strike."

The tarpon was a beauty, but not more than sixty pounds. A lot of fish, but not in the bragging class. When Syd had him up alongside, he told me to jaw gaff him and shove the jig out of his mouth. We could see the hook was just holding loosely in the side of his jaw. A lesser fisherman would not have been able to hold him beyond the first jump.

Before we reached the offshore rig, we tangled with a school of Spanish mackerel and in twenty minutes had five of them in the ice chest.

"Lots of folks raise the devil 'bout the oil, gas, and sulphur platforms the companies are building out here in the Gulf," Captain Max said. "But us that make our living fishing are pretty sure they don't do anything but good so far as the fish population is concerned. Fact is, if it wasn't for them I'd do better trappin' rats back in the marsh."

Before the day was over, I was convinced of one thing. Fishing was about as good as I had ever seen it. The platform we tied up to was a monstrous affair supported on columns that went down nearly ten fathoms to the bottom. By trying a number of different methods of fishing we finished filling the ice chest with an assortment that included a large cobia, several bluefish, and a wahoo that whistled by like a run-away torpedo and hit Don's lure so hard it nearly pulled him overboard.

My first saltwater venture off the Louisiana coast was all Don Eddy had promised, and more. The problem was that we had a towboat to catch the next day for the trip back up the Mississippi. I knew right from that day that I was coming back for more. What had intrigued me the most was the tales Captain Max and Syd told about pompano fishing around the rigs.

"The best time for pompano is anywhere between the tail end of October, on up into March," Captain Max said. "With two or three of us fishing we'll ice down a hundred or more in one day. We get the biggest ones in January, but whether you plan to fish with me or any of the other skippers you better get your reservations in early 'cause folks come down here by the droves and it's all we can do to handle 'em."

As luck would have it, I had to forego the trip that winter, but the next year I was on the island with reservation in hand. Again there were four of us aboard and in seven hours of fishing we had boated nearly a hundred and fifty pompano that ranged in weight from two to five pounds. Our biggest problem was not catching enough pompano, but resorting to all kinds of tricks to fight off the mackerel and blues that seemed determined to keep the pompanos from taking the yellow buck-tails with the dabs of shrimp on the hook tips.

We were using spinning tackle and we found the best method was to tie the 2-pound nylon leaders directly to the bucktails and then join the leaders to the 8-pound test monofilament lines with the smoothest blood knots (See Chapter XIV) we could tie. A swivel or a clip of any kind seemed to set the macks and blues wild and they acted as if they were cutting the line to protect the hordes of pompano that swarmed beneath the platform.

There are several types of fish in the pompano class that include the large permits, the round pompano, and the African variety. The type

Pompano

that invades the Louisiana coast in winter is the common pompano *(Trachinotus carolinus).* Their chief hang-out is around the offshore oil-drilling platforms and today they are the most popular light-tackle saltwater game fish along the Louisiana coast.

As a conservationist I inwardly shudder every time I hear of a new oil rig being erected anywhere along the coast, because each one is a potential bombshell and a distinct threat to swimming beaches, waterfowl, littoral wildlife, and especially to the propagation of fish life, so much of which depends on the shallows near shore as a hatchery and nursery ground for larvae and immature fish. If a pipeline breaks and cannot be repaired by divers almost immediately, the effects are certain to be devastating.

What it does to swimming beaches is obvious. The sand is befouled, the water is not fit to swim in, and there are few aromas more offensive to the human olfactory system than crude oil spread out over a wide area. The havoc to wildlife and the fish population is more subtle but highly detrimental.

If the world does not pollute and overpopulate itself into oblivion in the near future, many generations will pass before the devastating flood of oil that spewed up from the oil rig off Santa Barbara, California, is forgotten. Resort owners, ornothologists, conservationists in general, and ichthyologists in particular set up a hue and cry that was heard all the way across the nation. The same thing occurred in 1969 off the coast of Louisiana, but the effects of that unfortunate incident went almost unnoticed by the general population, because a strong and steady north wind pushed the oil away from shore and disbursed it in the far reaches of the open Gulf.

Had the wind been from the south the result would have been tragic and beyond repair. Oil spills are not restricted to the drilling platforms alone, and it will be a long time before the residents of Florida's Sun Coast in the vicinity of Tampa Bay will forget the tanker *Delian Apollon* that broke a seam while entering Tampa Bay on February 13, 1970. Then, too, there is the unforgivable practice of ships flushing their tanks at sea. No matter where it comes from, the results are the same. Oil and water do not mix. As a result, the oil floats on top of the water and goes whichever way the prevailing wind drives it. Waterfowl are the first and most obvious victims. Pelicans, gulls, cormorants, ducks, and all the others that spend part of their lives resting on the water are unaware of the deadly booby trap of which they are becoming victims when they splash in for a landing. Immediately, their feathers become coated with the thick, gooey mass, and when they try to take off they discover they can do no more than flounder along helplessly, and death is the almost certain outcome. Even if they could find a patch of clean water, no amount of splash and thrashing will remove enough of the clinging oil, and being unable to fly in search of food, they simply starve.

Certain surface-swimming fish make a habit of jumping and otherwise breaking the surface at frequent intervals. They, too, are unaware of the deadly film and get the oil in their gills, which act as a fish's lungs, and they soon succumb. Many rotted and bloated carcasses wash up on the beach and add to the general human misery.

The real damage is often not nearly so noticeable as a beach unfit for human habitation, or helpless birds dragging themselves along with spent wings. The vast destruction is back in the marshy fringes of seacoast swampland where the average human seldom ventures.

It is here that the deadly oil does its long-range damage. Animals such as muskrats, raccoons, and others that normally feed on small creatures and plants found along the shoreline are poisoned.

Worse effected still are the shallow mud and grass flats where shellfish such as oysters are found. The oil does not evaporate as gasoline would and it alternately rises and falls with the ebb and flow of the tide. Each time the oil settles on the grass or mud bottom a certain amount of it clings to every blade of grass and grain of sand. Here, in this piscatorial cradle, eggs and newly hatched fish so small they cannot be seen perish and so do the microscopic planktonic creatures upon which they feed. Death comes quickly and not in the millions or billions or trillions, but in numbers too astronomical even to begin to count.

Only time, tide, and storm will eventually disburse the oil particles and cover them with mud and rotting vegetation to a point where they are no longer harmful, but that may take years, and the diminution of wildlife and certain types of fish may have reached or crossed the threshold of oblivion.

One of the worst oil-rig disasters, one which spread the greatest oil slick, occurred in the northern Gulf on February 10, 1970, when a cluster of oil wells blew out. The explosion caused a fire which spewed crude oil into the Gulf for a month.

On August 26 of that year a federal judge in New Orleans fined the Chevron Oil Company $1 million for the disaster. The oil company pleaded no contest to five hundred violations of failing to equip its offshore wells with proper safety and antipollution devices. When laws with teeth as sharp as this are enforced, it should be certain that the oil companies will see to it that similar accidents are few and far between. Yet hardly a year passed before another holocaust was loosed off the same coast when another cluster of rigs blew. The resulting fire burned totally out of control.

The offshore rigs are huge steel platforms built many feet above the surface and supported by massive pilings. In the midst of these pilings are the pipes that reach down into the bowels of the earth beneath the Gulf and through which countless barrels of oil and gas are sucked up day and night, twenty-four hours a day.

The saying *it is an ill wind that blows no good* was never so true as when referring to the oil rigs. According to the natives of Grand Isle and Cameron and other villages along the coast, the fishing has always been good. There is no doubt that the endless array of bays and bayous have long been bountifully supplied with fish such as the speckled trout, redfish, flounder, and so forth, but it has been only within the past two decades that really big-time saltwater sport fishing has come into its own.

Maybe the abundance of amberjack, cobia, Spanish mackerel, barracuda, pompano, and others were always there. There is no way to turn back the clock and find out, but it was not until fishermen began investigating the waters beneath and around the platforms that they found they were actually in an angler's paradise. Today, it is estimated that nearly 90 percent of all the state's saltwater angling is centered on rig fishing, as it is popularly known. The remaining small percentage of offshore fishing is done by trolling in the open water.

The reason that the rigs have become such popular places to fish is quite logically because that is where the fish are found in the greatest numbers. The supporting piles are, in effect, nothing short of a man-made reef, and it is astounding how quickly the fish population begins to increase once construction is begun.

Those of us who have not been content to fish only from the surface know that sunken wrecks quickly become the homes of vast numbers of fish. Whether it be a huge ship or small boat, the action starts immediately, and any scuba diver who has explored wrecks either old or new knows how the chain of events takes place.

Once a solid object is under water, be it the hull of a ship or the concrete and steel footings for an offshore oil rig, creatures of the sea congregate within a matter of days. They are everywhere both in microscopic forms of animal life and plant spores. In order to live and grow they must find some solid object to cling to. Failing this they soon die or become prey of a host of other forms of life that subsist on them.

The first form of life on a solid object under water is almost sure to be a thin coating of what appears to be a smooth moss. Once it finds a foothold, it begins to take root and to grow, and almost at the same time come tiny forms of sea animals, such as the larvae of barnacles, sea squirts, hydroids, and limpets. Once these find a place to light, they, too, begin to grow and because they are there in ever-increasing numbers they attract tiny fish that feed on them. The growing numbers of smaller fish that are beginning to swarm around the solid sunken object soon attract the attention of even larger fish, and they move in to feed on the swelling population.

The oil, gas, and sulphur platforms offer something extra that the sunken ship cannot afford, and this is shade. Cobia and dolphin, for example, like to rest near the surface in shaded areas when they are waiting for food of their choice to come in range. Spanish mackerel, kingfish, and other types that are forever on the move use the rigs as feeding stations. Down below are the real heavyweights of the fish world: the red groupers, black groupers, and the giant of all groupers, the jewfish. Divers with whom I have talked, who work on the underwater structural parts of the rigs, report seeing jewfish that would exceed a thousand pounds in weight and have mouths large enough to swallow a refrigerator. One diver, John Luck, was working out of a bell with another, named Lee Gates. Suddenly, Gates realized that Luck was being swallowed by a monster jewfish. Through sheer brawn he managed to pull Luck free.

On another recent occasion, a diver friend of mine, Nick Zinkowski, was working out of a diving bell on the bottom when a giant jewfish actually stuck its head up into the bell entrance, not once, but time after time, while Zinkowski was working around one of the platform footings. When he returned to the bell to climb inside, the jewfish grabbed him by the legs and literally pulled off one of his boots while Nick's partner struggled to get him into the safety of the bell. If you have any doubt about the behemoths that lurk in the depths around the bottom of the rigs, just ask some or any of the professional divers who work down there. These are not just weekend skin divers who enjoy telling a tall tale or two, but professionals who have been at the business for years.

The oil companies and the crews who man the drilling platforms have been more than cooperative with the sport fishermen who have discovered the rig-fishing bonanza. They could, if they chose, refuse to allow the boats to tie up to the pilings. After all, each rig is as much private property as another man's boat or pier. The nice part about it is that they are willing for the fisherman to tie up and enjoy himself while he fills his fish chest. All they ask is that when one of the boats puts out a mooring line that it be done in such a manner as not to interfere with the drilling operation. They also expect the fisherman to keep clear when one of the work boats bringing supplies, equipment, and relief crews nears the platform. The true sportsman recognizes that he is, in a sense, a guest and is more than willing to abide by such common-sense rules.

The fabulous fishing along the Louisiana coast is not restricted to the bays, surfcasting, and rig fishing. These shores are becoming a mecca for the spectacular blue-water gladiators such as the sailfish, blue marlin, white marlin, bluefin tuna, and others that were simply unheard of and certainly not fished for there a few years ago.

The first broadbill swordfish *(Xiphias gladius)* taken on rod and reel in the Gulf was caught on July 21, 1969, by George M. Snellings III. He was fishing with Captain Bert Smith, skipper of the *Holiday* out of South Pass, Louisiana. Smith generally fishes his 45-footer out of Pompano Beach, Florida, during the winter, spending the spring and summer taking charters out from South Pass.

Snellings' fish struck a rigged mullet. The tackle was a 9/0 reel with 800 yards of line. The fight lasted almost twenty minutes, and when put on the scales at the South Pass weighing station, the broadbill weighed 112½ pounds, measured 8 feet 5 inches in length, with a 35-inch girth. Swordfish have been taken on occasions by research vessels using long lines off the coast of Louisiana, but it remained for Snellings to have the honor of capturing the first by rod and reel.

If you should want to fish as far south as possible in Louisiana you can take State Road 23 all the way down to Venice and go by boat to Port Eads at the very bottom of the Mississippi. A much quicker way is to charter a float plane in New Orleans and get there in forty-five minutes. When you arrive at South Pass, which is where Port Eads is located, you will know you are in big game fishing country. There is an automated Coast Guard lighthouse that can be seen seventeen miles at sea and a fine new marina with all the facilities, as well as slips for over a hundred boats. Several charter boats are also available.

Port Eads is also headquarters of The New Orleans Big Game Fishing Club. Not only is this club a fine organization of dedicated bluewater sportsmen, but it is performing a valuable service that is constantly adding to the store of knowledge about Gulf fishing. To do this, the club cooperates with the Louisiana Wildlife and Fisheries Commission by sponsoring a scientific survey in relation to all the important fishes. Almost all fish brought into the South Pass weighing station are examined in detail by a graduate marine biologist. Measurements are taken, the sex determined, and a study is made of its stomach contents. Such detailed analysis is certain to produce surprising discoveries. The outstanding one to date is that 90 percent of the blue marlin caught in these waters are females. The opposite is true in the Bahamas, where most of the blues are males.

Some of the best charter fleets and towns that cater to the saltwater fisherman in Louisiana are those of Cameron, in the western part of the state just south of Lake Charles, Intracoastal City at the northwestern corner of Vermillion Bay, Cocodrie on Terrebonne Bay, Grand Isle, which has already been discussed, and the towns of Venice and Empire. The latter are situated right on the Mississippi delta as it reaches out into the Gulf.

TEXAS

Texas fishing cannot adequately be described without resorting to the use of superlatives ordinarily associated with the Lone Star State. The state has an abundance of coastline. There are 367 miles of beach fronting on the Gulf and a grand total of 3,359 miles when the entire tidal shoreline is measured. If you are traveling from the east the first glimpse of the open Gulf comes when you turn south at Port Arthur on State Road 87 and down to the town of Sabine. From that point on it is saltwater fishing all the way down to Boca Chica, just a short stretch above the mouth of the Rio Grande River.

Much like the coast of North Carolina, the majority of the Texas coast is shielded from open water by barrier islands. For the saltwater angler, this means a double bonus in the form of two major types of fishing. There is the pounding surf on one side and the sheltered water of bays and lagoons on the other. Then, of course, there are numerous ports, both large and small, that are well supplied with charter and party boats that make daily voyages out on the Gulf to deep water.

My first sampling of fishing along the Texas coast occurred a number of years ago when a friend and I had the treasure-hunting bug and spent a period of time camping on that long, skinny finger of sand known as Padre Island. We failed to find a pot of gold, but it was a true end-of-the-rainbow so far as surf fishing was concerned.

Texans are quick to tell you that most of Padre Island is a National Seashore, and being Texans, they just can't help adding it is the biggest —which it is, all 81 miles of it. What is more, it is just about as wild and ruggedly beautiful as it was eons ago when the Gulf of Mexico was first formed.

The causeway at Corpus Christi is the northern gateway to this wonderful reach of seacoast wilderness. The island itself is over a hundred miles in length with the National Seashore near the middle. It is unpolluted and unspoiled, and the National Park Service is determined to see that it remains that way.

If your inclination is to go farther south, you might want to go all the way down to Brownsville and cross over to South Padre Island on the free Queen Isabella Causeway. It is a three-mile journey from Port Isabel to Isla Blanca Park, which is a real wintertime haven for the fisherman-camper on wheels. Down at the southern tip there are overnight shelters, cabins, and campsites. The cabins are equipped with bunk beds, stoves, electric lights, running water, refrigerators, and a moderate amount of necessary furniture.

It is possible to drive for many miles along the beach of Padre Island in a conventional automobile, but like any beach, there is also the ever-present problem of getting bogged down in soft sand. Therefore, for those interested in some real wilderness camping a long way down the island, it is advisable to use a car or truck equipped with four-wheel drive. In fact, it is the only safe way to make such a trip.

It is also important to remember that when the term "wilderness camping" is used, it means just what it says, and a bit more to boot. You might go on a wilderness camping trip in many areas of the country and not be overly concerned about drinking water. On Padre Island, the wise angling camper will give serious consideration to carrying along all the water he and those with him will need for the length of time civilization will be out of reach. It is easy to underestimate how much potable water just one person requires in a day's time.

Of course, there is the Gulf that invites swimming in the warm months, thus solving the problem of bathing. But you dare not fill the car radiator with salt water, nor will it work for boiling a pot of rice or beans. Until a person begins to keep close track of every ounce of water he uses, he seldom has any idea of the amount. Be honest with yourself and start adding up the ounces used from the time you get up in the morning until you retire.

It must be remembered that the morning glass of juice is largely water. Then comes the coffee or tea intake, or both, during the day, plus bottles of soft drinks, water used for cooking, and most important of all, just plain old-fashioned drinking water. Shaving, too, requires a certain amount of water, and toothpaste and the wet stuff in the Gulf are not exactly compatible. Then again, you may be one of those who gets rained on every time he goes fishing, but don't count on it down in the middle of Padre Island.

The best practice is to make a careful study of the logical amount of water that will be needed and then add a bit more for good measure. Most camper trucks are equipped with water tanks that afford an adequate supply for a short period, but it still makes good sense to augment the main reservoir with many extra gallons. Some of the best containers are plastic jugs that are common on the grocery store shelves. They can be thoroughly washed and filled with water that will remain safe to drink for days. The nice part about them is that they do not break, as do those made of glass.

There are two basic modes of transportation that may be used to take full advantage of the Padre Island National Seashore: an automobile along the beach and a boat along the inshore side of the island on the calm waters of Laguna Madre. But here again, once you leave Corpus Christi you are on your own except for a chance meeting with another boat. It is, therefore, necessary to plan in advance and be sure your larder is well stocked. Running out of gasoline for the outboard or camper is not as serious as exhausting the water supply, but it can be downright annoying.

The question of when is the best time to visit Padre Island cannot be answered without a few "ifs" and "buts." The winters along the coast can be unpleasantly cold when the northers are blowing. Again, if luck is on your side, the weather in midwinter can be comfortable. In winter the best fishing is to be found in the bays and this, of course, includes Laguna Madre. Then, too, there is the question concerning the type of fishing that appeals most to you.

There is no doubt that the greatest variety of fishing is to be found during the warmer months. From early spring to late fall, fishing is good on both sides of the island.

Padre Island averages about a mile in width and consists mainly of sand dunes with sparse vegetation such as rank grass, mesquite, and chili bushes. The dunes, some of which reach a height of fifty feet, are forever on the move. You may find a given stretch of the island ridged with formidable hills of sand one year and when you return to the same spot a year or so later they may be nearly gone or moved for a considerable distance.

Many types of birds are there in abundance, and other forms of wildlife consist mainly of raccoons, coyotes, and occasional droves of wild hogs. Lizards and snakes are also present. While not numerous enough to be considered a menace, it is a wise idea to keep an eye out for rattlesnakes when in heavy underbrush. This problem, however, exists along practically all southern coastal areas and is mentioned here only because it is possible to be a very long way from medical aid about halfway down the length of Padre Island.

Man's tenure of the island undoubtedly began a long time ago when the Indians went there to fish. The finding of flint points attests to their visits, but there is little to suggest they resided there on a permanent basis. The real history of this interesting island began about four centuries ago when Spanish sailors stopped off from time to time to salvage treasure-laden ships blown ashore by hurricanes that swept in from the Gulf. Many are the anglers and campers today who have found gold and silver coins in sufficient numbers to tantalize the imagination. There is always the wonder of whether or not one is only a few steps away from a large cache of real treasure.

The name of the island resulted from the period when a Spanish padre named Nicholas Balli founded a colony of ranchers along the southern end. He and those with him made an attempt to establish a cattle empire, but the experiment was a total failure. There simply was not enough grass to support the cattle, and the ranchers were frequently washed out by storms. The mainlanders began to refer to the long stretch of sand as "the Padre's island" and this was eventually shortened to Padre.

In viewing the island one would have no reason to suspect it could in any manner be associated with the sewing machine, but it does in a remote sort of way, and therein lies an interesting bit of Texas history and another intriguing story of a bona fide treasure that still lies hidden under the restless sands.

John Singer, brother of Isaac Singer of sewing-machine fame, was shipwrecked near the southern end of the island in 1847. Singer managed to get ashore and also to save his wife and son along with one of the ship's sailors. During the time they were castaways on the island they decided they liked it and proceeded to build a house. After they were well established, John Singer began to explore the area and on one of his jaunts he discovered a cache of gold and jewels reported to be worth about eighty thousand dollars.

Fearful that his wealth might be confiscated by the Union Army, by then rumored to be moving into the area, Singer followed the time-honored practice of digging a hole and burying his hoard. He then drew a map showing where he had hidden it, six miles due north of his front door. With his treasure thus secured, he and his family left the island.

After the Civil War Singer returned, fully expecting to unearth his fortune. He was positive he had made no miscalculation in drawing his map, but the topography was so completely changed by the shifting sands that he was unable to find any trace of his cache. The search became an obsession with him, and he continued to hunt until he died many years later.

Camping and fishing on Padre Island, with an occasional thought of buried treasure, is only a small part of the Texas fishing story. For the piscatorial landlubber there are numerous piers that extend well out into the Gulf. Many are free and provide excellent accommodations, including bait, tackle, plenty of parking space and camping ground. One good example is the 800-foot pier on the Gulf side of Padre Island just twenty-five minutes from downtown Corpus Christi.

Not to be overlooked are the fishing fleets of both charter and party boats to be found at all ports along the coast from Port Arthur to Brownsville. These boats are most active during the summer months when the bonito, kingfish, dolphin, tarpon, marlin, sailfish, and cobia are nearby in abundance.

Then there are the inshore schools of game fish that provide action around the calendar. This list includes speckled trout, flounder, sheepshead, gaff-topsail catfish, whiting, and croaker. Drum fishing begins in January and continues well into spring.

Any discourse on saltwater fishing in Texas would simply not be complete without a brief mention of my life-long friend, Jack Holt. Now with the Texas Department of Public Safety, Jack has led a Jack London-type life. He and I grew up together in Virginia, and after our ways parted he set out on a life of adventure of the type most people

Look out, fish, here they come! The time is early morning, the place is Port Aransas, Texas, and the destination is the open expanse of the Gulf of Mexico.

only dream. True to his nature of never doing things in a half-hearted manner, Jack has explored the coast of Texas for many years in search of the best fishing. Where does he go? He will hedge a bit, stretching his lanky frame and mentioning a good trip after reds off Mustang Island, or a time he practically had to fight off the trout, or the day he caught a monster shark in Port Mansfield Channel. When you pin him down he is likely to admit the Matagorda Bay area is his favorite.

For the angler who wants to try his luck in Matagorda Bay or Espirito Bay just to the south, the starting point is Port O'Connor. Once there you will have your choice of numerous different types of fishing. For instance, there is the huge jetty that protects the channel cut through the peninsula. Most conservationists, and the angling fraternity is full of them, take a dim view of man's tampering with nature. This time, however, the jetties worked decidedly in favor of nature and the fisherman.

The swift tidal flow through the opening increased the angling potentials by leaps and bounds. The channel invites vast numbers of game fish to enter the sheltered bay waters, and the fishing is outstanding along the jetty rocks themselves. Another bonus from the channel is the nearness to the deep water of the Gulf.

Corpus Christi has long boasted one of the best charter- and party-boat fleets to be found anywhere along the coast, and the skippers know their business and are proud of it. Tarpon are plentiful in the summer months there and all along the coast. The season extends well into October. The average Texas angler will restrain himself when he views a 6-foot silverking and likely say: "Wal, what did you expect, partner? It's a Texas tarpon, ain't it."

twelve ~~~~~~~~~~~~~~~~~~~~~

~~~~~~~~~
~~~~~~~~~

DANGEROUS MARINE ANIMALS

STINGRAYS

The afternoon was warm and the surface of the bay was smooth. It was early fall, and Charlie and I were wading about knee-deep across a grassflat, casting for speckled trout. Suddenly, Charlie let out a wild yell and I saw him drop his spinning rod.

"Stingaree!" he shouted and began splashing frantically toward the beach as if he had been set upon by a swarm of hornets.

Hurrying to his assistance, I was startled to see him collapse in the shallow water a few feet from shore. When I reached his side and helped him to his feet I could see he was in agony. By the time I had him stretched out on the beach he began retching violently.

"Felt it under my foot," he blurted between gasps. "Soft and slick. I knew I was on a stingaree, but he hit me before I could get off."

305

The stingray is basically a bottom-dwelling creature that frequents bays and inlets. He often covers himself with silt and is difficult for the wading angler to spot. The sheet of paper in the photo shows the location of the dangerous barb on the top of the tail.

Examining my companion's right foot, I saw the embedded tail spine of a stingray, or "stingaree" as it is known in some localities. It was a large one, nearly three inches in length, and had entered the soft flesh between the ankle and the Achilles tendon. Gingerly, I touched the spine and realized it had been driven in so deeply that extraction was going to be difficult.

Hardly five minutes had passed since the accident, but Charlie was already beginning alternately to shiver with chills and to gasp at hot flashes he said were sweeping over his body. By the time I had him back to my car, which was parked on a sandy trail of a road, I could tell he was becoming fairly ill. The muscles of his stomach were almost as rigid as a board, and he was complaining of a pins-and-needles sensation all over his body. He next told me that his arms and legs were growing numb.

By luck, we were able quickly to find a doctor who, because of his practice near the Florida coast, had acquired considerable experience in treating stingray wounds. Several weeks later Charlie was still unable to use his foot, but prompt medical attention had prevented serious complications. Unhappily, such is not always the case where stingray injuries are concerned. Gangrene may develop, and as a result, the foot, and sometimes the leg, has to be amputated. There are cases on record where death has been attributed to a stingray wound.

Close relatives of sharks, stingrays are flat, fishlike creatures that spend a considerable portion of their lives on or near the bottom in water ranging from several inches to several feet in depth. The three most frequently encountered by fishermen with unpleasant results are the Atlantic stingray *(Dasyatis sabina)* and the bluntnose stingray *(Dasyatis sayi),* which average between two and three feet in width. The third is the southern stingray *(Dasyatis americana)* that is known to reach a size measuring 5 feet in width, 7 feet in length with weight well over a hundred pounds. One scientifically unidentified specimen, but believed to be of the southern variety, was captured by commercial fishermen off Bradenton Beach, Florida. It measured 6½ feet across, was 10 feet long, and weighed nearly 600 pounds.

In general, the stingray is somewhat rhomboid in shape, with some more oval and others almost round. The tails of those mentioned above are as long, or longer than, the total body length. The eyes are located on the dorsal side and near the anterior portion. The mouth, nose, and gill slits are just below the eyes on the chalk white underside. The color on the top ranges from greenish tan to dark brown.

Depending upon the size of the individual, stingrays feed on amphipod crustaceans such as sand fleas and others. Worms, shrimp, and shellfish also form a part of their diet. The food is crushed by a series of knoblike teeth set deep inside the mouth. In order to eat, the stingray must descend upon his food, or near it, and then depend upon his nose to guide him to the exact spot.

Unlike the skates that lay black, horn-tipped eggs, known as mermaid's purses, the stingrays are ovoviviparous and give birth to living young that have first hatched within the female's body. A newborn stingray about the size of a man's hand enters his watery domain fully equipped with a small, but nonetheless dangerous, spine.

It is this barbed spine, located on the top of the tail about a quarter of the way back from the base, that makes the stingray dangerous. It is somewhat loosely attached to the tough hide. A close examination shows it to be a sliver of hard, bony substance with fifty or more recurved barbs on each side. When this needle-sharp spine is driven into flesh the serrated edges make extraction extremely difficult and the spine is frequently torn loose from the tail. The lost spine is quickly replaced by a new one that is forming beneath it and at times rays will

When attached to the stingray's tail this dangerous spine is coated with poisonous slime. The cleaned example in the photo is of average size and shows the recurved barbs that make its removal difficult once it is driven into human flesh.

be observed to have two fully developed spines. It is to be assumed in such cases that the older one was used, but with insufficient force to tear it free of the tail.

The spine is solely a weapon of defense, and the average fish is content to leave the stingray alone rather than run the risk of being struck by that venomous weapon. Sharks, however, as well as a few other fish, including large grouper, seem to ignore the spine. Many sharks have been caught with as many as a dozen stingray spines embedded in the flesh around their mouths; some obviously having been there a long while.

Unlike the fangs of many venomous snakes, the stingray spine is not hollow. The poison is contained in the coating of slime on the spine and beneath the recurved barbs. Therefore, the deeper the spine is driven into the flesh, the more serious the wound becomes, both from a standpoint of tissue injury and the excess of envenomation. Along with immediate pain, swelling near the point of entry is usually present. The flesh becomes ashen in appearance, later cyanotic, and then changes to a reddish color. The only practical first-aid treatment is to wash the wound with antiseptic and induce bleeding. The victim should be placed under medical care as quickly as possible.

Some otherwise perfectly rational people have an abnormal dread of venomous creatures and often this fear is magnified to such proportions as actually to bring on a heart attack. It is important when administering first aid to a stingray victim to reassure him that the incident of death from the poison is extremely rare.

There have been cases on record where people have died of fright after being bitten by a nonpoisonous snake. Where the stingray is concerned, the pain is often so intense that the victim has good reason to believe he has been mortally wounded, and it should be emphasized that while occasional deaths have been the result, it is generally because medical aid has been ignored and secondary infection has been the eventual killer.

The more common of the stingrays spend the warmer months of the year in the shallow water of bays and tidal estuaries. With the coming of winter they move offshore into deeper water.

Others found along the lower Atlantic coast and in the Gulf include the bluntnose, cownose, roughtail, and two species of butterfly stingrays. In the case of the latter two, the disk or "wings" are considerably exaggerated to the extent that they taper like the wings of a bird.

One of the most beautiful of the dangerous rays is the spotted eagle ray *(Aëtobatus narinari)*. They are common from the Chesapeake south and throughout the Gulf. The eagle ray is most often seen in offshore waters, but they occasionally venture into bays. They are black on the dorsal side, with sharply defined markings in the shape of complete and broken circles. These markings are often almost pure white, but they may occasionally be greenish yellow in color. The underside is almost pure white.

They sometimes travel in pairs or schools and are often seen making spectacular leaps that vault them ten or more feet into the air, frequently emitting loud croaking sounds as they jump. The adult spotted eagle ray is large, reaching a width of seven feet and weighing nearly five hundred pounds.

Discounting the remote possibility that one might accidentally land on a small boat as the result of an ill-planned jump, their only danger lies in the two or more large and highly venomous spines at the point where their long whiplike tail joins the body.

Several other rays jump as does the eagle ray. None, however, is quite so awe inspiring as the Atlantic manta ray *(Manta birostris)*, jumping in a school. They often grow to a width of twenty feet or more and weigh in excess of two tons. It is believed that the jumping occurs during the period when the young are being born. They are harmless creatures that swim swiftly through the water, often on or near the surface when feeding on shrimp, small fish, or plankton. This food is swept into their mouths with large cephalic fins situated on each side of the head adjacent to the mouth.

The stingray is occasionally caught by bottom-fishing anglers. A stiff

Fearsome as he may look, the Atlantic manta is harmless unless, of course, he happens to land on your boat after one of the high jumps for which he is famous. Mantas reach a width of twenty feet and weigh in excess of two tons. Such bulk can cause a considerable splash.

fight is certain to follow once it has been hooked, and if it is landed it should be treated with utmost caution, because the spine is equally dangerous in or out of water. The safest practice is to cut the line, because, as is the case with the shark, it is not easily killed. Of course, it can be bludgeoned with a length of pipe or heavy stick, but the tail should be carefully avoided while the *coup de grâce* is being delivered.

Despite its formidable weapon of defense, the stingray is an easily frightened creature. The danger of stepping on one can be greatly minimized if the wading angler will slide his feet rather than take conventional steps. Rays have a habit of settling on sandy or mud bottoms and covering themselves with silt in much the same manner as a flounder. Except for their exposed eyes, they are often completely hidden, and trying to watch for them is an undependable precautionary measure.

MORAY

There are two popular misconceptions about morays. One is that they are eels, and the second is that they have poison fangs. While it resembles an eel in that it has an elongated, snakelike body and is covered with a thick coating of slime, it is not an eel at all. Instead, the moray belongs to the family *Muraenidae.*

They have small rounded gill openings but have no pectoral or pelvic fins. They are not migratory, spending most of their time in the general area of salt water where their life began.

The common American eel, *(Anguilla rostrata)* is of the order *Apodes,* and its life cycle is entirely different. Hatched in the mid-Atlantic, the true eel is a catadromous creature that deserts the sea at an early age and moves far inland into lakes, ponds, and streams where it lives for ten years or more until it reaches maturity and is ready to

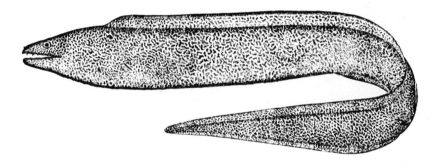

Moray

spawn. It then descends to the salt water and open ocean from which it came, and never returns.

The green moray *(Gymnothorax funebris),* which is found in southern salt water, is truly a fearsome sea animal to behold. Large specimens can and do inflict painful and serious bites, but contrary to popular belief, they do not possess poisonous fangs. They grow to a length of six to ten feet and some as thick as a man's thigh. Their large mouths are filled with needle-sharp teeth.

On several occasions I have been in a boat when one was landed and have caught a few of them myself. So certain are some fishermen that

The green moray is not an eel, nor does he possess poisonous fangs. His powerful jaws are filled with needle-sharp teeth, however, and he can inflict a serious bite. Morays are known to reach a length of ten feet and be as big around as a man's thigh.

they have hooked a deadly sea serpent that they become terrified. One man I was fishing with off the jetties near Panama City, Florida, caught a fairly large moray which gave him quite a tussle for a few minutes. When he finally got it up to the surface and saw the writhing creature, he became panic-stricken and threw his rod and reel into the water.

Oddly enough, the green moray is actually not green. Instead, its true color is a bluish gray and only appears to be green because of a yellow alga that clings to the thick coating of slime covering the entire body. It is the combination of the two primary colors that gives the moray its greenish hue, hence its name.

All told, there are well over a hundred types of morays scattered over all tropical and many subtropical seas. Research on some of these is sparse or entirely missing, therefore it would be presumptuous to state categorically that no moray possesses poison glands. It is safe to say, however, that none of those inhabiting the waters of the Gulf of Mexico or the lower Atlantic coast have them.

Along with the green moray, and sharing the same range, is the spotted variety, *(Gymnothorax moringa)*. This one is not quite as large as the green, but still of formidable size. He is easily recognizable by the liberal sprinkling of white or yellow spots, or both, on a dark, almost black background.

Both types are similar, being of a sluggish nature when in an unmolested state. They are essentially bottom-dwelling creatures and are found close to shore as well as out in water over a hundred feet in depth. They are seldom far from coral reefs or rock piles in which they spend most of their time. It is frequently stated that morays are nocturnal, but I have seen many of them caught during daylight hours, which would seem to indicate that they are just about as active at either time.

One episode in which I became personally involved with a moray occurred when my wife and I were on our way to Key West. Late afternoon had caught us as we reached Long Key. Since we were in no hurry and wanted to enjoy the automotive sea voyage in the full light of day, we decided to stop at a motel and spend the night. After dinner I took a couple of light spinning rods from the car and bought a bucket of live shrimp from the operator of the motel.

It was only a short walk down to the point where the Long Key viaduct connects that island with Conch and Duck keys to the west. Dorothy and I decided to spend a few hours fishing from the bank near the bridge abutment, just to see what might be active. As is generally our practice, I started out using artificial lures, while Dorothy dug a fat specimen out of the shrimp bucket.

After fifteen or twenty minutes of uneventful fishing on the part of both of us, Dorothy shouted that she had something and from the way her rod tip was acting, it was obvious that she had hooked onto some-thing big. Propping my rod against a slab of concrete, I picked up the flashlight and shined the beam down into the clear water. She had a green moray. All we could see was the head protruding from a length of rusted pipe.

When Dorothy would exert pressure on the line, the moray would allow himself to be dragged a short way out of the pipe, his mouth opening and closing rapidly as if trying to rid himself of the hook without going into full battle.

Remembering that I had seen a long-handled gig back at the motel bait shop, I left Dorothy with the flashlight in one hand and her tackle in the other, admonishing her to keep the moray's head as close to the pipe opening as possible. I knew that once he backed far enough inside, the light monofilament line would quickly be sawed in half by the rusted metal.

The gig consisted of a single tine with a barb about two inches back from the tip. The handle was about seven feet in length and made of hardwood.

"You'd be a lot better off just to break the line and leave that eel alone," the motel operator suggested. "Those devilish things will bite a plug out of you if you give them half a chance."

Thanking the man for his warning, I hastily explained that I was particularly interested in catching him so that I could photograph his mouth and tooth structure.

"You can't reach him from the bank," Dorothy said when I returned.

"I know it," I replied. "I'm going to wade in and when I get close enough I'll jab him when he sticks his head out far enough."

"Well, don't expect me to come to your rescue if you get in trouble," she said, with a bit of wifely concern. "I wouldn't get out in that water at night for anything in the world and certainly not with that hideous creature there."

With the flashlight in one hand and the gig in the other, I carefully waded out, keeping the light directed on the moray's head at the pipe opening. I knew the light had him confused and I was counting on that to keep him distracted until I could get near enough.

Perhaps he felt the vibration of my footsteps on the bottom, or maybe it was the changing direction of the flashlight beam as I drew nearer. Whatever the case, just as I was about to make a thrust with the gig the moray suddenly recoiled into the pipe and the line snapped.

"I can still get him," I said. "All I have to do is jab into the opening and I'm bound to stick him."

Stick him I did, and in the handful of seconds that followed I wished I had listened to Dorothy and the motel operator, and for that matter, I wished we had kept right on driving across the overseas highway that night all the way to Key West.

The point of the gig was needle sharp and I felt it plunge into the thick hide of the moray. An instant later I was struggling with a powerful and enraged animal. The moray literally boiled out of the pipe and began throwing one coil after another up the gig handle. Just where I stuck him was impossible for me to tell, but it surely was not in the head. In a frantic and stumbling rush, I began backing toward the beach and then I dropped the flashlight.

The moray must have been about five feet in length and larger around than my forearm. It felt as if he weighed at least thirty pounds. Time after time part of his body would slap against my hands and arms coating me with slime, and in the confusion I could see the beam of the flashlight which was still burning brightly on the bottom. From its submerged position it cast an eerie green glow over the area. Suddenly, the moray broke free and I nearly fell over backwards, so hard was I struggling to pull the creature ashore. When he was off, I was in water just above my knees and not more than ten feet from the shore, but it seemed to take forever to gain the safety of dry land. With each lunging step I imagined I could feel the slick body slipping between and around my legs.

What the moray actually did after he pulled free of the gig, I have no way of knowing. He may have made a few passes at me or he may have gone the other way. The salt water extinguished the flashlight by the time I had reached shore and we decided to give up that night's fishing. My clothes and arms were covered with slime and so was the gig handle. I scrubbed it clean before returning it to the motel manager and then went to our room and took a hot shower. I was glad the same man was not on duty the next morning.

Morays do not attack swimmers, but spear fishermen and skin divers have occasionally run into serious trouble with them. One particularly harrowing experience is reported by A.J. McClane in his *Fishing Ency-clopedia**.

In his account of the incident, McClane states that Lieutenant Rudy Enders was an instructor at the Navy Underwater Swimming School in 1961. Enders was looking for fish in thirty feet of water but had not speared anything at the time. He was on his way to the surface for air when a moray lashed out at him from a nearby hole and grabbed his right wrist. The bite was so severe, tearing tendons and ripping the flesh, that Enders was forced to spend several weeks in the hospital.

An odd sequence to this account occurred several months later when Enders was again diving at the same location. This time, and fortu-nately so, he had a diving companion, Scott Slaughter, with him. On this trip the moray came completely out of its hole and poised to bite Enders' neck. Slaughter shot the creature through the head, but it pulled free and vanished in the rocks. It was estimated that this moray was at least seven feet in length.

While the morays inhabiting the Atlantic and Gulf coasts of North America are not venomous, their bites are still dangerous, principally because they have powerful jaws and when they do bite the teeth are

*McClane's Standard Fishing Encyclopedia, A.J. McClane, published by Holt, Rinehart and Winston, 1965.

driven deep into the flesh. Also, their teeth, as with many other fish, carry a coating of mucus which can cause serious infection unless prompt medical attention is received.

Many fishermen are prone to cook and eat almost any type of fish they catch, sometimes if for no other reason than to say they have eaten something unusual. Since true eels are considered a delicacy in many parts of North America and Europe, it might logically be assumed that you could dine on the eel-like moray. But *don't!* The flesh of at least some morays is highly toxic and eating them could cause serious illness and possibly death.

There are plenty of fine food fishes to be had, and the safest and best way to deal with a moray is to cut off the head, clean up the slime in the boat, and get back to the business of angling.

PORTUGUESE MAN-OF-WAR

There are a vast number of coelenterates in one form or another found in salt water. Included in this phylum there are numerous types of jellyfish, many of which cause absolutely no harm to man. A few are capable of producing varying degrees of discomfort when they come in contact with the human skin.

There is, however, one member of the phylum Coelenterata, the Portuguese man-of-war *(Physalia physalis),* that should be avoided at all costs by everyone who frequents salt water. It is one of the most violent of all marine invertebrates and its stinging cells or nematocysts can cause severe injury and occasionally bring death to humans.

The Portuguese man-of-war is of the order *Siphonophora,* which are colonial similar to the corals and consist of many animals of the same species gathered together under one roof, as it were. Fortunately, the man-of-war is generally found in open water and is easily recognizable. At times, when a prolonged onshore wind blows, it may be driven into shallow water and is occasionally washed up on the beaches in vast numbers. Whether far out at sea, in shallow water, or washed ashore, a strictly hands-off policy is the safest course to follow.

These creatures have been described in many different ways, but probably the most graphic is to say that they resemble balloons floating along on the surface of the water. At times they are almost transparent, while again they are dark blue in color. Closer examination will reveal what appears to be a kidney-shaped bladder that has been sewn together along the top side. Just above this line of seemingly crude stitches there is a flattened crest that resembles a small sail. The color of this crest is blue tinged with pink.

The bladder, which ranges from five to ten inches in length, is the only part you may touch without regretting it. It feels like a partially inflated penny balloon. A word of caution, even here, is necessary. Don't squeeze too hard or the bladder, more properly the pneumatophore, may burst. It is filled with a poisonous gas that can cause serious injury to the eyes.

The really dangerous part of the Portuguese man-of-war is the mass of tentacles attached to the bottom of the float. These trailing tentacles, which resemble pale blue threads of monofilament, may be forty or fifty feet in length and sometimes even longer.

It is with the aid of these tentacles that the man-of-war feeds on small fish and other organisms with which it happens to come in contact. Each of the tentacles contains vast numbers of stinging cells called nematocysts, which resemble tiny spherical beads. Inside, these cells contain a coiled tube tipped with barbs. Under normal conditions, the man-of-war floats along on the surface with the tentacles trailing downward in a relaxed state. The instant a fish or even a tiny particle of plankton swims into or brushes against one or more tentacles, the nematocysts are activated and the coiled tubes spring out and stab into the flesh of the victim. A minnow the size of a man's finger may thus be impaled by several hundred harpoonlike arrows which are still attached to the tentacles. At the same time the action of the coiled tubes causes a reflex action on the part of the tentacle and it begins to contract, drawing the victim slowly upward toward the pneumatophore.

Except for plankton and other minute creatures, a small fish could easily break free of the coiled harpoon lines that have been released from the nematocysts were it not for a violent and quick-acting poison that has been injected into the victim. This poison is neurotoxic in nature and similar to the venom of a cobra and some of the extremely poisonous sea snakes of the tropical Pacific and Indian oceans. The victims are almost instantly paralyzed and dead by the time the retracting tentacles have drawn the creature up to the base of the pneumatophore. At this point the stomach organs of the man-of-war envelop the

318 DANGEROUS MARINE ANIMALS

fish and the body fluids are completely digested in short order by powerful enzymes.

When the human body comes in contact with the trailing tentacles and their countless nematocysts, the reaction is exactly the same as if they were touched by a small fish. My own personal contact with the physical agony that can be inflicted by the man-of-war came a number of years ago while swimming off the Gulf coast of Florida.

I had been properly warned by fishermen and others who frequented the salt water to give the blue balloons wide berth or suffer the consequences. Being of a naturally inquisitive nature and full of youthful enthusiasm, I wanted to find out if the stories I had heard were not greatly exaggerated. The first time I found myself swimming near a man-of-war I decided to investigate. Luckily it was a lone individual and lucky too that I was fairly near the beach, because like the fool who rushes in, I swam up beside the balloon and swept my right arm completely under it so that the mass of threadlike tentacles completely enveloped my arm from shoulder down to and including my hand.

I instantly knew that I had made a serious mistake. The sensation was almost identical to taking hold of a charged electric wire. Drawing back quickly, I started swimming for the beach while I wiped my arm with my left hand. Instead of subsiding, the pain grew more intense. By the time I had reached the shallow water I was becoming dizzy and severe griping pains were seizing first one part of my abdomen and then another. Pains also began to manifest themselves in my groin and armpits and it seemed that my fingers and toes were becoming paralyzed. Even more frightening was the fact that I could not seem to fill my lungs with enough air.

I had indulged in a dangerous prank that, had it not been for the fact I was in top physical condition and had youth on my side, could have cost me my life.

There have been numerous instances, in only one weekend, where a hundred or more people have been so severely "stung" by the man-of-wars that hospitals from Texas, around the Gulf, and up the Atlantic coast have been hard pressed to render aid.

In frequent cases, the respiratory system becomes so badly constricted that it is necessary for the patient to be placed in an oxygen tent and at times treatment must be continued for several days. Under certain conditions, death is the result.

In any case, the tentacles should be removed as quickly as possible and alcohol should be rubbed on freely to neutralize the venom. Itching can be controlled with calamine and other lotions that have been compounded to relieve the stinging of poisonous plants and the bites of insects.

Occasionally, after a hard blow, great stretches of the beach will be littered with the balloons. Take heed. The siphonophores may be dead, but their poison lingers after them. Many people have been subjected to stinging sensations on large portions of their body while sunbathing on what seemed to be a clear portion of the beach far below the storm-tossed bladders and other wrack. This is because they were lying on the invisible and still poisonous tentacles left on the sand.

Frequently, while trolling, an angler's lure will snag a man-of-war. Again, caution is the watchword. If handled carefully, the line may be slowly reeled in, making certain that all of the mass is confined to the lure itself. Even then the line and leader should be handled with care. The glob that clings to the bait or lure should be removed with a stick or gaff hook, and the work should be done over the side and not in the boat. A good practice after the lure has received a preliminary cleaning and dunking in water, is to place it in a plastic bag or wrap it in paper. Back at port, it can be properly cleaned with running water while the fisherman is wearing rubber gloves to protect his hands.

No one can discuss the Portuguese man-of-war without mentioning one of nature's strangest associations. This concerns a small fish, *(Nomeus gronovii)*. Known as the bluebottle fish, it is found nowhere else except in and around the tentacles of the man-of-war. This tiny fish seems to act as a decoy or Judus goat by attracting other fish. As a reward, it is allowed to feed unmolested on the solid parts of the captive fish not wanted by the man-of-war. For a considerable time after scientific investigation was begun, it was believed that the bluebottle fish was simply skillful at dodging the deadly man-of-war tentacles. More recent studies, however, have proved that the little fish is actually immune to the poison.

CATFISH, TOADFISH, AND PUFFERS

Probably more saltwater anglers are injured by catfish than any other fish that is normally caught. There are numerous species included within this group, but the two most likely to be encountered in southern salt waters are the gaff-topsail catfish *(Bagre marinus)* and the far more common sea catfish *(Galeichthys felis).*

Caught on light tackle, the gaff-topsail comes close to performing like a true game fish and one of three pounds or more is guaranteed to put up a rousing good tussle before he is brought to the net. What is more, he is a good food fish.

Once seen, the gaff-topsail is not likely to be mistaken for the more common variety. His thick body is blue gray on the back and sides with a silver belly. His most distinguishing physical characteristics are the exceptionally elongated rays of the dorsal and pectoral fins. He is frequently hooked on artificial lures and live bait.

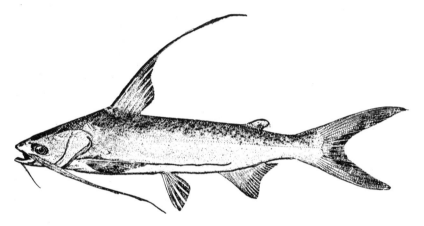

Gafftopsail Catfish

In contrast is the sluggish sea catfish which averages about two pounds, but has been known to exceed eight pounds. When the unlucky angler snags one of these scavengers, the best practice is to dispatch him with a stout stick and remove him with a pair of pliers and a hook disgorger. Extreme caution should be exercised to avoid contact with the sharp anterior dorsal and pectoral spines.

The sea catfish is a poor fighter while in the water, but he often becomes very active after being boated or beached and the three dangerous spines are extended. Most injuries occur when the angler is attempting to remove the hook from the mouth of a living fish. Because his body is coated with a film of slime, he will often wriggle free, even though the fisherman thinks he has him securely pinned down with the sole of his shoe. At this moment, while the catfish is flopping about, one of the spines is likely to be driven into the angler's flesh. A stinging or burning pain is instantaneous.

The method the catfish employs to inject its venom is similar to that of the stingray. The poison is located on the outer, or epidermal layer of the spine and is introduced into the victim's flesh by being rubbed off during penetration and extraction.

Over the years I have occasionally had the misfortune of being "stabbed" by catfish, and generally the pain from the wound has subsided in a period of time ranging from a few minutes to half an hour. Some years ago, however, while on a fishing trip at the tip of Cape San Blas on the northwest coast of Florida, I received a wound so severe that I thought for a while I was going to die.

My wife had caught a sea catfish that weighed about three pounds. In my attempt to remove the hook from his mouth the fish made a sudden flounce that drove one of the pectoral spines into my right leg just above the knee. It hurt at the moment, but I did not attach any special significance to it until a few minutes later when I started to walk along the beach. Suddenly, my right leg began to feel cold, and this reaction was quickly replaced with a pins-and-needles sensation.

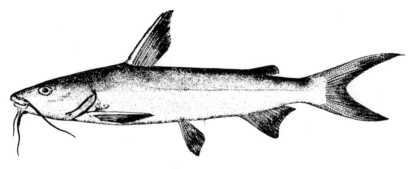

Sea Catfish

Looking at the puncture I saw that the small hole was surrounded by a white pallor. As I continued walking, I began to notice that I was losing control of the fingers on my right hand, and there was a distinct acid taste in my mouth. Sitting down in the shade of a palm, I again examined the wound and discovered the area around the puncture had suddenly turned fiery red and was extremely sore to touch. The next sensation was one of dizziness and then I began to vomit.

Attempting to call to my wife, I suddenly discovered my vocal cords seemed paralyzed. I was drenched in cold perspiration and my pulse was weak and very rapid. Then, almost as quickly as it had begun, the unwell feeling began to vanish and after about thirty minutes I was again normal.

Later, when discussing the episode with a physician, he told me that he had encountered several cases with the same symptoms following the puncture made by a catfish spine. In discussing some of the victims he had treated, he said that occasionally secondary infection sets in and that he had known of gangrene resulting from the wound. Further investigation has revealed that humans have died as a result of catfish poisoning.

There is no specific treatment and so the watchword is caution when handling a catfish. Unless they can otherwise be satisfactorily disposed of, they should be thrown back into the water where they will be eaten by scavengers. One of the most thoughtless acts a fisherman can do is to toss them on a dock or beach where someone may step on them. Shortly after my own severe encounter on Cape San Blas, I assisted in getting a three-year-old boy to the hospital after he had stepped on the dorsal spine of a dead catfish tossed aside by some unthinking fisherman. The child spent two weeks in the hospital, and it was well over a month before he was able to walk without limping.

Another dangerous fish found in southern salt water is the toadfish, which is a member of the family *Batrachoididae*. In some localities it is also known as the dogfish. This is certainly one of the ugliest fish that swims. It has a large head and mouth and generally a dark rusty color. Not only can it inflict a painful bite with its powerful jaws, but some species possess a pair of hollow fanglike spines on the dorsal fin. These spines are generally small, but nonetheless dangerous. When pressed into flesh, venom flows through these hollow spines in much the same manner as it does through a snake's fangs. As with the catfish, it is strongly recommended that the toadfish be killed with a heavy stick or length of pipe and handled only with pliers.

While they do not possess poisonous spines, the various species of fish generally known as puffers, swellfish, or porcupine fish of the order *Tetraodontoidea* should not be considered as food fish. There have been cases of illness and death resulting from the eating of their flesh. They are easy to recognize by their ability to inflate their bodies after being hooked until they resemble a balloon with fins. Occasionally, when

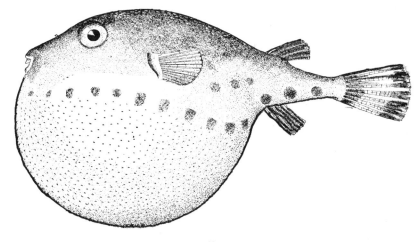

Puffer

pulled out of the water quickly, they will inflate themselves with so much air that they are unable to release it and will float like a cork bobber when tossed back into the water.

Considerable investigation is currently in progress concerning the edibility of the puffers, and while their flesh is not actually poisonous, their internal organs contain a concentration of neurotoxin. If properly prepared, the flesh is safe and edible, but the possible danger of contamination does not make them worth the risk.

ᴧᴧᴧᴧᴧᴧᴧᴧ
ᴧᴧᴧᴧᴧᴧᴧᴧ

THE RESTLESS WAVES

THE GULF STREAM

There is no question that the Gulf Stream has a decided effect on the type of fishing found in the Gulf of Mexico and all along the Atlantic coast. Were it not for its presence, the entire fishing picture would be drastically different from what it is. Indeed, should it not exist, the mode of life of a large part of the world would be dramatically different.

The name itself would seem to imply that the Gulf Stream originates in the Gulf and flows like a giant sea-going river around the tip of Florida and out into the Atlantic Ocean. There are some elements of truth in this belief, but it is only a small part of the story of one of the earth's most interesting and important ocean currents.

To understand the Gulf Stream more fully, it is necessary to reach far back into history for as much as a hundred million years. It was

324

during the late Cretaceous period, the age when the dinosaurs were becoming extinct and early mammals and flowering plants were becoming a part of the earth, that the continents of North and South America were connected by a great upheaval in the earth's crust. It was this that formed the Panamanian isthmus.

Until then, the North and South Equatorial currents swept westward across the Atlantic from Africa, through the opening between North and South America, and on into the Pacific. The forming of this great land dyke had a devastating effect on these powerful ocean currents. It was almost the same as would be experienced, in miniature, if someone should direct a stream of water from a garden hose into a shallow, round-bottomed pan. The relentless water from the open Atlantic began to swirl and then pile up along the eastern shore of Central America.

After what was undoubtedly a long period of confusion, with the currents seething about in different directions, a pattern began to develop. Striking the Windward Islands, the Equatorial currents split, with part of the water flowing into the lower part of the Caribbean Sea and another sweeping toward the northwest.

The flow that rushed toward the coast of Central America began to bend northward and push like a river through the Yucatan Channel and into the Gulf of Mexico. Here again, however, it is necessary to turn back the clock even further to look at the beginning of the Gulf of Mexico.

For countless eons of time the Gulf bore little resemblance to what it is today. Instead, it was partially dry land or a very shallow sea basin. Great rivers from the continent of North America were flowing into the area and bringing with them an endless flow of sediments. Finally, about the middle of the Cretaceous period, and before the Isthmus of Panama was formed, the steady flow of sediments caused the Gulf basin to begin to sink from sheer weight.

The eventual result was the formation of the body of water that today is the Gulf of Mexico, which covers an area of 600,000 square miles. The average depth is about 5,000 feet, dropping to its greatest general depth of approximately 2,000 fathoms in the southwestern part known as Sigsbee Deep. Here, even greater soundings of 14,360 feet have been made.

It was into this body of water that the northward flowing part of the Equatorial Current known as the Caribbean Current passed between the Yucatan Peninsula and the western tip of Cuba. Because the water was literally piling up in the Gulf, it had to escape in some manner, and as a result it formed a sweeping gyre and began to rejoin the parent current and flow back out through the Straits of Florida between the Keys and Cuba.

Early mariners who sailed along the Florida coast and westward through the Straits sensed this "river in the sea" and they drew certain conclusions as to where it was coming from. As they passed Key West and Dry Tortugas, they became convinced it was emanating from the Gulf, and one of the popular beliefs was that there were enormous fissures in the bottom out of which great submarine rivers were rushing.

In 1769, Benjamin Franklin became fascinated with the subject of the Gulf Stream. It was during this time that Franklin was Deputy Postmaster General of the Colonies. The curiosity of this investigative genius was aroused when he continued to hear complaints from the Board of Customs in Boston that packets crossing from England to the Colonies took as much as two weeks longer to make the trip than those from the Colonies going to England.

To explore the mystery, Franklin called on a friend, Timothy Folger, who had spent many years as a Nantucket sea captain. Folger gave Franklin the answer without delay. He said that on numerous occasions while out on whaling trips he had spoken with westbound ships and advised them to cross to the side of the Gulf Stream if they wanted to make better time. The proud English shipmasters, however, felt it beneath their dignity to heed the word of the unlearned colonist and seldom took the valuable advice that was offered. They stubbornly stuck to their course which was, in effect, the same as trying to sail up a river. A deviation in direction, either to the north or the south, would have taken them out of the stream's flow and thus increased their speed by several knots.

Franklin had an opportunity to study the Gulf Stream when he sailed aboard the packet *Pennsylvania* from England back to the colonies in the spring of 1775. He tested the temperature of the water by trailing thermometers from the stern. It occurred to him that if ships were equipped with thermometers that would register the temperature of the water, they could easily avoid the delay of sailing against the Stream's flow by staying to either side of the warm current.

This observation was not made public by Franklin when he reached Philadelphia on May 5, 1775, because the War for Independence had just begun and he had no desire to help the British warships expedite their Atlantic crossings.

Oddly enough, Spanish sailors had learned nearly two hundred years earlier that the shortest distance between two points was not necessarily a straight line, if distance was to be synonymous with time spent on the ocean. The Spaniards quickly discovered that the fastest round trip to the New World could be made by crossing westward in the Equatorial Current and then returning by following the Gulf Stream.

Together, Franklin and Captain Folger set about the task of drawing a chart of the Gulf Stream. When it was completed, Franklin sent it to Falmouth, England, where it received scant attention, and it was not until several years later that the chart was printed in France.

The speed of the Gulf Stream varies, as does its depth and width. At some points it moves along at barely three knots, whereas at others the rate is much greater. In 1513 Ponce de León noted that while sailing down the coast of Florida to the Dry Tortugas his three ships, although under good wind, were unable to stem the flow of the Stream. It is possible that he was in the vicinity of Fowey Rocks, located southeast of what we know today as Miami's Key Biscayne. Here, the speed of the Stream has been clocked at six miles per hour.

The vastness of the Gulf Stream, which Ernest Hemingway referred to as "The Great Blue River," is staggering to the imagination; billions of tons of water flow past a given point during a period of a single day. Rachel Carson, in her book *The Sea Around Us,* likened its flow to that of "several hundred Mississippis." Indeed, it may be equal to the volume of all the rivers of the world combined!

After sweeping through the Straits of Florida, the Gulf Stream turns almost due north and proceeds along the continental shelf until it reaches Cape Hatteras off North Carolina. At this point it begins a gradual curve to the northeast and its gyre continues in this general direction until it reaches the tail of the Grand Banks.

In 1969 the miniature submarine *Ben Franklin* made a twelve-hundred-mile exploratory voyage along the Stream from Palm Beach, Florida, to a spot off Boston. At times the sub traveled at a depth of six hundred feet and sometimes down to two thousand feet.

When the Stream reaches the Grand Banks, its deep blue color and warm temperature contrast sharply with the frigid green water of the Labrador Current. In winter the warmth of the stream is most noticeable. The line of cold and warm water is so sharply drawn that as a ship moves into the Stream from the colder water to the north, her bow may actually be in water twenty degrees warmer than that of her stern.

In 1498 when the Italian father-and-son team of John and Sebastian Cabot sailed from England to Nova Scotia and down to the Carolinas, they found that food they carried in the hold of their ship went bad after turning southward at the Grand Banks. It was difficult for the Cabots to grasp the meaning of this sudden entry into warm water, when only days before they had been battling icebergs and sailing through ice floes.

Where the Gulf Stream strikes the arctic waters of the Labrador Current near the Grand Banks, one of the densest fog areas in the world is created. From this point the Stream bends eastward toward Europe, and its warm water has a decided influence in mollifying the winters that would without it be almost unbearably cold.

There is a slight swaying effect on the part of the Stream that is noticeable as it passes the coast of Florida. Probably the most dramatic result in this sway took place in 1882 near Nantucket, Massachusetts. For over a century, commercial fishing vessels had depended to a large extent on their catches of tilefish. In that year, for some unexplained reason, the Labrador Current gained in velocity or the Gulf Stream leaned more to the south. Whatever the case, the result was a sudden influx of frigid water in an area where dragging for tilefish had become commonplace. The cold water had a devestating effect on the tilefish population and in a very short period of time the industry was ruined. Over four thousand square miles of the Atlantic Ocean was covered with dead tilefish. So complete was the destruction that not another fish of this species was caught for the following five years.

Gradually, the population began to reestablish itself and today tile-fishing is back to normal with an annual catch of some ten million pounds.

During the winter months, when the cold air from the north moves into the southern states, the migratory game fish react in one or two ways. Some simply move out into deeper water, while others turn south and head back for the tropical waters. With the return of spring, however, the fish such as sails, marlin, tuna, dolphins, mackerel, and others reverse their course and literally swarm into the Gulf and up the Atlantic coast, always influenced by the route of the Gulf Stream.

Man, with his inventive genius, is forever seeking to harness the forces of nature and make them do his bidding. Great rivers have been dammed, thus supplying the world with hydroelectric power and

The yellowfin tuna is found in the Gulf of Mexico and near the Gulf Stream on the Atlantic side. No, that's not tangled line on the angler's rod. It is chunks of sargassum weed that were picked up by the line during the battle.

spreading great lakes where none before existed. For all of his prowess, however, man has not been able to put a bridle on the Gulf Stream.

In 1878, when France was beginning its hopeless task of digging a great ditch through the Isthmus of Panama, there arose a hue and cry in Europe to put a stop to the project. Those concerned maintained that if Ferdinand de Lesseps cut the canal through the Isthmus as he had dug the Suez Canal, the result would be that the swift-moving Equatorial Current would once again rush unhampered into the Pacific, thus destroying the flow of the Gulf Stream.

Since the original conception of how the Panama Canal should be constructed was entirely unrealistic, those who fretted claimed that if the Gulf Stream was stopped a large portion of northern Europe would be subjected to unbearably frigid winters. Of course, it can only be supposition, but had the French managed to accomplish their task, the results might well have been catastrophic. With such a vast pile-up of water in the western Caribbean, there would have been only one way for it to go and that would have been straight through the canal. The American engineers, instead, chose to provide the passage with a series of locks, and the result was that the Gulf Stream continued on, following the same route it has followed for millions upon millions of years.

Contrary to popular belief, it has been found that the Stream does not follow one prescribed path through the Gulf all year long. Instead, its passage is in a constant seasonal change. During the early fall the current flow is predominantly northward through the Yucatan Channel and bending sharply eastward around the tip of Cuba and through the Florida Straits.

As the winter months approach, this distinct eastward rush begins to become less evident and the Stream spreads more and more in a northwesterly direction. During this period, it curves around the Campeche Bank and continues its course throughout the Gulf. With the coming of spring, the westernmost portion of the current is approximately south of the Mississippi delta. The main flow is forced south as it strikes the Florida shelf.

Throughout the summer months, it is starting to be pinched off north of the Yucatan Channel and an anticyclonic gyre develops in the mid-Gulf. This clockwise revolution continues to swirl until fall comes on, and once again the Stream begins to bend more decidedly around the western tip of Cuba.

Project EGMEX, which is a detailed study of the eastern Gulf of Mexico, was begun in the spring of 1970, and as it progresses will undoubtedly shed more light on the eddies and loop currents. Involved in the project are Florida State University, Florida Institute of Oceanography, the National Science Foundation, and other interested groups. If the study continues as expected, it may well be many years before all the facts concerning the Stream are finalized.

TIDES

Make no mistake about it, tides do affect fishing. The ebbing and flowing is as constant out in the middle of the ocean and along the shoreline as the rising and setting of the sun. Nowhere, however, is this fluctuation as important to the fisherman as in the tidal zone. This is the region, most often close to shore, where sand bars and mud flats are alternately exposed and covered by water.

It is here at the edge of the sea that every form of marine life is vitally aware of and dependent upon the constant changing of the tide. Everything from the endless array of sessile creatures such as barnacles and

Tides do affect fishing. This flat, exposed at the ebb will begin to stir with countless forms of life when the flood tide covers it with several feet of water.

bivalves to large game fish adapt their hour-by-hour existence to the coming in and going out of the tide. Even the seemingly aimless drifting of tiny planktonic forms of life are governed by this powerful and relentless phenomenon of the sea.

Although the habits and actions of fish that frequent the tidal zone are distinctly influenced by its movement, there are few hard and fast rules that can be applied. The reasons for this are as numerous as they are complex. A few of these seeming inconsistencies might well begin with the season of the year. For example, a particular fish might react in one manner to the tidal conditions in early summer and then act in a completely reverse manner in late fall. Again, there is the addition of ever-changing weather which must be considered in conjunction with any tide. To some fish, an incoming tide might, under normal weather conditions, be a signal for the beginning of a feast. Let a storm be in progress or in the making and those same fish might find conditions entirely contrary to their liking. Even the direction and force of the wind can and often does either encourage or discourage certain fish from reacting the same way from one tide to another. Another important factor to be considered in conjunction with fish behavior is the time of day that either high or low water occurs. For it is important to remember that while tides may be predicted for years in advance with astounding accuracy, the ebb and flow is not the same today as it was yesterday and it will be still different tomorrow and the day after that ad infinitum. The casual angler might catch a string of fish near the mouth of a pass on an ebbing tide at sunset one day and therefore conclude he could perform the same feat a week later at the same place. The most important point he would be overlooking is that a week later the stage of the tidal flow would be decidedly different.

Despite all the attendant conditions that accompany fish behavior, there are certain general rules fish follow and it is axiomatic that the greater the angler's store of knowledge about the tides, the greater are his chances of catching a fish. With all due respect to the venerated *Farmers' Almanac,* man has not yet learned to predict the weather far in advance. He can, however, tell what the tide will be doing at any given hour a month from now, a year from now, or even several years hence. Thus, armed with at least one certainty, the angler need only apply a knowledge of the habits of a given species of fish and local weather conditions and he has already won a third of the battle.

For anyone not thoroughly acquainted with salt water, the subject of tides is little short of a mystery. The observer cannot fail to notice that sometimes the water around docks and along the beach is higher than at other times. In a general sort of way he knows there is something called high tide and something else called low tide.

Should this person become interested in fishing, he has two choices open to him: he can ignore tides and just go fishing whenever the urge strikes him and maybe catch a fish, or he can study the tides and greatly enhance his chances of making a good day's catch.

Changing tides are a result of the gravitational pull of the moon and the sun. On a daily basis there are two types of tides—the *highs* and the *lows.* Twice each luna month there are two different types of tides that are known as *spring* and *neap* tides.

The spring tides, which have no connection with the season of the year, are far more powerful than the normal highs and lows. The reason is more easily understood when it is considered that the moon travels an irregular path across the heavens. It is when the moon is full or new and in line with the sun that the combined gravitational forces are joined, and pulling together, create the highest and lowest tides.

The neap tides also occur twice each luna month at the quarters of the moon when the gravitational forces of the moon and sun are pulling at right angles to one another. The high and low water marks during the neap tides are as a rule only half of those which occur during the spring tides. Also, during the neap tides the ebb and flow, or tidal currents, are considerably weaker than those that move the spring tides.

The science of calculating and predicting tides in advance is extremely complex. The United States Coast and Geodetic Survey, a branch of the Environmental Science Service Administration (ESSA), is charged with the responsibility of producing tide tables far in advance and uses a battery of machines and computers. Into these are fed no less than three dozen known factors concerning tidal changes. When this complex mathematical equation is finalized, the tables can show almost exactly when high and low tides will occur at any given location.

The revolution of the moon around the earth, combined with the rotation of the earth on its axis, results in the moon making its circle about once every twenty-four hours and fifty minutes. Because of this difference between the moon's revolution and the standard twenty-four hour day, tomorrow's high tide will be nearly an hour later than that of today and still nearly an hour later on the following day, and so on and so on. Even though the sun is twenty-seven million times larger than the moon, it has only half the effect on the tides. It is the nearness of the moon that enables it to exert its enormous gravitational pull on the sea.

In this interval of approximately twenty-four hours and fifty minutes, there will be two high tides and two low tides at any given point. This is so because the high tide that is directly below the moon has a correspondingly high tide on exactly the opposite side of the earth. In general terms, the angler can expect the high tide to be almost one hour later each day. Such a manner of figuring is convenient on a short-term basis, but over a period of months the missing ten minutes each hour makes a considerable difference.

The variation in the rise and fall of the tide in different parts of the world is considerable. For example, in the Bay of Fundy the flood tide may rise more than fifty feet, while at the other extreme there is frequently a variation of only about one foot in Florida's Tampa Bay. However, tides along the Atlantic coasts generally range between four and ten feet. The entire Gulf of Mexico has one of the smallest variations between high and low tides of any large body of water, frequently not changing more than two or three feet. Certain local conditions also result in the Gulf having only one high and one low tide each day. Much depends on the contours of the bottom. Tide charts may actually show two complete tides, but when luna conditions are right the second high tide may be so insignificant as to hardly be noticeable.

In large bays, such as the Chesapeake or North Carolina's sounds, high tide may vary by as much as twelve hours at different points in the same body of water.

On a larger scale, this same condition is present as one travels along the coast. It is therefore important to have tide tables that show the time of the highs and lows at the location at which you plan to fish.

When the current is flowing from open water toward land, the tide is said to be on the flood. When the flow is away from land, it is known as ebb tide. At the precise moment when the ebbing or flooding stops, the tide is said to be slack. Slack water lasts only a brief moment before the current reverses itself.

One of the major and entirely unpredictable factors that can cause a wide variation in an otherwise normal tidal condition is the barometric pressure. As the pressure rises the result is a depression in the water. When the barometer begins to fall and the atmospheric pressure decreases, the level of the water rises accordingly.

To a fish, the rise and fall of the tide might be likened to the effect of daylight and dark on land creatures. Just as there are nocturnal and diurnal animals on land, there are some fish that prefer to be most active during an ebb tide while others seem to wake up on the flood tide.

Many fish prefer to do most of their feeding when the tide is on the flood, or coming in. This is especially so in most bays, for as the water begins to rise, large areas of grassflats are covered with a depth of water suitable for them to swim in.

The grassflats are the natural home for many of the forms of food on which the average fish normally feed. During the period of low water when the grassflats lie either exposed or barely covered, the shrimp remain motionless. Instinct tells them that movement betrays their presence and they know that in the air above them are the terns and other sea birds gliding to and fro watching for that slight movement that will show them where another tidbit of food is hiding.

With the flooding tide, however, the grassflats begin to stir with life. The shrimp dart about with backward flipping of their tails, and minnows swarm in from the deeper channels. As the water deepens, the larger fish rouse themselves and head for those flats which represent their dinner tables.

This same renewal of activity is beginning to take place along the outer beaches. Swash channels are filling and the redfish, pompano, and others come in closer to reap the harvest of sand bugs, ghost crabs, sea worms, and small fish that have been out of reach when the tide was low.

Paradoxically, this "awakening" of bait on the flood tide does not always work in favor of the fisherman. Some fish, such as snook, that feed in mangrove-fringed bays, will go so far back into the tangle of roots on high tide as to be out of range, or in such a jungle that there would be no hope of drawing him out because of the snags. Under these conditions, the fisherman simply has to wait for the ebb tide and count on his quarry's not having been able to satisfy his appetite during the flood.

At other times certain fish will hesitate to enter bays, preferring instead to loaf around the mouths of passes and wait for the outgoing water to bring them a supply of shrimp, minnows, and crabs that have been dislodged and caught up in the swift current. The surf caster also capitalizes on this ebbing tide and devotes his efforts to breaks in offshore sand bars where striped bass, channel bass, drums, and others may be waiting for food to be swept out of swash channels near the beach.

Bridges often afford excellent angling spots even for fish that are prone to prowl the shallows when the tide is at the flood. They know that much of the food they depend upon will be found congregating in the shelter of pilings and in the shadow of the bridge itself.

It was mentioned earlier that storms have a bearing on fishing conditions. For some fish, pounding surf and roiled water near shore will cause them to cease feeding and sulk in the safety of deep holes and channels. Other fish take a completely different view of the situation and become more daring, coming closer to shore to reap the harvest of beach-dwelling bait that is sure to be dislodged by pounding waves.

As it is with all forms of fishing, what works best for one man may not work for another. The fact still remains, however, that tides do exert a strong effect upon the feeding habits of most fish, and part of the battle is knowing what the tide is doing and what it is going to do in the next few hours.

RED TIDE

We live in an age when man is becoming increasingly aware of the importance of the sea. The rapid growth of population has led to ominous predictions that widespread famine is almost certain in the next few decades. Many are convinced that in the not distant future there simply will not be enough arable land left to supply the world with sufficient food. Others, more optimistically, say that if properly farmed the sea will produce a virtually inexhaustible harvest.

With all its dire aspects, the almost inevitable crisis is not without some beneficial results. It has brought about an almost sudden awareness that no longer can we regard the sea as a catchall for everything unwanted and offensive on land. Albeit some people are convinced the awakening has come too late, at least an effort is being made to protect the sea from indiscriminate pollution.

One of the most ironic facets of human nature is that man has paid little heed to his own wanton destruction of natural resources, whether it be defiling rivers with pollutants, laying waste to vast forests, depleting the land of nutriments, or making the air unfit for breathing. Let nature go on a rampage, however, and shatter man's tranquillity with an earthquake, volcano, flood, hurricane, or other phenomena and immediately there is a great hue and cry that something must be done to control nature's tempestuous outbursts.

Because Florida is famous as a seaside resort for the nation, there are two natural happenings there that are certain to receive widespread attention by the news media. One of these, of course, is the passage of a severe hurricane that causes extensive damage. Running a poor second, but still definitely significant, is the occurrence of a red tide.

Both are highly newsworthy in that they lend themselves to shocking photographs and exciting stories of damage. Because hurricanes cause far more destruction over not only Florida but many other states as well, more is known about them, and the reporting is generally considerably more accurate, basically on account of a constantly building hurricane research program.

When the coast of Florida is suffering from a red-tide outbreak, however, the paucity of readily available scientific information results in the disbursement of much misinformation. As a rule, the general public is simply told that a given stretch of the Gulf coast is being plagued by an overblooming of a specific type of planktonic organism that is killing fish by the thousands or millions, and the stench of these putrifying fish is causing many tourists and residents to evacuate the area.

What is more, the photographer-journalist is not at a loss to record the event on film. He may aim his camera at vast windrows of dead fish washed upon the beach. He may photograph boats with seines collecting thousands of floating dead fish. And he will be able to show bulldozers and other heavy equipment going about the task of burying the remains in great trenches and covering them with tons of sand.

If the outbreak of red tide is severe and prolonged, the federal government may be stampeded into instituting crash programs of research to find methods of predicting and preventing future outbreaks. After all, nature has offended mankind, and the concerned public demands that something be done immediately to put a stop to it.

As a result, panels are formed, scientific research teams are organized, and vast quantities of valuable data are collected; but before any effective results can be obtained, the threat of the current red tide begins to subside, public interest wanes, and research grants are reduced or cut off completely.

Most experts in the field deplore these crash programs of research in times of emergency, contending that while such intensive studies doubtlessly increase the store of red-tide knowledge, the money is wastefully spent. Far better, they say, would be a more moderate but dependable budget that would permit a continuous study until the problem is solved. In this manner research duplication could be controlled and organized programs could be carried through to a logical conclusion.

As it now stands, the exploration of numerous avenues of research is begun, only to have the findings filed away when the crisis is past. There, the store of knowledge lies virtually forgotten. When the next emergency arises, there are often different investigators who, under pressure to find a solution, spend valuable time in research that is already available if they only knew where to find it.

There are several fundamental questions the average person wants answered about the red tide, such as: What is a red tide? What causes it? Where does it occur? How serious is it as a threat to commercial and sport fishing? Is it a human health hazard? Can it be predicted? Can it be controlled or stopped? Is it a natural phenomenon or the result of man-made pollution? Some of the questions can be answered specifically, some only partly and others must go either totally unanswered or, at best, are only understood in theories.

The first of the above questions can be answered with practically 100 percent accuracy. What is generally termed a fish-killing red tide is caused by the overblooming of vast numbers of a naked dinoflagellate —microscopic organisms known as *Gymnodinium breve,* not identified until 1948. When they congregate in vast numbers in a given area, they contaminate the water to such an extent that it actually takes on a reddish brown color, hence the name "red tide." *G. breve* is auto-trophic, requiring light for survival. Interesting, too, is the established fact that this dinoflagellate thrives in nutrient-poor water.

Viewed through a microscope, *G. breve* is seen to be a microorganism divided roughly into four quadrants on the ventral side, with a small nipplelike protuberance at the upper end. The width is about thirty microns and the length about twenty-five. Dense swarms appear red-dish brown in transmitted light. When referred to as naked, it means they have no shell or armor, as have some other related plankton. No ingested food has ever been found in them and it is suspected that *G. breve's* survival is quasi-holophytic to the extent that it obtains its food in the same manner as green plants.

Gymnodinium breve reproduces by division, or splitting into two parts as a binary fission. When conditions are optimum, several divi-sions may occur in a single day with each part quickly becoming a complete organism. Such rapid reproduction accounts for many of the swiftly growing overblooms that result in severe fish-killing red tides.

When *G. breve* begins to multiply at a critical rate, water, when dipped up from the affected area and allowed to stand in a container for a few minutes, becomes viscid, having a consistency closely resem-bling that of diluted syrup. To give some idea of the size of these microorganisms, twenty-five thousand of them would be able to circu-late freely in a mere thimbleful of water.

There is no question as to whether or not the red tide kills fish. All one has to do is stand on the beach during an outbreak and view and smell the vast numbers of dead and decaying fish floating belly up in the shallow water or littering the beach. Just *how* the fish are killed is somewhat more complex, yet reasonably well established.

Numerous scientists who have made detailed studies of the cause of death have slightly divergent views, but in general they agree that the fish dies of some form of respiratory failure caused by neurotoxins released by the cells of these dinoflagellates. When the fish swim into the toxic water the first symptoms are a loss of balance and a noticeable change of color pattern. The movement of the gill covering slows and the fish suffers intermittent periods of violent gasping, uncoordinated bursts of movement, and eventual death as in a form of suffocation. The time required for a fish to be killed varies with the type of fish and the concentration of *G. breve* that is present. Some have died in as short a span of time as ten minutes after being introduced to toxic cultures.

There seem to be no certain types of fish that are immune to the effects of the red tide. Often seen on beaches are such species as speckled trout, grouper, pinfish, mullet, catfish, and jacks. Many others are undoubtedly victims of the contaminated water. During the outbreak in 1946–47, sponge divers working off Marco, Florida, reported that the bottom was littered with dead mackerel, although these fish are not frequently found washed up on the beaches. Blue crabs have been observed feeding on dead fish floating on the surface, while conversely others have been found dead on the bottom. Horseshoe crabs *(Limulus polyphemus),* however, are frequently killed by the thousands and washed ashore.

One of the most popular misconceptions concerning the red tide is that it is strictly a product of the Gulf of Mexico, concentrating mainly along the west coast of Florida. This is far from the truth. Outbreaks of similar fish-killing tides are known to be worldwide, with documented reports of mass mortalities in such widely scattered areas as India, Chile, southwest Africa, Japan, southern California, the Gulf of Paria near the mouth of the Orinoco River in northern South America, and along the coasts of Texas and Mexico.

Why a red tide occurs is more difficult to explain. In almost every case, detailed investigation will seemingly be leading toward a logical set of conclusions, only to become clouded by documented evidence from past records or contradicted sharply by a pattern established in subsequent outbreaks.

There are, however, certain conditions that seem, by frequency of occurrence, to be conducive to a red-tide outbreak. Records show that the late summer and well into the fall are the most likely periods if a red tide is going to develop in a given year. Statistics also strongly indicate, with exceptions, that an autumn preceded by a spring and summer of excessive rainfall enhances the chances of a severe over-blooming of *G. breve.*

An abundance of sunlight for a protracted period of time, coupled with calm weather, with light to moderate onshore winds, will be conducive to producing a red tide of lethal proportions. A strong off-shore wind has frequently been observed to break up a red tide.

Therefore, if one were bold enough to attempt to predict an outbreak he would wait for a calm and cloudless September following abundant spring and summer rains. He would certainly have statistics on his side, but he should be fully prepared for the capriciousness of nature that could dash asunder his carefully laid plans. A good example of such contradiction was the severe red tide that began in November of 1946 after a comparatively dry spell and ceased the following September during a period of heavy rainfall.

Many investigators concerned with the seriousness of the ever-increasing problem of pollution are wont to blame the sporadic over-blooming of *G. breve* on careless sewage disposal and eutrophication of streams when fertilizer from farmland is carried into them by heavy rainfall.

While everyone is concerned with the topsy-turvy ecology that is threatening our environment, scientific investigation of a given problem must never resort to witch-hunting or making a scapegoat out of some-thing just because it is otherwise dangerous or objectionable. Toward this end, the red tide investigator must look closely at recorded history as an integral part of research. The red tide is not something new; reports began well over a century ago when the peninsula of Florida was little more than wilderness country.

This is in no way to be misconstrued as minimizing the seriousness of pollution, and it may well be discovered that, while not the single cause of red tide, man-made pollution may contribute to the frequency and extent of the overblooming of *G. breve.*

One popular misconception concerning the red tide is that it fre-quently spreads over hundreds of square miles. Even during a severe outbreak, the water affected is in streaks, rather than being diffused through a wide area. Frequently the intervening spaces between the toxic and "clean" water may be wide and fish are not harmed until they enter the areas of concentration. The first documented evidence of this was submitted in 1884 in a report by S.T. Walker concerning his observations during an outbreak four years earlier in the general area of Tampa Bay on the west coast of Florida. He noted that several commercial fishing vessels, which at the time maintained their catch in live wells in lieu of ice, would have contrasting luck in their ability to return to port with their fish. Even though the ships were within sight of one another during the return voyage, some would sail through streaks of "poisoned water" and all their catch would die. Others that were able to steer clear of the red-tide patches and streaks managed to make port with all their fish alive and well.

It is also frequently asked whether or not fish killed by the red tide are dangerous for human consumption. Here, the information is even more vague. There is technical evidence to prove there has been no definite tracing of human illness due to *G. breve*. It is known that fish caught in red-tide water have been eaten with no adverse effects. It is reported that people along the Indian Malabar coast harvest and eat fish killed by the red tide. At the same time, there are other reports that warn of illness due to eating fish taken from infected water. There are also reports of birds such as gulls, vultures, and cormorants that have been killed by eating such fish.

From a practical standpoint, the human consumption of fish by Gulf coast residents is sharply curtailed during, and for a time after, a red-tide outbreak. This is probably largely because of the adverse publicity that always accompanies an outbreak. Certainly there would be danger of human illness resulting from eating fish that had begun to decay, but this would be true if the fish had been caught in the purest of waters.

Suffice it to say, the general population is going summarily to cross seafood off their diet if they know or believe it is taken from red-tide waters. Such precaution, whether for real or imagined reasons, contributes, of course, to the financial loss in the area.

Apart from the unpleasant odor associated with rotting fish, the red tide in most respects has no serious effect on the health of the human population. An exception to this is a finely suspended mist that pollutes the air. This slightly toxic gas caused by the decomposition of the dinoflagellates, when borne on strong onshore winds, is sometimes noxious and may be temporarily injurious to people suffering from certain respiratory ailments.

It is important, too, to note that occasionally large patches and streaks of discolored water are mistaken for the fish-killing red tide caused by *G. breve*. Dr. Robert F. Hutton, marine biologist, states that discoloration can be caused not only by red tide, but also by a blue green alga, *Skujaella (Trichodesmium) thiebauti*. He reported that in 1960 discolored water that appeared between St. Petersburg and Sarasota,

Florida, was caused by the serious *Gymnodinium breve* which was responsible for large fish kills. But, in addition, there were other concentrations that caused discolored water during the same year—*Gymnodinium splendens, Acartia tonsa,* and *Labidocera aestiva.* In the case of the latter three blooms there was no apparent damage to fish.

In the final analysis, the most important question to be answered is whether or not the fish-killing red tide can be eliminated. Much headway has been made under laboratory conditions, but from a practical standpoint the red tide is no more under control than it was when first discovered.

Copper sulfate has been used for many years by Japan to protect its oyster beds. The same has been used to a limited extent off the Gulf coast of Florida. Numerous chemicals have shown promise, but fortunately modern scientists are reluctant to recommend the widespread use of an agent destructive to one of nature's offenders until sufficient evidence is available to determine beyond a shadow of a doubt that harmful side effects will not be produced.

The extensive and indiscriminate use of practically nondestructible hydrocarbons such as DDT for mosquito control is viewed by many ecologists as one of mankind's biggest blunders. The wholesale damage to valuable estuarine nursery grounds is inestimable.

At the present time there is no sure-fire cure for the red tide, and while it represents a serious loss to those concerned with sport and commercial fishing, it is far better to proceed with caution than to open another Pandora's box.

fourteen ~~~~~~~~~~~~~~~~

~~~~~~~~~
~~~~~~~~~

TOOLS OF THE TRADE

TACKLE BOX

The seasoned fisherman who has spent a good number of years in quest of saltwater game fish instinctively knows exactly what type of equipment he wants to carry when he goes out on the briny.

Each year, however, there are literally thousands of newcomers to the game of fishing who wander into a tackle store for the first time with little or no knowledge of what kind of tackle they want or need.

As a rule most tackle-store dealers are good sportsmen and if they have the time they will be more than willing to lend a helping hand to assist the neophyte in getting started with the correct hook, line, and sinker.

Left to their own devices, there are those hapless souls who will purchase a polyglot mixture of equipment that would only partially serve their needs. With not too much stretching of the imagination they might leave the store with a reel big enough to battle a tuna to gaff, a rod designed for fly-fishing in a mountain stream, the wrong size line, not enough hooks, and an assortment of junk that never should have found its way onto the dealer's shelves in the first place.

The distressing results are that all too often the new fisherman has probably left a lot of money in the store and when he does get around to trying his luck he will discover that he could have caught as many fish with a willow pole and a bent pin.

It would take a weighty volume to outline exactly what types of tackle are best suited for all types of fishing, but there are a few basic guides that can be followed, and the best place to begin is probably with the tackle box.

A few short years ago tackle boxes were of two types: those made of wood and those made of metal. Both had their advantages and both had their drawbacks. Unless skillfully made, wooden boxes were heavy and likely to come unglued when exposed to the elements. The metal boxes were generally lighter, but they would rust unless given the proper care after each fishing trip.

The first real forward step came in the manufacture of plastic tackle boxes. With today's technical advances the fisherman can buy a plastic box that is strong, durable, and one that requires only a minimum of care.

As for the size box to invest in, the answer naturally depends on how much equipment the individual angler plans to carry along. Since we are concerned here with the beginner, it would be well to strike a happy medium and choose a box of average size. One about fifteen inches long, seven inches deep, and eight inches wide should adequately serve the purpose. Tackle stores generally have a good supply in stock that range from twice this big to half the size. Boxes of the size suggested will generally have two trays that fold back on hinges once the lid is opened.

The trays are shallow, being about one and one-half inches in depth, with divided compartments designed to hold various size lures. In the bottom of the box there is enough space to carry bulky objects such as a spare reel, line, plastic bobbers, boxes of hooks and sinkers, and a first-aid kit.

Hooks are quite logically one of the most important items in any tackle box and the assortment should be wide and plentiful. The size of a hook is determined by measuring from the eye, to which the leader is attached, to the bend, which is the bottom of the curve. The manufacturers have two methods of designating the hook sizes, i.e., No. 1 and No. 1/0. When marked with a single figure the hooks become smaller as the figure increases and those with the slant sign increase in size along with the number.

With the advent of inexpensive little plastic boxes, manufacturers have started putting hooks of certain sizes in individual boxes. This practice may cost a fraction more, but is by far the best. After all, who wants to scramble around through a Chinese puzzle to find a No. 6/0 when the wind is blowing and the boat is rocking and there are fish waiting to be caught. Also, as you begin to run low on one particular size you can tell it at a glance and make a note to pick up another box the next time you visit the tackle store.

In addition to sizes, hooks also come in at least a dozen different designs. They carry such names as *Eagle Claws, Sproats, O'Shaughnessys, Wide Bends, Carlisles,* and so forth. A good bet is to start with a selection of Eagle Claws and O'Shaughnessys. Stick with these until you become an expert and then branch out and become more selective.

Hooks should never be tied directly to the fishing line but should be separated by a swivel to prevent the line from winding up and kinking. A swivel with a safety-pin clamp at one end will also allow you to change hooks and lures without a lot of fuss and bother. Just be sure to have an assortment, also individually packaged, to match the general size hook you will use for a particular size fish.

Leaders are a bit more complex. In general, they should be considerably stronger than the strength line you are fishing with and are necessary to prevent a fish from cutting the line with sharp gill covers or sawing the line in half as he runs around a barnacle-incrusted piling. As an example, a spinning outfit with a 6-pound test line should use a 15- or 20-pound test leader.

Leader material comes in three main types. One is single strand monofilament, another is braided cable, and the third is single strand stainless steel. The monofilament and braided cable are best for small and medium-size fish, while the stainless steel is more serviceable for the larger ones that are caught while trolling and bottom fishing in open water.

Let's suppose now that you have decided on the tackle box that best suits your own needs or personal preference, or both. You have a working knowledge of hook sizes and know something about leaders and swivels. The following is a list of articles that should also be included in the tackle box:

1. A good quality knife. This is an absolute must. You will probably have a penknife in your pocket, but a sheath knife is valuable for cutting bait and skinning certain type fish.

2. A pair of pliers. These are needed for crimping lead sinkers and making minor repair jobs to various articles of tackle and other gear. Choose a pair with wire cutters at the base of the jaws. The cutter comes in handy when snipping off steel leaders, and there are times when the only way to remove a hook is to cut it out.

3. Fish scaler. Most bait fish, such as mullet, should be scaled before cutting for bait and it is often desirable to scale your catch before returning to dock.

4. Snap-type fish stringer. If you plan to put your catch into an ice chest, then the stringer can be eliminated, but if not, the stringer is necessary to keep the fish alive. Hook the fish on the stringer through the bottom jaw only. This gives them a chance to breathe and keeps them alive longer.

5. Hook hone. Carborundum makes a good one about the size of the average man's ring finger with a precut groove so burrs can be removed from both sides of the point with one operation.

6. Hook disgorger. These come in handy when the fish gets the hook all the way down in his gullet. It saves time and also prevents cut fingers when dealing with fish that have sharp teeth.

7. Fish mitt. Gloves used to be the only answer when handling fish with sharp fins and gill covers. Today, the answer is a plastic fish mitt with a pronged metal insert in the palm. The mitt is virtually puncture proof and has really solved the problem of preventing cut hands.

8. Insect repellent. It seems that noisome insects can turn up at the most unexpected places. A word of caution here: *Be sure to remove all traces of the repellent before handling bait or lures.*

9. Spare line. Carry at least one spool of spare line because few things can bring a fishing trip to a quicker halt than having a big fish strip your reel.

10. Floats or bobbers. These come in a wide variety ranging in size from a small marble to an ostrich egg. The primary objective of a float is to keep the bait off the bottom, so the size of the float should be sufficient to support the amount of lead used.

11. Sinkers. Here again there is a wide variety. Some, like the barrel

type, are made to slide along the line. Others clamp on and stay wherever placed along the line. There are also large sinkers designed to carry a lure or bait deeper in the water when trolling. A good idea is to select an assortment.

12. First-aid kit. Some of the hardy members pooh-pooh such "sissy" additional gear, but they are the same ones who groan the loudest when they have to be treated for blood poisoning. Make no mistake about it, a scratch from a hook or fish fin can cause real trouble, but the trouble can generally be prevented with a dab of antiseptic and a Band-Aid if used immediately.

13. Suntan lotion. Seasoned anglers are well acquainted with what the sun can do in southern climes. If you are a newcomer you might be surprised to discover that you can come home from a day on the water with a case of sunburn even though it was a cloudy day. *As with the insect repellent, keep the lotion off bait and lures.*

14. Screwdriver. Best bet is to keep it small. Screws that hold the reel together have a habit of working loose and from time to time you may want to change hooks on a plug.

15. Lures. This includes artificial minnows, spoons, spinners, feathered jigs, bucktails, and an unending collection of special types, some of which are made of soft plastic and resemble everything from worms to shrimp. It has long been a debatable subject as to whether the colors of lures are made to please the fish or the fisherman. Each angler sooner or later settles on certain basic lures for his particular brand of fishing. In the beginning the only hope is to buy a collection of all and give each a try.

After the basics are neatly installed in the new tackle box, there will undoubtedly be a few empty spaces to fill. If you are a pipe smoker you should carry a package of pipe cleaners; a can of lighter fluid always comes in handy, especially when your lighter runs dry; and by all means leave room for a small compass.

KNOTS

A fisherman may invest in several hundred dollars' worth of the finest rods, reels, tackle boxes, and other angling paraphernalia, but no matter how good his tackle and how much he knows about the wiliness of the particular fish he is going after, he is in for a lot of disappointments if he doesn't know his knots. There is more to it than just knowing how to tie a number of knots, because not all knots are good knots when it comes to fishing lines. Especially is this true since the advent of monofilament. The simplest of all is the overhand knot and it is probably the first everyone learns to tie. Regrettably, many fishermen will use this same knot, generally several of them tied one on top of the other, to fasten a leader or line to a hook, sinker, or swivel. Laboratory tests have proved that the common overhand knot reduces the line's strength by 50 percent, whereas properly tied knots allow the line to maintain nearly all its rated strength through the length from reel spool to hook. Results of electronic tensil-testing equipment and high-speed (slow-motion) film have shown that the wrong kind of knots reduce the built-in line strength.

To test the hazards of using the simple overhand knot one has only to take a length of thread or light string, tie an overhand knot in the middle, then with the ends of the thread wrapped around the fingers of opposing hands, exert a steadily increasing pressure until the strand breaks. The chance that the break will occur right at the spot where the overhand knot was tied is almost 100 percent.

There are hundreds of different knots, and each has been developed down through the years to serve its own special purpose. For the average fisherman, however, there are only a few basic ones that are necessary, but it is important to know which ones they are, how they should be tied, and the purpose they serve.

Before beginning a discussion of the various types of knots it should be mentioned that the instructions for tying are from the viewpoint of a right-handed fisherman. The southpaw should have no trouble reversing the procedure, since it is his nature to do so as a matter of course.

Basically, a line of any type has two parts. One of these is the *end* and the other is the *standing part* of the line. The term end is, of course, obvious. The standing part is the main section, or that above any loop or bend that may be formed near the end.

A helpful hint to anyone learning to tie an unfamiliar knot is to allow plenty of spare end or ends, as the case may be. Few phases of knot tying are more exasperating than trying to be parsimonious with the line and winding up working like a clumsy jeweler replacing the hairspring in a small watch.

They are not always needed, but two tools that are handy to have nearby are a pair of needle-nose pliers and some sharp cutting tool such as a pair of nail clippers. Then, alas, for those not blessed with perfect vision, a pair of reading glasses of the proper magnification will come in handy.

One final suggestion is to practice tying a new knot with a limp line of reasonably large diameter. It enables the beginner to follow more easily the progress of the knot he is attempting to tie.

Blood Knot

One of the knots of primary importance is the blood knot. It is most useful when joining two lengths of line of approximately the same diameter. For example, an angler will notice a frayed spot somewhere

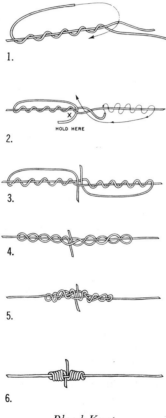

Blood Knot

*Knot drawings courtesy of E.I. Du Pont de Nemours & Company, Wilmington, Delaware.

along the length of the line he is casting. Often this frayed, and naturally weakened, spot will have been caused by the line chaffing against some underwater obstruction. When such a flaw is noticed there are three alternatives. One is to ignore the worn place and hope that not too much of the line strength has been reduced. The second is to replace the line with a new one. If this is impractical, then the answer is to cut out the offending length and rejoin the line with a strong, even knot that will pass smoothly through the levelwind guide, or over the tip-top guide on a spinning reel. The blood knot is the best one to use.

The way to tie a blood knot is to lap the two strands across one another so that about four inches of each end are extended. Hold the junction where the lines cross between the thumb and forefinger of one hand. Grasp one of the ends of the line and wrap it loosely around the standing part of the other line five or six times. Double the loose end back and place it between the lines at the point where you began twisting.

Next, shift the partly formed knot to the thumb and forefinger of the opposite hand and wind the end of the second line around the standing part for the same number of turns in the opposite direction from which you wound the first end. The second loose end is then returned to the open loop at the center of the knot and inserted through on the *opposite* side from which the first end was pushed. The result will be a loosely tied blood knot. The next step is carefully to draw the loops together by alternately pulling on the two loose ends and the standing parts, drawing the coils tighter and tighter together until the knot is firmly set. The ends should then be snipped off at the knot.

Improved Clinch Knot

Equally important to the blood knot is the improved clinch knot. This is the one often used to attach a line to a lure, swivel, or the eye of a hook, and it is ideal for monofilament lines.

To tie the improved clinch knot, the end of the line is first run through the ring to which it is to be tied. Double back three or four inches of the end over the standing part of the line and wind around six or seven turns, holding the eye of the hook or lure between thumb and forefinger. Next, pass the free end through the loop of line formed at the hook eye, then through the larger loop that was formed when the line was doubled back over the twisted part. Take hold of the loose end with the fingers of one hand, hold the hook with the other, and exert

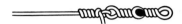

Improved Clinch Knot

an even pressure until the coils are drawn tightly together. It is good practice to leave about a quarter of an inch of the end of the line showing at the point where the excess is snipped off, since the big fish will likely exert more pressure on the knot than one is able to do when tying it.

Improved End Loop

There are times when an angler finds a need for a loop at the end of his line. This is especially important when a snap swivel is not to be used and the fisherman has reason to believe that he will need to change lures frequently and does not wish to tie a fresh knot each time.

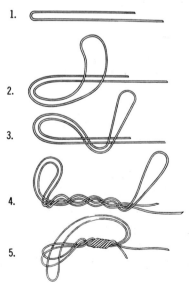

Improved End Loop Knot

The improved end loop is also valuable in joining leader material to the smaller diameter line, in which case the same loop knot is tied in both leader and line. One of its most valuable uses is that it eliminates the need for other hardware such as swivels and clips, and often this is important when one wants to take full advantage of the "wiggle" that is built into a particular lure.

To tie the improved end loop properly, several inches of the end should be bent back over the standing part. In case the lure and line to be used are of small diameter, about six inches of double back will suffice. If the lures are going to be on the large side, then more line will be needed to tie the knot.

After the line has been bent back in a "U" shape, a bend in the double line should be formed and the part with the loop wound about five turns around the double standing part of the line being held with the other hand. Next, return the "U" end of the line to and through the loop that was formed when the line was first bent back against itself. Slowly pull the knot tight, leaving as much of a loop as desired. The excess part of the end may then be cut off and there will be a slip-proof loop in the end of the line.

To make use of this knot, slip the loop through the eye of the lure, pass the lure through the loop, and draw up tightly. Changing to another lure is simply a matter of pushing some of the loop through the lure eye to gain slack and reversing the installation procedure.

Dropper Loop Knot

From time to time it is desirable to form a loop near the end of a line but not right at the end. One practical use for such a loop would be a place to attach a sinker. Of course, a three-way swivel might be the most perfect answer for such a case, but such swivels are not always available in every tackle box and it would also necessitate the task of tying three improved clinch knots, one to each swivel ring. When the three-way swivel is not available and the fisherman wants to include a sinker in a hurry, the dropper loop knot is a quick way to solve the problem.

To tie this knot, a loop about the size of a baseball is formed at the desired location in the line. Then, with the end of the line make about seven overhand loops or windings around the bottom of the large loop. When this is done, pinch a small loop at the top of the circle directly above the windings and push it through the center of the overhand windings. When the small loop is all the way through, secure it with

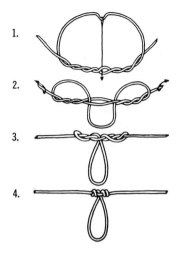

Dropper Loop Knot

a pencil, pipe stem, or a finger and gradually pull the standing line from both ends at the same time. The result when drawn tight will be three windings on either side of the loop. The knot will not slip and the loop will remain the same size as it was when the knot was tied.

The biggest problem with the dropper loop is that it is a form of overhand knot and will weaken the line where it is tied. The extra windings, however, give it added strength above the common overhand knot and there are times when the speed with which it can be tied outweigh the loss of strength. As an added precaution the sinker should be attached to the dropper loop with a lighter test line. Then, should the sinker become snagged on some bottom obstruction, the weaker leader will break, thus leaving the main line intact.

Perfection Loop Knot

There are times, especially when using flies and other small lures, that it is desirable to tie a loop at the end of a monofilament line that is less bulky than the improved end loop. Such a knot, then, is the perfection loop. As with the dropper loop, the construction of the perfection loop sacrifices some of the line strength, but again, there are times when loss of strength is more desirable than bulk.

This is a relatively simple knot to tie since it involves the forming of two loops at the end of the line and then pushing the lower loop through

354   TOOLS OF THE TRADE

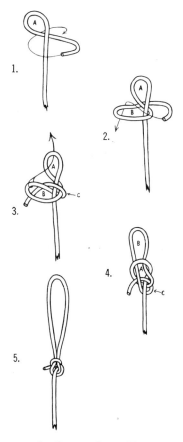

Perfection Loop Knot

the upper one. If not properly learned, however, the results are likely to be an overhand slip knot that will reduce the line strength by half.

The proper procedure for tying the perfection loop is to grasp the line so that about six inches extend above the thumb and forefinger. Next, form a loop to the left with the end of the line passing *behind* the standing part. Hold this crossing spot and make a second loop over the top of the thumbnail with the end again passing *behind* the now partially tied knot. The next step is to fold the end of the line across the top of the intersection of the two loops which is being held between the thumb and forefinger. At this point lift the bottom loop up through the top loop and slowly draw the knot tight by pulling on what has now

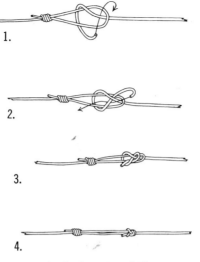

Tucked Sheet Bend Knot

become the top loop. When firmly set, the excess end of the line may be clipped as close as an eighth of an inch, leaving a strong loop that will not slip or come untied. The finished perfection loop can be made as large or small as needed at the stage of tying by adjusting the second loop just before tightening.

Tucked Sheet Bend Knot

Let us suppose light tackle with a fly or small lure will be used. The lure has been tied to the end of the leader with the improved clinch knot, and a perfection loop is at the opposite end. The leader should now be joined to the main line with an equally small knot. An excellent knot to know at this point is the tucked sheet bend. It is an easily tied knot and has the advantage of finishing so that the end of the line is pointing downward toward the leader. Thus, it is less likely to cause trouble in casting or in forming a protuberance that will snag wisps of fine sea grass often found drifting in salt water.

To tie the tucked sheet bend, hold the leader loop in the left fingers and pass the regular line through the back side of the loop. Then, run the line around the loop on the outside and tuck the end under the standing part of the line at the point where it first entered the leader loop. Next, reverse the direction of the line end and cross the top of the leader end under the near side of the line loop that has been formed around the loop in the leader. Draw up tight and snip off the excess. When completed there will be a trio of knots from the end of the line, through the leader, and onto the lure.

Double Surgeons' Knot

It is often desirable to join a heavy leader, or one of larger diameter, to the end of monofilament line. If the angler is past the tyro stage when he would resort to a wad of overhand knots tied together, he is likely to resort to the blood knot, but the results are usually a jumble. It will be recalled in the discussion on the blood knot that it is recommended the lines be nearly the same diameter. When the difference is great, the best knot to tie in a hurry is the double surgeon's knot.

The double surgeons' knot is simply a double overhand knot, but the fact that it is *double* and used at the ends of two lengths of line allows

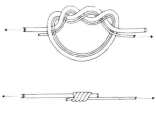

Double Surgeons' Knot

the weaker line to maintain almost all its built-in strength.

The way to tie this simple and valuable knot is to lay the end of the leader and the end of the line parallel to one another. Then, treating the two lines as one, tie a simple overhand knot and then run the two ends back through the loop so that two overhand knots are present. At this point draw the knot together slowly and evenly. Clip off the ends, and the lines are securely joined.

Besides the overhand knot, two of the worst where monofilament lines are concerned are the *square knot,* and worse still, the *granny knot.* The square knot will hold fairly well in cuttyhunk and some of the braided lines, but neither are of any value when using monofilament, because the ends of the line simply slide through the loops.

The above seven recommended knots are especially selected with monofilament in mind, but they will work equally well with all diameters of braided line.

There is one knot that the angler should know when he plans to use

*Overhand Knot—not recom-
mended*

stainless steel wire, either as a leader or the main fishing line. This is called the *haywire twist,* and as the name implies, is not so much a knot as the formation of a slip-proof loop at the end of a wire line.

To form the haywire twist, bend several inches of the wire back and across the standing wire. Hold this crossing point with a pair of pliers or between the thumb and forefinger. Begin to secure the loop by carefully winding the end of the wire around the standing portion so that each twist is carefully laid beside the one that precedes it.

Each of these windings should be made as tight as possible by exerting pressure on the end of the wire. Eight or nine is not too many turns to make. At that point stop. Bend the end of the wire in an "L" shape and begin to work the end backward and forward. Under the strain of constant bending the metal will quickly become fatigued and will break off smoothly right at the end of the final twist. Never, repeat NEVER, cut the end of the wire off with a pair of cutters. The reason for not doing this is that a fraction of an inch of needle-sharp wire is almost certain to be left and in the excitement of boating a fighting fish, someone will be likely to receive a bad cut on the hand or fingers from this sharp projection.

As previously mentioned, the number of different types of knots is almost endless. The above are only a few of the fishing knots that, when properly learned, will provide the average angler with enough different kinds to handle just about any situation that may arise.

TACKLE

When it comes to the subject of tackle, there are two sorts of fishermen to be considered. One has been engaged in the sport for a number of years and during this time has accumulated a wide and varied assortment of equipment to suit the types of angling he enjoys the most.

He knows just what rod, reel, and specialized pieces of gear he is going to take with him when he goes out after a certain fish.

Angler number two has made a few trips out on the briny and has caught a bad case of that old malady known as fishing fever. He may have gone out on a charter boat where everything was furnished as part of the overall price, or he may have been fishing a few times with friends who had plenty of the correct tackle to loan him. Sooner or later, however, the neophyte angler decides he wants to buy his own equipment.

If his chosen sport was golf, he would need only to walk into a pro shop and buy a set of clubs of a size most suited to his build, a box of balls, a pair of shoes, a package of tees, and a few other minor accouterments which the pro might suggest, and he would be equipped to play the game anywhere in the world.

If fishing is to be his sport, he walks into a tackle store and instantly discovers that the problem is considerably more complex. The first question asked by the clerk would be: "What kind of fishing do you intend to do?" Unless you really are able to give a concise answer, then the question might as well have been: How long is a string? or Why is a duck?

Unlike golf, fishing is many sports wrapped into one, and the angler can spend as little or as much as his purse and desires dictate. Many a bragging-size fish has been caught on nothing more complicated than a cane pole, a length of line, a piece of lead, and a hook, with a cork stopper for a float.

One of the biggest mistakes a beginning angler can make is to spend money on mismatched tackle and pieces of equipment for which he has no practical use. Just a few months ago I saw a pathetic example of this. The only exception was that the man did not spend his own money, but the results were the same.

The poor fellow had devoted nearly forty years of his life working for a large company in the Midwestern part of the country. He was well liked by all the employees as well as the management. When it came time for him to retire, it was common knowledge that he was going to move to Florida and enjoy his leisure hours pursuing the sport of fishing. The various departments of the company passed around a number of hats so that a nice going-away present could be presented by each. Shortly after he moved into his new home, he called me and asked if I would stop by and see what he had received in the way of

To the victors belong the spoils. There can be little doubt that, with the aid of the flying gaff, the mate on this boat off the Louisiana coast is only a second away from bringing this big one aboard. But take another look. You may have missed a touch of tragic humor. If you still fail to see it, look closely at the angler's tackle, and you will notice the rod was snapped in half during the battle.

presents. I thought I detected a note of sadness in his voice. When I arrived, I was led out into the garage where he had everything spread out on the new concrete floor.

"Just look at this," he said, waving his arm above the assortment of presents in a dejected gesture. "There isn't a piece of equipment here that didn't cost well over a hundred dollars. It just makes me want to sit down and cry when I think of all those nice guys spending their hard-earned money on all this. None of it is worth a plugged nickle for the type of fishing I want to do."

Scattered about in the collage of equipment I caught sight of a gleaming 12/0 reel, a sonic depthfinder of the type designed to be mounted on the bridge of a cabin cruiser—the man did not even own a boat, nor did he plan to buy one—a superb example of a fly rod and reel combination that would have been the pride and joy of a fisherman whose quarry would be rainbow trout in a mountain stream, and half a dozen other valuable articles.

My only suggestion was that he try to swap his gifts for more practical equipment from some understanding dealer. The average reputable tackle-store operator will make an honest effort to help a customer outfit himself with equipment that is at least fairly well matched. The trouble is that today every place from hardware stores to department-store chains is in the tackle business and all too often the man behind the counter does not know how to help in the selection of the proper tackle, even if he had the time to do so.

The four basically distinct types of saltwater fishing tackle are deep sea, surf casting, small boat, and the type best suited to fishing from bridges and piers. To complicate the issue, the latter three can include spinning, revolving-spool, and in some cases, fly-casting tackle. And still further, one will often serve equally as well for entirely different types of fishing. In mentioning the methods of fishing that attract many anglers, party-boat fishing has been omitted because most of these boats supply equipment best suited to their brand of fishing.

The largest and usually the most expensive of the aforementioned types is the heavy tackle used in pursuit of such ocean-going heavy-weights as the tunas, marlins, swordfish, and large sharks. It would be pointless in a book such as this to attempt to suggest the size reels, rods, and types of line for the beginner to invest in. Should he elect big-game fishing as his specialty, he will undoubtedly make dozens of trips on charter boats and gradually develop his own opinion as to what type of heavy tackle is most suited to his needs.

In the long run, fishing from bridges and piers attracts more begin-ning saltwater anglers than any other type. Just behind these are the anglers who fish from small boats and those who engage in surf casting. The reason that bridge and pier fishing is the most popular is threefold: first, the angler does not have to be an expert and there is generally someone on either side of him to show him the ropes; second, bridges and piers are within easy reach of anyone traveling coastal highways; and third, the type of tackle can literally be anything from a handline to a cheap drugstore rod and reel.

Whether the bridge or pier fisherman uses spinning tackle or the revolving-spool equipment, the important element to be considered is that it be sufficiently strong to bring a large fish up from the water to the platform of the bridge or pier. The result is that a rod of medium weight with plenty of backbone should be selected. The reel can be of any size from a small freshwater bait casting to one considerably heavier in the event the angler tangles with a large fish, which is frequently the case. For those who have moved along to the stage where they enjoy pitting their skill against a fish with light tackle, it is impor-tant that they have some means of lifting the hooked fish out of the water. There are two ways this may be done. One is using a weighted snatch hook that may be lowered on a stout cord after the fish has admitted defeat and is lolling about on the surface. Another is with the aid of a large net, which is also attached to a piece of rope. This is lowered from the bridge until it is a foot or two underwater and the fish is guided over the top. The net is then pulled up, and after the angler has finished untangling his fishing line he can rebait his hook and get back to the business at hand.

When fishing from a small boat, there could be so many possibilities that the tyro might be prone to throw up his hands and justifiably ask how he can tell if he is going to catch a dozen trout or tie into a sixty-pound cobia, channel bass, or maybe have to battle it out with a big tarpon.

The answer to such a question is that there is no way he can tell. That very enigma, however, that confounds the beginner is one of the most interesting facets of saltwater fishing. I have had so many reels stripped down to bare metal that I shudder at the total price of lines, lures, leaders, swivels, and clips I have sent off to Davy Jones.

The ideal solution to the problem is to carry along several different size rigs and thus be prepared for any eventuality. If I had to choose just one rod-and-reel combination, I would invest in what might be generally categorized as light saltwater spinning tackle. This would be a rod about seven feet long, with an open-faced reel with a spool that would hold about 250 yards of 8-pound test monofilament line.

The fisherman in the next boat down the launching ramp might shake his head and say he would favor a medium-size boat rod with a revolving-spool reel, with or without a level wind. Again, he might say he would prefer to take his chances with a heavy-duty bait-casting rod with matching reel. If I were partial to the revolving-spool reel, I think I would choose the latter of the two.

The conventional bait-casting reel dates well back into the nineteenth century, and there is considerable doubt as to who actually should be credited with the invention. The basic principle is a revolving spool that is connected to a crank on one side of the reel. In the early days they were single action, in that one complete revolution of the crank handle caused the spool to turn once around. Next came the multiple gear ratio that enabled the spool to make three to four turns to one revolution of the handle. In the early 1900's the level-wind mechanism was added to factory-built reels and the result was that now the line was automatically laid evenly from one end of the spool to the other as the angler retrieved his cast.

Today, the angling fraternity is fairly evenly divided between the time-honored conventional reel and the newer spinning reel that began showing up in limited numbers before World War II. It was not until after the war, however, that they began to gain in popularity.

The actual origin of the spinning reel is as obscure, if not more so, as that of the revolving spool. The principle is that the weight of the lure carries the line off a fixed, or motionless, spool during the cast, and a bail or some similar grasping device guides the line back onto the spool, which rotates during the retrieve.

As with so many fishermen of my vintage, I grew up using the revolving-spool bait-casting reel and I well remember the day about twenty years ago that I decided to start hinting well in advance of Christmas that I would like to have a spinning outfit. My wife consulted with Santa Claus and decided that by cutting a few corners here and there I would find what I wanted under the tree.

Today, after millions of casts and a satisfying number of large and small fish, I can laugh about it. It was not a laughing matter, however, that first winter day that I walked out on the end of a low dock and began to experiment with the art of casting with a spinning outfit. First, I knew it represented a considerable investment, because Dorothy decided that if I was to have a spinning outfit I was going to have a good one and they did not come cheap. The second problem was that, while I considered myself in the lower expert class with a fly rod and bait-casting tackle, I knew absolutely nothing about spinning. Worse still, I did not even know anyone who could give me a few basic pointers.

All I had was the little booklet that came with the tackle, which included a few sketches that showed how to grip the rod and minipulate the reel during the cast and retrieve. It would be nice to say that my first cast was perfect and I landed a big fish to go with it. It would also be a lie. I doubt that I ever welcomed a cold windy day more simply because it discouraged curious onlookers from coming out on the dock and watching me perform in my hour of travail.

Happily, I can say that whoever was responsible for authoring and illustrating the tiny booklet knew what he was talking about, and after all my fingers stopped moving like wooden pegs the tackle began to work. With a growing sense of confidence, I found that before the Christmas turkey was out of the oven I had mastered the basic principle of that new form of casting. I returned to the house almost numb from the cold, but with a sense of inner warmth that comes when a person begins to understand a problem.

I knew I would never discard my conventional gear, but I was convinced that spinning was destined to be my favorite form of fishing tackle. This conviction grew as I discovered that I could cast a quarter-ounce lure twice as far as I could throw a two-ounce plug with my older tackle and bring a 12-pound snook to the landing net while using only 4-pound test line.

Spinning, however, is not the tackle for everybody, at least not yet, and probably never will be. It has certain limitations, and then there is still the matter of personal choice. There are those who have spent many years perfecting the art of fishing with conventional revolving-spool reels and this often includes everything from the lightest bait-casting rigs to heavy-duty tackle.

Spinning runs the gamut from ultralight, light, medium, heavy-duty, and even extra heavy-duty equipment. These rods range from six to eleven feet in length. For a very long while all good rods were made of split bamboo, cut into strips and fitted together with extreme precision. Some were real works of art, and I still have a split bamboo bait-casting rod and one for fly-fishing that I occasionally take out just for old-times sake.

Fiber glass is the rod material of today and probably will be for a long time in the future. There are two basic types of fiber-glass rods. One is a tapered hollow tube made of glass threads closely woven over a mandrel and bonded with any of several formulas of resin. When the mandrel is removed, the result is a light, powerful tube. The second is made of long threads of fiber glass laid parallel over a core of balsawood which remains in the rod after it, like the hollow one, has been bonded with resin. The line guides and handles are fitted to the rod blanks after they are completed.

What makes fiber-glass rods so superior, whether solid or hollow, is that they are practically impervious to salt water, sand, heat, and humidity; something that could not be claimed for those made of split bamboo. It is unquestionably one of the greatest boons to rod construction to come along since man first tossed aside the willow pole. Of even more importance is that a really first-class rod is within the price range that the average fisherman can afford.

While on the subject of price, however, a word of caution is worthwhile. As with every new product, there is always the poorly constructed imitation that can be bought for a "bargain." I, for one, would rather have a good quality rod and reel, even if I had to carry my tackle in a paper bag. The safest course to steer in the purchase of rods and reels is to depend on the fishing tackle companies that have been in business for a considerable length of time. They advertise extensively in most fishing magazines and the fact that they have remained in business over the years proves that they make good tackle. Because the business is so competitive, the prices of a given quality rod or reel of brand A is likely to compare favorably with brands B, C, and D.

The tackle to avoid is brand X that is sold at enormous "bargain" prices and especially in stores that are not in the fishing tackle business. The safest bet is to go either to a sporting goods store or the sporting goods department in a recognized chain store. Then, if the rod breaks or the reel comes to pieces under normal usage, you at least have a place to go back to and lodge a complaint. Hackneyed as the phrase may be, you get what you pay for.

Another important consideration, when purchasing a rod and reel, is to make certain they are reasonably well matched. A heavy-duty reel on a light rod, or vice versa, is almost as ridiculous as buying a set of tires that will not fit the wheels of your car.

Surf-casting tackle is entirely different from the ones discussed above. They can be either of the spinning or revolving-spool type, but the rods are considerably longer and stronger, as are the reels that are used on them. They are also equipped with much longer butts and are primarily designed to cast large lures or heavy bait. The average length is ten feet, and with such long rods, casting is done with the use of both hands, one near the butt tip and the other close to the reel.

Just as glass has supplanted bamboo rods, synthetics have also invaded the line industry. This is another important advancement, especially for the saltwater fisherman. It was only a few years ago that many of the best lines were made of natural materials such as linen and silk. This required that the final chore after a fishing trip was to wash the line. This generally meant stripping the line off the reel and letting it pile up in a bucket of fresh water. If you were extra conscientious you then spooled it onto a large frame or wound it around the back of a chair until it was dry and ready to go back on the reel.

Happily, with the synthetics such as Dacron, Nylon, Perlon, Terylene, and others, the task of washing and drying the line is a thing of the past. While rods and lines are unaffected by salt water, do not be lulled into false complacency and neglect to wash the salt from rod guides and the reels. This can generally be done with a stream of water from the garden hose, and after a few shots of oil and grease on your reel you are ready to put the tackle away in less than five minutes.

In the synthetics, there are two types of line. One is monofilament and the other is braided. Monofilament is, in my opinion, superior to braided line for those of relatively low breaking tests. As the strength of the line increases, so does the stiffness. For light spinning tackle, 4-to-8-pound test line is ideal. This enables the angler to cast a very light lure a long distance. It also has the added advantages of being virtually invisible underwater and being nonabsorbent. When using heavier tackle and heavier lures, or in trolling, monofilament of a much heavier test may be used.

Braided line is good for the revolving-spool reels because it is more limp in the heavier tests. It is also less elastic, but not as durable as monofilament where abrasion is concerned. When using braided line on the reel it is often advisable to add a monofilament leader of fairly heavy test to prevent fish with scissorlike jaws and razor-sharp gill covers from cutting the line off during the fight.

In summation of the best all-around one type of tackle for the beginner, it is essential that the newcomer first decide on the type of fishing he will like best. He should then put his money in a recognized brand of rod and reel. If the tyro insists on buying his tackle before he is acquainted with the various phases of saltwater fishing, he will not be throwing his money away if he chooses a medium-weight spinning outfit. Of course he will miss the excitement of battling it out with a scrappy three-pound speckled trout or a puppy drum and he will not be properly equipped to engage in surf fishing for heavyweights.

On the credit side, however, he will have a set of equipment that will enable him to fish from a bridge or pier, he can troll, still-fish, or cast from a boat, and he can catch fair size fish from the beach.

NATURAL BAIT

There are many saltwater anglers who will fish with nothing but artificial bait, contending that to do otherwise takes the sport out of game fishing. For every one of these, there are others who would not consider going fishing without natural bait. They claim their method is just as sporting as sticking strictly to artificials.

The pathetic part about those who do favor natural bait is that a sizable percentage of them are restricted to whatever type is being sold at their favorite marina or nearest baithouse. Many times, in fact most of the time, they could have a wide variety of natural bait within a few yards of the places they plan to fish. They simply do not know what is available.

The average baithouse is usually limited in the variety of bait they can keep on hand. The most popular is live shrimp, which they keep in large tanks of running water. Those baithouses also generally maintain a supply of frozen squid and occasionally some keep iced fish, such as mullet and menhaden.

Here and there, on rare occasions, you will find an establishment that makes a specialty of natural baits and has practically every type available. Such places are few and far between and consequently the average saltwater angler just buys several dozen live shrimp, which he tries to keep alive as long as he can in his bait bucket. If he cannot get the live ones, he will take frozen shrimp or frozen squid.

Almost any fish will now and then get himself hooked on an artificial lure. Some types do so with such regularity as to make natural bait a waste of time. But, by and large, most fish are carnivorous creatures and since flesh is their diet they will often insist on the real thing or refuse to bite.

Therefore, it behooves the saltwater angler at least to have a working knowledge of the types of bait that are available to him and then know how to go about the business of catching a supply.

One of the most plentiful sources of natural bait comes in the form of the sand bug *(Hippa talpoida)*. In various parts of their range they are also known as kippa crabs, mole crabs, and sand fleas. Whatever their local name may be, they are excellent bait for many different kinds of fish, especially for channel bass and other surf-running species.

Sand bugs live in large colonies between the tide lines wherever the beach is sandy. They are most active during the warmer months. It is frequently necessary to walk for a quarter of a mile along a stretch before you might suddenly spot a colony that is very likely to number in the thousands.

Again the wise fisherman will do well to pay heed to the birds; especially the shore birds of the sandpiper class that are often seen scurrying along on their stiltlike legs right at the water's edge. When a large flock of such birds are noticed to be actively digging in one place with their beaks, it is quite likely they have discovered a colony of sand bugs and are feeding on them.

Go to that spot and stand motionless for a minute or two. Human eyes are not nearly as sharp sighted as those of the birds, and it will take a bit of looking before you are able to spot the heaviest concentration and hence the best place to dig.

Watch the area around your feet just as the wave recedes and while the sand is still in a semifluid state. If you don't actually see the bugs themselves, you will notice a movement in the sand and frequently see their feathered antennae that will be visible momentarily on the wet sand. They will appear as a "V" with the two branches pointing toward the water.

Making a fast grab for the spot, your fingers will close around a small creature about an inch and a half in length and shaped like an egg. The curved carapace covers most of the sand bug's body, but if you turn it over you will see the creature is well equipped with legs designed for digging and a flat tail that folds forward to protect the underside.

The sand bug is a fast-moving creature of the tide line that has no permanent hole or resting place. When a wave breaks on the beach, he pops up and while the foam and sand are churning around him he sweeps his antennae back and forth to catch organic matter. As the wave recedes the sand bug scurries backward with his legs kicking furiously to dig far enough down to be completely covered until the next wave breaks on the beach.

After you have located a colony there are two ways to catch them. One is to get down on your hands and knees and let the waves wash around you while you grab a bug here, miss one there, and search for the sign of another. The other method is to nail a six-inch board about two feet in length onto the end of a stick about the size of the average garden rake handle. With this primitive hoe you can stand in the middle of the sand bug colony and chop down while the water is swirling back out around your ankles. A standard garden rake will serve the same purpose if a piece of hardware cloth is wired securely to the tines. Once the sand has lost its fluid state between waves the sand bugs can still dig back in, but their progress is slower, and with a wooden hoe or modified rake you can pick up more at a time and still not get the seat of your pants wet.

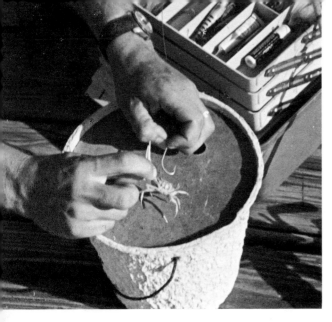

Fiddler crabs such as the one shown in this photo make excellent bait for sheepshead and many other game fish. Fiddlers are easily captured on the inshore flats of many southern bays.

Sand bugs will survive for a considerable length of time if kept in a ventilated bucket that has been loosely packed with wet sea grass. Because they are almost entirely aquatic in nature, they will die quickly if allowed to dry or if the container in which they are to be kept is left in the sun too long. Conversely, they will drown if placed in a bucket of water.

When they are ready to be used for bait, the hook should be pushed through from the underside so that the point and barb breaks through the carapace near the rear. This way they will remain alive and struggling for a longer period of time and stand a better chance of attracting a passing fish's attention.

Another fine member of the Crustacea class is the fiddler crab *(Uca pugnax)*. These little creatures average about the size of the first joint of a man's middle finger and bear some resemblance to the common blue crab, except that their carapace is rounded on the side instead of being pointed. They are gregarious in nature, but unlike the sand bugs they are more frequently found in vast numbers on the lee or marshy sides of islands and along the sandy mud flats of bays.

Colonies of fiddler crabs are easy to spot. At low tide—the best time to collect them—they are often seen solemnly marching in droves or scurrying about on eight stiltlike legs over the flats. Their presence is also disclosed by the fact that the area where they live is pocked with hundreds upon hundreds of finger-size holes that may extend obliquely for as much as three feet below the surface. Around the tops of the holes will be found little balls of sandy mud which the fiddler has rolled up and carried to the surface.

The difference between the male and female is readily obvious. Both sexes are about the same size, but one of the male's claws, quite often the left, is greatly enlarged. This huge chela serves no purpose except when the mating season is in progress. At such times the males engage in battle and fight one another with their claws. Their habit of waving these enlarged chela in a to-and-fro motion is responsible for the name "fiddler." In a sense, the male is at a distinct disadvantage when he eats because he has only one small feeding claw whereas the female has two. However, he seems to do fairly well.

The male's large chela can deliver a painful pinch on an unwary finger. They should be grabbed by the claw or from behind so that they are unable to bring their weapon into play. Better still, wear a pair of cotton work gloves and pick them up as fast as you can.

When catching them, they can be tossed in a bucket until you have time to finish the roundup. Then they, as with the sand bugs, will survive much longer if the bucket is loosely packed with wet sea grass.

One of the good things about fiddler crabs is that they can be kept alive for a week or more by packing them, with damp grass, in plastic bags and storing them in the refrigerator. With this in mind you can spend an afternoon laying in a good supply of fiddlers and several days later you will have them ready and kicking when it comes time to go fishing.

When putting a fiddler on a hook, many live-bait anglers remove the male's large claw. They do this because if he touches bottom grass, rocks, or a barnacle-crusted piling, he will hang on so tightly that he is likely to be lost when the line is pulled up. Hook the fiddler through the lower right- or left-hand side just where the legs join the body. The tip of the hook should protrude up through the carapace.

Blue crabs *(Callinectes sapidus)* form a large part of the diet of many game fish and because of this they are a favorite bait with fishermen. They can be used whole or in halves or broken into small chunks.

While it is a far cry from game fishing, crabbing itself can be an interesting sport. In the warmer months they are most often caught in brackish water near the mouths of streams and well up into larger rivers. They are omnivorous and will eat practically anything from shell fish, carrion, vegetation, and one another.

Even more excellent bait, and also a table delicacy, are soft-shelled crabs. Blue crabs shed their shells one or more times during the summer months and these "shedders" or "peelers" are most vulnerable to hungry fish at this time. The crab sheds his old shell in order to grow. The carapace begins to break loose first and when this happens the crab simply backs out of his old shell, legs, claws, and all. The hindmost pair of legs are paddle-shaped and used for swimming.

At this time he is flabby and completely unable to defend himself and barely able to swim. As a result, he seems to know ahead of time that he is about to shed and will seek the sheltering edge of a rock, sunken log, or any submerged object that will afford him maximum protection from predators.

Once out of his old shell, he is prone to lie motionless until his new shell begins to harden. This generally is accomplished in a matter of twenty-four hours or less. When he begins to move again, he has a fresh set of claws and legs, plus a glistening new carapace. What is more, he is much larger than when he began to shed. If the summer is long and there is plenty of food available, the crab may have to go through this ordeal several times during that period.

There are three primary methods of catching crabs and it is up to the fisherman's own inclination as to which way he wants to go about the crabbing game. The simplest and least complicated is to just pick up a crab net and a bucket and wander along the shore in about ankle- to knee-deep water. When a crab is spotted, the crabber scoops him up in the net, drops him in the bucket, and keeps on looking. The most productive spots are under and around old piers, the edges of jetties, and places where sunken logs are prevalent. At times, under piers, there may be as many as two or three crabs around the base of each piling.

Another method that is successful in catching crabs is literally to fish for them. Unless you want to make it more elaborate, the tackle can be as rude as that used by the earliest human fishers of the sea—a ball of cuttyhunk or any heavy twine, a crab net, and a bucket. Bait can be anything from chicken necks to fish heads and it does not have to be fresh. Tie the bait on the end of the string and let it down to the bottom. If you are in a good crabby place it won't be long before you will begin to feel a steady tug on the line and then you pull back, but slowly. The crab will generally hang on with his claws at least until he has been lifted to the surface. At that point you simply reach down with your net, scoop him up, and dump him in the bucket.

The third method of crabbing is a bit more elaborate and requires the use of specially constructed boxes made of wide-mesh hardware cloth. Ready-made traps can be bought at many tackle stores, but the principle is the same. The four sides of the box are hinged at the bottom and connected to a bridle that is attached to the main haul line. When let down to the bottom and tension is relaxed on the haul line, the four sides flop out flat.

The bait is the same as above, except that it is tied to the mesh bottom. This type of trap may be set out in numbers and the haul lines are buoyed with large cork or plastic floats. After a waiting period of anywhere from fifteen minutes to an hour the crab fisherman pulls up on the haul line, which in turn causes all four sides of the wire box to close at once. It is drawn to the surface, the trapped crabs removed, and the trap is rebaited for another waiting period.

Whatever the method used, the conservation-minded angler will toss the female crabs back over the side. There is no problem in distinguishing a male crab from a female. Simply turn them upside down and notice the hinged plate on the plastral side. On females this plate is a large half circle. The same plate on the male is connected at the rear just as with the females, but tapers sharply to a thin finger pointing forward.

Eggs are laid in the summer months and when a female is ready to spawn she will produce as many as a million or more eggs. When the female is carrying the orange-colored eggs beneath the plastral plate, she is often referred to as a sponge crab, berry crab, or cushion crab. If she is carrying a large number of eggs, which frequently she does, the mass will cause the plate to bulge away from her body.

If it were a case of survival, I would not hesitate to keep both sexes because either are good to eat and it certainly does not make any difference to the fish you will be seeking to catch. If every egg that was hatched was allowed to grow to maturity, it would not be long before the oceans would be vastly overpopulated with crabs. This, however, is not the case. Only a small percentage live to reach maturity, because they form such an important part of the diet of many fish and other creatures of the sea. Thus, by tossing back into the water one single female crab, the angler is striking a minute but nonetheless meaningful blow to stem the gross waste of our dwindling natural resources.

One of the best baits for such fish as sheepshead, bonefish, and many others is the plentiful and easily obtained hermit crab *(Pagurus pollicaris)*. These are found in abundance in the shallow waters of bays.

The hermit crab is another of nature's oddities in that it has a soft thick body that is totally lacking any form of protection except for the head and a pair of stubby claws. Recognizing his vulnerability the hermit "moves in" on the first empty shell it can find. Popular abodes of the hermit are the shells of the tulips, periwinkles, bonnets, or any other that is of suitable size.

To take up residence in an empty shell the hermit crab simply backs in so that his soft body is protected. He moves about with the aid of his legs and pincers. When trouble threatens, he withdraws and remains in his shell until he feels it is safe to continue moving about the bottom in search of food. This act of moving into some other creature's abandoned shell for protection would be oddity enough, but it does not stop there. As the hermit crab continues to grow, he begins to look for a larger abode. In his lifetime he may change shells three, four, or even five times. Unless by chance he happens to find a shell of the same type he has outgrown, he may wear a different armor with each move.

When collecting a supply of hermit crabs for bait, it is best to search the margins of bays and in tidal pools at low water. They are easy to spot, because they are active and move along the bottom with remarkable agility for a creature so seemingly clumsy. Since he feels secure in his shell, he will allow you to approach close to him before he withdraws.

The hermit's shell is easily cracked open with a tack hammer and the living creature withdrawn, but while they make excellent bait, they are difficult to keep on a hook unless you know the proper procedure. Tie a small piece of sewing thread around the shank of the hook you plan to use. Then spear the crab through the hard part near the head and tie the soft body onto the shank with several wrappings of the thread.

Live eels are another superb form of natural bait that often prove irresistible to such game fish as striped bass, cobia, bluefish and others. The eel is a catadromous creature that is hatched in the depths of the Atlantic and migrates shoreward as it begins to grow. The females range far inland where they live in fresh water until they reach maturity. At that period of their development they have grown large and begin a sometimes fantastically long journey back down through streams and ponds until they are met by the males that have remained in salt and brackish water.

The eels caught in bays and tidal streams will frequently be the male of the species, and unless catching them for bait or food, they can become an unmitigated nuisance to bottom fishermen. I know of no other creature that can so thoroughly foul an angler's line, be as difficult to remove from a hook while at the same time shedding his abundant slime over an angler's clothes and the bottom of the boat. There are many gourmets who consider properly prepared eels an epicurean delight. Personally, I don't care for them.

I do like to catch eels when there is a chance that I can use them for bait. The mouths of rivers, tidal streams, and shallow parts of bays are likely fishing spots. If they are to be kept alive they must be treated in the same manner as any bait fish. Freezing often solves the problem of keeping them. When thawed, they can be almost as effective as fish getters as the live ones, if the fisherman keeps his rod tip moving so that an "alive" action is imparted.

If you can get live eels there are two good ways to hook them. One is through the lips, the other is the two-hook rig, which is especially recommended if the eel is fairly large and may be picked up broadside by a striper or cobia. When this happens, you may feel a sudden powerful tug and the fish either turns loose or cuts the eel off behind the head. The two-hook rig is simply a second hook made fast to the eye of the first hook with a length of leader material. It is then strung along the side of the eel and tied to the eel's body with several windings of thread. This method also works well when trolling. Of course, wherever live eels are used, a swivel should be attached just forward of the hook to prevent the eel from wrapping itself around the line and causing a tangle.

Putting a live eel on a hook can be a messy job, even if he is held fast with a pair of fish grippers, which often succeeds in killing him. The best, if not the only, way to handle a live eel is to wear a pair of dry cotton gloves. Grasping him with a piece of toweling or burlap will also work if gloves are not available. Whatever the kind of cloth used, it must be dry or you are right back where you started with your bare hands slick with slime and an endless flow of expletives directed at whoever suggested using eels for bait in the first place.

An excellent way to rig a dead eel for trolling or surf casting is with the aid of a long needle, leader material, and two hooks of the proper size, or one hook and a metal squid. Tie the leader to one of the hooks, then thread the leader on the long needle. The needle is then pushed forward through the eel's body from a point just behind the vent and out of the eel's mouth. The leader is then pulled tightly so the shank of the hook near the vent will be drawn into the eel's body with the bend and point exposed. The second hook, or the hook on the squid, is pressed through the eel's head with the exposed part of the hook protruding from the top of the head. The leader from the tail hook is made fast to the swivel on the metal squid. This is then tied to the leader on the line. Several eel baits can be prepared in advance and kept on ice until needed.

Shrimp is unquestionably the most popular all-round bait when fishing southern salt waters. There is no doubt that live shrimp are the best, but frozen or iced shrimp will work almost as well for a whole host of fish.

From a practical standpoint, the best supply of shrimp is the nearest baithouse, but should you happen to be umpteen miles from nowhere when you run out of bait, you can catch your own supply if you have had the foresight to bring along the necessary equipment. They can be scooped up with a small mesh seine with a handle on each end. Small shrimp are found in abundance on grassflats in bays. A fine mesh dip net may also be used to dip them from the grass that borders the mouths of streams flowing into bays.

Dead shrimp can be placed on the hook in a number of ways. They can be hooked through the bony part of the head section, hooked through the tail, or when you are after the big ones, several can be threaded on a single hook.

Hooking live shrimp requires a bit more caution. The safest way is to push the hook through the thick fleshy portion of the tail. Another good way is to hook him through the head, but unless you want to be fishing with a dead shrimp, be sure your hook misses the dark spot just behind the eyes. It is this dark spot that contains the shrimp's vital organs and if ruptured by an ill-placed hook the creature will die instantly.

If there is a plentiful supply of shrimp to be had, they can be used whole or chopped to form a chum line that drifts with the current. Fish are attracted to this flow of chum, and the angler hooks on a live or dead shrimp and lets it mingle with the free offering. The results are often fantastic.

Another type of natural bait that is frequently available right under a surf fisherman's feet is shellfish that can be generally classified under the heading of bivalves. Some of the most common are the calico clams, sunray venus, scallops, and the common black mussels. Many types of bivalves are found in shallow water and can be dug out with a rake or simply picked up by hand. A small oyster, known as the coon oyster, grows on the exposed roots of mangrove trees. Any of these shellfish make good bait, but they often must be tied to the hook to avoid their washing off.

Some bivalves with thin shells work well for large bottom feeders such as the drums by cracking the shell slightly and inserting the hook through the muscle. This allows the juice to escape and attracts any passing fish interested in such a diet.

Squid is another popular bait and it is equally effective offshore and in shallow water. The squid can be used whole, especially when trolling, or cut into chunks or strips. The flesh is tough. Because the cephalopod is a plentiful and standard diet of many fish, it makes good bait.

Big fish eat little fish. What is more, most fish are entirely piscivorous and if, for example, conditions were right, you could bait your hook with a small bluefish and catch a big bluefish. They don't care about their young. Some fish will even tear members of their own school apart if one happens to become injured.

It therefore behooves the fisherman to bait with small fish when he is after larger ones. Mullet, menhaden, spot, pinfish, shiners, and most minnows are good bait. They can be used alive, dead, or cut into strips.

Of these, mullet and menhaden are used for bait in southern salt water more than perhaps any other single types. Mullet are plentiful but they are an unusual fish in that they feed on microscopic animal life and forms of plant life. They can, under certain conditions, be caught on hook and line, but this is rare and much too involved for this pupose. Most fishermen rely on fish houses for their supply of mullet bait, but they can also be caught with a cast net or snagged with weighted treble hooks. They are difficult to keep alive and both bunkers (menhaden) and mullet are generally packed in ice and used either whole or cut.

Pinfish and shiners are perhaps the easiest bait fish to catch, and if kept in live tanks with a good flow of water, they will remain in a frisky condition for a considerable length of time. The question often is not *how* to catch shiners and pinfish, but rather *how not* to catch them. They are ardent and skilled bait robbers. When they are needed, however, it is generally a simple matter to use a small hook with anything from a barnacle to a tiny piece of bacon as bait. They can be caught in abundance around docks, bridges, piers, and even in the open waters of bays.

On the way out to more productive fishing grounds, it is a general practice to stop off at a selected spot and rig up a spinning rig and catch as many pinfish and shiners as you think you will need.

If the pinfish or shiner is to remain alive after it is placed on the hook, it should be hooked in one of three places. The first is through the top part of the mouth with the hook protruding forward of the eye. This will allow the bait to continue drawing water through its mouth and over the gills. The second is through the flesh just below the dorsal spines. The third is through the upper or lower part of the caudal peduncle. In either of the latter two methods, it is important that the hook is not passed through the spine. If this is done, the bait will die quickly.

Bloodworms are favored along the Atlantic coast for such fish as striped bass, trout, flounders, channel bass, and others. Bloodworms can be kept alive for a week or more if stored in damp grass and away from heat. The proper way to attach them on a hook is for the head and a portion of the worm's neck to be placed parallel to the shank where it is held fast by several loops of a small rubber band. This method allows the worm to squirm and twist about and the movement is attractive to fish.

Almost any small creature that lives in or close to the tide line is food for some kind of fish. A small mesh seine dragged through the waves close to any beach is almost sure to trap numerous types of minnows and other creatures. It is interesting to experiment with anything that gives any suggestion of being something a fish might like to eat.

Fishing with natural bait certainly takes less skill than the use of artificial lures. It also often involves a certain amount of physical labor to catch a supply, but it can frequently spell the difference between a fishless day and one that is filled with excitement.

ARTIFICIAL LURES

Tucked away in a far corner of an upstairs closet I have a box large enough to house a small dog. It is filled almost to the lid with a conglomeration of artificial lures that I have bought, made, and been given over more years than I care to mention. They are made of wood, plastic, rubber, metal, leather, feathers, cork, bucktail, and several other substances I am not sure I could quickly identify.

This hook-studded mass should be taken out and buried, but for some reason I cannot explain to myself, and certainly not to my wife, I am unable to part with them. Secretly, I guess I plan at some future date to dump the entire mass out on my workbench and try to resurrect the ones that might still be serviceable. When I am completely honest with myself I know I will never get around to the task, but every so often I clean out my tackle box and continue to add to the collection.

I am certain that sentimentality plays a part in my inability to divest myself of this mausoleum of memorabilia. Now and then when I poke about in the box I spot first one lure and then another that conjures up almost total recall of just where it came from and what type of fish chewed it so badly and why the hooks are straightened out the way they are or why some of them have no hooks at all.

Time was—as Eugene Fields wrote of the little toy dog and the little toy soldier—when each of these lures were "new and passing fair." Always, however, before I have a chance to become melancholy, I am sure to find some strange-looking device that is so ridiculous that I almost find myself laughing in the sheer wonderment of why I ever thought it would catch a fish in the first place.

It is entirely possible that some student of psychology will earn his doctorate by making a thorough investigation of the reasons that fishermen buy lures. If I could add up all the time I have spent standing before the lure counters in a thousand tackle stores, I am quite sure I would find where a good portion of my life has gone. I am equally certain that if I could get back all the money I have spent on lures I could retire for a year or so.

There would be no possible way to ascertain for sure just when man first conceived the idea of tricking a fish into striking at something made to look like food. Aelian spoke of men using artificial flies as far back as the third century A.D.

The list of different types of artificials is practically endless. At one time or another, you can be sure that someone has made some kind of a lure to resemble everything a fish ever ate, including insects, minnows, worms, frogs, eels, mice, birds, snakes, and a whole host of other objects that have been dreamed up in man's mind.

Some of the most popular forms of artificial lures fall into categories such as plugs, flies, spoons, bugs, squid, jigs, or a replica of a large worm or small eel, depending on how you look at it.

Flies and popping bugs are most popular with the fly-rod angler.

Plugs, spoons, and metal squid are favored by the fisherman with the bait-casting rod, and numerous variations of each are fair game for the man with the spinning tackle. Unlike the telephone, the electric light bulb, the steamboat, and the airplane, there are no Bells, Edisons, Fultons, and Wrights to take credit for being the sole inventors of the basic forms of artificial lures.

The patron saint of all fishermen, Izaak Walton, certainly was aware of the equivalent of some of today's artificial minnows, as evidenced by the following paragraph from his venerable book *The Compleat Angler:*

> And here let me tell you, what many old Anglers know right well, that at some time, and in some waters a *Minnow* is not to be got, and therefore let me tell you, I have (which I will shew to you) an *artificial Minnow,* that will catch a Trout as well as an artificial *Flie,* and it was made by a handsome Woman that had a fine hand, and a live Minnow lying by her: *the mould or body of the Minnow was cloth, and wrought upon or over it thus with a needle: the back of it with very sad French green silk, and paler green silk towards the belly, shadowed as perfectly as you can imagine, just as you see a Minnow; the belly was wrought also with a needle, and it was a part of it white silk, and another part of it with silver thred, the tail and fins were of a quil, which was shaven thin, the eyes were of two little black beads, and the head was so shadowed, and all of it so curiously wrought, and so exactly dissembled, that it would beguile any sharpe sighted Trout in a swift stream. And this Minnow I will now shew you, and if you like it, lend it you, to have two or three made by it, for they be easily carryed about an Angler, and be of excellent use; for note, that a large Trout will come as fiercely at a Minnow, as the highest Hawk doth seize on a Partridge, or a Greyhound on a Hare.*

One time-honored story credits the invention of the plug or wooden minnow to James Heddon of Dowagiac, Michigan. According to recorded facts, it seems Heddon was whittling a small chunk of wood as he sat beside a millpond one summer afternoon in 1889. Wearying of his pastime, Heddon flipped the small stick out onto the still water of the pond. Instantly, the surface was shattered as a black bass mistook the scrap of wood for some form of food and grabbed it in his jaws with the same enthusiasm he would have displayed in attacking a mouse that might have fallen from an overhanging limb.

Such a piscatorial mistake might have gone unheeded by a nonfisherman, but to angler Heddon the faulty judgment on the part of the bass fired his imagination. If, he reasoned, another similar piece of wood were carved in the general shape of a small fish, painted and studded with hooks, would not other bass be prone to make the same mistake?

Whether or not James Heddon was the first man actually to attach hooks to a block of wood and begin catching fish is secondary to the fact that in the next decade or so several dozen companies were manufacturing and selling artificial minnows. Among the front runners in the business, aside from James Heddon, were William Shakespeare (not to be confused with the Bard of Avon), Pflueger, and Worden.

In the early years of the twentieth century no less than fifty companies were engaged in the business of making wooden minnows, and since there were no hard-and-fast rules, countless anglers carved and painted their own versions of the hook-studded lure, which soon became generically known as the *plug*.

In the beginning, plugs were cigar-shaped pieces of wood with hooks and a ringeye to attach the line. It was not long, however, before practically every conceivable shape was devised. The front end was grooved and sloped to cause the plug to dive deeper the more rapidly it was retrieved. Metal lips were added to achieve the same purpose; some were cut in half and hinged to increase the wobble as they traveled through the water; others would dart from one side to the other in the manner of a wounded minnow; spinners were added first to the front end and then the back end and finally to both ends, and each manufacturer waxed eloquently on the fish-catching prowess of his particular creations.

I doubt that it has ever been done, and I am sure I would not know how to go about it, but if a poll were ever taken I would hazard a guess that red-and-white colored plugs would rate highest on the list. After that would be every shade of the rainbow and every possible combination of colors.

Like the ever-changing forms of dance and music, one type of plug has had its hour in the sun, only to be replaced by something radically different a short while later. There are anglers who are convinced that fish grow wary of certain types of lures when vast numbers have taken up residence in the millions of tackle boxes about the country. This, to other anglers' thinking, is just so much bunk. They maintain that it would be impossible for such caution to be passed on from one generation of fish to the next.

My own experience has been that a lure may work wonders one day, or on one tide, for that matter, and then become totally ineffective on the next. I like to think that I have developed a reasonably good understanding of where fish at least *should* be under a given set of conditions. When they refuse to strike what I first start casting their way, I can see no sense in flogging a dead horse and I start trying out everything in my tackle box. My reasoning is that fish have a habit of specializing for a few hours, or even days, on one particular type of readily available bait. When such bait is closely duplicated by a certain type of lure the chances are enhanced that one will catch fish. When that particular type of natural bait becomes temporarily in short supply, or as old Izaak would have said, "is not to be got," the fish will shift to another fare, and again, it is close duplication that does the trick.

The question of color is a never-ending topic of debate among anglers. Some swear by one or a combination of colors while others go along with some of the better scientific minds and say that a fish's eye cannot distinguish color. There are those who contend that lures are painted to attract the fisherman rather than the fish. Just about the time I get myself conditioned to throw in my lot with one group or another, something comes along to confound the theory and I keep on buying lures. At least, I know I am in good company, no matter what side I take.

Here is a thought on which to cogitate: Just suppose all lure manufacturers came to a unanimous agreement. If a fish cannot see color, why bother? From that moment on all lures, flies, bugs, spoons, plugs, and all the rest would be painted a dull gray. Of course it will never happen, but if it did you can bet there would be a new hobby, probably known as "color your own lure." The piscatorial ophthalmologist may be right, but it is going to be a long, long time before the day comes when all lures are painted gray.

The only definite stand I will take is that if I were to be cast away on a desert island and could have only one artificial lure, it would be a supply of yellow bucktail. I might not catch fish with every cast, but I do not believe I would go hungry.

A few years ago when the age of plastics arrived, lure manufacturers found a whole new vista opening. They discovered that the weight of plugs could be drastically reduced simply by making molds that would produce two identical sides that could be fused together, thus forming hollow plugs. Another bonus was that the plastic could be impregnated with color or left clear and others could be put together with a strip of shiny metal on the inside to cause the plug to flash and glitter in the light. It will be a long time, however, before wooden plugs are a thing of the past. Many are still made and there are times when nothing else will serve as a substitute.

After rigid plastics came the discovery of soft plastics, and still another field was waiting to be explored. Rubber had served well in the same capacity for a long while, but improper storage, too much heat, and a variety of other conditions dictated a relatively short life span. Now the angler can find artificial eels, frogs, shrimp, minnows, and so forth, that not only look like the real thing, but feel real to the touch.

Certain lures, such as flies, bucktails, feathered jigs, spoons, and spinners have been practically unchanged over the years. Where flies are concerned the old silk thread has largely given way to the more durable synthetics, but there are still a legion who swear silk is best. The colors, patterns, and sizes are the same for time-proven standbys, but the list of recognized fly patterns continues to grow.

When I first took up fly fishing I became obsessed with the art of tying my own flies. By the time I had learned the difference between a hairwing Royal Coachman and a Quill Gordon and could tie a reasonably respectable Parmachene Belle, I found I had to learn the difference between wet and dry flies.

The nonfly-fisherman may look through the felt or wool pages of a fly book and crudely proclaim that, except for size and color, they all look the same. In doing so he automatically invokes the ire of the purist, or dedicated fly-fisherman. A Blades' Hackle nymph may bear a resemblance to a Darbee's Stonefly nymph just as a Squirrel Doctor may resemble a Night Hawk, but for the angler who knows his patterns there is a considerable difference. In some cases there may be only a nuance between one fly and another, but the slight variation in the lay of the hackle or color of the head is vital to the true fly-fisherman.

Be it streamer fly, plastic eel, or floating plug, the most important thing for the angler to learn is the proper method of presenting and retrieving any artificial lure. Some should be worked in short jerks, others twitched along the surface or the bottom, while still others catch more fish with a slow steady retrieve. It all depends on the individual lure, the time of day or night, the set of the tide, the type of fish, the mood the fish is in at the moment. Simple, isn't it?

The facts are that artificials do catch fish and I would rather catch them by that method than any other way yet devised. At the same time, I am not opposed to turning to natural bait if that happens to be what the fish wants at the time.

fifteen ~~~~~~~~~~~~~~~~~~~~

~~~~~~~~~~
~~~~~~~~~~

THE RECORD BOOK

INTERNATIONAL GAME FISH ASSOCIATION

If you fish long enough in salt water, the chances are that sooner or later you will catch a fish so large that your instinct tells you, you have caught a record. It might be a barracuda, sea bass, cobia, flounder, speckled trout, or any of two dozen other types.

You might make your catch from a skiff, the end of a fishing pier, out on a charter or party boat, or you might take him while surf casting from the beach. This has nothing to do with fishing tournaments, rodeos, or fishing roundups where you pay an entry fee and fish your heart out for a few weeks in hopes of winning a new car or a set of tackle or something like that. This is a really big fish you caught on a regular fishing trip for fun, and you know that it is a lifetime fish that you have always dreamed about.

What in the world do you do with it? You take it back to the nearest scales and have it weighed, show it to your friends, wish you had money enough to have it mounted, and maybe remember to take a picture or two, and that is about it. All the while you know that somewhere there is an organization that keeps records of big fish. Time after time in newspapers, magazines, and books you have read something that goes like this: ". . . according to the IGFA records the largest yellow-bellied, broadbill something or other was caught by Roy Whatshisname on February 3, 1962, while fishing from Cape Broken Hull. . . ."

If the fish you caught was big enough to arouse sufficient interest, there is a chance that the news will get to the outdoor writer of the local newspaper. If it does, you may even get a telephone call. The columnist will ask if you registered your fish with the IGFA. When you admit you did not, the man on the other end of the phone is likely to sigh audibly and tell you that if the fish was as big as you said you have missed a good chance.

A good chance at what? What does IGFA mean? Where is it located? How do you make contact with the organization? Is it a club you join? How much are the dues?

It is really surprising how many conscientious fishermen who spend

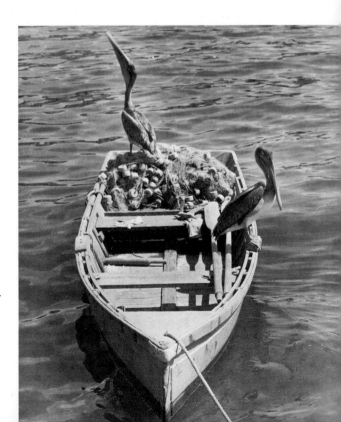

Two old fishermen just waiting for the tide to change.

their leisure hours in pursuit of game fish do not know the answers to
these questions. There is no way of knowing how many record-size fish
have been cut into steaks or fillets and relegated to the freezer, or maybe
just used to fertilize the azaleas. One cannot help but harken to the
analogy from the lines of Thomas Gray's *Elegy:* "Full many a flower
is born to blush unseen, and waste its sweetness on the desert air."

The initials IGFA stand for International Game Fish Association.
The headquarters are located at 2190 S.E. 17th Street, Fort Lauderdale,
Florida 33316. Contact may be made by mail or telephone. IGFA is
not a club and there are no dues, neither are there any individual
memberships. On the other hand, fishing clubs are welcome as members
if the club is not comprised solely of commercial or charter-boat fishermen. The IGFA will want to know the approximate number of members, names of club officers, and the one designated to receive
correspondence.

The IGFA has no restrictions or limitations based on race, color, or
creed and it has no local, national, or international political affiliations.

The IGFA was organized in June, 1939, as a result of the desire of
prominent anglers and clubs all over the world to have a central clear-
ing house for marine fishing problems and records. Interest in it was
especially strong in the United States, England, and Australia. The
purpose in the beginning, as today, is fivefold: 1) to encourage the study
of game fishes for the sake of whatever pleasure, information, or benefit
it may provide; 2) to keep the sport of marine game fishing ethical and
to make its rules acceptable to the majority of saltwater anglers; 3) to
encourage this sport both as a recreation and a potential source of
scientific data; 4) to place such data at the disposal of as many human
beings as possible; 5) to keep attested and up to date charts of world
record marine fishes.

The organization had its inception when Dr. William K. Gregory
and Michael Lerner were in Australia on the Michael Lerner Australia-
New Zealand Expedition of the American Museum of Natural History.
At this time they met Clive Firth, one of Australia's leading anglers,
and discussed with him the formation of the IGFA.

When Gregory and Lerner returned to the United States, many
letters were written to outstanding individual anglers, fishing clubs, and
tackle manufacturers to discuss the possibilities of such an organization
and to ask for their ideas on the subject.

On June 7, 1939, the IGFA was formally launched at a meeting which was attended by Lerner, Dr. Gregory, Van Campen Heilner, who was then affiliated with the Department of Fishes and the American Museum of Natural History. Also present at this meeting was Miss Francesca La Monte, Associate Curator of Fishes with the Department of Fishes and Aquatic Biology, American Museum of Natural History. Miss La Monte had also served as science leader on several of the Lerner expeditions.

The first IGFA president was the above-mentioned Dr. Gregory. At that time he was chairman of two American Museum of Natural History departments; Ichthyology and Comparative Anatomy. He was also professor of paleontology at Columbia University. He remained president until his retirement from the Museum in 1943, when he was succeeded by Lerner. In July, 1960, William K. Carpenter was elected president and Lerner became founder-chairman.

Six months after its formation, IGFA had two member scientific institutions, ten member clubs, and was represented in twelve territories. By 1969 the organization had grown to the extent of including twenty-four scientific institutions, approximately six hundred clubs, and maintained representation in seventy territories.

Each year the IGFA publishes a chart titled: "World Record Marine Fishes." In it are listed a total of forty-two fish which the organization considers to be game fish. In addition to this number, six species of sharks are listed, along with the true fish, for a total of forty-eight.

In the case of all listings, the common name is given first, followed by the scientific name. After this comes the weight of the record fish, the length, and the girth. It also lists the place the fish was caught, the date, and the name of the angler.

The record pages are divided into six parts depending upon the test of the line, beginning with lines having a breaking strength of twelve pounds or less and graduating up to one hundred and thirty pounds. Each of the record classes is based on the wet testing strength of the actual line used in making the catch, whether linen or synthetic.

All claims must be filed on IGFA forms, which may be obtained from headquarters at the address listed above or from member clubs. Along with details of the fish being entered, these forms require information concerning the tackle used. It also must be stated on the application form the type of bait and the method of fishing, such as trolling, casting, and so forth, by which the catch was made.

Enclosed with the application must be a sample of the line that was actually used to catch the fish being entered. Photographs are desirable in any case and are a must where certain species of fish are concerned. In any event, photos of the scales used to weigh the catch as well as the tackle must be included. If the photograph is sharp enough to show detail clearly, the fish, weighing scales, and tackle may be included in a single photograph.

After the form is filled out, it must be signed by at least two witnesses and the angler must have an affidavit properly notarized. All the rules and regulations governing the method of making the catch are printed on the back of the application form.

Basically, the rules may be summed up by stating that they are written in such a manner as to cause the catching of a record-size fish to be an honest contest between man and fish. Many otherwise record catches are automatically disqualified by the IGFA if strict adherence to these rules is not observed.

Some anglers are not in full agreement with all the rules set down by the IGFA. This is to be expected, because it is seldom, if ever, that people as a whole agree entirely with any set of rules whether it be the fixing of public utility rates or laws pertaining to highway traffic.

Some take umbrage at the IGFA rule which states that metal lines are prohibited. They contend that stainles steel lines are at times the only logical way to catch certain types of fish when they are running deep. Others are opposed to the IGFA rule that says only two hooks may be used, thus automatically disqualifying a fish caught on an artificial lure equipped with treble hooks. They contend that certain fish, such as the snook, spotted weakfish, and others are regularly fished for with such lures and it is just as sporting as with two single hooks.

By and large, however, most sports fishermen accept the rules and regulations set down by the association. One of the rules states that the angler must fight the fish from beginning to end without help from anyone, except when the fish is brought alongside. Then another member of the fishing party may take hold of the leader while the fish is being brought to gaff. Also, there may be an additional person handling the gaff. During the actual fight, however, it is strictly one man against the fish.

Sometimes this rule can have some comic and again pathetic overtones. I recall one blue-water trip I was on when a friend of mine hooked a particularly large blue marlin. The battle was being waged in full accordance with IGFA rules and all aboard, including the angler, were reasonably confident a new record was about to be established. Then the unexpected happened. The man holding the rod was overtaken by a sudden case of mal de mer. Perhaps it was the excitement, the heat, or the slow steady roll of the boat, or maybe it was a combination of all three. Whatever the case, the angler began to acquire that sickly green hue that frequently accompanies sea sickness. Beads of perspiration broke out on his face and he suddenly grabbed the mate by the arm and indicated by gesture that he take over the rod while he made a dive for the rail.

Five minutes later he resumed his position in the fighting chair and continued the fight until the huge fish was brought up beside the boat. At this point he pulled out a pair of wire snippers and cut the trace. For a few minutes we thought the charter-boat skipper was going to drop dead from apoplexy.

"I had a record," my friend sighed, "but since I would not have been able to swear that all the rules were followed, I would rather see that old blue go free."

Thus, the age of honest men is not entirely a thing of the past. In a somewhat similar situation, I happened to be on board a different boat when another angler fishing with a 9/0 reel, a seven-foot tubular glass rod with a 22-inch butt and 80-pound test line tied into a real monster of a tiger shark. Everything was going along in high gear until for some reason one of the two wing nuts that were used to clamp the reel onto the rod began to work loose. So loose, in fact, that the reel was about to slip out of its socket. The hard-working fisherman tried time after time to adjust the reel and tighten the wing nut, but the shark seemed to sense the dilemma and put on a new burst of speed. The skipper knew better, but I guess he just could not endure the suspense of standing by and watching the tackle fall apart. Before the angler knew what was happening, the skipper squatted beside the gimble and ran the wing nut back up on the bolt and cinched it with a quick twist of a pair of pliers.

This time it was the angler who lost his temper. There is nothing to be gained by quoting his words. Suffice to say, he upbraided the skipper in terms not generally used when one gentleman speaks to another.

He continued the fight with the tiger shark and it was boated, but the angler refused to have any more to do with it. No photographs, no name, and no notice to anyone. The next day the skipper towed the possible record far off shore and let it sink to the bottom.

Such are the rules of the game as seen by the IGFA, and a great many

A highway sign for the boating angler.

fishermen insist on following them to the letter, no matter how much it hurts at times.

For those who wish to see their names entered in the IGFA record charts, it is suggested that they write to the association, get a copy of the application blank, which is free, and a copy of the "Bylaws and Rules." There is a small charge for this booklet to cover the cost of printing and mailing. Study the rules carefully, and if you decide your brand of fishing coincides with the IGFA stipulations, you will then be ready to enter that big one you are planning to catch in the near future.

"Remember, you can't catch fish with your hook out of the water."
—Lead Line Louie

INDEX